TO SAVE THE WILD BISON

TO SAVE
THE WILD BISON

Life on the Edge in Yellowstone

MARY ANN FRANKE

UNIVERSITY OF OKLAHOMA PRESS : NORMAN

Also by Mary Ann Franke

Yellowstone in the Afterglow: Lessons from the Fires (National Park Service, 2000)

Library of Congress Cataloging-in-Publication Data

Franke, Mary Ann.
   To save the wild bison: life on the edge in Yellowstone / Mary Ann Franke.
      p. cm.
   Includes bibliographical references (p.).
   ISBN 0-8061-3683-9 (alk. paper)
      1. American bison—Conservation—Yellowstone National Park. 2. American
bison—Yellowstone National Park—Public opinion. 3. Public opinion—Yellowstone
National Park. 4. Americans—Yellowstone National Park—Attitudes. I. Title.

QL737.U53F73 2005
333.95'9643'0978752—dc22

2004063667

The paper in this book meets the guidelines for permanence and durability of the
Committee on Production Guidelines for Book Longevity of the Council on Library
Resources, Inc. ∞

1 2 3 4 5 6 7 8 9 10

Contents

Illustrations

Photographs

Graphs

Maps

Preface

During my first summer in Yellowstone, as a volunteer for the National Park Service in 1996, I discovered the park's literary as well as biological diversity. There are dozens of books about its unusual geology of geysers and the microbiology of hot springs, its mostly commonplace vegetation, its various species of wildlife; there's even a book on Yellowstone amphibians and reptiles, which are small in number and influence. But why had no one written a book about the remarkable Yellowstone bison since Mary Meagher's Ph.D. dissertation was published in 1973? The animal better known as the buffalo has provoked the good, the bad, and the ugly in attitudes toward wildlife in the United States. And much has changed for the bison in the last thirty years, both in Yellowstone and in herds across the country. Yes, the debate about how bison are to be managed in Yellowstone is inflammatory and still unfolding, but neither lawsuits nor lack of clear answers has deterred the writing of many books about wolves in Yellowstone.

The Yellowstone bison's small presence on the bookshelf may be a token of the way in which an animal that looms large in the abstract realm of American iconography has been overlooked when it comes to the physical world of wildlife that Americans regard as part of their heritage. Wildlife managers in the Yellowstone area are apt to describe the bison as having been "left behind" in this country's progress in wildlife preservation. Although elk and deer also endured a period of intense slaughter in the nineteenth century, they have been allowed to return to many parts of their former range as free-roaming wild animals that may be hunted, provide food for predators and scavengers, and participate in the vegetation recycling process despite the problems they may cause when they wander onto roads and in fields of grain.

To tell the story of why wild bison are nearly absent from our picture of twenty-first-century wilderness and to describe the effort to save the wild bison in Yellowstone became my reasons for writing this book. As someone who has benefited from hindsight when summarizing the long history of a human endeavor, I was amused by the occasionally mistaken notions of those who spoke their minds before me, and humbled by the realization that my own pronouncements may sooner or later seem just as quaint or foolish. But insofar as this book contains any nuggets of lasting value, it is because I benefited from the assistance of many minds more knowledgeable than my own about Yellowstone bison, the park's history, and recent controversies. Of the many scientific opinions I cite in this book, none has been subjected to the hindsight that Mary Meagher's work has. Through her long career in Yellowstone she has contributed more to an understanding and appreciation of the Yellowstone bison than anyone has before or is likely to ever again. She has also left a long paper trail in the park archives that helps explain the peculiar turns taken by bison managers in Yellowstone.

John Varley, director of the Yellowstone Center for Resources, encouraged me to write a book that he knew he wouldn't entirely agree with, because of a goal we share: to save the wild bison. That made it easier for me to obtain the assistance of people who work with him at the park, especially Rick Wallen, Glenn Plumb, and Wayne Brewster. Also helpful in their areas of expertise were Paul Schullery, Rosemary Sucec, Doug Smith, Kerry Gunther, Dan Reinhart, Lee Whittlesey, Jim Peaco, George Nell, Kevin Schneider, and Roger Anderson, who first suggested to me the idea that the Yellowstone bison had a life on the edge.

For providing balance to the charisma of Yellowstone, I am grateful to Keith Aune of Montana Fish, Wildlife and Parks; Jack Rhyan of the Animal and Plant Health Inspection Service, USDA; Steve Torbitt of the National Wildlife Federation; Fred DuBray of the InterTribal Bison Cooperative; Josh Osher of the Buffalo Field Campaign; and Bob Frost of the United States Animal Health Association.

Tami Blackford and Jim Caslick read an early draft of the manuscript in its entirety and offered many suggestions that left their mark on the finished product. Having written a fine book that has been a valuable resource for me, *Preserving Yellowstone's Natural Conditions: Science and the Perception of Nature*, James Pritchard also provided a thoughtful manuscript critique. His most important advice led me to look for the fence between wild and civilized and, instead of sitting on it, realize that it is too flimsy to support the weight of my ties to both.

A brief history of bison in Yellowstone National Park

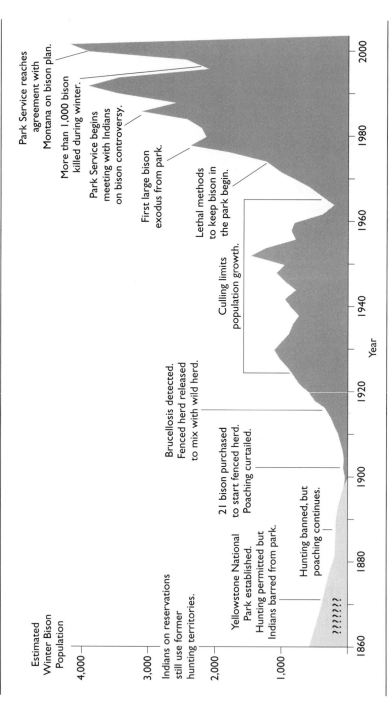

Wildlife counts in Yellowstone are always subject to error because of the unknown number of animals that may go undetected, but estimates made before 1900 were especially unreliable because they were often based on hunches and chance observations rather than a systematic survey.

Introduction

On an overcast morning in March, when spring is not yet even a sunlit twinkle in the snows of Yellowstone, a police escort accompanies a procession of vehicles leaving the park. The somber faces suggest a funeral cortege. None of the 41 bison in the trucks is dead, but they are on their way to the slaughterhouse. Five miles north of the park, the convoy passes an overlook on the Gallatin National Forest where a sign explains the importance of this "wildlife migration corridor." The sign refers not to the state highway, but to the adjacent land where "tasty grasses and shrubs on snowfree hillsides invite thousands of hooved animals to escape the arctic storms that swirl into Yellowstone. . . . Wildlife knows no boundaries."

It's a nice thought, but not always true for the wildlife shown on the sign—elk, mule deer, pronghorn, bighorn sheep, coyotes, mink—and even less for the bison, wolves, and bears that are not represented. In addition to the boundaries set by suitable habitat, many wild animals in the Yellowstone area experience the limits of human tolerance. At this time in the region's history, the bison is more restricted than other species, and its future as a wild animal is more uncertain. The threat is not extinction by way of the slaughterhouse, but obliteration of what makes these bison wild, what makes them special on a continent that is now home to hundreds of thousands of bison raised as livestock on commercial ranches.

Long before the first hamburger and milk shake, Bessie the Cow was a wild animal that had to live by her wits and strength to survive her predators. Like bison, cattle began their evolution in Asia and spread across Europe

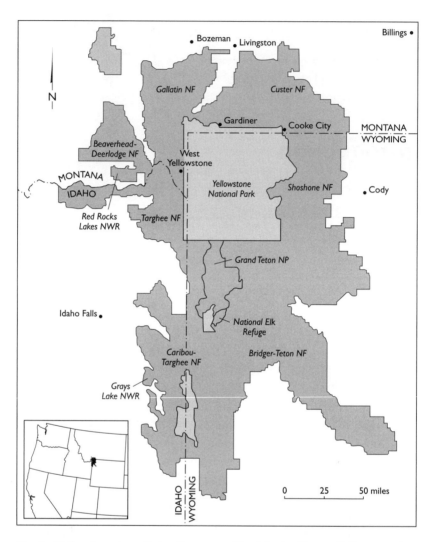

Greater Yellowstone Area. Federally managed land in the Greater Yellowstone Area includes two national parks (NP), two national wildlife refuges (NWP), and six national forests (NF).

and Africa in roaming herds. But while ancient civilizations figured out how to domesticate cattle as a source of food and labor, the bison remained an animal that had to be hunted with spears. Wild cattle, known as aurochs, became extinct, and bison adapted to colder, drier climates, enabling them to cross the Bering Strait to North America, where they lived in enormous herds for millennia. Then Europeans arrived with their domestic cattle and diseases, and they found that the bison and the people already living in America were obstacles to their progress. The native people got smallpox and were called Indians, though they had nothing to do with India, and the bison got brucellosis from the cattle and became known as the American buffalo, even though the bison is only distantly related to the buffalo of Asia and Africa.

The adjective "wild" comes from "willed," suggesting self-willed, willful, or uncontrollable.[1] It also suggests why the wild inhabitants of America were regarded as something to be conquered by white settlers in the nineteenth century. "There is no law which human hands can write, there is no law which a Congress of men can enact, that will stay the disappearance of these wild animals before civilization," said Representative Omar Conger of Michigan, who argued against legislation to protect the country's dwindling bison herds in 1874. "They eat the grass. They trample upon the plains on which our settlers desire to herd their cattle. . . . They are as uncivilized as the Indian."[2]

History proved Conger wrong about the U.S. Congress, but 20 years passed before it enacted such a law, and more time before it could be enforced. By then, the free-roaming Indians had been assigned to reservations, and the only wild bison left in the United States were in Yellowstone. Bison were not valued as part of the landscape until they became scarce, which was about the same time that an appreciation for unsettled land became a mark of the truly civilized person.[3] Even so, as the history of Yellowstone vividly demonstrates, attitudes toward wildlife have continued to change. After visiting the park in 1902, President Theodore Roosevelt wrote, "To any lover of nature it could not help being a delightful thing to see the wild and timid creatures of the wilderness rendered so tame. . . . It was amusing to read the proclamations addressed to the tourists by the Park management, in which they were solemnly warned that the bears were really wild animals, and that they must on no account be either fed or teased."[4]

Today's Yellowstone bears really are wild, and most of today's lovers of nature want wildlife that must track down its own food, rather than animals that have been rendered tame by doughnuts. When unhampered, wildlife displays a continuity that has become scarce in our transient civilization — an attachment to the land and routines passed from one generation to the next.[5] Yet wildness is a matter of degree, and wildlife in national parks often represents a compromise between uncontrolled nature and the interference demanded to manage a park with human visitors and neighbors.

Today's bison population in Yellowstone is in some ways an embarrassment of riches, far larger than anyone predicted when culling to control herd size ended in the 1960s and nature was allowed to take its course. In retrospect, it is possible to regard that loosening of reins on the park's bison and elk populations as an extension of social changes that were occurring in American culture in the name of human liberation. But there was a scientific as well as political rationale for adopting the policy that came to be known, not quite accurately, as natural regulation. After park personnel reduced the bison herd to fewer than 300 in 1966, it was expected that nature, in the form of severe winters and limited winter range in the park, would keep it from growing much past 1,000.[6] Yet in recent years the bison count has exceeded 4,000, perhaps more than this part of the Rocky Mountains ever accommodated before, and perhaps for reasons that are not altogether natural. While elk numbers may be limited by wolves and by hunters outside the park, neither wolves nor the proposed hunting of bison that leave the park is expected to significantly reduce the bison herd.

The bison evicted from Yellowstone that March morning were among 280 whose lives came to an unseemly end in the spring of 2004 because they crossed an invisible line in search of greener pastures. They were following routes that bison used when the herd was far smaller, and may have used long before there was a Yellowstone National Park. The ostensible reason for killing these bison is the remote possibility that they could transmit brucellosis back to cattle, causing the cows to miscarry their calves. There is more to it than that, however, for the only evidence of brucellosis transmission to cattle in the Yellowstone area has incriminated elk and they are not subject to deportation at the park border. Even if brucellosis could be eliminated from the Yellowstone bison, their movement outside the park would have to be controlled because the animals pose a risk to human safety and private property. But it is the methods intended to reduce the risk of brucellosis transmission from the Yellowstone bison herd that raise questions about what kind of animal we want wild bison to be.

Although the National Bison Association, whose mission is to promote bison ranching for profit, believes that bison are too unruly to be considered "domestic," nearly all commercial herds contain some cattle genes as a result of crossbreeding. The bison ranchers decide which animals breed based on their potential for producing meat, and the more aggressive bison are unlikely to be chosen. Even in noncommercial herds, cattle hybrids are often present and the "wildness" of the bison is questionable. Their natural instincts may be domesticated by fenced pastures and periodic roundups for tagging, vaccination, and culling to limit herd size.

It's too late to save the wild aurochs; thousands of years of selective breeding to satisfy human desires have engineered dairy and beef cows so that they cannot defend themselves against predators and have difficulty mating or giving birth without human assistance. But in Yellowstone the bison cows still swing their horns to rebuff bulls unworthy of fathering their calves, and the bulls fight it out with each other, occasionally to death, for the privilege. They are a difficult prey but an important food for wolves and grizzly bears, which feed on the carcasses of bison not strong enough to survive the park's harsh winters. At one end of the rainbow are those who regard the Yellowstone bison as a resilient and thriving animal that could recolonize the Great Plains, restoring biodiversity to native grasslands and economic well-being to declining rural communities, if only we would get out of the way. Under the thunderclouds are those who believe Yellowstone bison are struggling on overgrazed habitat, using roads groomed for snow-mobiles to leave the park in the winter, and suffering from a contagious disease that threatens the livelihood of ranchers and carries a potential weapon of bioterrorism. An animal with an illustrious past, the bison that now roams Yellowstone has a life on the edge—the edge of its historic range, the edge of livestock officials' tolerance, and the edge between the wild animal it still is and the zoolike exhibit it could become if subjected to the kind of livestock management practices typically applied to bison herds.

As concern about brucellosis in wild bison has increased over the decades, the National Park Service and the three states that intersect in Yellowstone have responded in various ways, including wishful thinking, tape-recorded wolf howls, lawsuits, boundary patrols, hunting, and ship-ment of infected bison to new owners. Much has been learned through trial and error, and much effort has gone into working out compromises that address the interests of wildlife, livestock, and human communities in the Yellowstone area. However, as envisioned by those in a position to make the decisions, liberating the Yellowstone bison from the politics of brucellosis will require not only many boots on the ground, but significant advances in wildlife medical technology. Even if "wildlife medical technology" is not an oxymoron on the order of "wildlife zoo," a strategy of such complexity comes at a high ecological and financial cost, while the goal of eliminating brucellosis from the much larger elk population remains even further out of reach. The government agencies involved push forward with plans to eradicate brucellosis in the expectation that solutions lie around the next corner of research, and the controversy generates enough political heat to open congressional purse strings for funding. Wherever people must arrive at policies to manage wildlife populations whose lives interfere with their own, debates are increasing about the price we are willing to pay, the process used to arrive at solutions, and what it is about wildlife that should be saved.

The first bison to receive the death penalty for crossing the park boundary in the fall of 2001 was killed in the Gallatin National Forest in the presence of six Montana Department of Livestock agents, two Gallatin County sheriffs, two highway patrol officers, one Yellowstone park ranger, and some reporters and protesters. Government employees shot the bull because they could not capture him. He had been hazed repeatedly back into the park during the previous month but kept leaving, and a landowner had complained about property damage. According to a Yellowstone spokesperson, the bison had become increasingly belligerent and charged some of the people who were hazing him on horseback.[7] Some people regard that bison as exactly the sort that must be eliminated, an uncivilized animal that has no place outside the park. Other people believe he was exactly the bison we must try to save, the wild bison.

TO SAVE THE WILD BISON

PART ONE

BISON WITHOUT BORDERS

Creator Sun took some of the mud, as he had done when he made Mudman. And with his hands he molded a thing with four legs on it, a head and the body. The Mudman was astounded. Creator Sun made the thing's nostrils and held it up to his mouth. He blew very hard into this thing's nostrils and said to it, "Now breathe the air from me, my breath, and live with it like my children are now living with it. Eat the grass to fatten you and those in the same likeness as you are that will all roam this land some time soon. Abound this land and become the food of my children."

—Percy Bullchild, *The Sun Came Down:
The History of the World as My Blackfeet Elders Told It* (1985)

Bison herd in Hayden Valley (1972). Courtesy of Yellowstone National Park.

CHAPTER I

Coming to America

When the U.S. Treasury asked him to redesign the nickel in 1913, sculptor James Earle Fraser's goal was "to achieve a coin which would be truly America, that could not be confused with the currency of any other country." The result, however, was "a sad failure as a work of art" in the eyes of zoologist William Hornaday. "The buffalo head droops and it looks as if it had spent its life in a small enclosure."[1] Fraser's model had posed in the Bronx Zoo, but the image seemed unsuitable for an animal that for thousands of years had abounded in large herds roaming wide-open spaces.

The image of the Indian sculpted for the other side of the nickel with the motto "LIBERTY" was paradoxical in its own way, yet inextricably linked with that of the buffalo. The oral histories of some Indians speak of both the first people and the first buffalo being formed out of earth or coming from a place underground. Based on limited fossil and archeological evidence, mostly from underground, scientists have fleshed out a variety of scenarios in which the ancestors of both the American Indian and the bison, as it is scientifically known, first came to this continent from Asia. While these theories remain a matter of debate, the more widely held views on bison evolution do seem to go a long way toward explaining why modern bison look and behave as they do.[2] Hornaday's objections notwithstanding, the American bison does have its head set low to the ground, perhaps because that's the most efficient position for a large animal that must spend a large portion of its life fattening on grass.

The buffalo head nickel, which was minted from 1913 to 1938, was designed by sculptor James Earl Fraser to be a distinctly American coin. Courtesy of Yellowstone National Park.

The bison belongs to the bovid family of species, which includes cattle, sheep, and other hoofed animals and in which both the males and females have unbranched horns. Bovids may have begun evolving into separate species in southern Asia 20 million years ago. Those that remained in the south became cattle and true buffalo, which have no hump, such as the African cape buffalo and the Asian water buffalo. Bovids that expanded their range northward into a drier, grassier habitat began appearing as a humped animal with short horns protruding from the sides of its head. Some of the herds moved west into Europe, where today they are known as wisents, a woodland bison that browses on the leaves of shrubs and trees and carries its head higher than its American cousin. Other bison traveled east across Siberia and spread throughout most of North America during the Pleistocene epoch, when thick ice sheets extended across much of the northern hemisphere for intervals lasting thousands of years. During these periods of glacier advance, so much of Earth's water was frozen that sea levels dropped hundreds of feet and the Bering Strait became a broad grassy plain traversed by bison, mammoths, mastodons, and camels and by the carnivores that preyed on these animals.

Among the Missing in Greater Yellowstone

The Greater Yellowstone Area of today, which includes Yellowstone and Grand Teton national parks and the surrounding national forests, is often referred to as an "intermountain" region, where the mountains extend into the surrounding plains. This topography obscures the demarcation between the Rocky Mountains and the Great Plains, a boundary that in many places is no more obvious to the eye than is the one around Yellowstone National Park. About 25,000 years ago most of the Yellowstone area lay under an ice cap thousands of feet thick, with little plant or animal life of any kind. But all things must come to an end, even the 1.6 million–year Pleistocene epoch, and a warming trend had melted most of the ice by 14,000 years ago, evidence of the transition to the Holocene epoch, in which we still bask today.

As the glaciers receded northward, some animals retreated with them into Canada, including the caribou and musk ox, while in greater Yellowstone, bison and human inhabitants moved in. People were using Yellowstone's high country at least 11,000 years ago to obtain obsidian for blades, points, and other tools. With a thick point attached to a spear or dart, they could kill a large animal when jabbed at close range. Anthropologist George Frison has identified two ways of life that were evident in the Wyoming and southern Montana area about 10,000 years ago: that of the plains-basin and the foothills-mountains.[3] The plains-basin people lived in larger bands and developed techniques for driving bison herds over cliffs or into arroyos, where the animals trampled each other to death. But the foothills-mountain people may have depended more on bighorn sheep and mule deer, for little evidence of bison has been found in the archeological record. Stone tools discovered along the shore of Yellowstone Lake, at an elevation of 7,700 feet, include a point stained by bison blood that is about 9,000 years old.[4]

Most of the large species that were present in North America as the Pleistocene came to an end did not survive anywhere on the continent. The community of large grazers and predators of which the bison had been part for millennia, through warm times and cold, changed abruptly. The disappearance of mammoths and mastodons, as well as earlier forms of bear, cheetah, and lion, has been attributed to climate change or a growing population of human hunters, or a combination of both. Large mammals that emigrated to North America during the Pleistocene became adapted to extremely low temperatures but not necessarily to deep or ice-hardened snow that makes foraging difficult; the northern climate was generally dry until the warmer Holocene began. Some traits that had been advantageous in the Pleistocene, such as large size and thick pelage, may have become liabilities. Bigger is not always better in the survival-of-the-fittest competition. Larger mammals tend to have longer gestation periods, take longer to reach sexual maturity, and be more likely to confront rather than flee from predators.

The archeological record shows that as the bison bones that appear in the fossil record were becoming smaller, hunting gear was becoming more sophisticated. The stabbing spear was replaced by a spear attached to an atlatl that could be hurled farther or at a moving animal without loss of force. This would have reduced the advantage of size in prey species and favored animals that could conceal themselves or flee quickly. Using various assumptions about hunting efficiency and the population density of humans and prey, scientists have constructed computer simulations to demonstrate that even relatively small numbers of relatively inept hunters could have brought about the demise of so many large mammals.[5] Not everyone believes that computers can tell us what happened 11,000 years ago, but animals that were stressed by climate change would have been more vulnerable to predation, and the growing impact of human hunting could have pushed some species over the edge.

When Smaller Is Fitter

The bison survived the transition to the Holocene, but the bison we know today is smaller than its ancestors, one form of which stood up to eight feet tall at the shoulder and had horns that spanned more than six feet. So which came first, the smaller bison or the more proficient bison hunter? Did bison hunting become more widespread and successful during the Holocene because the bison became smaller and less dangerous, or did the bison become smaller at least partly because more intense hunting pressure eliminated the large bison who matured later and were less likely to survive to sexual maturity? Evolution is a slow process, and like the human species, whose physical and mental traits do not always seem well suited to the challenges of life in the twenty-first century, the modern bison is the cumulative result of adaptations that earlier versions of the animal made for survival, some of them in very different circumstances from those in which the bison lives today.

Lacking the possibilities for concealment from predators that are available in wooded habitats, species that adapt to life on the open range may surround themselves with large numbers of their own kind as a substitute. The larger the group you're in, the more herd members there are to marshal a defense, and the more likely that a predator will pick on someone else. The herding behavior that bison developed as protection against wolves would have been impossible with a six-foot horn span and appetite to match, but it favored a smaller bison. The larger the herd, the more the bison had to keep on the move, traveling to find ranges with enough forage for everyone, and the more difficult it became for an individual bison to attain a large size.

By about 5,000 years ago the bison had become an animal with essentially the same traits as the one that became known as the American buffalo. With most of its large predators and grazing competitors gone and its svelter size, the bison was just the right animal to fit into an ecological window of opportunity that opened on grasslands that became known as the Great Plains. It thrived in an environment that required enduring drought-stricken summers, frigid winters, and attacks on its young by wolves and bears. Numbering in the tens of millions, the American buffalo extended its range west over the Rocky Mountains and east of the Mississippi. It became one of the most numerous large mammals that has ever existed on Earth, reaching its maximum population size and density about 2,500 years ago. Compared to its ancestors, the modern bison may be a dwarf, but by surviving through a period that eliminated bigger species, the bison was left standing as the largest land mammal in North America. A bull bison may weigh as much as 2,000 pounds; the females up to 1,000 pounds.

According to a legend of the Blackfeet, whose territory once spread from Canada to the northern edge of the Yellowstone Plateau, they had difficulty killing bison until Creator Sun showed them how to drive the bison over a cliff into a *piskan*, an enclosure made of branches and rocks. Bison that survived the fall were dispatched by people wielding clubs and lances. Many-Tail-Feathers, a Pikunni Blackfoot elder, described how the piskan changed his ancestors' lives. "How happy the men and women were as they sprang into the piskan and with their flint knives and stone-axes and hammers began butchering the animals—a whole herd of buffalo decoyed

As they get older, these two calves will become darker in color, grow their horns and humps, and look less like cattle. Courtesy of Yellowstone National Park.

and killed with ease; enough meat for the whole tribe for many days. . . . It is no wonder that the hunters sang and sang and gave praise to Sun for his helpfulness."[6]

At Ulm Pishkun in central Montana the quantity of bones excavated to grind up for fertilizer and cattle feed during the 1940s indicated that 10,000 bison had died there from about 1000 to 1500 A.D. Evidence of 238,000 bison was found in bones at the Highwood site.[7] But even with help from Creator Sun, a successful bison drive depended on having enough bison nearby; the momentum of the moving mass of bison could push hundreds to their death. Any notion that such behavior indicates the bison's stupidity may be dispelled by the many incidents in which humans have trampled each other to death when attempting to flee in a panic through a confined area. Bison are not the only species for which a herd mentality has been both a defense and a vulnerability.

CHAPTER 2

A Removable Resource

The controversy over management of wild bison in Yellowstone that intensified during the 1990s raised the question of whether large bison herds were native to the area or were the result of what Euro-Americans did after they arrived. For several thousand years before that, the wildlife community in the Yellowstone area probably remained largely the same, and humans were part of that community and having some effect on it, though different effects than today. That much can be discerned from fossils, archeology, and Indian oral histories, but such evidence offers few clues as to how many animals there were and whether some species were less or more common than they are today.[1]

Speculations about wildlife abundance prior to the park's establishment in 1872 have suggested several possible scenarios. Bison and other ungulates may have been scarce in the intermountain area because their numbers were kept low by Indian hunting or because the habitat does not naturally support large ungulate populations, especially during periods of deep snow.[2] According to another scenario, more intensive Indian hunting in the area around the Yellowstone Plateau "doubtless contributed to concentrating game animals in the future park."[3] Yet another perspective suggests that wildlife populations were on a rebound as the Euro-American frontier moved west, because hunting pressure was relieved when Indian populations were reduced by European diseases that often arrived before the settlers themselves.[4]

The National Park Service has traditionally viewed Yellowstone as a place where the pre-1872 human population was too small to have significantly affected wildlife. While that would be consistent with evidence believed to provide "abundant proof that today's native ungulates and their predators were common residents of the park area for thousands of years,"[5] this scenario sounds suspiciously like wishful thinking. Yellowstone is widely thought of as a premier wildlife park, and many people would prefer to think that it's "natural" for it to be chock-full of large animals even if the reason they are present there now is that it is not safe for them to leave.

The few references in Indian oral histories and Euro-American accounts of bison hunting in the future park do not suggest a large bison population there before 1872. Historians Paul Schullery and Lee Whittlesey examined hundreds of written reports from the nineteenth century that mentioned bison in the Yellowstone area. They found evidence that bison were abundant in lower river valleys and grasslands on the edge of and beyond the Greater Yellowstone Area, and were widely but more sparsely distributed in higher-elevation sites. The only mention they found of a large bison herd within bellowing distance of what would become Yellowstone National Park appeared in the journal of A. Bart Henderson, a prospector. Henderson mentioned seeing "thousands of buffalo quietly grazing" in 1870 near the head of Hellroaring Creek, an area that he called Buffalo Flats and still goes by that name, lying just beyond the park's north boundary. However, other journal entries suggest that Henderson, unaware that researchers would one day pore over them for evidence of wildlife, used "thousands of" to mean "lots of." Henderson also reported seeing thousands of hot springs and minerals, and catching thousands of fish.[6]

Feast and Famine among the Indians

When the buffalo first came to be upon the land and hunters tried to coax them over the cliff for the good of the village, the buffalo did not want to go. They did not relish being turned into dried flesh for winter rations, they did not want their hooves and horns to become tools and utensils, nor did they welcome their sinew being used for sewing. A young woman who saw her people facing starvation said to the herd, "If you run off the cliff, I will marry your strongest warrior."

As the other buffalo went over the cliff, a big bull lifted the woman between his horns and carried her to his village. When her father came looking for her, he was trampled to death by the buffalo. A magpie brought the woman one of her father's bones and she sang over it until he returned to life.

The buffalo were amazed. They said to the woman, "Will you sing this song for us after every hunt? We will teach your people the buffalo dance, so that whenever you dance before the hunt, you will be assured of a good result. Then you will sing this song, and we will all come back to life again."

—Traditional Blackfoot story[7]

In U.S. popular culture "American Indian" came to mean nomadic tribes who lived in tepees and shot buffalo with bows and arrows while riding bareback. However, that way of life was led by only some American Indians and for scarcely 200 years, and it was largely a reaction to European influences: the introduction of horses and European diseases and the possibility of an easier livelihood through the fur and hide trade. For thousands of years before that, the immense bison herds on the Great Plains provided only a partial source of subsistence for a relatively small number of tribes living near them.

Before Yellowstone National Park was established, small bands of Indian hunters and gatherers made up most of the human presence in the Yellowstone area, but larger, outlying groups used it during summer. After the bones of a bison began eroding from a cliff of billowing steam vents above Yellowstone Lake in the 1990s, archeologists found that they bore obsidian flakes from tools that left butchering marks more than 800 years ago.[8] Indians may have chosen the site because the steam made it a warm place to camp and prey could be cornered against the lakeside cliff. These people would have faced the same challenge as do wild animals inhabiting the area today: foraging and hunting activities had to be efficient enough so that the energy expended to obtain food was not greater than that which could be derived from the food.[9]

By early in the eighteenth century, tribes west of the Continental Divide—known today as the Bannock, Coeur D'Alene, Kalispel, Nez Perce, Salish, and Shoshone—had acquired horses and crossed the Yellowstone Plateau to hunt bison to the east. Coming from the east, the Blackfeet, Crows, and Wind River Shoshones traveled through the area to hunt and fish, obtain obsidian, and use the hot springs for religious and medicinal purposes.[10] More Indians came through the Yellowstone area as the bison herds diminished elsewhere. While trapper Osborne Russell was traveling in Bannock territory west of Yellowstone in 1835, the chief showed him where "upwards of a Thousand Cows were killed without burning one single grain of gun powder."[11] But the bison were soon gone from west of the Rocky Mountains, perhaps the combined result of snowstorms, the burning of many grains of gunpowder by Indians who had abandoned their arrows, and hunting by fur trappers who abandoned their traps as easterners abandoned their beaver hats for those made of silk.

Since the bison no longer came to the Bannocks, the Bannocks began going to the bison east of the mountains. The Bannocks were friendly with the Shoshones who shared their territory on the Snake River Plain, but their relations with other tribes in the Yellowstone area were often hostile, and heavy snowfall kept the higher elevations inaccessible much of the year. To avoid enemy camps and the most difficult terrain, the Bannocks passed over the Gallatin Range to Mammoth Hot Springs, across the Black-tail Plateau, up the Lamar River Valley, and through the Absarokas along what is now the east side of the park. Their 200-mile route became known as the Bannock Trail, but it was also used by the Flatheads, Nez Perce, and Shoshones.[12]

Describing the Blackfeet in the 1830s near the mouth of the Yellowstone River on the upper Missouri, the artist George Catlin wrote, "The buffalo herds, which graze in almost countless numbers on these beautiful prairies, afford them an abundance of meat; and so much is it preferred to all other, that the deer, the elk, and the antelope sport upon the prairies in herds in the greatest security; as the Indians seldom kill them." But it wasn't all powwows and potlucks. Catlin also saw how dependence on the buffalo could lead to times of deprivation. After visiting a Mandan community on the upper Missouri River, he observed, "Buffaloes, it is known, are a sort of roaming creatures, congregating occasionally in huge masses, and strolling away about the country from east to west, or from north to south, or just where their whims or strange fancies may lead them; and the Mandans are sometimes by this means most unceremoniously left without anything to eat."[13]

Leave No Bison Behind

The bison herds did not begin losing ground as soon as Euro-Americans and their horses arrived on the continent. In the early 1600s bison were still expanding their range east of the Mississippi River, possibly drawn to grasslands that Indians created by burning woodlands where today wood-lands have returned.[14] Bison range eventually extended from northern Florida to central New York in the east and from Mexico to the Great Slave Lake in Canada's Northwest Territories. However, the population was never as dense east of the Mississippi, and it was short-lived. White settlers dispatched the animals because they disrupted farming and livestock grazing and because the meat and hides helped tide the settlers over until their first crops could be harvested.

West of the Mississippi, a bison population of perhaps 30 million was reduced to fewer than 1,000 by the 1890s. This extermination is sometimes attributed to greedy Euro-American capitalism or a genocidal campaign against the Indians, but the explanation is both less dramatic and more complicated. Many government officials did hope that fewer bison would mean fewer Indians or at least resign the Indians to life on reservations, and many Euro-Americans did try to make money off the backs of bison, but the population was shrinking before industrial-strength slaughter began in the 1870s and before the government noticed its effect on the Indians. Both the Indians and the Euro-Americans responded to the opportunities available to them in ways that may have combined with periodic drought to start the bison population decline in the 1820s.[15]

Although "No part of the buffalo was wasted" has become an article of faith in the folklore of many tribes, most people exercise such thriftiness only when it is necessary, and the Indians were not an exception. Indians may have boiled up every last bit of bone and gristle for soup when meat was scarce, but buffalo jumps and other hunting techniques could produce a surfeit of carcasses. When more animals were killed than a community could consume or make into dried pemmican before the meat spoiled, the Indians took the prime cuts and left the rest. The Crees and Piegans con-sidered it imprudent to let any animals from a hunt survive, because they would warn the rest of the herd to stay away. The Cheyennes and Arapahos believed that buffalo came in endless numbers from a place underground, and so they had no reason to worry about using them up.[16]

In their traditional beliefs many Indians regard animals as intermediaries between human beings and supernatural forces, with each creature having its own role in a single interrelated community. In some cultures, as expressed in Buddhism and certain other Eastern religions, the belief that humans share a universal spirit with other animals leads to the conviction that killing them is wrong except in self-defense. But in aboriginal cultures in which animals are an important source of food, the prey species may be seen as giving itself to its human brethren willingly, fulfilling its purpose in life. The rituals for hunting and using animal flesh that developed among aboriginal cultures have been interpreted as a way to relieve the guilt that people would otherwise feel about consuming sentient creatures and to give people a sense of control over the natural elements on which their lives depend.[17]

That is one way to understand tribal customs for "calling" the buffalo before a hunt. Among the Cheyennes and Blackfeet, for example, certain men who disguised themselves in buffalo robes and imitated the animal's movements and sounds were believed to have a special power for luring buffalo into a corral or over a cliff. Although "buffalo jump" is the English term that came to be used for sites where a herd was driven off a precipice, many people suspect that the buffalo did not so much jump as fall, and they did not all die a sudden death. Today most meat eaters do not watch their next meal being slaughtered and have no desire to do so. When the Indians had no choice, the bison slaughters were by all accounts joyous occasions, but if you were watching and listening as several dozen or several hundred buffalo plunged over a cliff and lay mangled and bawling, hooves kicking, horns thrashing, and blood flowing as you butchered them, you would want a way to make sense of the suffering endured on your behalf. Anthropologist Elizabeth Atwood Lawrence has suggested that by regarding the buffalo as sacred and honoring it through ceremonies, the Indians made a "communal ritual reconciliation" with the "buffalo nation."[18] The animal does not really die, because its soul remains part of the universal spirit; eternal return is assured for both buffalo and humankind by fulfilling reciprocal obligations that maintain the harmony of the natural world.

With horses, it no longer took a village to hunt a bison herd; a few good men on horseback could cover large areas and bring back enough meat for everyone before it spoiled. When a family's belongings had to be pulled by dogs on a travois, tepees were often made with fewer than ten bison hides, but with horses to carry the load, a 14-hide tepee became commonplace.[19] Europeans regarded the nomad's life as uncivilized, but many Indians of this period enjoyed a more comfortable and healthier existence, with more time to devote to art, religion, and recreation and to caring for the young and old, than did European peasants bound to a life of drudgery in the field.[20]

By the 1820s, Indians were no longer killing buffalo just to feed, clothe, and shelter themselves. Buffalo robes became currency in the trade for guns, blankets, cooking pots, and whiskey, and buffalo became ammunition in territorial conflicts between tribes. Predictions about the eventual disappearance of the buffalo were heard in the 1840s not only among federal authorities and missionaries pushing an agricultural agenda but also among the Indians. Many-Tail-Feathers said his father burned down the Pikunni piskan because he'd had a vision in which a buffalo bull came to warn him: "With your piskans you are rapidly killing off us buffalo. . . . So this I say: stop using your piskans if you would prevent something dreadful happening to all of your kind."[21]

As the buffalo herds shrank and white settlers encroached on the tribes' territories, the Indians fought with each other and with the U.S. Army over access to hunting grounds. At an 1851 meeting at Fort Laramie to define their hunting territories, the tribal leaders accepted the eastern third of what would become Yellowstone National Park as part of the Crow nation. The treaty commissioners' goal was to minimize conflicts between the tribes and assure the safe passage of white settlers as they migrated west through Indian lands, but the accord could not end the competition for an increasingly scarce resource. In his annual winter count, a traditional depiction of events on buffalo hide, Bad Head of the Blackfeet designated 1854 as the year "when we ate dogs."[22] The commissioner of the Bureau of Indian Affairs reported that "the great diminution of the buffalo and other game" had pushed the Plains Indians to such "destitution as to compel them to plunder or steal from our citizens or starve."[23]

When General George Crook worried that the wanton killing of buffalo by his allies, the Crows and Shoshones, would foil their plans to sneak up on the Sioux in 1876, the Crows explained, "Better kill the buffalo than have him feed the Sioux."[24] The Euro-Americans were not the only ones to think that the buffalo of my enemy is better off dead.

Tenacity of Purpose

The herding defense used by bison to protect their calves from predation by wolves was of little value against hunters on horseback, but the bison did become warier of humans. Approaching hunters could trigger a stampede that resulted in winded horses and fallen riders instead of dead buffalo. Colonel Richard Dodge observed, "A buffalo can run only about two-thirds as fast as a good horse; but what he lacks in speed he makes up in bottom or endurance, in tenacity of purpose, and in most extraordinary vitality. If a herd is not overtaken in 500 or 600 yards, the chase had better be abandoned, if any regard is to be had for the horse."[25] Sometimes the buffalo killed the horses by goring them, leaving the rider vulnerable to a similar assault. Both Indians and white hunters began staking their horses and approaching the herd downwind by crawling through vegetation. If the first shot proved fatal, the herd rarely moved more than a short distance, and several dozen buffalo could be killed before the herd became so alarmed that it stampeded. Zoologist William Hornaday, who hunted buffalo in 1886, commented on how the other buffalo "cluster around the fallen ones, sniff at the warm blood, bawl aloud in wonderment, and do everything but run away."[26] The Indian belief that the buffalo gave themselves willingly appeared to be true, even for hunters who hadn't said the right prayers.

John James Audubon was among the young men who went West to see the sights, not kill the buffalo, yet became caught up in the thrill of the chase. Traveling up the Missouri River in 1843, he wrote, "Even now, there is a perceptible difference in the size of the herds, and before many years the Buffalo, like the Great Auk, will have disappeared; surely this should not be permitted."[27] Audubon intended to try buffalo hunting just once, but one chase led to another and to eventual remorse. His companion, Edward Harris, wrote afterward, "We now regretted having destroyed these noble beasts for no earthly reason but to gratify a sanguinary disposition which appears to be inherent in our natures. We had no means of carrying home the meat and after cutting out the tongues we wended our way back to camp, completely disgusted with ourselves and with the conduct of all white men who come to this country."[28]

Technological advances brought guns that made it easier to kill buffalo and new uses for buffalo hides. The demand for cattle hides to make the leather belts that drove industrial machinery outstripped the supply, and by 1850 more than half of the hides tanned in the United States had to be imported from Latin America.[29] This provided an incentive for tanners to experiment with soaking buffalo hides in a strong lime solution to create an elastic leather for industrial belts. Buffalo leather also became fashionable for use in padded furniture and other interior decor. If it now took 12 to 20 buffalo hides to make a tepee, how many would be needed for textured wall paneling for the library in Andrew Carnegie's home?

The new tanning process made the buffalo's hide worth nine times as much as the rest of the animal combined, and unlike buffalo robes, which were taken from animals killed in the winter, summer skins were preferred for tanning. This created a year-round market for buffalo, ending the reprieve that the buffalo once had during the rutting season.[30] But it was the "iron horse" as much as the flesh and blood horse or industrial belts that doomed the buffalo. The first transcontinental railroad, constructed in the 1860s, divided the population into what were referred to as the northern and southern herds, and as railroad tracks spread across the Great Plains, they made it easier for hunters to get to the buffalo and to get the buffalo hides to market, along with the cattle that were replacing the buffalo on the range. The railroads brought in more settlers and, especially after the Civil War ended, more soldiers to fight the Indians and make the plains safer for the white settlers and their cattle. The soldiers and railroad workers who labored to turn the plains into the kind of place where buffalo would no longer roam subsisted largely on buffalo meat, and the railroads that were carrying the buffalo away promoted tourist excursions that glamorized a land that still had buffalo in it, stimulating a demand for buffalo robes and buffalo wall panels in the East and for train stops so that passengers could shoot at the buffalo still to be seen through the window.

CHAPTER 3

A Park Is Born

While the railroad helped bring the last large bison herds down, it may be considered poetic justice or just a perversity of history that the railroad also brought Yellowstone National Park into being. The idea of setting aside such a park was already aloft when construction of the Northern Pacific began in 1870, and the railroad's president, Jay Cooke, needed backing for the route through Montana Territory. Nathaniel Langford, who had been Montana's chief tax collector but not yet seen the geysers to the south in Yellowstone, persuaded Cooke to "expedite the sale of Northern Pacific Railway bonds by popularizing the region through which the line was to be built."[1] Ten square miles of Yosemite Valley and a nearby redwood grove had been granted to the state of California in 1864 "to be used and preserved for the benefit of mankind," which meant that tourism soon altered its wild character. Yellowstone's promoters would have liked to have had its geothermal wonders granted to Montana, but the geysers were all in Wyoming Territory, which was not inclined to relinquish them. A federally administered park seemed the best alternative.

When Langford organized a group to explore the Yellowstone area, fear of an Indian attack caused the men to obtain a military escort. They did cross paths with a large group of Crows on the Yellowstone River, but the meeting was without incident. Although the 39 million acres granted to the Crows by the 1851 Fort Laramie Treaty had been reduced to 8 million in an 1868 treaty, their land still included a narrow strip that would become the northern edge of the park. However, the only people thought to actually reside within the future park were some nomadic bands of Shoshones, probably no more than 400 people with a few horses. Among the Shoshones they were known as the Tukudikas, which means "Sheep Eaters," the name by which they became known among white people, because they hunted bighorn sheep. Two other Shoshone groups who frequented the area in and around the park were the Agaidikas (the Fish Eaters) and the Kukundikas (the Buffalo Eaters), who later became known as the Eastern Shoshones.[2] Four decades before, the artist George Catlin wrote of the "splendid contemplation" to imagine seeing such Indians in a "nation's Park," where "by some great protecting policy of government," they would be "preserved in their pristine beauty and wildness . . . the native Indian in his classic attire, galloping his wild horse, with sinewy bow, and shield and lance, amid the fleeting herds of elks and buffaloes. What a beautiful and thrilling specimen for America to preserve and hold up to the view of her refined citizens and the world in future ages!"[3] Geologist Ferdinand Hayden, who undertook his own expedition through the proposed park, spoke to congressmen not of the Indians but of the worthlessness of the area for anything other than tourism: it had no valuable minerals or timber, and the terrain was too steep and sparsely vegetated for livestock grazing.[4] Instead of being preserved in the park as if they were a museum exhibit, as Catlin had envisioned, the Indians were overlooked when the boundaries for Yellowstone were set.

For the Benefit of the Poachers

Preservation of the park's "fleeting herds of elks and buffaloes" also received scant attention. More than a century later a *New York Times* reporter would perpetuate the valiant myth that the bison's "near-extermination helped inspire the creation of Yellowstone," but this was not so.[5] The goal of the Yellowstone Park Act of 1872 was to protect the area's natural "wonders"— its geysers and hot springs. The secretary of the interior was "to provide against the wanton destruction of the fish and game found within said Park, and against their capture and destruction for the purpose of merchandise or profit." But the bill's sponsors did not ask for the absolute protection of wildlife, a notion that did not exist at the time, nor did they propose how to prevent "wanton destruction," however that might be defined. Fishing and hunting for sport were assumed to be an appropriate activity in a park, and hunting for food was a necessity because no other source of provisions was available. As for the Indians, the idea of a preserve where hunting and even plant collecting would be prohibited would have struck them as an especially bizarre idea of the white man.

Supporters of the Yellowstone Park Act promised to request no funding for the park's administration, and none was provided. Langford visited the park only twice during his five years as the unpaid first superintendent, and the park was of benefit to poachers, who visited often. In the winter of 1874–75, thousands of elk were reportedly killed solely for their hides near Mammoth Hot Springs, where the headquarters were located. The park's bison were fewer in number, but they increased in value as herds diminished elsewhere in the country. The same economic depression that pushed Jay Cooke into bankruptcy in 1873 drove other men into hide hunting; it was one of the few thriving businesses.

Hunting on Unoccupied Lands

The decline of Indian populations during the nineteenth century did not translate directly into less Indian use of the Yellowstone area. Increasing agricultural settlement and mining camps in the Rocky Mountains made long-distance travel more difficult for Indians, but it also eliminated some of their traditional fishing and hunting places, which increased the importance of the still unsettled Yellowstone Plateau. Alliances of Bannocks, Shoshones, and other tribes from west of the divide continued to move through Yellowstone in the 1860s as they competed with the Sioux, Cheyennes, and Arapahos for the shrinking bison herds on the plains and as winter hunting in the mountains became more necessary. For the Crows the upper Yellowstone River served as a refuge from the more heavily armed Sioux, who traveled brazenly through portions of Crow territory in the late 1860s.[6]

In 1868 the Crows and Shoshones signed treaties with the U.S. government that permitted white settlers to use much of the tribes' former territories, including most of what would become Yellowstone National Park. Although the treaties often gave tribal members off-reservation hunting rights, government officials generally regarded these provisions as a temporary measure to gain time, reduce hostilities, and save government funds by enabling the Indians to support themselves. The expectation was that as white hunters and settlers entered these lands, game animals would diminish and the Indians would have to start farming. Many of the Bannocks and Shoshones had been moved onto reservations by 1872, but they didn't always stay there. The agent for the Lemhi Reservation complained that the Sheep Eaters were prone to "roaming from point to point in the mountains, making the reservation rather a convenience than a home."[7]

In 1874 the Bannocks gave up their annual hunt in the Yellowstone country, but their meat rations on the Fort Hall Reservation were gone by January, and so they were compelled to hunt. When rations ran out the following winter, heavy snow deterred most of the Indians from leaving to hunt, and the agent reported that many came to his office "begging most piteously for food, stating that their children were crying for bread, which I well knew was the truth."[8] Consequently, about 500 Indians—nearly half those on the reservation—left the following winter for their former hunting grounds.[9] Some Sheep Eaters were living in the park until at least 1879, when they were induced to settle on reservations in Idaho and Wyoming.

Impressions of bison numbers in the park in the 1870s were equally vague. When George Bird Grinnell, who later became publisher of the weekly journal *Forest and Stream*, took a 13-day trip through the area in 1875, he was distressed by the "terrible destruction of large game" but referred to "abundant" bison.[10] Philetus Norris, who was appointed super-intendent in 1877, estimated that 300 to 400 bison were residing in the Lamar Valley on the north side of the park, in addition to any that might be residing in the park interior. But he believed that bison would soon be eliminated from the entire country unless the animal could be made useful through domestication. He recommended that "two or three spirited, intelligent herdsmen" be allowed to raise livestock in the Lamar Valley, where they could also capture and gradually domesticate the wild bison calves. "Judicious slaughter and sale of their flesh, pelts, and furs, and also of those still wild," Norris believed, "might render them permanently attractive and profitable to the park and to the nation in its management. . . . If our people are ever to preserve living specimens of our most beautiful, interesting, and valuable animals, here, in their native forest and glens of this lofty cliff and snow encircled 'wonderland,' is the *place* and *now* the time to do it."

Norris did induce a rancher to put some cattle in Lamar Valley in 1877, but the Nez Perce slaughtered them for traveling rations that September. Efforts to force the Indians onto a reservation in Oregon caused 750 men, women, and children to flee through the park with 2,000 men from the U.S. Cavalry in pursuit. The Indians spent 13 days in the park, where they pastured their horses, accosted some tourists, and sought a safe passage across the mountains. More than 300 of the Nez Perce escaped into Canada, but many died during the ten-week, 1,170-mile journey, and the rest surrendered to reservation life.[11] Rebellion among the Bannocks on the Fort Hall Reservation broke out the following summer, and the last band of 60 insurgents took a detour through the park, raiding horses and frightening tourists, before they were restrained by a platoon of soldiers and Crow scouts in Montana. Neither the Nez Perce nor the Bannock uprising was directed at the park itself, but they tainted the park's relationship with Indian tribes for decades to come. The first park headquarters was constructed in 1879 on a hill that offered the "best defensive point against Indians."[12]

However, the slaughter of the cattle in Lamar Valley and other problems with hungry Indians did not dampen Norris's hopes for domesticating the park's bison. In 1878 he suggested that the park had "several excellent sites" for this purpose and that "in any or all of these localities the bison can be at least as easily reared as domestic cattle, with its flesh fully equal and its nearly black curly robes far more valuable than those of the buffalo of the plains." Norris also reported that "the intelligent members of the legislature of Montana" had passed a law to "protect bison in certain counties in Montana Territory" by inflicting a fine or imprisonment for up to six months for anyone caught killing the animal. But with no one employed to patrol the ranges or monitor the sale of hides, the law had no discernible effect. In *Forest and Stream* Grinnell lamented that Montanans were not "far-sighted enough" to enforce the game laws and thereby preserve one of the "greatest attractions" in a park that "draws so many strangers to their land . . . but in our ever-busy, bustling West every man is so intent on the accomplishments of his own private business ends, that he has little or no time to devote to the public good."[13]

A Little Decency

Like Superintendent Norris, most Euro-Americans in the nineteenth century believed that the "wildness" of both Indians and buffalo meant that they were destined to be conquered. Popular accounts of the buffalo, not unlike those about Indians, often described a violent species losing out to slaughter by humans and the forces of nature—blizzards, disease, and the hardships of nomadic life. In 1873 Interior Secretary Columbus Delano said, "I would not seriously regret the total disappearance of the buffalo from our western prairies, in its effect upon the Indians, regarding it rather as a means of hastening their sense of dependence upon the products of the soil and their own labors."[14] Some Indians would have none of it. "Now, you tell us to work for a living, but the Great Spirit did not make us to work, but to live by hunting," Chief Crazy Horse of the Oglala Sioux is reported to have said. "You white men can work if you want to. . . . We do not want your civilization! We would live as our fathers did, and their fathers before them."[15]

Despite the prevailing wisdom that the removal of the buffalo herds was a form of progress, seven western states and territories had enacted protective laws by 1883. Even though the laws were ineffective and sometimes passed only after the last buffalo had died, they were evidence that completely obliterating the herds was thought reckless, and some lawmakers regarded the commercial hide hunting as reprehensible—it violated treaties, provoked war with the Indians, and wasted meat when people were going hungry. Hard at work on behalf of the Indians, Representative Greenburg Lafayette Fort of Illinois introduced a bill in the U.S. Congress that would make it "unlawful for any person who is not an Indian to kill, wound, or in any manner destroy any female buffalo of any age, found at large," and another bill to tax buffalo hides, which he hoped would make the market unprofitable. The Committee on Territories recommended that the first bill be passed. When Jacob Cox of Ohio cited Delano's opinion "that the civilization of the Indian is impossible while the buffalo remains upon the plains," Fort replied, "I am not in favor of civilizing the Indian by starving him to death, by destroying the means which God has given him for his support." With such arguments presented for and against, the buffalo protection bill passed both houses but was ignored by President Ulysses Grant, who let the legislative session adjourn without signing it.[16]

In 1876 Fort tried another bill to preserve buffalo "for the use of the Indians, whose homes are upon the public domain, and to the frontiersmen, who may properly use them for food." He cited the money that would be saved if the Indians on reservations did not have to be fed with government-purchased cattle. The bill passed the House by a vote of 104 to 36 in February, but it faded in the Senate, and after Custer's defeat at the Little Bighorn intensified sentiment against the Indians, it had no chance of passage. Still, no one proposed a bill ordering the army to exterminate the buffalo, and evidence that the U.S. government contributed materially to or actively promoted the slaughter of buffalo is slim.

"While it may not be as satisfying an explanation for those who prefer the federal government as proximate cause in most evils," historian Dan Flores could find no evidence of a government plan to end the Indians' use of buffalo.[17] That was taken care of by men who were out for their personal gain. Even if Grant had signed the protective legislation, the government would have had no realistic means of enforcing it. The Canadian government prohibited the commercial slaughter of buffalo in 1877, but the number of buffalo in that country continued to decline until it bottomed out at several hundred in the 1890s. There was no precedent for federal legislation protecting any animal. The U.S. government was at that time no more capable of saving the American buffalo than it was of saving the lives of settlers who died of starvation during the locust plagues of 1875. The difficulty of such a mission would become even more apparent after the military took over the administration of Yellowstone in 1886.

Apprehension among the Cattlemen

In 1879 the hunters who had pursued the southern herd for eight years discovered that only a few thousand buffalo remained—not enough to support another hunting season. An estimated 500,000 buffalo still inhabited eastern Montana when the railroad reached Miles City in 1881, and the entire northern herd numbered about one million. In northern Wyoming that year, the *Cheyenne Leader* warned that "so many buffaloes are reported between Fort Fetterman and Fort McKinney and through the Little Big Horn Valley as to cause serious apprehension among the cattlemen in regard to the grazing."[18] But two years later, estimates of the northern herd had dropped to 75,000, and a cordon of hunting camps that stretched across Montana prevented many buffalo from escaping to Canada. In 1884 white hunters were joined by Chief Sitting Bull and nearly a thousand of his braves from the Standing Rock Agency in slaughtering about 10,000 buffalo in the Dakota Territory, the largest remaining herd.

In the Yellowstone area, Indians began hunting more elk, but the abrupt end of buffalo led to famine for many. Nearly one-third of the 1,800 Piikani Blackfeet died of malnutrition at their agency on Badger Creek in the winter of 1883–84. Some struggled along on muskrats, gophers, and grass, and a few survived by butchering their horses and dogs, but others considered the horse and dog sacred in a way different from that of the buffalo, a way that made eating them forbidden. Accustomed to buffalo meat and the life of the hunt, the Blackfeet resisted changing their ways even in the face of starvation. They found cattle meat to be unpalatable, and they feared that it carried the white man's diseases, as their tribe suffered its first outbreak of mumps shortly after their first taste of it.[19]

Some buffalo were brought down by men who hunted for sport rather than for food or profit, and sport hunters would later have a large role in wildlife preservation. In 1879 a wealthy group led by dude rancher Howard Eaton arrived in an area of the Dakota Badlands they considered a "sportsman's paradise."[20] But when 25-year-old Theodore Roosevelt came for his buffalo hunt four years later, he had difficulty finding one to shoot. In 1885, after buying a ranch in the Dakota Territory where today a national park bears his name, Roosevelt concluded that the buffalo had to make way for white settlers. "We wanted the game preserved," he later explained, "but chiefly with the idea that it should be protected in order that there might be good hunting which should last for generations."[21] Sportsmen like Roosevelt and Grinnell believed that the buffalo slaughter was necessary for the country's economic growth. "The Indian, the buffalo, the elk, deer and moose will disappear; from many sections they have already done so," wrote Grinnell in 1882. "This was to have been expected, and while it may be deplored, it cannot be avoided. The interests of civilization demand that the country shall be settled and improved, and sentiment cannot be permitted to stand in the way of such improvement."[22]

Excellent Hunting in the Park

After the big southern and northern herds were gone, some bison remained on the headwaters of the Yellowstone River, too few and too far from the railroad to be of interest to the hide hunters. Indian use of the northeast part of the park dropped off as gold prospectors established camps along the boundary.[23] The U.S. government wanted to encourage mining and the extension of railroad lines north of the park, and in 1880 the Crows were persuaded to sell the western fifth of their reservation, including the narrow strip along the park's north boundary. The white sightseers for whom the park was intended did not want to see Indians, and Superintendent Norris sought to persuade them to stay away. After visiting the Crow, Bannock, and Shoshone agencies in 1880, he said he had their "solemn promise" not to venture north of Heart Lake, "thus averting in future all danger of conflict between these tribes and laborers or tourists." In 1881 he reported that "decimation by war and disease, with the occupancy of intervening regions by whites, guarantees future safety from the Blackfeet; a nearly impassable mountain range and a cordon of military posts and armed ranchmen, from the Sioux." But he knew that Indians still entered the park, and he wanted the army to set up a military post on Yellowstone's west boundary to keep out Indians from the Fort Hall and Lemhi reservations.

The Indians were no worse than the U.S. government at keeping promises, but some resisted life on the reservation and continued to hunt in the park, often avoiding notice by staying away from the few areas where tourists were concentrated. White people were still permitted to hunt in Yellowstone, however. "Although severe and dangerous, hunting in the Park was excellent sport, and the only recreation I enjoyed during the season," Norris claimed in 1880, when he estimated the park had about 600 bison in three herds. To advance Norris's plans for semidomesticated ungulate herds in the Lamar Valley, Harry Yount was employed as a gamekeeper that year. One of the first white men to spend an entire winter in Yellowstone, Yount resigned after one year in frustration over the impossibility of his job, and recommended that what the park needed was a police force.[24]

After traveling through Yellowstone in the summers of 1881 and 1882, General Philip Sheridan disparaged the park's adequacy as a game reserve and urged Congress to nearly double the size of the park by extending the boundary 40 miles to the east and 10 miles to the south. "This extension would not be taking anything away from the people, as the territory thus annexed to the Park can never be settled upon," he claimed. Sheridan's primary concern was that the hide hunters were reducing the game available to sport hunters such as himself. Although his advice was not followed, the Forest Reserve Act of 1891 set aside areas around the park that later became part of the national forest system and Grand Teton National Park. At the time, Sheridan's recommendation to enlarge the park seemed beside the point, given the government's failure to prevent poaching within its existing area, but his request to station troops in the park to protect the game animals was also turned down. Grinnell, who described the Department of the Interior as "that sink of corruption," also urged sending in the cavalry because the park was "overrun" with hide hunters who "laugh defiance at the government.[25]

The Retention of a Few Buffaloes

In 1883 the secretary of the interior issued regulations to "prohibit absolutely the killing, wounding or capturing at any time" certain animals in Yellowstone, including "any buffalo, bison, moose, elk, black-tailed or white-tailed deer, . . . or any of the small birds commonly known as singing birds."[26] Despite his cynicism just a few months before, Grinnell lauded the policy as one that "will rejoice the heart of every man throughout the land who is far-seeing and intelligent enough to appreciate the importance of preserving from utter extinction the noble game with which, in some few locations, the grand old Rocky Mountains still teem. . . . While it may not all at once wholly prevent the killing of these animals, its moral effect can scarcely be overestimated."[27] But Grinnell did overestimate the effect, for poachers could be penalized only by expulsion from the park, and moral considerations did not weigh heavily with them. Settlers around the park resented game laws and did not believe that they would benefit from game protection as growing animal populations dispersed from the park.

With encouragement from General Sheridan, Senator George Graham Vest of Missouri made six unsuccessful attempts in the 1880s to pass legislation that would curb hunting in the park. Even Buffalo Bill Cody, who claimed to have killed 4,280 buffalo, urged protection of the park's game and noted that wholesale butchery "does not find favor in the West as it did a decade or so ago."[28] But opposition came from railroad officials, mining interests, and real estate speculators who wanted tracks laid across the park to transport tourists and haul ore from mines on the former Crow reservation. Representative Louis Payson of Illinois, who was being paid to lobby on behalf of the railroad, assured the House that, except for Mammoth Hot Springs, there was not "another object of natural curiosity within 40 miles" of the proposed railroad. "I cannot understand the sentiment which favors the retention of a few buffaloes to the development of mining interests amounting to millions of dollars." For Representative William McAdoo of New Jersey, Yellowstone served the higher purpose of preserving wilderness, and he pleaded with his colleagues to "prefer the beautiful and the sublime . . . to heartless mammon and the greed of capital." Representative Samuel Cos of New York also believed that utilitarian criteria were irrelevant. He saw support of the park as a matter of preserving "all that gives elevation and grace to human nature, by the observation of physical nature." At the conclusion of his speech the House applauded and the railroad's request for a right of way was denied.[29] For historian Roderick Nash this rebuff was a seminal moment in the development of attitudes toward wildlife protection. "Never before had wilderness values withstood such a direct confrontation with civilization."[30]

In endeavoring to withstand their confrontation with the white man in Yellowstone, the Indians' success was more fleeting. After a horseback trip through the park with his wife and 17-year-old daughter in the summer of 1885, New York attorney George Wingate reported that "the Indian difficulty has been cured, the Indians have been forced back on their distant reservations, and the traveler in the park will see or hear no more of them than if he was in the Adirondacks or White Mountains."[31] Wingate was mistaken; the Indians were there, and they dared to behave as if their presence was permitted. They remained largely on the park's outskirts, but instead of moving surreptitiously in small bands as white poachers did, they still hunted in large groups. This fact, and their technique of setting fires to dislodge game animals, made the Indians' presence impossible to overlook, but lacking any jurisdiction over them, park officials could do little more than insist the Indians leave the park.[32]

David Wear, a retired army officer who was appointed superintendent in 1885, disparaged his predecessors for having allowed game to be "shot with impunity and marketed at the hotels without interference." In February 1886 *Forest and Stream* reported that there were "two or three herds of buffalo of not more than 60 each," that frequently crossed the park border, "travelling short distances for grazing purposes," and the journal advised adding this area to the park.[33] Congress ignored such recommendations and canceled funds for paying the superintendent and his staff, compelling the secretary of the interior to request assistance from the secretary of war. By August 20, 1886, Captain Moses Harris and 50 cavalrymen from Fort Custer had arrived to take over at Yellowstone.

Grinnell described the troop's confrontation with a band of Bannocks a month later, "when the Park was thronged with visitors." This is difficult to picture, given that visitation for the entire year was probably less than 5,000—not even half the number of visitors in the park on a single September day now. Still, it must have been quite a sight when the Bannocks, whose number was variously estimated at 50 to 100, appeared "in such warlike array as to give rise to much anxiety and excitement among the tourists, causing many of them to shorten their stay in the Park." The Bannocks were also induced to end their stay, but as soon as the soldiers left them, they started two forest fires to drive game out of the park and, "withdrawing into the mountains to the west, continued their hunting operations secure from interruption by the troops."[34]

Captain Harris and the army officers who succeeded him were referred to as "acting superintendents" because military administration of the park was expected to be only a temporary measure, but it lasted for 30 years. From Mammoth Hot Springs, where the park headquarters were later designated "Fort Yellowstone," the cavalrymen patrolled the boundary and major points of interest, arresting poachers and expelling squatters, wood-cutters, and vandals. In 1887 Harris was "practically certain" that no bison had been killed in the park during the last two years. But he cautioned, "My impression is that they have been heretofore somewhat overestimated, and that at the present time they will not exceed 100 in number." A man ahead of his time, or at least ahead of Philetus Norris's, Harris responded loftily to a Canadian offer to sell bison to Yellowstone: "It is not the policy of the government to endeavor to make this Park attractive by making a collection of domesticated animals, but rather to preserve the reservation in its natural condition and to protect the existing game animals so that they may breed in security."[35]

However, the members of Troop M knew little of the park's animals or its natural condition, for their assignments in Yellowstone often lasted less than a year, and most of them could not ski, which was the only means of travel through the park during the long winter. When the War Department learned that a man had been arrested for skinning three bison, Harris was ordered to discharge the prisoner who had been detained "without authority of law or military regulations."[36]

Although he complained about the white poachers, Harris believed that a band of Indians could cause more destruction during a summer hunt than all of the white hunters combined and that Indian hunting was an "unmitigated evil" that threatened the park's purpose. He despaired that his efforts were futile as long as Yellowstone continued "to afford summer amusement and winter sustenance to a band of savage Indians." Grinnell also denounced Indian hunting in the park, describing in *Forest and Stream* how the Crows, Shoshones, and Bannocks used the area to obtain their winter supply of meat. "The injury done by Indian hunting parties to the forest and the game in and near the Yellowstone Park is so serious that it demands immediate attention. . . . It is clear that these Indians ought not

to be allowed to leave their reservations except in charge of some responsible white man who can be held accountable for their actions."[37]

Grinnell was known to be sympathetic toward the Indians' plight and
had used his influence with Theodore Roosevelt and other politicians to
address mismanagement of the reservations, and he tried to maintain the
high moral ground. "We are not among those who believe that the Indian
has no rights which should be respected. On this point we are quite
prepared to stand upon our record. When, however, the Indian does
anything antagonistic to the general welfare he must be restrained." But it
was the unrestrained white poachers who were seeking out the few bison
in the park; the Indians were hunting for food and took any game they
could find. And despite Harris's best efforts, poachers continued to kill
bison in the park and then flee with the heads and hides. Those averse to
the risk of entering the park camped just outside the boundary and waited
for the bison to wander out.

Wanted Dead or Alive

*Under different circumstances, nothing could have induced me to engage
in such a mean, cruel, and utterly heartless enterprise as the hunting down
of the last representatives of a vanishing race, but there was no alternative.
The philistines were upon them, and between leaving them to be killed by
the care-for-naught cowboys, who would leave them to decay, body and
soul, where they fell, and killing them ourselves for the purpose of
preserving their remains, there was really no choice.*
                    —William Hornaday, "The Passing of the Buffalo," 1887[38]

While the taxidermists of Livingston were tanning bison hides from Yellowstone and shipping the heads to ornament Victorian parlors, the taxidermist
of the National Museum in Washington, D.C., wanted to obtain enough
whole bison to mount an exhibit. William Hornaday's inquiries in the
spring of 1886 brought grim news: outside of Yellowstone there was only a
band of six or eight bison in southwestern Dakota—too few to justify the
search—and about 200 in scattered bands in the Texas Panhandle—too
difficult to reach, or the hunters would already have killed them—and
some bison near Big Dry Creek, 90 miles north of Miles City in Montana.

Hornaday left for Montana in May, killed a bull that was too old to be
of any value except for its skeleton, and loaded a live calf into the baggage

car for a train ride to Washington, where it died from eating too much damp clover. But about 35 bison were said to be roaming farther north in the rugged butte country, and Hornaday returned there in the fall to search across "great yawning ravines and hollows, steep-sided and very deep, and bad lands of the worst description."[39] After searching for 18 days, Hornaday's party found bison that spooked at the slightest movement and could easily outdistance horses over the tortuous terrain. Most of the old bulls bore the scars of rifle shots. A review of Hornaday's subsequent book, *The Extermination of the American Bison*, explained these bison were "changing from the old-time fat, sleepy beasts that the hunter could shoot down by the score from his stand, to a race of alert, keen-eyed, greyhound-like animals that were ever on the go, and were all muscle."[40]

Hornaday's expedition came to collect 20 bison and left with 23. Like Audubon, Hornaday discovered the thrill of the chase. He lamented having to spend so much time preparing specimens instead of pursuing bison, and took off for just one more hunt, on which he killed a bull with four old bullets in his carcass. The skinning of another bull could not be finished before darkness, and when the men returned to the site the next morning, they found that Indians had stolen the skin and edible meat, broken a bone to get the marrow, and smeared the head with red and yellow paint in defiance. Hornaday was bitter toward Indians for the rest of his life. A magazine article he wrote about the expedition began, without any sense of complicity: "At last the game butchers of the great West have stopped killing buffalo. The buffalo are all dead!" Not quite, but Hornaday lamented the lack of federal protection for the remaining bison: "Another fact that stares us unpleasantly in the face is that with the exception of the wild buffalo in the National Park, all of which will eventually either wander out or be frightened out and killed, unless the Park is inclosed by a barbed wire fence in time to prevent it, the National Government has not a single buffalo on any of its reservations, nor anywhere else in charge of anyone in its employ."[41]

But Hornaday soon had a group of six buffalo standing in lifelike postures, placidly sniffing at clumps of wax grass and bending to drink from a pool of glass in the National Museum.[42] The American Museum of Natural History, which craved an exhibit of its own, sent an expedition that searched the same area of Montana for three months in 1887 without finding any of the bison that remained there in the badlands, protected by the local cowboys.[43] No, the buffalo weren't all dead when Hornaday returned from Montana with his specimens. Sam Bedson, a penitentiary warden in Winnipeg, bought four bison calves and one bull from some Indians in 1877 and gradually built up a herd of nearly 100 animals. In Texas Charles Goodnight captured some of the wild calves left in the Panhandle in 1878, nursed them with domestic cows, and eventually had a herd of 125. There were still wild bison in the Panhandle when Charles Jesse Jones made four annual trips starting in 1886, during which he acquired the name "Buffalo Jones" and more than 60 calves, some of which survived the journey to his ranch in Garden City, Kansas. All of the adult bison that he roped died. As Jones explained it, the animals "took fits, stiffened themselves, then dropped dead, apparently preferring death to captivity."[44] During his last trip to Texas in 1889, he released carrier pigeons to take periodic reports back to Garden City, from where they were wired to the *Chicago Times* so that the nation could be kept abreast of his ordeals as buffalo savior.[45]

Jones expressed remorse for his previous career as a buffalo hunter, and his efforts to "save" some wild buffalo may have salved his conscience, but he wanted to make a fortune and expected that hunters would pay large sums to shoot his buffalo. Most of the 95 buffalo he purchased from Bedson reached his ranch alive, having taken the train from Winnipeg. By 1892 he was able to sell ten buffalo for $1,000 each. The buffalo was now worth more alive than dead. Jones tried to domesticate them as beasts of burden and even designed a buffalo-drawn streetcar system for Garden City, but the project never got going because the buffalo declined to follow directions. Jones lost his money speculating in real estate, and when he had to sell his herd in 1895 to pay off debts, 45 of the animals went to Michel Pablo and Charles Allard, half-blood Indians who had a herd on the Flathead Reservation in Montana. The Flatheads sometimes returned from buffalo hunts with orphaned calves, and Pablo and Allard had started their herd in 1884 by purchasing some of these animals. With the addition of Jones's buffalo, their herd became the largest in the United States and numbered about 300 in 1896.[46]

The Happy Poacher

Although privately owned bison herds were growing, the future of the wild bison in Yellowstone remained precarious. Soon after taking command at Fort Yellowstone in February 1891, Captain George Anderson learned of E. E. Van Dyck, who was suspected of having sold bison heads to a

Livingston taxidermist. Van Dyck was arrested on the Lamar River in possession of beaver traps and held in the Fort Yellowstone guardhouse for more than a month, but there was nothing he could be charged with. After capturing two bison calves on Specimen Ridge the following June, Charles Pendleton crammed them into beer cases lashed to mules and took them north of the park, but they died before he could get them home. When Pendleton returned to the park for replacements, he ran into a patrol and was arrested, but all that could be done was to order him to limit his movement to the road from Cooke City to Gardiner, which he immediately ignored. He was briefly confined in the guardhouse and his belongings were confiscated. But many of the poachers used cheap guns and old horses and wagons, whose loss would mean little, and with taxidermists paying upwards of $300 for a head, the poachers were willing to take the slight risk of getting caught. Anderson amassed so much confiscated equipment that he lit bonfires to burn it.

Anderson pleaded with Secretary of the Interior John Noble for legislation that would impose penalties for poaching and other offenses in the park. He tried to make the most of evictions by having poachers marched on foot across the park, accompanied by a mounted soldier, and expelled at the opposite boundary. In his annual report for 1891 Anderson claimed to have "abundant evidence" that "the buffalo are contented and quiet in the Park." The following year he estimated the bison herd at "certainly not less than four hundred" and declared that "their perpetuity within the park is thoroughly assured, and a steady and gradual increase may be looked for." *Forest and Stream* expressed confidence in Anderson's ability to manage the park. "He has infused the heedless, happy-go-lucky tourists who desire to carry away everything they see with a wholesome respect for the law, while the deliberate law-breaker is mightily afraid."[47] Much of the local populace, however, lacked a wholesome respect for Anderson and regarded the soldiers patrolling the park not as the heroic vanguard of wildlife protection but as an imposition of martial law by the "Czar of Wonderland."[48] Under Yellowstone's previous administration, many settlers had treated the park as they did unsettled land elsewhere—open to timbering, grazing, and hunting.

Despite Captain Anderson's assurances, the winter of 1893–94 was a profitable one for poachers on the park's west boundary, who took 116 buffalo. Southeast of the park, Indians reportedly killed 19. Crossing the park's east boundary, two men brought in supplies on a hand sledge and established a camp on Astringent Creek, where they intended to kill buffalo. But they quarreled, and one of them, Edgar Howell, drove his partner out and remained there alone. In February a scouting party that went into Pelican Valley to report on the buffalo came across a sledge trail that appeared to head toward Cooke City. When Felix Burgess, a civilian scout, and Private Troike were sent in to investigate, they found snowshoe tracks that led to a tepee and six buffalo heads hanging from trees. The heads had been wrapped in gunnysacks and hoisted there to keep wolves from getting at them.[49]

Continuing down to Pelican Creek, Burgess and Troike heard rifle shots and found Howell removing the head from one of five buffalo carcasses. Neither Howell nor his dog realized they had visitors, and Burgess dashed 200 yards in snowshoes to get within pistol range despite missing two toes that some Crow Indians had cut off. When Burgess was within 15 feet, he told Howell to drop his knife and raise his hands. The men spent the night at the Canyon Hotel, where Howell was reported to be "chipper and gay." He seemed glad to have been brought in out of the cold and ate 24 pancakes at breakfast, acting as if he were an honored guest. "If you don't think it's a hard trail from Cooke City to Pelican Valley, you just try pulling a toboggan over Specimen Ridge," he said. Back in Fort Yellowstone, he resided in the guardhouse, and plans were made to turn him over to Wyoming territorial authorities for conviction under the Wyoming buffalo protection law. However, the law made no provision for transferring someone from the park for punishment, and Howell had to be released after barely a month. Burgess's big toe, which had quadrupled in size during the mission, had to be amputated.

However, Howell's case was distinguished from previous catch-and-release arrests by the presence of a correspondent for *Forest and Stream*, Emerson Hough, who happened to be in the park to report on poaching activities. Grinnell published Hough's story, along with an editorial pleading on behalf of the Yellowstone buffalo, "the most curious ornaments, the rarest of the living wonders of our American Wonderland." He charged that Congress, "by its continued neglect, encourages the evil-minded to believe that they may penetrate even here and destroy this last remnant of a race long nearly extinct."[50] Grinnell and some influential friends also went to Washington and presented such a persuasive case that a bill "to protect the birds and animals in Yellowstone National Park, and to punish crimes in said park" was introduced by Representative John Lacey of Iowa less than two weeks after

Howell's arrest. The Lacey Act, as it became known, blew through Congress in a gust of outrage and was signed into law by President Benjamin Harrison on May 7, 1894. It prohibited the transport of animals from the park and imposed jail sentences of up to two years, fines up to $1,000, and forfeiture of equipment used while committing the crime. It also provided for a U.S. circuit court commissioner and deputy marshals to be assigned to Yellowstone and funds for constructing a jail in Mammoth Hot Springs, and eventually the park received funds to hire three more scouts.

Although Howell could not be tried under the law, which was passed after his arrest, he was expelled from the park and forbidden to return without permission. Howell was not easily cowed, however, and he was arrested several months later when Captain Anderson found him sitting in the barber's chair at the Mammoth Hot Springs Hotel. He was fined $50 and sentenced to a month in jail, but he appealed the case and soon went free. Rather than defend himself as a man just trying to make a living, Howell bragged that he'd killed 80 buffalo the previous winter. He wrote blithely to the editor of the *Livingston Enterprise* of the daring that had enabled him to elude park patrols for so long and to survive the winter in Yellowstone. "I was doing what a great many more would do if they had my courage and ability."[51] In 1896 Howell was refused permission to travel through the park, but a year later he was employed at Yellowstone as a scout to apprehend poachers.

Mourning the Buffalo

The Lacey Act had long-term consequences for wildlife protection in national parks by putting teeth in anti-poaching laws, but the number of buffalo in Yellowstone continued to decline. For some poachers the increased risk of getting caught was offset by the larger potential profit. Shortly after the Lacey Act was passed, Captain Anderson told the secretary of the interior that taxidermists were paying $500 for a buffalo head, which they could sell mounted for $1,500, and a "rich and anxious customer" might pay a good deal more.[52] In 1895 *Forest and Stream* warned that "no matter how earnest and energetic they may be," the few troops stationed in the park could not adequately patrol the west boundary, and that unless the state of Idaho provided some assistance, the few buffalo remaining in the park would be eliminated.[53] "A wild buffalo is looked on as a small fortune walking around without an owner," *Recreation* magazine explained in 1901.[54]

Officers of the Sixth U.S. Cavalry with buffalo heads, probably taken from poacher Ed Howell in 1894. Courtesy of Yellowstone Photograph Archives.

Anderson was especially annoyed that the poachers operated with the apparent cooperation or at least sympathy of other local residents, but he did receive occasional anonymous tips from people who were either concerned about the loss of wildlife or resentful of the poachers' success. "I will drop you a few lines as a favor for the buffaloes as they are about extinct," read a letter from Gardiner that told of the capture of several calves in the park and was signed "A Friend to the Buffalo." Reporting on what had been observed west of the park, an informant advised, "If you make an investigation and search about the hunters and fishermen's cabins about Henry Lake you will find where some of your Bison has gone to." Another note specified that Dick Rock of Henrys Lake "has in his possession three young Buffalo calves supposed to have been caught in the Park."[55]

Over time, the prices offered by taxidermists dropped as buffalo became available from private herds, and as tourism and support for game protection in Yellowstone communities increased. But the wariness that may have saved the few buffalo in the park may have also prevented their number from growing. They endured winter in the remote Pelican Valley, where forage often had to be excavated from under deep snow, and some may have starved to death rather than move to lower ranges where men with guns waited. Aside from the buffalo in Dry Creek, Montana, which were gone by 1899, the only wild herd outside Yellowstone numbered about 30 in Lost Park, Colorado. They were looked after by local ranchers, but poachers diminished the herd until the last four were found dead in 1897.

Except for the herd on the Flathead Reservation, living buffalo were no longer part of Indian lives, but some tribes tried to maintain the old traditions. At the Red Cloud Agency in Nebraska, the Oglala Sioux prepared for the delivery of government-purchased cattle as they had once prepared for a buffalo hunt. When the animals were released into the corral, the Indians staged a mock hunt in which cattle were chased on horseback, slaughtered, and butchered in the traditional way. This practice continued until 1897, when the U.S. government thought it best to end this form of cultural expression and build a slaughterhouse. "The meat was to be killed by butchers and cut in the white man's way," explained Fire Thunder, "which cut short the enjoyment of raw entrails while still hot." In his winter count No Ears designated 1897 as the year "they burned down the slaughter-house" because that was how the Indians responded.[56]

That was the year after four buffalo were sent from Goodnight's Texas herd on a two-week journey by way of Fond du Lac, Wisconsin, to the end of the Northern Pacific's branch line at Cinnabar, Montana, and then hauled on wagons to Yellowstone Lake, where they traveled by barge to Dot Island, a place named for its teensiness. E. C. Waters, president of the Yellowstone Lake Boat Company and part-time resident of Fond du Lac, had purchased the buffalo to be in a "zoological garden" for the viewing pleasure of tourists who took his steamboat from West Thumb to the Lake Hotel. He also had some elk moved to the island for the summer. Few tourists were pleased and some considered the animals' internment inhumane. Nonetheless, Waters tried to attract more business in 1899 by requesting permission to add a few Indians "to be kept in their wigwams" on the island during the summer.[57] The secretary of the interior gave his consent but stipulated that any Indians who left their reservation for this purpose must be "entirely willing to go" and must return to their reservation promptly at the end of the season.[58] Waters may have been unable to persuade any Indians to spend the summer on Dot Island, for no evidence has been found that the display ever included them.[59]

The National Association of Game and Fish Wardens and Commissioners, which held its annual meeting in the park in 1907, was aghast at the "pitiful" condition of the animals on Dot Island.[60] The acting superintendent, Samuel Young, ordered Waters to remove the animals from the park, but they were confined near the Lake Hotel at the end of the summer as usual. In October Young had the pens taken down. He wanted the eight buffalo and seven elk driven from the park because they were infected with mange, but the following June, one of the buffalo was seen near the lake "disturbing traffic and endangering the lives of tourists by frightening horses, etc., along the stage road."[61]

CHAPTER 4

Not Just Another Buffalo

Like the American Indian and the West Indies, neither of which has anything to do with India, the American buffalo was misnamed by confused Europeans. Few of them knew or cared that in 1758 the Swedish naturalist Carolus Linnaeus had assigned the American buffalo a scientific name, *Bos bison*, setting it apart from the European bison or wisent, *Bos bonasus*, and putting both animals in a different genus from the African cape buffalo (*Syncerus caffer*) and the Asian buffalo (*Bubalus arnee*). It was Linnaeus who devised the system of two-part Latin names for plants and animals: the first part for the genus and the second for the species. Each genus, which is broadly defined as a group of plants or animals with characteristics that distinguish it from other groups, may include any number of species. Similar-looking animals are generally considered different species if they cannot mate without human assistance or produce healthy, fertile offspring. To recognize significant differences within a species, biologists may use a third name to indicate subspecies.

Members of the Bovid family spread from southern Asia to locations all over Earth in forms ranging from the musk ox of Alaska to the Philippine *tamarau*. Like the bison, some of these species now exist in both wild and domesticated forms, but some exist only as wild animals and others only as domesticated animals. Domestication occurs when animals are bred in captivity to emphasize traits valued by humans rather than those that would result from natural selection. By classifying the American bison as *Bos bison*, Linnaeus put it in the same genus as cattle, which by then existed only as domestic livestock, and taxonomists have been debating the merits of this idea ever since. In 1849 the British naturalist Charles Knight gave the bison a genus of its own, *Bison,* and this classification came to be widely accepted.

While the Linnaean system provides biologists all over the world with a standard naming format, it does not prevent disagreements about taxonomy, the science of classifying specimens. Evolution generates living things across a spectrum of characteristics, not in tidy categories. Taxonomic debates are often between "lumpers," who emphasize the similarities between specimens and put them in the same group, and "splitters," who focus on the differences between specimens and put them in separate groups. The development of DNA testing has cast doubt on many taxonomic as well as courtroom verdicts and has generally supported a trend toward lumping. Studies of bison and cattle genes suggest that although they may have gone their separate ways on the evolutionary tree more than four million years ago, and bison ended up with 14 pairs of ribs and cattle only 13, deep down inside the animals are still closely related enough to belong to the same genus.[1] Some taxonomists are again classifying the American buffalo as *Bos bison,* but this shift has not yet been officially accepted by the scientific bodies that sanction such changes.

In North America the "plains bison" and the Canadian "wood bison" are now considered to be the same species, and some mammalogists also regard the European wisent as the same species.[2] The three forms of bison have demonstrated their ability to mate with each other and produce fertile offspring, but the wisent is the most visibly and ecologically different of the three. It has a less pronounced hump, smaller head and forequarters, and hairier tail, and its horns project forward rather than up. The wisent was extinct in the wild by the 1920s, but a small number of captive wisents have been used to reintroduce herds on public lands in Europe and Russia.

The domestic dog, *Canis familiaris,* is the most diverse species on Earth, existing in a wide range of physical forms and behaviors. Although this diversity is the result of human manipulation, any two animal populations with a common ancestor begin to diverge unless there is some exchange of genes. After mutation and natural selection have operated independently in each of the populations for long enough, eventually they become different species. But "eventually" is a gray area, and decisions about when speciation occurs can appear arbitrary rather than scientific. Fossils do not provide irrefutable evidence as to how far back one must go to find the common ancestor of the North American and European bison, but it may have been tens or hundreds of thousands of years.

The Elusive Mountain Bison of Yellowstone

Early reports of wildlife in the park often referred to the "mountain" bison or buffalo. According to Superintendent Norris in 1880, these animals "differ materially from the buffalo of the Great Plains, being more hardy, fleet, and intelligent" and having hides that were "darker, finer, and more curly." He also believed that they were "the most keen of scent and difficult of approach of all mountain animals" during the summer and fall. After his trip through Yellowstone in 1885, George Wingate described the so-called mountain buffalo as "smaller and more active than the buffalo of the plains" and "wary in the extreme"—"unlike the common buffalo, which is a stupid animal." Even though he considered the common buffalo to be "almost as extinct as the dodo," Wingate predicted that it was so difficult to kill the mountain buffalo that "it is probable that they will be able to keep up their struggle for existence for a long time to come."[3]

This mountain buffalo was thought to be the same subspecies as the wood bison, *Bison bison athabascae*. Wood bison are generally both darker and larger than plains bison (*B. b. bison*) and have a more angular hump and less distinct cape and chaps. The contemporary Yellowstone bison are not considered significantly different in size or color from other noncommercial bison in the United States. In her 1970 Ph.D. dissertation on the Yellowstone bison, Mary Meagher referred to the original bison in the area as *B. b. athabascae* and the current population as a "hybrid herd," a result of the 21 plains bison brought to the park in 1902.[4] But references to the Yellowstone bison as a "hybrid" remained infrequent, perhaps because such a status seemed to confuse claims of the herd's uniqueness that were used to argue against lethal efforts to eliminate brucellosis from the herd. In 1985 Meagher acknowledged that "today most authorities view the original Yellowstone bison as a northern and perhaps slightly larger form of plains bison."[5] A 1998 study on brucellosis in the Yellowstone area published by the National Academy of Sciences referred to "the original bison" that inhabited "the valleys in the Rocky Mountains" as "*B. b. athabaska*," but Canadian zoologists typically regard the wood buffalo as an animal that has been unique to their own country.[6]

It probably makes no difference at all to the Yellowstone bison if it were once a different subspecies or a different "form" of the plains bison. But to the conservation biologist, if the original Yellowstone bison were genetically different from the plains bison, then something was lost after 21 plains bison were brought to the park in 1902. National Park Service director William Mott said in 1987, "Although past actions taken to supplement the Yellowstone herd were based on accepted wildlife management practices of the time, given modern ecological understanding, this hybridization is unfortunate in that it may have caused a loss of genetic integrity of the Yellowstone bison herd."[7] Consequently, while the Yellowstone bison is generally regarded as "one of the shining successes of wildlife conservation,"[8] Yellowstone historian Aubrey Haines described the introduction of plains bison as "a failed enterprise based on a noble idea." While it succeeded in ensuring the park "an adequate number of buffalo," it was "a biological disaster in that the inevitable cross-breeding between imported plains buffalo and the local mountain buffalo resulted in hybrid animals not really typical of either strain."[9]

Examining the question through a microscope rather than the lens of history, some biologists have come to a different conclusion. A genetic study of three wood bison herds and eight plains bison herds on public land found that the Yellowstone herd "clumped together [statistically] amidst the other plains bison populations," suggesting that "the indigenous animals in this park were in fact plains bison."[10] Whether there is a significant genetic difference between animals referred to as wood bison and plains bison remains a matter of dispute, given the relatively short period that has elapsed since the two forms could have begun diverging as species (possibly no more than 5,000 years ago) and the fact that by now even the most remote wood bison herds in Canada have been affected by interbreeding with plains bison. Physical differences such as size and coloring can be a short-term response to an animal's habitat rather than the result of the wood bison's evolution in smaller herds with a more sedentary existence than that of the nomadic plains bison.[11]

Because they don't seem to have any genetic basis, some differences in appearance are no longer considered relevant for purposes of taxonomy, but current methods of DNA testing may not be capable of detecting all significant genetic variations. It could be that biologists are still looking at the animals genetically through the equivalent of a weak microscope.

The Bovine Melting Pot

But what about the kind of genetic diversity that, like the multitude of dog breeds, results from human meddling rather than the geographic separation of animal populations? When James Derr, a geneticist at the Texas A&M College of Veterinary Medicine, began analyzing the hair follicles of bison, he found widespread evidence of cattle genes. He concluded that only about 5 percent of the 300,000 bison in North America were in herds that did not contain cattle hybrids.[12] Although natural interbreeding is known to have occurred occasionally in the centuries since cattle were first brought to North America, most of the hybridization is the result of human intervention. Ranchers once tried to breed bison with cattle to produce a domestic animal with the hardiness of bison and the docility of cattle. But the "cattalo" did not turn out to be the best thing since barbecue sauce. Domestic bulls were rarely interested in mating with bison cows, the mating of bison bulls with domestic cows resulted in a high mortality rate for the cow and her calf, and male offspring of either combination were often born dead and almost always infertile.[13] Nonetheless, most of the public and private bison herds that were established after the widespread slaughter of wild bison in the nineteenth century began with bison from ranches with cattalo.

The genetically pure bison include those in U.S. national parks (Badlands, Grand Teton, Theodore Roosevelt, Wind Cave, and Yellowstone) and a few private herds. Other herds on public land, including those at Custer State Park and the National Bison Range, were found to have some cattle hybrids. The proportion of cattle genes in these animals is usually too small to make a difference in their appearance, but large enough to concern conservation biologists. Some recommended removing these animals from the gene pool, but others objected that doing so would diminish the genetic diversity of the bison population in other, undesirable ways. Culling bison that carry cattle DNA might eliminate certain bison genetic lineages. In any case, current technology would not permit eradication of all cattle genes from bison, because it can only detect mitochondrial DNA, which is inherited from the mother, not nuclear DNA, which includes genes from the father.

The bison in Yellowstone, like most on public land, are isolated from other herds. This limits the genetic diversity within the herd to the genes that have survived there and whatever changes occur as a result of mutation, genetic drift, and natural selection. But this isolation permits greater genetic diversity to be maintained within Earth's total bison population, because it decreases the likelihood that rare traits will be lost.[14] An analogy can be made to a small town with a few family-owned restaurants. The choice of places to eat may be limited, but they are unique to Smalltown. If a new highway brings in Dairy Queen, Pizza Hut, and Taco Bell, Smalltown will have more dining options, but Mom's Diner may be driven out of business and her buffalo stroganoff will be no more.

Loss of genetic variation may diminish a species' capacity to adapt to changes such as global warming or the introduction of exotic species or diseases. Genetic traits were lost when the bison with a six-foot horn spread became extinct or hybridized with some other form of bison thousands of years ago. The difference now is that humans are in a position to make choices about what gets saved and what does not, and some believe that Earth's environment will be healthier for humans if species are not lost or altered as a result of human actions. And some people value diversity for its own sake; they want to live in a world that still has a place set aside to ensure the survival of both Mom's Diner and the Yellowstone bison.

PART TWO

PRESERVING THE SURVIVORS

There is no doubt that the country can well afford for many years to utilize in the preservation of a few hundred of these distinctively American mammals the amount of land requisite for showing them in an approximation to their natural condition. . . . The display now of a little intelligent regard for the survivors of the massacre, a little consideration for the pleasure and instruction of our successors in the land, would be a seemly manifestation of regret for the irreparable. The buffalo had to go under the working of a great natural law of which reckless hunters were only the unconscious instruments of application, but we can get around this law, in a small way.

—George Bird Grinnell,
"Pleading for the Buffalo," *New York Times*, 1905

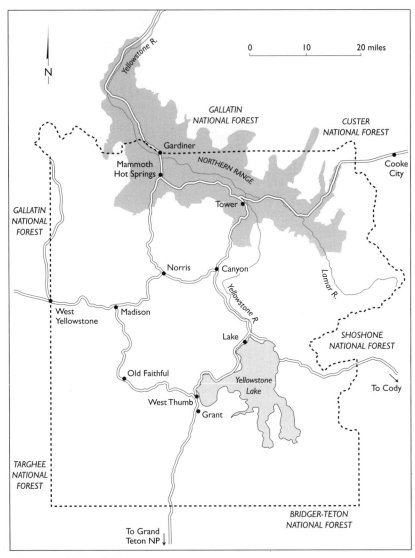

Yellowstone National Park

CHAPTER 5

For the Great National Playground

Often thought of as a timeless place untouched by human hands, wilderness is also a concept shaped by human values that change over time. The American wilderness of the nineteenth century was widely regarded as a place to be "settled and improved," as George Bird Grinnell put it in 1882.[1] However, the more that the unsettled land became settled, the more that some people idealized untouched nature as a source of physical and spiritual renewal. Jack London's *The Call of the Wild* was an immediate best seller in 1903, and it remained one of the most widely read American novels for decades. The wild called to a dog named Buck, who was stolen from the comforts of a California ranch and sold to haul sleds in the Yukon. Instead of a tragedy, Buck's story is an allegorical triumph in which the hero casts off his civilized ways and attains the "summit of life" in the wilderness.[2]

Buck's progress from domesticity to wildness appealed to readers in the early twentieth century who felt some qualms about the loss of the American frontier and the increasing industrialization of their culture.[3] Yet however much untamed nature may be revered in theory, most people prefer to be in places that are less wild, and human progress has been largely marked by increasing interference with nature. Even the naturalist John Muir struck a note of resignation when he said in 1897, "I suppose we need not go mourning the buffaloes. In the nature of things they had to give place to better cattle, though the change might have been made without barbarous wickedness."[4] In *Our Vanishing Wildlife* (1913) William

Hornaday wrote, "Out West, there is said to be a feeling that game and forest conservation has 'gone far enough.' . . . Many men of the Great West, — the West beyond the Great Plains, — are afflicted with a desire to do as they please with the natural resources of that region."[5]

Historian Donald Worster has described a struggle between rival views of humans' relationship with their natural environment: the "arcadian," which seeks to preserve a peaceful coexistence with nature; and the "imperialist," which labors to establish man's dominion over nature.[6] These two views have coexisted, peacefully or not, within the National Park Service, and sometimes within the same person. While director of the Park Service, Horace Albright wrote an article for the *Saturday Evening Post* in 1929 called "The Everlasting Wilderness," which set forth his conviction that nearly all of Yellowstone remained as "primeval" as before the area became a park, and that all national parks should be "preserved forever in their natural state." These delusions of pristine grandeur sprang from a romantic view of national parks that retains a firm grip on the public imagination today. But as other parts of the West were transformed by agriculture, forestry, and mining, Albright and other "imperialists" transformed Yellowstone conceptually and physically into a park that was perceived as manageable — a park without Indians or other frightening creatures, a park with hotels and paved roads. Yellowstone embodied the cultural transition from wilderness as an unruly and intimidating place to nature as a pleasant landscape for wholesome recreation.[7]

The passage of time has brought greater awareness that instead of a patchwork of wilderness and nonwilderness, the surface of Earth is a continuum of land and water ranging from largely unaffected to highly altered by humans. Just as there is some pioneer plant capable of sprouting in an urban corner of cracked pavement, there may be no corner of Earth, however remote from human residents, that has entirely escaped human influences. The wilderness that Euro-Americans thought they were conquering in the so-called New World has been described as "widowed" rather than virginal: it already bore the imprint of both the long presence of Indians and their abrupt population decline as a result of European diseases that arrived before European settlers.[8] The 1963 Leopold Report, prepared at the request of the secretary of the interior, proposed that the goal of wildlife management in the national parks should be to recreate "a reasonable illusion of primitive America."[9] This was an illusion from which Indians were apparently absent, for the report made no mention of them.

Yet in the centuries before the settlers arrived, Indians affected the Yellow-stone area by hunting, plant gathering, obsidian mining, and setting fires, as would Euro-Americans by suppressing fires, reducing predators, feeding wildlife, and starting a new herd of bison.

Fool Experiments

The decline of Yellowstone's herd of wild bison led to a repudiation of Captain Harris's 1888 pronouncement against introducing "domesticated" animals in the park. As early as 1893 Captain Anderson suggested such a purchase to bolster the bison herd.[10] Instead the Smithsonian Institution gave the park $3,000 to construct a corral in which captured bison could be protected. "If this plan succeeds we will be able to retain a small herd and keep them nearly in a state of nature," Anderson believed. The secretary of the Smithsonian, Samuel Pierpont Langley, had something different in mind: "The plan of inclosing the animals was intended both for security against unlicensed hunters and to 'gentle' those which might later be transmitted to Washington," he explained years later.[11]

In 1895 a stockade enclosing a square mile was baited with hay near a bison trail in Hayden Valley. But the snowfall was light that winter, and the corral was considered a failure when only eight bison entered it. The Smithsonian then considered a proposal to capture the park's bison for immediate shipment to its zoo, an idea that Grinnell thought ridiculous. "Here is a proposition for the lawful extinction of the wild buffalo in the United States which is most extraordinary, and could have been made only by people who are ill-informed respecting the animal in question and of the regions which this herd inhabits," he sneered in *Forest and Stream*. "The capture and close confinement of the adult buffalo of this herd would mean to them death as certain as the bullet of the poacher could bring. . . . It will not be time to try fool experiments with them until after they have become more numerous than they are at present." Well-informed readers could take comfort in Grinnell's assurance that the Yellowstone terrain would defeat any attempt at "wholesale capture."[12]

News that money was being spent in an effort to confine Yellowstone's bison reached the enterprising and cash-strapped Buffalo Jones. In 1896 he offered to corral the bison for $200 a month plus expenses if he succeeded or $500 if he did not.[13] The following year when Jones learned that $5,000 had been put forward for the Yellowstone herd's protection, he made another grandiloquent plea to the secretary of the interior. "Unless heroic measures are adopted at once, the remaining few will meet the fate of their kind before another year passes," he wrote. "Having had many years of active experience in capturing and rearing over one hundred head of these noble animals, I am confident the only thing to do is to corral the remaining band, and hereby reproduce a herd that every true American will be proud of."[14]

"Unfortunately, no action was ever taken by the Department upon these propositions," said Colonel Henry Inman in a lionizing biography of Jones in 1899, "and the United States lost forever its greatest race of native animals."[15] Inman's conclusion was premature, but *Forest and Stream* had already buried the buffalo alive, announcing in 1897 that Congress was responsible for "the destruction of the last considerable herd of wild buffalo in the United States—those which ranged in the Yellowstone Park. . . . Reports made this spring concerning the buffalo show that the numbers in the Park are not under thirty nor over fifty. . . . This stock is too small to warrant the hope that the Yellowstone Park herd will ever re-establish itself."[16]

The park's managers were almost as pessimistic. In his report for 1896, Anderson admitted, "Whether or not I shall be able to save them remains a doubtful problem. The forces of nature and the hand of man are alike against them, and they seem to be struggling against an almost certain fate." Colonel Samuel Young, who took over from Anderson in 1897, consulted with the superintendent of the National Zoological Park in Washington, D.C., and decided that corralling the park's bison would not be feasible because many of the adults would "fail to adapt themselves to even slight restraint, and die in consequence."

In 1900 Jones succeeded in getting a bill introduced in Congress that would establish a 3,300-acre reserve in New Mexico to populate with 150 bison, but nothing came of the plan. He also tried to persuade Congress to move the Yellowstone herd to New Mexico to benefit from the milder winters there. From 1900 through 1903 Congress appropriated only $5,000 a year for game protection in the park, and that was not expected to cover travel expenses for the bison. It was used to buy hay for elk and deer in winter and to pay a clerk and two civilian scouts. The scouts could not effectively patrol the park's 3,500 square miles, especially in deep snow, and months passed between their visits to some outlying points. The soldiers' low pay made them susceptible to bribes. In 1902 one soldier allegedly made a deal to drive two bison out of the park so that poachers could get them.[17] The shortage of funds led one critic to conclude that "the project to purchase new stock to infuse fresh blood into the badly inbred and rapidly dwindling herd of bison must be given up." He compared this negligence to the political influence evident in the $113,000 appropriation for roads for the benefit of the Yellowstone Park Transportation Company, which cut hay and pastured stock in Hayden Valley, driving bison from their range.[18]

Nothing but Pure-Bred Buffalo

All that is left of the once mighty herds that roamed the plains are perhaps twenty-five, which have taken refuge in the wildest and most inaccessible part of the Rocky Mountains set aside as a national park. They are so extremely shy that they can only be seen in winter, and only by those able to penetrate to their mountain fastness on skis. . . . It may thus be seen how difficult it is to keep any track of these animals—to learn their exact number and what the increase or decrease has been during the year.
—Peter Holt, describing his experience
as a Yellowstone scout in 1903[19]

In January 1902 the U.S. Senate passed a resolution requesting the secretaries of the interior and agriculture to provide

any facts which they possess with reference to the preservation in the United States, or the Dominion of Canada, of the buffalo, or American bison, informing the Senate whether such animals are dying out or are on the increase; to what extent they are running wild or are being domesticated, and whether such as remain are of pure or mixed blood; and also informing the Senate whether any steps ought to be taken by the United States for the preservation from extinction of such animals.

According to the report submitted by Interior Secretary Ethan Allen Hitchcock the following July, the total number of bison in the United States was "175 mixed and 968 pure-bloods," nearly all of them in captivity. Canada had "600 running wild in the Great Slave Lake Country and 44 pure bloods in captivity."[20]

In addition to the four that E. C. Waters kept at Yellowstone Lake for tourist viewing, the 1902 census reported 23 bison running wild in the park, and there could have been at least that many that went unnoticed. But the motivation for establishing a captive herd in Yellowstone seems to have had more to do with gratifying park visitors than with preserving the bison from extinction. As Major John Pitcher told Hitchcock, "The little herd that we have left in the park has been a matter of great interest to the public, and inquiries are constantly being made about it, but as far as I know not a buffalo has been seen by the tourists for a number of years." Pitcher requested authority to "catch up all the young buffalo that were left" and confine them under the army's care. "By doing this each year, I believe we can soon start a new herd at very little cost."[21]

The species no longer seemed at risk of extinction, nor was there an appreciation yet of the ecological role played by a wild animal in its natural habitat. It did not matter to people then that Yellowstone had been a different place when many bison were there to graze upon its grass and provide calves for its predators and carcasses for its scavengers. On the contrary, the Yellowstone environment was being deliberately altered by efforts to remove its wolves, coyotes, and cougars because their effect on other wildlife was considered undesirable. As understood at the turn of the century, the role of buffalo in Yellowstone was to be easily seen in the "pleasuring-ground for the benefit and enjoyment of the people," as set forth in the act that established the park.

Encouraged by a rising tide of public support, Pitcher requested $30,000 to buy 30 to 60 bison and construct an enclosure for them. When Hitchcock included the estimate in the bison census report to Congress, he explained, "With these animals in a national reservation, under governmental supervision, it is believed that a herd of pure-blooded American bison may be domesticated, which will increase in numbers, and the herd now running wild in the park may be also benefited by the introduction therein of new blood." The bill considered by Congress appeared to have Buffalo Jones's fingerprints on it, for half of the requested $30,000 was to be used to establish "an experimental station for cross-breeding various animals of different genera, with a view to obtaining breeds of sheep, goats and cattle capable of enduring the Western winters without shelter or feeding." Although that scheme was rejected, Congress did appropriate $15,000 as of July 1, 1902, to "restock a portion of Yellowstone Park with buffalo."[22] Jones was 58 years old and serving as sergeant at arms for the Kansas legislature when he obtained an appointment from Hitchcock to become Yellowstone's game warden.

Because Jones and other ranchers had crossbred buffalo with cattle, Pitcher wrote to the 11 known buffalo owners specifying that "we want nothing but pure-bred buffalo."[23] One of the buffalo owners was Dick Rock, who had eluded the army's attempts to catch him poaching. On February 17, 1903, he offered to sell the park a bull, one of his four "Full Blood" buffalo of unknown provenance, for $400. He also proposed catching the calves in the park for $50 each and the yearlings for $100. Pitcher wanted to pursue this idea, but a month later, when Rock was feeding a bull that he had "tamed" to be saddled and ridden, the animal pinned him against a wall and fatally gored him.[24]

Pitcher received offers from six other buffalo owners, including Howard Eaton, a dude rancher with a personal interest in seeing buffalo herds return to the West. Eaton had taken an option on buying 60 buffalo that Charles Allard had left to his family on the Flathead Reservation. By February 1903 Yellowstone had purchased 18 buffalo cows from Eaton for $500 each and three bulls from Charles Goodnight in Texas for $460 each. The cows and bulls were obtained from different herds to reduce the risk of inbreeding. That spring five of the cows that had been pregnant when they left the Flathead Reservation bore healthy calves. Pitcher's annual report that year stated, "The increase in the herd this year was not as great as was hoped for, but was due to the fact that many of the cows purchased were quite young and all were badly shaken up in transporting them from their range to the park."

The buffalo were branded "U.S." on the left hip in large letters, as was done to the government's horses, and on the horn in small letters. "It is our intention to feed and handle the new herd of buffalo in the same manner that domestic cattle are handled in this country," Pitcher explained. The herd was enclosed near Mammoth Hot Springs where they could be seen throughout the year by tourists using what was then the busiest park entrance. Pitcher ventured his opinion that "if we succeed in raising a new herd of buffalo under fence they will become very tame, and when the herd is sufficiently increased in numbers we can gradually turn them loose in the park and they will become so accustomed to seeing people about them that they will not be frightened out of the country or driven into the high mountains by the appearance of the summer tourist." A local editor commended Pitcher: "While zealously guarding the interests of the Park, he never loses sight of the fact that it is the great national playground and that the people have rights there."[25]

The Exceedingly Wild Ones

Describing the park's other 22 buffalo, those found near the head of Pelican Creek in the winter of 1902–03, Pitcher said, "This herd is exceedingly wild, and will probably never increase in size, and may possibly die out completely." He considered Pelican Valley to be "exceedingly unfavorable country" as winter range for them, because of the heavy snowfall. "The only way that they can keep alive is by grazing on the few places kept open by the hot springs." It was the thermal features, not the buffalo, that propelled the park's establishment, but it may have been the thermal features more than the park's establishment that provided a refuge far from commerce where those buffalo could survive. A small enclosure was constructed near the herd and baited with hay, but Pitcher vetoed Jones's plan to try to drive the buffalo into it, because he feared that they might be injured.[26] Instead, Jones took one of the Goodnight bulls in a wagon to the enclosure to serve as a decoy. On a scrap of paper dated January 19, 1903, Jones wrote: "Dear Major. Arrived yesterday with only one frozen ear. Snow only about 2^1/2 ft. 15 buffalo were within 100 yds of corral this morning."[27] The wild buffalo passed close to the corral but showed no interest in meeting the bull. A trail left by the bull indicated that he eventually left the corral and traveled half a mile to join the other buffalo, but he returned alone after several days.

To increase the size of the fenced herd and give it "three distinct strains of blood," Pitcher sent Jones with scouts Peter Holt and James Morrison to try to capture newborn calves from the wild herd that spring. Pitcher acknowledged that the mission would be "an exceedingly difficult and somewhat dangerous matter." Holt was dubious about their prospects. "The snow is still too deep for a horse and the warm sun so weakens the snow that it will not bear up a man, even on skis," said Holt. "Would the buffalo give up their young without a fight, in which men handicapped by skis tied on their feet would certainly get the worst of it?"[28]

Holt left Fort Yellowstone on May 5, 1903, with Jones, Morrison, and three foxhounds trained to hunt mountain lions, but no blankets. They intended to stay in outpost stations during their trip, the first one at Norris, 21 miles away, but Morrison was skiing under the influence of alcohol, and they had to spend the night in a miserable cabin at Crystal Springs without bedding or fire. The following night at the Grand Canyon of the

Yellowstone, the sight of a toboggan gave Jones the idea of harnessing the dogs to haul their packs. The dogs were willing but ran into trouble going downhill, when the rear dog would take off, "pursued by the awful toboggan," pulling the other two dogs off their feet as he dragged them along.

On May 10 the men found 14 buffalo with two new calves, but the animals fled from the intruders, who could not keep up with them in the slushy snow. The next morning while the snow was still crusted, Holt skied downhill as the herd ran past below him and he caught both calves with his hands. He could not let go of one in order to tie up the other, and looked up for someone to assist him. Instead he saw a buffalo cow returning "with head lowered and at a furious gallop." Holt released the calves and fled, feeling for the pistol in the holster at his belt. "I would only use this as a last resort, but precious as was the buffalo's life to me, mine was more precious."

However, the buffalo cow turned her attention to one of the calves, nosing it onto the trail and then running back to the rest of the herd. Holt tied up the other calf and, after crossing Pelican Creek, "wading almost to my armpits amid the chunks of ice," found the second calf where it had lost the trail. In his own more flamboyant account of the capture, Jones said, "Holt was game, and the gait he took up over the hills and down the valleys was one not known to even the Norwegians themselves."[29] When Holt approached, the calf rolled his eyes and pawed the snow. "As I got alongside of him," Holt recalled, "he curled his little tail over his back and began butting at me furiously." Morrison arrived and tried to pet the calf, "but he was hostile and would accept no overtures of peace."

The men departed the next morning with the two calves tied atop sacks of hay on the dog-powered toboggan. At Pelican Creek the men unhitched the dogs, rolled up their pants, took off their boots, picked up the toboggan with the calves, and waded across. "It was below zero and not a very agreeable job, but it had to be done," Holt thought. "The dogs reluctantly entered the water and they were a dejected and sad-looking lot when they emerged on the opposite side. We had to step barefooted into the snow and it seemed we would surely freeze before we could get our feet dressed again."

Jones said that the calves would drink condensed milk mixed with water, and the men tried feeding them, one holding the calf with its nose up, while another pried open the calf's mouth to pour in the milk. "A little of this would be swallowed and the balance spattered upon us as we floundered about in the snow," Holt recalled. After a feeding attempt the next day had similar results, the men feared their precious charges would starve. But when they reached Yellowstone Lake, the winter keeper for the E. C. Waters Boat Company offered them the use of a milk cow. The scouts took the calves to the stable and saw to it that the cow fed them, while a soldier at the station fed Jones, who was suffering from snow blindness.

The men left the calves with their milk supply until a wagon could be sent to collect them. In Washington the Department of the Interior authorized a payment of $15 to George Evers, who looked after the calves at Yellowstone Lake, and $50 to purchase a cow to provide milk for them in Fort Yellowstone.[30] Jones sent a note to President Roosevelt with photos of some cattalo robes "which I know you will appreciate" and of the two calves. "They are both bulls, would have named one Teddy, but we have one already of that name."[31]

Unlike the stuffed bear named for Roosevelt in 1902, the Teddy buffalo did not capture the public imagination, and the following winter, the unidentified bull that Jones had taken to Pelican Valley was found dead on the ice of Yellowstone Lake, where the animal had apparently starved. "His pawing and nosing around in the snow covering the ice showed the hopeless struggle he had made for life," Holt noted.[32] The other captive buffalo were carefully tended, but even though "every effort was made to save her," one cow died in 1904 after breaking her leg by running into a badger hole in the pasture. Pitcher later acknowledged that Jones was helpful in starting the new herd, but then "his usefulness in the park ended absolutely." Jones was angered by Pitcher's refusal to let him sell the horns, hides, claws, and teeth of park wildlife that he found, and he became involved in a dubious scheme for a navigable balloon contest held at the St. Louis World's Fair in 1904.[33]

"For the past two years he has apparently become interested in other matters to such an extent that he has neglected his duty as buffalo keeper," Pitcher wrote to the secretary of the interior in 1905. The captive herd produced 12 calves the previous year, but only six in 1905, and two of them died. Jones resigned later that year to establish a cattalo ranch in Arizona.

Buffalo on Tour

The tendency of early Yellowstone managers to value the buffalo as a tourist attraction rather than as wild animals in their natural habitat reflected an

These two bison calves, shown with Buffalo Jones may have been among those in the captive herd that received milk from a domestic cow rather than a bison. Courtesy of Yellowstone Photograph Archives.

already engrained American love of show business and conviction that the public can be edified through entertainment. Western artist George Catlin organized what may have been the first "Wild West show" in the 1830s with an entourage that included hundreds of costumed Indians on horseback, ceremonial dances, and a buffalo hunt. Catlin profited from the show financially, but he genuinely wanted to rally support for what he regarded as noble savages who were victims of Euro-American settlement.[34]

Fifty years later Buffalo Bill Cody's show portrayed the frontiersmen as courageous and the Indians as bloodthirsty obstacles to progress. Like Buffalo Jones, Cody kept his fame as a buffalo hunter aloft by a certain amount of hot air. In elaborately staged battles complete with the rattle of gunfire and galloping horses, Cody was often the hero, arriving just in time to save a wagon train from the Indians. But like Catlin, Cody believed his show conveyed important messages about the central drama of American history: the conquest of wilderness and its inhabitants. Along with several dozen bison, the show featured celebrities like Annie Oakley and Chief Sitting Bull. The bison's brush with extinction made the animal interesting to audiences, but the show emphasized hunting bison rather than preserving them. The 1883 program included "Lassoing and Riding the Wild Bison" and other acts in which cowboys shot blanks at the animals and the Indians used blunted arrows. But the thrill of bison hunts that Cody had experienced was impossible to reproduce because the bison became accustomed to milling around in the arena and mostly ignored their pursuers.[35]

More than 80 shows with frontier themes toured the United States and Europe near the turn of the twentieth century, and many included live bison. In 1905, a year after appearing in Theodore Roosevelt's inaugural parade, the 76-year-old Geronimo was released from military prison again to participate in a "buffalo hunt" at a show in Oklahoma put on by Joe, Zach, and George Miller. Geronimo stood in a touring car with a Winchester rifle as he was driven past 65,000 spectators and 62 buffalo. After he shot one of the buffalo, 300 Ponca Indians on horseback played their assigned part by yelling as they came over the hill and engulfed a wagon train. Geronimo was glad to accept his appearance fee, but preservationists objected to the killing of buffalo for entertainment. President Roosevelt called the show a "disgraceful exhibition," but two years later he asked the three Miller brothers to bring their cowboys, Indians, and buffalo to the "Jamestown War Path," which was the "amusement section" of the Virginia town's 300th anniversary celebration.[36]

Journalist Ernest Harold Baynes became interested in buffalo when he saw the private herd of Austin Corbin, a railroad magnate with a game preserve in New Hampshire. "Jumping onto me and butting vigorously at the slightest provocation," the two calves that Baynes borrowed with the idea of trying to use them as beasts of burden delighted him. "I liked to see this spirit of self-protection, and I admired the splendid courage of these handsome little beasts; it would surely prove an important factor in the effort being made to preserve the race from extinction." Baynes wrote to prominent persons and published dozens of articles recommending that the federal government establish several herds. Instead of regarding the bison as the commissary that enabled hostile Indian tribes to hold out for so long, Baynes depicted the animal as the saving grace for thousands of pioneers who would have suffered greater hardship if not death without it. Baynes also had the fuzz shed by buffalo spun into yarn and knitted into gloves that proved to be warm and durable, but he admitted that "the question of how to obtain the wool from the living buffalo has not been clearly solved."[37]

President Roosevelt encouraged Baynes in his efforts, which included inviting 14 men to form the American Bison Society in 1905 with William Hornaday as its first president. Given that the bison's "fitness for longer survival in the wild state was long ago thoroughly disproved," Grinnell saw the matter as "wholly one of sentiment," but he supported Baynes's proposal for captive herds on federal land.[38] The membership also included Andrew Carnegie, artist Frederic Remington, and Gifford Pinchot, a wealthy Pennsylvanian who was the first head of the U.S. Forest Service. These men regarded the bison slaughter of the 1800s as an inevitable consequence of a growing economy, but they lamented the loss of heroic physical challenges that seemed inevitable in industrialism. Historian Andrew Isenberg believes that the preservation of the bison was not an end in itself, but a means to the preservation of an imagined frontier way of life. "It was the extinction of that culture, more than the disappearance of the bison, that the preservationists feared."[39]

While the eastern gentry were building bison castles in the air, Michel Pablo faced a dilemma with his 600 bison on the ground at the Flathead Reservation in Montana, the largest herd in existence. Charles Allard's heirs had sold their bison in small lots, but Pablo refused all offers and struggled to protect his herd from poachers. The Dawes Act of 1887 had reduced the Flathead Indians' claim to little more than first choice of sites for 160-acre homesteads; early in 1906 the federal government bought the remaining land and opened it to settlement by non-Indians. Having lost his range, Pablo tried to sell his bison to the federal government. President Roosevelt and Secretary Hitchcock were interested, but Congress thought the price too high and offered only grazing land that was too small for the herd. Still nursing a grudge against Indians for vandalizing his bison specimen in Montana, Hornaday did not bring the American Bison Society to Pablo's aid.[40]

When Pablo inquired about leasing land in Canada, the Canadian government offered to buy the herd instead. They were already responsible for a large herd that had survived in Wood Buffalo National Park. In 1906 Pablo signed a contract under which he would be paid $200 for each bison delivered live to central Alberta. Pablo hired cowboys and one cowgirl to build a 26-mile fence from the Flathead River to the railroad at Ravalli, Montana. They were able to drive 180 bison cows along the fence, but no bulls followed suit. The herd had never been herded before, and many of the animals took off, stampeding across the plains or climbing cliffs where a horse and rider could not follow. Pablo also tried rounding up the animals into a corral and having them pulled by horse teams to Ravalli. There the bison were loaded onto reinforced stock cars for the 1,200-mile ride on five railways. The shipments contained fewer bison as the animals became more wary of capture, but the herd continued to grow and five years passed before the last shipment was made.[41]

The Canadians expected to buy 350 bison, and with the cost of delivery and fencing at the new Wainwright Buffalo Park, this required an appropriation of $95,150, a major government outlay at the time. The most obstinate bison never made it onto the train, and some died en route, and some elk disembarked in Canada, apparently a by-catch of the roundup. But Canada ended up receiving and paying without complaint for 703 bison, including some born en route. Acquisition of those bison had become a matter of national pride, a way of outdoing the Yankees.[42]

Commercialized Salvation

President Roosevelt created another game preserve in 1905 by setting aside 59,000 acres of the former Kiowa-Comanche reservation in Oklahoma for what would become the Wichita Mountains National Wildlife Refuge. With its membership swelling to 236, the American Bison Society felt shamed by the loss of Pablo's herd to Canada and succeeded in lobbying Congress to fence 8,000 acres at the refuge for bison. Most of the 15 bison they donated to the refuge had been bought from a Wyoming rancher. The society also initiated a bill to establish a herd in the Adirondack Mountains that passed both houses of the New York legislature unanimously but was vetoed by the governor, who doubted there had ever been any bison in the Adirondacks. Undeterred, the Bison Society commissioned Morton Elrod, a biology professor at the University of Montana, to survey an area in that state for a possible bison preserve. The criteria for its selection seemed to be less about bison habitat than about tourism. The chosen site west of the Continental Divide was not thought to have been part of the bison's historic range, but it had previously been part of the Flathead Reservation and was conveniently located near the same train station through which Pablo's herd was passing on its way to Canada. Elrod wrote enthusiastically of the site: "Tourists or visitors may step off the train at Ravalli and in five minutes be on the range."[43]

After Roosevelt signed the bill to create the National Bison Range there in 1908, the American Bison Society raised $10,000 to purchase bison for it. Hornaday solicited contributions from more than 150 cities and received much favorable publicity for his cause, but the support was not unanimous. "Why any intelligent person should care about the preservation of these moth-eaten, ungainly beasts, when their room might much better be taken up by modern blooded cattle, beautiful to look at, are conundrums no one answered," protested the *Indianapolis Star*.[44] In letters sent to wealthy if not intelligent businessmen, Hornaday appealed to their sense of honor. "It was the business interests of the country, represented by men who wished to procure buffalo hides to sell at $2.50 each, that practically exterminated the American Bison millions. Now that an effort is being made to preserve the species for the benefit of posterity, the businessmen of the United States have no option but to take hold and help!"[45]

Andrew Carnegie chipped in $250, roughly the cost of one bison, and the society met its goal in less than a year. Hornaday expressed his delight at "the splendid support the undertaking received from the women of America," whose interest in birds was well known but who had not been expected to respond with "unflagging industry" to collect money for such an ungainly beast.[46] Hornaday was disappointed, however, that aside from a good showing in Montana, the project received paltry sums from the Great Plains states. Nearly half the money came from New York, but every state contributed something except four that were closely associated with the slaughter of the nineteenth century—Texas, Kansas, and the Dakotas.

Hornaday did not mention that the country's first two bison preserves were established on former Indian reservation land, or that most of the bison purchased for the National Bison Range were descendants of the Pablo-Allard herd, which had previously resided there. The Indian had no place in the vision of an untouched America that the Bison Society was trying to incarnate on game reserves. Historian Isenberg concludes that the same social and economic forces that led to the near-extermination of the bison in the nineteenth century contributed to the bison's return to the landscape in the twentieth century. Preservationists "saved the species not as a functioning part of the plains environment, but as a functioning part of the American economy: a curiosity, tourist attraction, target for hunters, and domesticated beast. This piecemeal and commercialized salvation owed itself to the limitation of an Eastern preservationist ideology based on nostalgia and recreation, and to the perception of Western ranchers that a profit could be made from the few remaining bison."[47] But Hornaday realized that truly wild bison were missing from the landscape of American recreation. In 1913 he noted that "at least one-half of the public interest attaching to the Yellowstone Park is based upon its wild animals . . . wild mountain sheep, antelope, mule deer, elk, grizzly bears and white pelicans, roaming free . . . the few wild bison remaining keep as far as possible from the routes of tourist travel."[48]

When the fence went up on the National Bison Range for the 37 new arrivals, about twice as many bison left from Pablo's herd still roamed free on adjacent land. Pablo, who could be held liable for any damage they caused, proposed a hunt at $250 a head to eliminate the herd, but the Montana attorney general declared that with the opening of the reservation to settlement, any bison that could not be rounded up would be regarded as wild animals under state game laws. Pablo could not legally kill or sell them, so he had to relinquish his claim to the animals. But the state of Montana had no way to protect them, and the only unconfined bison outside Yellowstone disappeared into the arms of poachers.[49]

In 1912, when efforts were underway to create a game refuge in Nebraska, the Bison Society argued that the National Bison Range was too remote for tourists, and the new refuge would be "more readily accessible."[50] The 14,000-acre site was located at Fort Niobrara, which the army had abandoned in 1906 after it was no longer needed to control the Sioux, cattle rustlers, and horse thieves. Roosevelt had already designated it a bird sanctuary. Eight bison were enclosed at what would become the Fort Niobrara National Wildlife Refuge, six of them donated by a Nebraska rancher who'd bought them from Buffalo Jones, and two sent by Yellowstone National Park from its fenced herd.

The American Bison Society also lobbied for establishing Wind Cave National Park, which then received congressionally funded fencing, 14 bison from the New York Zoological Society, and six bison from Yellowstone. Franklin Hooper, who succeeded Hornaday as the society's president in 1914, described its mission as one of "bringing men back to nature," because "there is already a strong and world-wide reaction against the artificial life of the city."[51] But except for the small herd of "exceedingly wild" ones in Yellowstone, bison in the United States had become a captive species.

Making Hay in Yellowstone

To increase the fenced herd in Yellowstone as quickly as possible, the bison were managed as livestock. Any instincts that jeopardized the well-being of other herd members were suppressed; unruly bulls were put in separate pastures; calves were bottle-fed and taken from their mothers to prevent injuries. By 1906 the fenced herd had grown to 57, including three bison that had been captured as calves from the wild herd. This was too many animals for the enclosure near Mammoth Hot Springs, so most of the herd was moved to a larger facility built on 600 acres in the Lamar Valley. The site offered some of the best year-round bison forage in the park, but Major Pitcher said that it was chosen partly because "with comparatively little work in the way of clearing and ditching for the purpose of irrigating it, almost any quantity of hay can be raised."

Winter feed for other park animals was already being cultivated in Yellowstone. In 1903, after settlement north of the park had reduced the pronghorn's winter range and increased the number of hunters waiting there, a four-mile fence was constructed along the boundary near Gardiner. This was intended to help keep wildlife in the park and prevent livestock from grazing on the 50 acres of alfalfa that were irrigated for pronghorn, deer, and bighorn sheep that congregated along the fence. Pitcher believed the park's ungulates should be treated "in the same way that cattlemen handle their range stock," which meant that in case of deep snow, there should be "a number of haystacks scattered about the range" to help the animals survive "the dangerous period, which in most cases would not continue for more than a week or two." The captive buffalo grazed on native grasses in fenced pastures during the summer and were fed hay through the winter, but as the fenced areas became overgrazed, hay feeding was extended into the warmer months. Because obtaining hay was difficult and expensive in the Yellowstone area, more than 400 acres in the Lamar Valley were eventually cleared of willows, cottonwoods, and sagebrush so that the land could be plowed and seeded with native and nonnative grasses.[52]

As the confined herd increased in size, so did the intensity of the fighting and injuries among the bulls. In cattle ranching, any bulls beyond the number needed to impregnate the cows may be considered excess, and the ratio of bulls to cows may be kept as low as one to eight for greatest

For many years, a group of bison bulls was brought from the Lamar Valley to a corral near Mammoth Hot Springs where they would be seen by more park visitors during the summer (circa 1920). Courtesy of Yellowstone Photograph Archives.

efficiency. Starting in 1907, some of the Yellowstone bulls were driven to the corral near Mammoth Hot Springs each summer to serve as a tourist attraction and reduce violence during the rutting season. After Major Harry Benson became acting superintendent in 1908, he commented favorably on the "show herd" of 14 bulls and the thousands of tourists who stopped to see them during the summer. Although the Lamar Valley herd was eventually left out on the open range during the day to lessen the grazing pressure on the fenced pasture, Benson reported in 1910 that they were becoming "quite tame and tractable." Nonetheless, he wished he had a way to dispose of some of the old bulls entirely.

Benson's successor, Colonel Lloyd Brett, also felt that the number of bulls was a problem despite the bison's apparent docility. "By constant herding during the summer the herd has become used to being driven, and as a rule is handled with but little trouble on the range," he reported in 1912; yet by 1915, when the herd had grown to 259, he wanted to eliminate at least 100 bulls. By then, the fenced pasture had been abandoned, and the Lamar herd was remaining on the open range all summer, gradually moving into higher slopes along the headwaters of the Lamar River. Range riders periodically rounded them up and drove them back toward the corral. Several attempts were made to drive some of the old bulls into the mountains instead to join the wild bison, but they always returned to the Lamar Valley. In 1917, when the Lamar herd had grown to 330, the decision was made to castrate more than half of the male calves to simplify management. The superintendents' annual reports, which previously had distinguished between the "wild herd" and the "fenced herd," began referring to the latter as the "tame herd."

The growing elk population was also causing problems. During the winter of 1910–11, many elk drifted down along the Yellowstone River and out of the park, where they damaged ranchers' haystacks, fields, and fences. Montana set aside a strip several miles wide around the northwest corner of the park as a game reserve, and Wyoming also designated areas as winter range for elk, but it was proposed that Yellowstone feed the elk during the winter. Colonel Brett objected that feeding would be costly and that it would have to be continued indefinitely because the animals would become dependent on it and increase in number until the herd was reduced by some other means.[53] In 1916 more than 800 elk were shipped from Yellowstone to start herds in 13 states that no longer had them, but history proved Brett right. As the shipment of elk out of the park was increased, so was winter feeding, and the elk population continued to grow. Instead of accepting winter mortality as part of nature's plan for population control, park managers saw it as an avoidable cause of death and bad publicity.

The Risks of Domesticity

Despite some losses to disease, the Lamar bison herd also continued to grow with the help of winter feeding. Hemorrhagic septicemia, a form of blood poisoning caused by a parasite, killed 22 bison in 1911. The herd was then vaccinated against the illness, but it recurred in 1919 and 1923, each time taking less than one-tenth of the herd. The disease had also been seen occasionally in elk, deer, pronghorn, and bighorn sheep in the park, but only during or after periods of confinement. Testing for brucellosis was first done in 1917, after two cows in the Lamar herd miscarried. Brucellosis is caused by a bacterium, *Brucella abortus*, that may be transmitted through oral contact with the afterbirth or milk from an infected cow. Blood samples taken from the two cows were seropositive, which means they contained antibodies against brucellosis, and the cows had presumably aborted their calves because they were infected with the disease. In humans, the disease is known as undulant fever because the symptoms include an intermittent high temperature and other flulike symptoms that can recur for months or years. No cure has been found for undulant fever, but it can be treated with antibiotics. It is rarely contagious or fatal, and it does not affect human reproduction.

When brucellosis was discovered in Yellowstone bison, it was not known how long it had been present in the herd or whether it was caused by the same bacterium and affected bison in the same way as it did cattle. Although fetal loss in the Lamar herd may have been present but too infrequent to raise suspicions until 1917, brucellosis was reported in Montana cattle shortly after the turn of the century, and in 1916 the United States Livestock Sanitary Association formed the Committee on Contagious Abortion in Cattle to promote control of the disease. Brucellosis often causes infected cows to abort the first time they become pregnant, but if the infection becomes chronic in a herd over a period of years, many of the animals develop an immunity that enables them to clear the bacteria from their bodies.[54] Park managers were apparently not concerned about brucellosis, for no other bison were tested for another 13 years. A two-page "Summary of the History of the Yellowstone Buffalo Herd" that was prepared by park staff in 1922 mentioned the septicemia outbreak but not brucellosis.

Evidence of the disease was found in elk when they were first tested on the National Elk Refuge in 1930 and in Yellowstone National Park in 1931, but how long the herds had carried brucellosis and how they acquired it have also remained matters of speculation. Although more than half of the 471 bison tested from 1930 to 1933 were found to be seropositive, doctors from the Montana Veterinary Research Laboratory observed that the disease did not seem to have impaired the herd's fecundity, and testing was suspended for another eight years.[55] Abortions were known to occasionally occur both in the Lamar corrals and on the range, but they were not necessarily caused by brucellosis. The launching of the Cooperative State-Federal Brucellosis Eradication Program in 1934 was less a means of addressing the disease than a way to pay ranchers to reduce their cattle herds during a period of economic depression and severe drought. Nearly half of the 12,000 herds tested that year had animals that had been exposed to brucellosis.[56] In 1935, when 500 elk from Jackson Hole were to be sold in Minnesota, one-fifth of the tested blood samples were found to be seropositive. However, testing was not resumed in Yellowstone until 1941 even though the park continued to send bison and elk to start or join other herds.

The Park Service Takes Over

The responsibility for park administration was transferred back from military to civilian personnel in 1916, after years of delay caused by the Department of the Interior's lack of funds to employ a park staff and maintain the facilities. The National Park Service Act was signed into law that year, creating a separate agency to oversee the parks. Horace Marden Albright, a 29-year-old attorney in the Department of the Interior who was instrumental in getting the legislation passed, went on to spend 10 years as one of Yellowstone's most influential superintendents before becoming director of the National Park Service.

While this transformation in park management was under way, a new field of study was emerging that would eventually transform how people thought about wildlife in parks. In contrast to traditional natural history, which emphasized the study of individual animal species, ecology was more broadly concerned with the interactions between animals and their habitat. However, this shift was not readily absorbed by park managers who believed that wildlife needed human assistance to satisfy tourists. Both Albright and Stephen Mather, the first National Park Service director, focused on increasing park visitation as a way to build a political constituency, increase congressional appropriations, and protect the parks from commercial development.[57]

Consequently, Albright regarded wildlife largely as a tourist attraction and never embraced the goal of protecting an untouched nature. Rather like the man who puts a woman on a pedestal so he can look up her skirt, Albright protected wildlife so that visitors could enjoy seeing it at close range, even if it meant sacrificing the animals' dignity and autonomy. Under his leadership the park's roads were rebuilt to automobile standards, interpretive services were established, concessioners were encouraged to provide new accommodations for tourists, and tourists were encouraged to feed bears from their automobiles. Bison were also part of the entertainment. As Albright told the American Bison Society in 1919, "Visitors to the park are becoming more and more interested in the bison herd and henceforth it will play a much more important part in the operation of the park as a playground than it ever has before."

Although Albright seems to have been the first superintendent to call the Lamar Valley facilities the "Buffalo Ranch," he referred to the Lamar bison as "the so-called tame herd." As Albright explained it, the herd was "not tame at all except that it was provided with hay in winter and was kept under control by the gamekeeper." He described the annual roundups in Lamar Valley as "about the last opportunities to see in this country the fearful and impressive buffalo stampedes."[58] In his 1925 annual report these bison were called "the main herd," numbering 764.

With the focus on the large bison herd available for visitors to see, little attention was paid to the wild herd that had, despite the kidnapping of four of its calves, survived without any assistance except protection from humans. Although the wild herd was at least as big as the captive herd in 1902, it grew far more slowly; only 66 bison were counted in Pelican Valley in the winter of 1924–25. Were it not for the introduced herd, concern about inbreeding in the wild herd would have remained. But how low a bison population can drop and for how long before inbreeding causes genetic problems is not well understood. Inbreeding in the wild herd may have resulted in some infertility or deformities that contributed to its low growth rate. But many of the bison herds that thrive on public land today have descended from relatively few founding members. The Henry Mountains herd in Utah is descended from 23 bison shipped from Yellowstone in the 1940s, not all of which were likely to contribute genes to future generations, yet the herd is now maintained at about 400 animals that have shown no evidence of genetic problems.

A Thrilling Representation of the Old West

Like his predecessors, Albright faced the problem of how to feed the growing herd in the Lamar Valley and "keep them from drifting down to the settlements."[59] Each year the "main" herd consumed more hay, which led to seeding and irrigating more land in the park. In 1921 a drift fence was constructed across the Lamar Valley to keep the bison from interfering with the haying operations. Albright sent bison to any public entity willing to pay for shipping and handling, but he soon found that not enough animals could be removed that way. Bison were being slaughtered on the National Bison Range, where the population peaked at 700 in the mid-1920s. The Northern Pacific Railway, which served the resulting steaks in its dining cars, assured passengers that the meat was "as savory and tender as the Indians and pioneer hunters ever tasted" and was evidence of the bison's successful preservation.[60] Still, the tide had turned from alarm about having too few bison to the dilemma of having too many bison mouths to feed.

Although this would not be permitted today, Hollywood came to Yellowstone to film *The Thundering Herd* in 1924, as the park was the only place where such a large buffalo stampede could be staged. Courtesy of Yellowstone Photograph Archives.

In 1923 Mather approved Albright's request to kill several "outlaw" bulls that "graze alone in the hills," one of which had already been shot by a ranger after the bull killed two horses. Albright's suggestion that Yellowstone establish a pemmican plant as possibly "the only feasible way of dispensing of buffalo meat in large quantities" was not pursued, but he was given authority to sell or otherwise dispose of surplus buffalo.[61] However, Albright's concern about reducing the Lamar herd did not diminish his pleasure in showing it off to distinguished visitors, on whose behalf it became customary to stage a stampede.

When Hollywood decided to film Zane Grey's story "The Thundering Herd," one of the first difficulties was casting enough humps and horns in motion to fill the scenery. The screenplay called for a stampede of epic proportions, and the two largest private herds available each had fewer than 500 buffalo. Instead Albright agreed to have the buffalo keeper, Bob LaCombe, and 18 rangers round up about 700 bison from the Lamar herd, a job that took several weeks. Afterward Albright proudly reported that 16 of the buffalo had gone on to become extras in Hollywood, where they were sent to help finish the movie. "It is a picture which will make the blood of every American boy tingle, and men with young hearts will find that the fighting between the hunters and the Indians will carry them back to the days of their youth when they were thrilled by the red-blooded accounts of the daring deeds in the '70s," the *New York Times* reported in 1925.[62] But before seeing the movie himself, Albright had a statement tacked on the end that not a single animal had been hurt in the filming. In fact, the movie contained many daring scenes in which horses fell, ran at high speed into the sides of covered wagons, and slipped on ice. None of these were filmed in Yellowstone, but the movie's release brought protests about abuse of the park's buffalo. Mather claimed that only one buffalo was actually roped and thrown, and that the animal "was none the worse for the experience."[63] Rumors abounded that the herd was stampeded eight or nine times a day and that many animals had been killed while the crew feasted on buffalo steaks, but Albright continued to refer to the bison in the Lamar Valley as "the famous Thundering Herd."

Albright installed the "Buffalo Jones Museum and Zoo" in the log cabin where the former buffalo hunter and park game warden had lived. Behind the cabin's "very interesting collection" of buffalo pictures and paraphernalia, the zoo included "four very tame bears, a badger, several coyotes, a pet buffalo calf, and a number of different species of birds," as well as the usual buffalo bulls visiting for the summer from the Lamar herd. Albright also organized a "Buffalo Plains Week" in 1925 to promote Yellowstone. He invited some Crows to camp in the park and assist in the annual roundup of the Lamar herd at the end of the summer. "That this herd of close to 800 head will give every patron of the exhibition a thrill that will be long remembered there can be no doubt. . . . We know what a wonderful spectacle is the herd in stampede."[64] Afterward, he described the event as a "colorful pageant" presented by "a score or more of Crow from the nearby reservation dressed in their regalia and war paints of other days, and a few real western cowboys." It was a big hit with tourists, who were taken in "old time stagecoaches" to see the roundup and the Indian camps, which were "a vivid reminder of the fact that not so many years ago the ancestors of these very Indians roamed and hunted over the lands in this vicinity," Albright wrote. Simulating these bygone "facts" would have been difficult without a herd of bison accustomed to being corralled.

Mather gave Albright permission to have 17 bison killed as part of Buffalo Plains Week, and 86 were shipped live to public and private owners that year. Most of *The Thundering Herd* extras soon left Hollywood for

Catalina Island, off the coast of California, where their stampeding skills were put to use in another movie based on a Zane Grey novel, *The Vanishing American*. This 1925 epic was said to "put the plight of the Indians in the context of the inevitable march of history where one culture crushes another." Also part of the inevitable march of history, the bison never left Catalina Island, where they became the founding members of a herd that is now kept at about 200 by a nonprofit organization dedicated to the preservation of Catalina Island, even though bison were an introduced species.

In 1927 Albright proposed that several hundred bison be confined on Pelican Flats during the summer for tourists to see. The chief ranger, Sam Woodring, and buffalo keeper Bob LaCombe advised that enclosing this site would be impractical, and they suggested a location on Antelope Creek instead. There the topography provided some natural barriers, and only six miles of drift fencing would be required to enclose about 2,500 acres for 150 to 200 steers and bulls. "This arrangement should provide a splendid show herd that will attract large numbers of visitors and materially increase the travel over Mt. Washburn and through Dunraven Pass," Woodring explained, using terms that would appeal to Albright. "Incidentally, the cow and calf herd would greatly benefit." Viewed from an era of different attitudes toward wildlife, this statement hits two discordant notes. Woodring considered the effect of the separate pasture on the bison cows and calves only "incidental" to the effect on tourists; and he regarded keeping the adult males separate from the cows and calves, a standard practice in livestock operations, as "beneficial," even though the bison management goal at that point was not to increase the herd or the amount of marketable meat. However, construction of the new enclosure was deferred. Yellowstone managers sold bison to a meat dealer for the first time in 1927 and then built an abattoir at the Buffalo Ranch to slaughter bison for market.

In Canada more than 2,400 bison were killed from 1922 to 1924 to prevent overpopulation at Wainwright Buffalo Park. In addition to public outrage, the slaughter produced widespread evidence of tuberculosis, and symptoms of brucellosis were apparent in some animals. More worried about public opinion than the diseases, the Canadian Park Service relocated most of the remaining bison. Although the Canadian government's purchase of one-way train tickets for 709 bison from Pablo's herd had seemed extraordinary in 1912, that turned out to be a mere prelude to the transfer of the 1920s, when 6,673 of their "plains buffalo" descendants were shipped to Wood Buffalo National Park. This was done despite objections raised on behalf of the 2,000 disease-free "wood buffalo" at the park. Half of the shipped bison may have died during or soon after the six-day, 620-mile trip by train and barge, but the survivors thrived in their new home. In 1926, after bison were seen south of the Peace River, which formed the park's southern boundary, the Canadian government expanded the park by more than half, making it five times as large as Yellowstone. Nonetheless, by 1929 Wood Buffalo National Park also had abattoirs to slaughter excess bison for the meat market.[65]

CHAPTER 6

Under More Natural Conditions

The overall trend in Yellowstone wildlife management during the twentieth century was toward more "natural" conditions, letting wilderness be wild, with ecological processes instead of humans determining the fate of individual animals. But the change proceeded by fits and starts, with different species subject to different policies, and abrupt transitions reflected political and administrative constraints rather than just a gradual learning process. For example, Yellowstone's initial policy of predator removal was intended to protect human life and property, including livestock. With that rationale, bears as well as wolves, coyotes, and mountain lions were killed. As the emphasis shifted to protecting the animals most popular among visitors, bears were removed from the enemies list, but pelicans and otters were added, because they ate trout that might otherwise be caught by fishermen.

During the 1920s, as part of the movement toward more ecologically based wildlife management, predator control in national parks began falling from favor. Yellowstone's bison and elk herds grew substantially during the first three decades of the century, along with a concern that they would have to be reduced by some means to prevent habitat degradation and starvation. National Park Service policies were revised in 1931 to halt the killing of predators except "when they are actually found making serious inroads upon herds of game or other animals needing special protection." However, coyote trapping was still occurring in Yellowstone after elk herd reductions by slaughter began in 1934. Other changes toward more natural conditions in Yellowstone also occurred sporadically. Winter feeding of ungulates ended in the 1940s, but the feeding of bears at park dumps was allowed to continue until the 1960s. The diversion of hot springs for public bathhouses and the stocking of lakes and rivers with fish continued until the 1950s. Wildland fires were automatically fought until the 1970s. More recently the Park Service goal of removing the effects of human interference in ecological processes has led to new interference in the form of wolf reintroduction. Intensive management of that species is expected to continue indefinitely in order to restore what are regarded as more natural conditions in Yellowstone as a whole.

Returning the Yellowstone Bison to a Wild State

By the 1920s the Lamar bison herd had begun finding its own way toward more natural conditions. As the herd expanded its summer range, it began mingling with the wild herd, and starting in 1932, no effort was made to distinguish between the two herds in population counts. Castration of calves ceased in 1931 because, as chief park ranger George Baggley explained, "the resulting animal is not a true buffalo and detracts from the appearance of the herd as a whole."[1] But many of the bison were still consuming artificially cultivated forage including both native and nonnative grasses. Baggley believed that winter feeding would probably always be necessary as the only means of keeping the herd from drifting into the elk's lower winter range and "possibly even outside of the Park."

The Lamar Valley is part of what is referred to as the northern range, about 378,000 acres of grassland and forest lying in the lowest area of the park and extending beyond the park boundary to private and U.S. Forest Service land. Albright obtained private funding to pay for a study of elk on the northern range by William Rush, a Forest Service biologist whose work helped establish the idea that wildlife policies should be based on scientific research rather than managerial or public whims. Although his 1932 report focused on elk, which is by far the most abundant large animal on the northern range, Rush mentioned the effect that other animals had on the "carrying capacity" of the range. "The buffalo herd is kept at about 1,000 head and there does not seem to be any good reason why this number should be changed," he observed.[2] This figure became the accepted goal, but it was soon interpreted as a winter count of 800 on the northern range so that the calving season did not boost the population over 1,000. "I have no hesitancy in recommending a reduction of the herd to 800," said

Baggley. He thought it would "permit a better balance as regards their relation to other Park animals" and reduce the need to dispose of surplus animals.[3]

Albright intended that the Park Service would rely on other agencies for scientific expertise, and it lacked staff with credentials in wildlife management. The first formal wildlife surveys of the national parks were conducted in 1929, when George Wright used inherited money to support a two-year leave of absence from his position as a naturalist at Yosemite. The surveys he produced with the help of several other former ecology students from the University of California at Berkeley were well received, and the Park Service gradually began funding a Wildlife Division based at Berkeley.[4]

In their 1934 "Report on the Current Status of Large Mammals in the National Parks," Wright and Ben H. Thompson noted, "Bison always have held a unique position among the park animals because of the intensive management necessary to prevent their extermination. Now that their perpetuation is assured, radical changes will be made in the buffalo program." They believed Yellowstone had recently ended a period "devoted to building up a new herd by every means at human command" and had begun one that would be "devoted to the task of returning the Yellowstone herd to the wild state insofar as the inherent limitations of the park will permit."[5] A natural sex ratio of about one to one was to be maintained in the Lamar herd, and management was to be limited to three activities: an annual roundup, which was considered necessary as long as there was a "surplus" to slaughter; winter feeding at the Buffalo Ranch, which was considered necessary as long as the herd must be "held within present park boundaries"; and disease prevention and treatment. Wright and Thompson believed that under this management program, "there will be once again a wild herd of bison in the United States." They did not specify the criteria by which they defined bison as "wild" nor whether any effort should be made to eliminate brucellosis. They noted that an estimated 40 percent of the herd was "affected" by the disease and that the 88 bison that were tested in 1934 would continue to be monitored "to determine prevalence and progress of infection, effect on reproduction, period required to attain individual immunity, if any, and probable general effect on the future of the herd."

Outlaws, Cripples, and Good Breeding Stock

Summarizing bison management in Yellowstone during the prior three decades, Wright and Thompson reported that a total of 297 bison had been

An abattoir was constructed at the Buffalo Ranch in 1928 as the number of bison slaughtered in the park to limit herd size began to increase. The meat was sold to wholesalers (circa 1930). Courtesy of Yellowstone Photograph Archives.

shipped alive from the park, 682 had been sent to the slaughterhouse, and "48 outlaws and cripples have been destroyed." (During this same period Yellowstone also shipped more than 3,300 elk to zoos and parks across the United States and Canada.) Although part of a new wave of ecologists who did not discriminate between "good" and "bad" wildlife species, Wright and Thompson were still of a mindset that could refer to individual animals as "outlaws" or "cripples" for failing to meet standards of acceptable conduct or appearance. Despite the "radical changes" Wright and Thompson reported in bison management, the impulse persisted to enhance visitor enjoyment regardless of the means. The small corral for bison near Mammoth Hot Springs was regarded as unsatisfactory, not for the bison, but for visitors, who could not photograph them "without having one or two fences appearing in the picture," as Baggley explained. To remedy this problem, 530 acres on Antelope Creek was fenced in 1935 for about 30 bison, which were driven into a five-acre corral near the park's main loop road during the day.

Once a year, rangers on horseback continued to round up as many bison as possible and herd them to the Lamar Valley for culling. This was usually done around Christmas, when "all available rangers and most anybody that could ride a horse" were mobilized for the operation in subzero weather, one of the participants later recalled. "It was a wild stampede for the corral," with some riders assigned to hide in ravines where they could head off bison that tried to escape toward higher country. The horses were shod with sharp steep calks, but "once in a while you'd look back to see how many [riders] had suffered spills or horses had fallen."[6]

In 1934 the Crow and Oglala Sioux became the first tribes to receive shipments of live bison from federal land. Not coincidentally, that was the year that Robert Summers Yellowtail become the first Indian to be appointed a reservation superintendent. Yellowtail cajoled white ranchers on the Crow Reservation in Montana to return 40,000 acres to the tribe and borrowed trucks to transport the bison 350 miles from Yellowstone. The Crows received a total of about 200 bison during the 1930s, mostly from Yellowstone and the rest from the National Bison Range. Journalist Frank Ernest Hill in the *New York Times* lauded the new government policy that had made establishment of these herds on tribal land possible. "This policy holds that the Indian is intelligent, that he has a valuable culture of his own, that if encouraged to adapt himself in his own fashion to modern conditions he can become fully self-sustaining and will make an important contribution to American life as a whole." Hill also noted that although "the white American has found no place for buffaloes in his economy," the buffalo's "hardiness"—its ability to "graze successfully in rougher, colder, and more barren lands" than domestic cattle—was something to appreciate given the drought-stricken condition of much western range.[7]

The Oglala Sioux began with 43 bison on a fenced pasture at the Pine Ridge Reservation in South Dakota, nine of them from Yellowstone and the others from Wind Cave National Park. Although the bison selected for slaughter at Yellowstone included "old bulls, dry cows, steers, and any crippled, deformed, or diseased animals," the opposite criteria were applied when filling requests for live shipment, because the new owners wanted "good breeding stock or a nearly perfect specimen for exhibition purposes," as Chief Ranger Francis LaNoue explained. An exception to that policy was made in the second bison shipment to the Crow Reservation, in which about half of the 96 animals were considered good breeding stock and the rest were animals that the park wanted to eliminate from the herd. LaNoue believed this decision was justified by the large number of bison the Crows had received. Because ordinarily the fittest bison were selected for live shipment, LaNoue advised against trying to use live shipment to control

Yellowstone bison population, 1900–1940

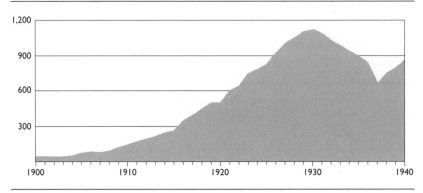

The Park Service began killing bison in the 1920s to limit the population size, but population goals were not set until the early 1930s.

herd size over an extended period. "It is unlikely that we will have many requests like that of the Crow Reservation where numbers taken are sufficient so that some inferior animals can be taken from the herd."

Reducing Elk and Bison on the Northern Range

In their 1934 report Wright and Thompson called for an end to the winter feeding of elk because it had "proved so much more harmful than beneficial." Although they were generally opposed to meddling with the landscape or wildlife for the sake of tourists, Wright and his colleagues believed that in order to combat the "harmful effects of human influence" and restore the "primitive state" of the parks, humans sometimes had to interfere with nature in a big way. They recommended reducing the northern elk herd, which was then estimated to number 12,000 to 14,000, by 3,000 a year until it could be sustained without artificial feeding. With drought affecting the range in the late 1920s and early 1930s, a population crash was believed to be imminent. Claiming that the herd was on the "brink of disaster," Wright warned that the next severe winter would bring "hideous starvation and wastage."[8] From a humanitarian standpoint, shooting the elk seemed preferable.

As with the accuracy of early wildlife population estimates, observations of habitat degradation made in the 1930s are difficult to evaluate in retrospect. Opinions were usually based on aesthetics rather than quantitative measurements, and long-term data were not available for comparison. By the time wildlife ecology and range management were professional disciplines, the native grazing system in most of the United States had been replaced or altered by domestic livestock operations with different goals and effects on the landscape. Under the prevailing range management dogma, heavily grazed ranges were evidence of too many animals. The goal was therefore to manage the northern range so that elk "productivity" was as steady as possible and mortality was kept to a minimum.[9] To address these concerns, the Park Service, Forest Service, and Montana Game Commission cooperated on a program that reduced the northern elk herd by about 3,300 during the winter of 1934–35. One-fifth were shot by rangers in the park and most of the others were shot by hunters outside the park. But even after a similar reduction was made in 1936, Adolph Murie, a highly respected wildlife biologist, believed the condition of the range required removing another 4,000 elk. At the end of the decade, the northern elk herd remained at about 11,000 and the bison herd on the northern range had been reduced to 582.

The 20-year tenure of Edmund Burrell Rogers as Yellowstone superintendent that began in 1936 was described by historian Aubrey Haines as one "dominated by expediency and diplomacy," and Haines credited Rogers with accommodating a tripling in annual visitation despite the "appalling obsolescence" of park facilities.[10] Unlike park visitors, the bison population was periodically culled, and it increased by only half during Rogers's term, but it also required park managers to adapt and make do. With the winter bison population in Pelican Valley back up to 136, it was tallied as a separate herd again, and 71 bison were relocated from Lamar Valley to Hayden Valley and Fountain Flats. These areas had once been part of the bison's winter range in Yellowstone, but the relocation was not done in the name of "ecosystem restoration," as it might today. Instead, as Rogers explained, "this was done in an attempt to scatter the herd over a wider range and provide more opportunity for park visitors to see buffalo running free and wild." As their size and ranges increased, the two new herds merged and were referred to by various cumbersome names, including the "Hayden Valley–Nez Perce–Firehole herd." Since the 1970s, bison in this area have often been referred to as the "Mary Mountain herd."

Rogers found that the buffalo show corral on Antelope Creek was popular among visitors, but the daily routine of driving the animals into it ended in 1937. Instead, the buffalo were left to roam in the large fenced pasture several hundred yards from the road, where they could be seen "in a more desirable setting even though they are at a greater distance." After 35 years of having to be there for visitors, liberation from the show corral was only a small step for Yellowstone bison, but a large step for Yellowstone bison management. In 1939 Rogers concluded that this compromise between natural conditions and visitor proximity had been the right thing to do. "Many favorable comments were received regarding the method of display in a large enclosure which simulates natural conditions," he reported.

A Formula for Carrying Capacity and Confusion

Another Yellowstone tradition bit the dust in 1939 when instead of a horseback roundup of the Lamar herd for culling, the rangers began drawing bison to the corral by baiting them with hay. This eliminated one form of physical human interference, but it provided no spectacle for tourists. The change was consistent with a policy that the Wildlife Division had developed in 1932 and the National Park Service officially distributed in 1939: "Presentation of the animal life of the parks to the public shall be a wholly natural one." The policy also called for an end to artificial feeding. "Every species shall be left to carry on its struggle for existence unaided, as being to its greatest ultimate good, unless there is real cause to believe that it will perish if unassisted." However, the policy recognized that keeping ungulate populations within the carrying capacity of the range would necessitate limiting their size artificially.[11]

In an effort to determine the northern range's carrying capacity, park ranger Rudolph Grimm used a figure of three acres per elk for the six-month winter season. This was based on Rush's data and "observations of the feeding habits of elk."[12] Grimm calculated a "forage acre factor" of 0.16 (based on the quantity of forage plants present that elk were likely to consume) and multiplied it by the number of range acres (145,437) to arrive at a carrying capacity of 7,756 "elk units." To allow for the overlapping diets of other ungulates, he reduced this number to 7,059, but that would leave room for only 245 bison on the northern range, each of which was assumed to use up 1.5 elk units. And the 7,059 elk figure was an "average winter carrying capacity"; it dropped to 4,781 during February and March, according to Grimm's estimate.

Traditional estimates of carrying capacity made in this way by livestock managers referred to the number of animals that would provide the highest economic return on a sustainable basis. This differs from the more recent concept of "ecological" carrying capacity, which is the number of animals that a range can sustain without human assistance. Ecological carrying capacity varies from year to year, depending on environmental factors, but it is generally larger than economic carrying capacity because each animal does not have to justify its existence by being a worthwhile investment. However, this difference was not generally recognized by wildlife managers until the 1970s, and it is still not accepted by some of those who criticize Yellowstone officials for allowing the range to become "overgrazed."[13]

In a peculiar attempt to explain how elk had thrived on the northern range for decades in numbers far in excess of his computed carrying capacity, Grimm noted that, "apparently due to the almost yearly recurring forage shortage, a stamina has developed in the surviving animals that permits them to live through such periods without suffering permanent physical injury so long as the dearth is not excessive." Grimm therefore concluded that the "true carrying capacity for the winter range under conditions that prevailed during the winter of 1937–38" would be a compromise between the average and the low carrying capacity figures. This came to 6,307 elk, plus 900 for the range north of the park.

In 1940 Daniel Beard, a wildlife biologist who would later become superintendent at Everglades and then Olympic National Park, reported that the "artificiality" of bison in national parks was inevitable. "The 'wildest' herds in the United States today are in Yellowstone," Beard argued, "but even they are not living as they did in a primitive environment. I suspect that now that the species has been saved, we should think of its future in federal areas where it must be maintained in semi-domestication."[14] However, Newton Drury, who became director of the Park Service that year, was determined to "work toward the ideal of placing all species, including the bison, as rapidly as practicable upon a self-sustaining basis."[15] A consensus within the Park Service favored reducing the Lamar herd to the "computed carrying capacity of the winter range" in order to eliminate the presumed need for winter feeding, but there was no consensus about what that number was.[16]

Without any elaborate calculations Drury issued an order in 1942 to reduce the Lamar herd by 200 animals, and this was done by slaughtering 193 bison and shipping 17 from the park. Nonetheless, more than a hundred bison headed north out of the park the following winter, the most severe since that of 1919–20. For park managers this large exodus was evidence that feeding alone would not keep bison in the park. Most of the bison returned within several weeks, along with complaints about damage to ranchers' haystacks and fences. Some of the bison traveled 30 miles to Carbella Flats, and one was reported on a ranch 50 miles from the park. The following August, nearly 150 bison were seen outside the park's northeast corner near Lake Abundance.

By 1943, when the parkwide winter bison count was 964, Drury had accepted the theory that Yellowstone's carrying capacity was about 350 bison for the northern range and 300 for the rest of the park. The increasing number of bison that spent the winter in the park's interior without artificial feeding was considered proof that the Lamar herd could be weaned from its "boarding house habits."[17] To help meet that goal, 405 bison were removed from the Lamar herd, leaving a count of 352. Drury also issued orders to stop using the fenced pasture at Antelope Creek and announced his intention to eliminate the Buffalo Ranch buildings and irrigation system because they were inappropriate in a national park. When 68 of the 313 bison in the Lamar herd left the park in the mild winter of 1948, their movement was regarded as evidence that before ranchers settled in the area, the bison's range had "probably extended down the Yellowstone valley to, or perhaps below the present town of Livingston," which is 50 miles from the park boundary.[18]

The changes in bison management and the reduction in the northern elk herd roused some opposition in surrounding communities and sportsmen's groups, but the Park Service's chief biologist, Victor Cahalane, staunchly defended the new policy. "A hundred nationally known scientists were first consulted for their opinions of these measures," he claimed. "They almost unanimously approved."[19] But among those who objected was a nationally known nonscientist.

Albright's Last Stand

Horace Albright was gone from the National Park Service but not forgotten. He corresponded energetically with people in high places and remained influential on conservation issues.[20] As Yellowstone superintendent, Albright had come to believe that the problem with bison was how to manage the population "under nearly natural conditions and at the same time get it near the main highways where it can be easily and safely observed," and he never swerved from that illogical goal.[21] Differing fundamentally from

Drury on the role of wildlife in a national park, Albright opposed the reduction in the Lamar herd and the elimination of fenced bison pastures. "It is argued," he wrote in 1944,

> that the law governing National Park administration requires that everything must be kept as nearly as possible in its natural state, and hence there must be no artificial care or direction of bison. The question is, can these herds, widely separated and with half of the total number of animals ranging on high altitude plateaus often swept by violent snowstorms accompanied by intense cold, survive without reserves of hay in the lower valleys and the facilities of the buffalo ranch for dealing with disease? The answer is "no." Even the Lamar River herd, if not fed in periods of deep snow or under blizzard storm conditions, will move down the valley and out of the Park into towns and farms, and in such drifts there is always the possibility of excessive losses of bison as well as great property damage by the restless hungry animals.[22]

As usual, Albright's concern for the Yellowstone bison was matched by his concern for the Yellowstone tourist, who he predicted would have "hardly one chance in a thousand of seeing one animal in a week's stay" after the herd was reduced. Albright lamented that under the new policy, "the bison must never be rounded up for any purpose, not even a few fine animals for the Antelope Creek enclosure. We all know that most visitors to Yellowstone would be unlikely to see the bison even if they were near at hand unless they should be pointed out."[23]

Cahalane countered that "700 healthy, vigorous wild animals were worth more than 1,200 animals lazily waiting for hay. No one is interested in sightseeing domestic cattle." He believed that feeding, fencing, and culling had changed the appearance and nature of the Lamar herd. "Members of the 'tame' herd do not seem to be as vigorous, as energetic, as hard, or as glossy-coated as those of the original herd of wild animals that has continued to exist and increase in Yellowstone without man's attention." Comparing the Lamar herd to the bison described by fur trader Alexander Henry in North Dakota in 1800, Cahalane asked, "Is the buffalo of today 'sagacious, alert, wary?' No, he is heedless, dull, almost stupid. Man must take the predator's place in keeping the herds within natural bounds, and thus from eating themselves out of house and home."[24]

Writing to Drury, Albright contended that the national parks were "not biologic units where animals can live in natural conditions the year round." He insisted that the display pastures were "absolutely essential," and that the public was entitled to "full opportunities to enjoy the animal life of the parks" even if this required "some small measure of artificiality in living conditions of the animals." According to Albright, George Bird Grinnell, "the grand old man of wildlife conservation," had watched the roundup of the big herd in Lamar Valley with tears streaming down his cheeks and said it was "the greatest sight that his eyes had beheld since 1876 when he was a reporter attached to Custer's staff on the plains." In response, Drury pointed out that Yellowstone was not a "complete biologic unit" for elk, deer, or pronghorn, yet no longer did the park "feed them hay and otherwise manage their lives."[25] Nonetheless, perhaps because his family had donated the land, in 1948 Laurance Rockefeller succeeded in pressuring the Park Service to provide 20 Yellowstone bison for a display in the Jackson Hole Wildlife Park. Drury hoped the scheme would fail, but bison remained in the enclosure long after it became part of Grand Teton National Park in 1950.[26]

Avoiding Public Criticism

Limited brucellosis testing resumed in Yellowstone in 1941, after a seven-year lapse, with four veterinarians using various methods to check blood samples from 200 bison at the Buffalo Ranch. They found that from one-third to two-thirds of the animals were "reactors or suspects."[27] Reactors are animals whose blood contains antibodies for brucellosis and are therefore considered seropositive; suspects are those whose test results are inconclusive. From 1941 on, only seronegative bison were to be used for live shipment from the park. However, of the 400 bison removed in January 1944, only three were shipped live, and blood tests were not used to determine which bison were slaughtered. Instead, a simpler selection process was used. "Since it was desired to retain the most independent and self-sufficient members of the herd, the earliest arrivals on the feeding grounds were trapped without regard for sex or other considerations," explained Cahalane.[28]

But later that year, a report that Yellowstone was shipping brucellosis-infected bison was made at the annual convention of the American Veterinary Medical Association. The blood test can detect only the presence of antibodies an animal may create to fight the bacteria, not the *Brucella abortus* itself. Therefore, an animal that is carrying the bacteria may test seronegative if the blood sample is taken when antibodies are absent or too sparse to be detected. Nonreactors from an infected herd are not assumed to be brucellosis free unless they have completed an approved quarantine period.

The veterinarians' complaints led to the suspension of live bison ship-ments from Yellowstone and an investigation by Erling Quortrup of the U.S. Fish and Wildlife Service. In his findings Quortrup downplayed the significance of brucellosis in the Yellowstone bison and supported the continued shipment of nonreactors to other herds. He could not find any evidence of undulant fever among American Indians or other people who had handled bison carcasses in the past, and he noted that the bison may have acquired "a natural immunity" to the disease through years of expo-sure, as suggested by the rarity of abortions and gross lesions. He believed that "if control methods are to be instituted, this should be done to avoid public criticism and to facilitate future live shipments rather than to safeguard the herd itself." He also supported feeding the Lamar herd during the winter to reduce defections from the park.[29]

A brucellosis vaccine for cattle had been approved in 1940, but its effects on bison were unknown. Quortrup's position was "If all the calves could be handled annually, I would unhesitatingly recommend vaccination; inas-much as this is impossible, the value of vaccination is open to debate." Don Coburn, the next veterinarian assigned to the case by the U.S. Fish and Wildlife Service, recommended vaccinating all calves and eliminating all seropositive adults despite the logistical difficulties, but the Park Service considered such measures unrealistic because of the impossibility of cor-ralling all of the bison and the prospect that even a "clean" herd could be reinfected by elk. In addition to the 38 bison that drowned in January 1946 after breaking through the ice and becoming trapped in the Yellowstone River, 200 bison were slaughtered, most of them seronegative, to reduce the Lamar herd to about 350.

Coburn did vaccinate 86 untested calves and yearlings during the 1946 roundup. The next year, nearly half of these bison were tested and vacci-nated again, including three reactors. Another 78 untested calves were vaccinated in 1947, along with 13 tested yearlings, including nine reactors. The next phase of Coburn's study, which was to determine the likelihood of bison transmitting brucellosis to elk, was canceled due to lack of funds.

Superintendent Rogers reported to his superiors, "In our personal discussions with Dr. Coburn it is clear to us that there is no present objective of establishing a disease-free herd in Yellowstone."[30]

Improving the condition of the northern range did remain an objective, but an elusive one. The relative abundance of native ungulates that inhabited the area before the arrival of Euro-Americans "has not been, and probably cannot be, definitively determined," stated Yellowstone ranger Wayne Alcorn. "This leaves some doubt as to which species are chiefly responsible for the over-grazed winter range, and which ones should be reduced to bring the large game animal population into natural balance once more," he explained, assuming that a numeric balance had once existed. However, in his enumeration of the reasons why it was not possible to return the Lamar bison "to a truly natural existence," Alcorn noted that the presence of brucellosis in the herd "made it highly desirable to trap periodically as large a number of bison as possible for testing, vaccination and removal of reactors."[31]

Reduce, Remove, Reconsider

The Buffalo Ranch had a squeeze chute stronger and heavier than those used to hold cattle in place while they are being worked on, but it was not suitable for bison calves. When vaccinations were given during the 1946 roundup, some of the calves were eight months old with eight-inch horns, and it took four men to safely pin a calf so that a blood sample could be taken and an inoculation given. The animal was held down while the sample was rushed to the warming shed, because the blood would often freeze before the test had been completed and another sample would have to be taken.[32]

No bison were removed in 1947, but the Buffalo Ranch facilities were remodeled to handle the large reduction planned to get the population back down to about 350. Now there was a wood-burning stove to provide heat for the building, and a series of chutes with gates that could be remotely controlled by one man using a system of ropes and pulleys to sort the bison into different corrals for slaughter, shipment out of the park, or veterinary attention. One bison was separated from the herd at a time and worked into the squeezer, and a gate closed, preventing forward or backward movement. One side of the squeezer was hinged at the bottom and operated with a heavy lever that clamped the bison into a viselike grip, and four small trap doors were positioned so they could be opened to vaccinate, take blood samples from, and apply ear tags to the animal.

The Park Service director lifted the embargo on shipping live bison from Yellowstone in 1947 because of the presumed progress in reducing brucellosis. The following January, 309 bison were corralled and 54 nonreactors were vaccinated and shipped; of the 181 bison that were slaughtered, only 32 had been identified as reactors or suspects. This practice was repeated during the bison removals conducted periodically until 1966: in order to meet the reduction goal, nonreactors were slaughtered along with reactors and untested bison. The effect of the herd reduction on brucellosis was therefore negligible.

Winter feeding of the Lamar herd, which had been discontinued in 1946, resumed in 1948 because the roundup and reduction activities had caused "critical range forage conditions" in the Lamar Valley. Summarizing the results of the 200 bison that were tested, Rudolph Grimm reported that the "incidence of infection" had been reduced from 62 percent in 1941 to 15 percent in 1948.[33] That was mistaken; what had been reduced was the percentage of bison that were reactors to the test or suspects, indicating that they may have been exposed to brucellosis. The actual infection rate in the Lamar herd was not known, and given the fallibility of the blood test, the apparent reduction in seroprevalence was not evidence that the partial vaccination and herd reduction program had had any effect. (Even with the more reliable tests that are used now on slaughtered bison, park managers are cautious in estimating infection rates, but about half of the Yellowstone bison whose blood was tested in the 1990s were seropositive, and probably no more than half of those seropositive bison were infected with brucellosis.)[34]

In 1949 brucellosis specialists at the National Institutes of Health rendered their opinion that efforts to test and vaccinate bison at Yellowstone and Wind Cave national parks should be suspended because of "the great difficulties and expense" and because no effort was being made to control the disease in livestock on nearby ranches. Furthermore, the NIH doctors believed that even if brucellosis eradication were possible in those bison herds, it could be detrimental to them because "clean" herds would be more susceptible to an "explosive outbreak of brucellosis with an accompanying storm of abortions" if the disease were transmitted to the bison by elk or by livestock on the surrounding ranges.[35]

The Park Service adopted this position but reinstated the embargo against live bison shipments from Yellowstone in 1951 because of concerns about brucellosis. By then, Superintendent Rogers had approved a plan to reduce the Lamar herd to no more than 125 so that the bison could be kept in the Buffalo Ranch corrals during elk-trapping operations and would not get in the way as they had previously. The following January, 131 bison, both reactors and nonreactors, were killed at the Buffalo Ranch pens, and 111 bison that could not be baited into the corral were shot on the open range. Another 81 untested bison were kept in a corral until April 8; they dropped 15 calves before their release, none of which were viable.

In 1952 Montana began a more concerted effort to eliminate brucellosis from livestock in the state. In most cases brucellosis eradication has required slaughtering the entire herd in which an infected animal is found, or testing the entire herd and slaughtering those that are seropositive; the remaining animals are vaccinated, quarantined, and periodically retested until they pass the requisite quarantine period. Strain 19, the vaccine used until RB51 was approved for cattle in 1996, was considered only 67 percent effective in preventing infection and abortion in cattle and of uncertain effectiveness in bison.[36] The blood test used to determine if the animal was seropositive was even less reliable, especially since inoculation with strain 19 often caused animals to produce antibodies that made them seropositive on subsequent tests. That made it difficult to determine how much, if at all, the vaccine contributed to brucellosis eradication in a herd. With or without an effective vaccine, if the test-and-slaughter process is repeated in a confined herd over a long enough period, eventually all the *Brucella abortus* bacteria are eliminated, along with both infected and uninfected animals.

Participation in the livestock program was voluntary at first, and many livestock owners did not volunteer. As Park Service managers would in subsequent decades, the ranchers objected to the inaccuracy of the blood test and believed that the herd reductions were more detrimental than was brucellosis. The risk of people getting undulant fever from infected livestock had diminished because of pasteurization requirements for dairy products.

As Much Progress as Possible

In Yellowstone, officials still considered a parkwide test-and-slaughter program impossible. But several hundred bison were culled about every other year, and in 1953, after a group wandered across the park's east boundary into the Absarokas, three were legally shot by hunters for the first time in

Montana since the 1880s. The park's bison count reached a record high of 1,477 the following year. But in 1956, on Edmund Rogers's last day of work as Yellowstone superintendent, he sent a memorandum to his superior confirming the need to reduce the population to 425 because of "the deteriorated condition" of the range.

The bison count was whittled down again, and the embargo against live bison shipments was breached on behalf of a Wyoming rancher who apparently had political connections. Having obtained a contract to trap bison for purposes of herd reduction, Bud Bosolo took 143 bison from the Lamar herd in 1962, regardless of test results, and 357 untested bison from the Mary Mountain herd in 1963.[37] That was the first herd reduction done outside the Lamar Valley, and it was possible because helicopters were used for the first time to drive the bison into a trap.

In July 1964, after the U.S. Department of Agriculture (USDA) "strongly recommended" that Yellowstone undertake "a major brucellosis control program," the National Park Service headquarters issued instructions calling for "the immediate development" of a program that would include testing all bison in the Mary Mountain herd and reducing the herd by removing reactors and suspects.[38] That did not happen. According to the "Long Range Wildlife and Habitat Management Plan" that Yellowstone superintendent John McLaughlin signed in October, the Lamar herd would be tested to the maximum extent possible with existing facilities, but there was no provision for trapping more bison if the number of reactors found fell short of the reduction quota; nonreactors would be killed instead, and no plans were made to test the Mary Mountain herd.

Yellowstone's shorter-term "Bison and Habitat Management Plan" for 1964–65 began with the cheerful notion "The least wildlife management necessary in national parks, the better the management, is an agreeable statement to most of us." However, the plan acknowledged that "it is necessary for us to make as much progress as possible each year toward a brucellosis-free bison herd," even though it would not be feasible to trap all of the bison in the park. Another change was the inclusion of the Pelican Valley herd in the program for the first time, with 94 bison to be removed "in accordance with long standing management goals" that allowed for 180 in that herd. A survey by the Soil Conservation Service had found that more than half of the Pelican Valley range was "in less than good condition" and that "present knowledge indicates that this deterioration resulted from excessive bison and elk use." However, because no trap had been constructed

Yellowstone bison population, 1940–1970

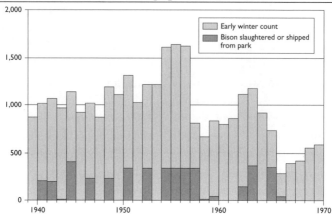

in Pelican Valley, the bison were to be shot without testing them first. The chief ranger notified his men that "this program will be difficult, and one undertaken in close cooperation with personnel of the Division of Animal Disease Eradication [USDA] and Mr. Ricks of the Quick Freeze Packing Plant of Livingston."

Yellowstone had been conducting aerial bison censuses since 1949, and these were assumed to be more accurate than those previously done by rangers on skis, but what was counted from the air did not always match what was found on the ground. When the time came to reduce the Pelican herd to 180, the rangers could find no more than 175 bison. They shot 34 anyway. In the Lamar and Mary Mountain herds, 320 bison were removed (both reactors and nonreactors), leaving 388 bison counted in the park. Although the elk removals of the 1960s attracted far more attention because of the much larger number of animals killed and the concerns of hunters, the bison herd was much more drastically reduced.

A Token Eradication Program

Whatever commitment the Yellowstone staff felt to "minimize" brucellosis in the park's bison herds, it was weaker than the desire to reduce inter-ference with the animals. At a staff meeting McLaughlin held in April 1965, the consensus favored "a token brucellosis eradication program" that was incidental to "habitat management" (i.e., overgrazing) concerns. The plan for the next winter was to remove 100 bison from the Mary Mountain herd because the prior winter's reduction goal had not been met, to test and vaccinate animals that were trapped in connection with the removal, and then to hold off for at least two years before trapping any more bison. The ordeal of unweaned calves that were subjected to repeated driving and trapping was troubling. But the Animal Disease Eradication Division (ADE) was not satisfied with Yellowstone's plans for a token effort. It wanted as many calves as possible vaccinated in all herds every year. As for the research on brucellosis in elk that Yellowstone staff believed should be done before launching an aggressive campaign against brucellosis in bison, "ADE doesn't appear to be at all interested, indicating if we get bison brucellosis reduced, the elk brucellosis may take care of itself, and further, that there's really no reason to be so concerned about brucellosis in elk."[39]

Park Service officials in Washington, D.C., were willing to propose a more aggressive program for eliminating brucellosis in bison than were Yellowstone managers. In May 1965 the assistant director of the Park Service wrote to ADE officials to explain that "fulfillment of our primary responsibility for conserving all components of the natural ecosystem . . . should not be construed as a debasement of our responsibilities for attempting to achieve brucellosis-free bison herds." Plans were drawn up to construct a trap and holding facilities in Pelican Valley so that testing could begin there. However, Yellowstone was excused from undertaking any immediate action in Pelican Valley by pleading lack of funds for both the construction and the staff needed to conduct a more intensive corralling effort.

The following winter, even an intensive corralling effort of the Mary Mountain herd failed to accomplish much, according to the park's 1966 wildlife report, because "the usual concentration of animals" in the herd's winter range did not show up. The usual concentration of bison may have no longer existed, or the bison that did exist may have found it prudent to winter elsewhere or were able to do so because of the mild winter; and the Mary Mountain bison that were on their customary range had an attitude that thwarted trapping operations. While some of the bison observed during the helicopter drives were described as "flighty," the solitary bulls were often impossible to move at all, and the mixed groups sometimes escaped when the lead cows became experienced in turning back underneath the helicopter.[40] This learned behavior was reinforced in bison that tested seronegative because after they were released from the trap, they were subject to more helicopter herding along with the untested bison. As a result, only 50 were removed that winter, including 5 that died at the site

This photo was taken as a helicopter was being used to drive bison to a trap near Nez Perce Creek in 1966. Courtesy of Yellowstone National Park.

from injuries and 19 that were reactors or suspects. The other 73 nonreactors and untested bison were released, including 8 calves that were vaccinated.

This reduction left the park with a bison count of only 266, and a bison herding experience that provided further evidence of "the desirability of reducing harassment by conducting trapping operations only every two or three years or when winter conditions permit maximum trapping efficiency." Therefore, the wildlife management plan for 1966–67 explained, no bison trapping, testing, vaccinating, or removals were to be done that winter. And after the next winter count found 397 bison, none were done the following year either, and plans to build a trap in Pelican Valley remained on hold.

Other Infected Bison Herds

Managers of other bison herds had already made or were undertaking more aggressive efforts to eliminate brucellosis. The bison that the Crow Reservation had received from Yellowstone and the National Bison Range had grown to a herd of more than 700 by the late 1940s, and they were leaving their 14,000-acre range and mingling with cattle. When many of the harvested bison tested seropositive in 1953, pressure for brucellosis eradication increased. The U.S. Fish and Wildlife Service eventually determined that the only practical solution was to eliminate the herd. The range was converted to a cattle operation, but the Crows started over in 1972 with 50 bison from Theodore Roosevelt National Park, and they now maintain the brucellosis-free herd at about 1,000 bison.

The 20 bison sent to the Jackson Hole Wildlife Park in 1948 were tested and vaccinated before they left Yellowstone, but reactors were found in 1963, when the group was next tested, and all 13 adults in the herd were killed. The nine calves and yearlings were vaccinated and soon joined by 12 bison from Theodore Roosevelt National Park. Grand Teton National Park, which had taken over the herd, agreed to a program to vaccinate all calves and test adults every three years, but it was suspended when the herd became free roaming in 1969. Evidence of brucellosis later appeared, and the herd remains infected.[41]

The 23 bison selected to start a free-roaming herd in Utah in the early 1940s were also tested and vaccinated before they left Yellowstone, but reactors were found when the next testing was done, on seven bison carcasses in 1961. The herd occupies a range of about 600 square miles in the Henry Mountains, most of which is administered by the Bureau of Land Management, but the bison are the responsibility of the Utah Division of Wildlife Resources. In the spring of 1963 they were able to vaccinate 12 yearlings in a herd of about 80 by using two airplanes to drive them to terrain where they could be shot with an immobilizing drug. Three of the yearlings died as a result of the procedure, but a corral was constructed, and the following fall, 69 bison were driven into it using two planes, a helicopter, and 10 men on horseback. Any "excited" bison were tranquilized, but five animals died from injuries received during capture, and five others apparently died from the testing or vaccination procedures or general stress.[42] Fourteen calves were vaccinated and released along with the yearlings that had been vaccinated the previous spring. The 27 surviving adults were also released, but the 10 that were considered reactors or suspects were marked so that hunters would know which ones they could shoot. Additional testing of the blood samples found more bison that should have been marked as reactors, and 4 of the 11 marked bison were not shot until the Division of Wildlife Resources finally located them after the 1964 hunting season.[43]

As a brucellosis eradication effort, the Henry Mountains program seemed to have been long on unintended casualties and short on results. No further vaccinations or live testing was done, but perhaps because the herd was relatively small and dispersed, the *Brucella abortus* apparently failed to perpetuate itself. No further evidence of brucellosis has been found in tested carcasses. Today the herd is maintained at about 400 bison through hunting.

The Wichita Mountains National Wildlife Refuge began vaccinating bison in the 1940s, but bison and elk suspects were found during routine testing in the 1964 roundup. Over a period of years, all bison that could be captured were tested, all seropositive bison and those that could not be captured were killed, and the herd was reduced from 781 to 345. The herd has been considered brucellosis free since 1974 and is maintained at about 600 by auctioning live bison. Both Custer State Park, which then had more than 2,000 bison, and the adjacent Wind Cave National Monument, with 250 bison, began programs of testing, vaccination, and slaughter in 1963. Custer's herd has been designated brucellosis free since 1973, but Wind Cave did not achieve that status until 1985.[44]

In Canada the bison shipped from Wainwright Buffalo Park to Wood Buffalo National Park in the 1920s brought both brucellosis and tuberculosis with them. The diseases were confirmed there in the 1950s, when the bison population numbered about 10,000. Until the 1980s, Wood Buffalo was considered remote from cattle grazing, and transmission to domestic livestock was not a major concern, but the health of the bison population itself was. Tuberculosis can be fatal to bison, and it makes the animal more vulnerable to other causes of death, such as winterkill and predation. In 1953 a scheme was worked out in which the Royal Canadian Air Force would conduct a search-and-destroy mission of all the bison so that they could be replaced with disease-free animals, but the plan was rejected as too extreme. Instead, a test-and-slaughter program was conducted until 1962, but according to government reports, the experiment did more to supply meat for northern communities than it did to eliminate disease from the herd, which remains infected.[45]

An Infringement on the Sanctuary Idea

In Yellowstone the perceived overgrazing of the northern range remained more worrisome than was brucellosis in bison. From 1956 to 1962 an average of 1,774 elk were removed each year, most of them killed in the park, including animals that might otherwise have left the park for areas where they could have been shot by hunters.[46] Enraged local communities that depended on the business generated by sport hunting demanded changes to the federal laws that prohibited hunting in Yellowstone. U.S. senator Gale McGee of Wyoming convened hearings in Bozeman, Montana, to consider the issue. Elk hunting was permitted in Grand Teton as part of the political compromise needed to establish the park, but the Park Service continued to oppose hunting in Yellowstone for a variety of reasons. It would be impossible for hunters to remove enough elk to meet the reduction goal; their pack animals would damage the range and disrupt other wildlife; and a large public hunt might cause elk to avoid humans in the park, so visitors would see fewer of the animals that now wandered in plain view.[47] Cahalane assured the Park Service director that "with a few selected marksmen, the necessary killing can be done with minimum disturbance and in the briefest time. Such conditions cannot be duplicated by inviting in the general run of hunters, many of whom can't distinguish between species and can't shoot accurately at their targets. . . . The official reduction by killing is an infringement on the sanctuary idea, but it is not as damaging and violent as public hunting."[48]

A survey in 1961–62 showed continuing deterioration of the northern range, and the experts were certain it could support only half the estimated herd of 10,000 elk. Elk removals in the park peaked in 1962, when 4,309 were shot in the park, 310 were trapped and shipped live, and only 125 were killed outside the park by hunters.[49] This triggered an uproar in local communities and "letters from schoolchildren in faraway places," and the remaining elk produced a bumper calf crop the next spring.[50] Public doubt about the pronouncements of the range experts increased as elk reductions seemed to have no effect on the condition of the range, and statements made by the Park Service took on a more defensive tone:

> The NPS does not plan to continue to sacrifice its capital, the soil, in a vain effort to save a few hundred elk for a winter or two so they can die of starvation. No responsible authority questions the poor condition of the northern range or the fact that more elk will ruin it. And, if in the final judgment of the years of study and experience the experts and the administrators should prove utterly wrong, natural reproduction on understocked range will restore any desired herd size in a relatively short period of time. True, aspen and other browse recovery is less than it should be, and much of the range is still overgrazed, but we know we are moving in the right direction in our management plan for range recovery.[51]

The controversy over elk reductions in Yellowstone and Rocky Mountain national parks prompted Secretary of the Interior Stewart Udall to
appoint the Special Advisory Board on Wildlife Management in the National
Parks in 1962. The committee of prominent scientists and conservationists
was chaired by A. Starker Leopold, Aldo Leopold's son and a professor at
the University of California at Berkeley. The 1963 Leopold Report, as it
became known, affirmed the principle of carrying capacity as the calcula-
tion of how many animals a range could support, and the goal of restoring
a "balance" between animal populations and their habitat. The committee
also supported the use of direct reduction to limit elk populations and stated
that removal programs at some parks had not been large enough; future
removals would "have to be larger and in many cases repeated annually."[52]

The Park Service worked with the U.S. Forest Service and the states of
Montana and Wyoming to develop a long-range plan for the northern range
that called for continuing to remove enough elk to maintain the herd at
5,000. It also advocated removing about 200 pronghorn and up to 45 bison
from the northern range. To prevent elk slaughter in the park, the Wyoming
Game and Fish Commission agreed to take the excess animals, even though
the state did not want them, and 4,543 elk were trapped and moved outside
the park over a four-year period. In 1965 Superintendent McLaughlin
avoided what he called the "distasteful practice" of slaughtering animals in
the park by trucking live elk and bison to a commercial slaughterhouse, a
change that he regarded as "one of the highlights of this year's wildlife
management program," with all of the hides, horns, and processed meat
turned over to the Bureau of Indian Affairs for distribution to reservations.

The use of a commercial slaughterhouse is more sanitary for humans
and makes it easier to put more of the carcasses to good use. But for some
people, live shipment is not only distasteful but also hypocritical for wildlife
managers, because killing wild animals on the land where they were born
is surely more humane than subjecting them to confinement and a truck
ride to the slaughterhouse. Nonetheless, McLaughlin hoped the new policy
would reduce public criticism of the elk culling. Yellowstone wildlife biologist Bill Barmore wrote optimistically to a concerned citizen, "I think we
have finally convinced the local public that an undesirable ungulate-
habitat situation has existed in the Park a long time, that serious habitat
damage has taken place, and that the situation must be corrected. . . . I
think the forthright stand taken by the National Park Service on the basis
of good factual information has impressed people." But Barmore thought

the "violent criticism" of "a local minority" had abated primarily because elk were no longer being killed in the park. "Fortunately, with newly developing techniques, we should not have to shoot large numbers of elk in the Park in the foreseeable future."

However, Yellowstone announced plans in February 1967 to immediately shoot 600 elk in the park because removals during the previous two winters had been insufficient. In the park's Annual Wildlife Report that year, Barmore attributed the resulting outcry in local communities to "widespread public misunderstanding of our elk program." But the fury over the loss of 600 elk expressed by residents of states where more than 100,000 game animals were harvested each year sprang from more than just a lack of good factual information or a passion about hunting; it indicated a resentment of Park Service dictates. Wyoming governor Stanley Hathaway insisted that the elk be trapped instead of shot, and Senator McGee held a hearing in Casper on March 11. The Park Service announced that it had stopped killing elk in Yellowstone as of that day. Hathaway asked for 1,000 elk to be relocated to Wyoming ranges, but after about half that number had been shipped, ranchers who did not want the elk consuming their hay persuaded the governor to rescind his demand.[53]

The Park Service did not promise that elk culling was over forever, but no elk have been killed in Yellowstone for the purpose of limiting herd size since then. If negative publicity were the only reason for this policy shift, Yellowstone managers could have resumed the bison culling that was suspended in 1966 because of operational difficulties. The bison program was far smaller and less conspicuous and controversial than the elk reductions. The bison were not of interest to hunters, and pressure was mounting to do something about brucellosis in the bison. But Yellowstone's 1964 "Long Range Wildlife and Habitat Management Plan" turned out to be short-lived, and 30 years passed before the next Yellowstone bison was killed because it tested positive for exposure to brucellosis. Park managers had reasons besides public opinion for changing the elk management policy, reasons that also applied to bison.

CHAPTER 7

The Imbalance of Nature

Metaphors are often used to describe the unfathomable: there are shifting plates beneath Earth's crust and black holes in outer space; glaciers are said to "calve" even though they are disintegrating rather than reproducing themselves. As a metaphor, "the balance of nature" is more an expression of cultural values than science. The concept suggests stability and resilience, and natural environments that are predictable if enough facts about them are known.[1] By 1930 the English ecologist Charles Elton was certain that a balance of nature does not exist. "The numbers of wild animals are constantly varying to a greater or less extent. . . . Each variation in the numbers of one species causes direct and indirect repercussions on the numbers of the others, and since many of the latter are themselves independently varying in numbers, the resultant confusion is remarkable," he wrote.[2] But few people wanted to exchange the comforting balance of nature for the resultant confusion, and Charles Elton was largely ignored.

Assumptions about the balance of nature have often gone unquestioned because they are grounded in religious convictions.[3] A beneficent Creator might reasonably be expected to provide us with a world capable of balancing supply and demand. But even for those without strong religious beliefs, the balance-of-nature concept has been so powerful and appealing that it has continued to affect how people explain natural phenomena despite considerable evidence to the contrary. Instead, evidence of imbalance in the natural environment is often attributed to what humans have done or failed to do. Those who believe that divine intervention affects the course of human events may try to maintain a desired balance of nature through prayer, sacrifice, or other rituals intended to bring good weather and ample food or to keep away disease and pestilence. Those who believe in the power of scientific knowledge try to use human intervention to rectify perceived imbalances in nature. The idea of a symmetrical, mechanistic nature may seem odd to those who regard nature as the antithesis of technology—something wild rather than civilized—but it has appealed to land managers who want to be able to improve on the portion of nature they have to work with.

So it was at Yellowstone in 1946, when park ranger Rudolph Grimm stated, "It is our responsibility to maintain in a natural condition the range plant cover as well as the wildlife population of this range. In order to attain such a state, we must bring about and maintain an equitable balance between the amount of range forage produced and the number of animals using this range."[4] People generally accepted an attitude that emphasized human control over nature, and regarded nature as something that could be kept in balance through careful manipulation. It did not seem to occur to park managers then, or for many years afterward, that there was nothing "natural" about an "equitable balance." Nature doesn't always play fair.

A Reasonable and Effective Alternative

After culling ended in Yellowstone in the 1960s, elk and bison increased dramatically in number and expanded their range. "Balance" remained a desired goal, but the controversy grew over how it was to be defined and achieved. There was an increasing recognition that balance was a largely subjective rather than scientific measurement, that wildlife species could be considered out of balance if they threatened human life or livelihood, if favored species declined, or if some animals were in poor condition and died because they could not survive the winter. Some people believe that "nature knows best," and if left to itself, nature would find the right balance between ungulate populations and forage, and that the large increases in the elk and bison populations that occurred after culling ceased were merely evidence that the ecosystem was returning to its natural equilibrium. Others believe that the Yellowstone ecosystem had been altered too much by humans for park managers to realistically consider leaving nature to itself and that without human intervention to compensate for human disturbances, something "unnatural" or otherwise unacceptable was happening to ungulate populations and their habitat. Were the apples simply being allowed to fall where they may, or were they rolling—or being pushed—too far from the tree?

Along with a shift in elk management policy after the public uproar in the spring, the year 1967 was marked by a change in Yellowstone management. Jack Anderson, who had been superintendent at Grand Teton National Park, took over at Yellowstone and brought with him Glen Cole, who had studied the elk in Grand Teton. Already at Yellowstone were wildlife biologists Bill Barmore and Mary Meagher. Soon after arriving at Yellowstone, Anderson met with the biologists and two veterinarians from the U.S. Department of Agriculture to discuss the brucellosis issue. Anderson stated that "a new look was being taken at the entire bison management program" and that no further reductions would be made unless research demonstrated their necessity. Echoing an old refrain, the group voiced concern about the impact of bison management policies on the Yellowstone tourist. "Reservations were expressed about the consequences of past brucellosis control programs in greatly reducing visitor opportunities to see bison during the summer," Meagher noted in her record of the meeting.

While acknowledging the uncertain origin of *Brucella abortus*, the park biologists used the possibility that the bacterium was native to Yellowstone as a rationale for the new bison management policy. "Very possibly brucellosis arrived on this continent with the bison as they crossed the Bering land bridge during the Pleistocene," and bison may have developed a natural immunity to it, explained a 1967 briefing statement. "In Yellowstone's bison, *Brucella abortus* occurs, from all evidence at hand, naturally— that is, the bison and the *Brucella* organism have evolved together for some hundreds or probably thousands of years. Therefore, *Brucella abortus* within Yellowstone bison cannot be considered a disease, in the sense that the bison or the bison population is suffering in any way, but rather an organism that simply coexists within these animals."[5]

The briefing statement pointed out that brucellosis appeared to have little effect on the Yellowstone bison, but even if it did, that would help keep the population at a size the habitat could support. The park biologists doubted that wild bison could transmit brucellosis to cattle, but dismissed the question as "academic" because the "boundary control program" would provide "a reasonable and effective alternative" to a test-and-slaughter program by enabling livestock interests to maintain brucellosis-free cattle and the Park Service to maintain wild bison "in the habitat and under the conditions to which they are native."

The Most Favored Form of Management

The goal of maintaining wildlife without human interference had been around in some form since the park's establishment, but questions about what constituted natural conditions grew more contentious during the 1960s. Some biologists were skeptical of the assumption that ungulates will overpopulate and destroy their habitat unless reduced by humans. The Park Service does not generally object to hunting outside national parks, but the belief that a wildlife population must be culled in order to maintain the species at some presumably ideal number was becoming suspect. Glen Cole suggested that situations of imbalance would be corrected through natural means, a process referred to as "natural regulation." Evidence of natural regulation may be seen when a population increase leads to lower rates of reproduction and calf survival, or to higher rates of mortality because of predation, more competition for food, or disease.[6] Although ungulate grazing affects the environment, Cole doubted that a herd could wreak havoc on the range, because mortality rates would equal birth rates before this occurred, keeping the population density below the range's ecological carrying capacity.[7]

For some people the idea of an animal species regulating its population level is a romantic notion similar to the illusion that aboriginal groups always lived in harmony with their environment. People become nomadic when they use up the resources necessary to their way of life in one area and must move on. Wouldn't nonhuman creatures use the same survival strategy to accommodate a growing population if they could find suitable habitat? Reproduction, emigration, and mortality rates in wildlife may change gradually as population density changes, or there may be thresholds at which abrupt shifts occur. But for natural regulation proponents, it does not matter if some people regard certain environmental changes as undesirable—too much or not enough wildlife, too many fires or too few trees—what matters is that the changes are the result of "natural" processes. If all processes are functioning in what is regarded as a natural fashion, then by definition the results are natural and therefore acceptable as long as they do not result in the loss of human life or damage to private property. Those who object to Yellowstone's so-called "Let It Burn" policy may be told that the park also has a "Let It Snow" policy, even though it sometimes results in flooding downstream of the park boundary.

Cole's view of natural regulation emphasized food, rather than predation, as the key limiting factor. This was convenient, given that wolves, once the ecosystem's most significant predator, had been exterminated. According to Cole, a major brake on population growth under natural regulation would be starvation in winter, which seemed wasteful to hunters and inhumane to many people. But Cole believed that if the elk were allowed to restore their migratory pattern along the Yellowstone River instead of being stopped by a firing line of hunters at the park boundary, enough of them would leave the park so that dispersed hunters could hold the northern herd to 5,000 to 8,000 elk.[8] Bison culling in the park also ended, but because of brucellosis, bison were subject to hazing or removal if they crossed the park boundary.

The "Guidelines for the Management of Ungulates in Yellowstone National Park," issued in December 1967, stated that the park's primary purpose was to preserve, and provide visitors opportunities to see, "the natural scenery and the native plant and animal life as it occurred in primitive America." A portrayal of "primitive America" was defined as "having natural conditions where scenery and 'balance of nature' in ecosystems are not altered by man"; "balance of nature" was understood to mean "dynamic balances" between animals and their sources of food. By stating that "the most favored form of management is to rely upon natural controls to regulate animal numbers whenever possible," the guidelines marked a radical shift in ungulate management at Yellowstone. However, they still allowed for "limited selective control of ungulate numbers" in certain situations, including when it would "compensate for disruptive influences that result from man's actions outside [park] boundaries"—which is what previous park managers thought they were doing when they culled the elk and bison herds. The guidelines also contained a murky pledge that "all control must be selective to favor animals seen and photographed by park visitors."[9] While the days of "good" and "bad" animals at Yellowstone may have come to an end, some animals were still more favored than others, and some animals were falling more out of favor with livestock officials.

Resolutions and Rebuttals

At its annual convention in 1968, the National Association of State Departments of Agriculture passed a resolution calling on the Department of the

Interior to "take immediate action" that would lead to "the early eradication of brucellosis in bison on the national parks." C. F. Layton, the Interior Department official who prepared the response, pointed out that the 230 bison at Theodore Roosevelt National Park in North Dakota and the 121 bison at Badlands National Monument in South Dakota were brucellosis free; the small display herd in Grand Teton had been purged and replenished; and Wind Cave, which had begun vaccinating calves in 1946 and initiated a test-and-slaughter program in 1963, was expected to eradicate brucellosis in its 250 bison by 1970.[10]

The bison in Yellowstone were another matter, however. Using terms that had already appeared in statements by Yellowstone staff and would be repeated in subsequent decades by their successors, Layton wrote that the brucellosis problem in Yellowstone was "unique," that the possibility of transmission to cattle from the bison was "remote," that Yellowstone bison (then numbering about 500) "represent the only completely wild, free-ranging bison herd left in the United States," and that intensive ranch-type management or total herd replacement would "tend to jeopardize the wild nature of the herds." Efforts to eradicate brucellosis would therefore remain subordinate to other objectives, such as maintaining the "ecological integrity" of the bison.

Although the Park Service had only recently gotten religion in regard to maintaining the "ecological integrity" of the Yellowstone bison, park staff maintained that brucellosis control "for its own sake" had never been done at Yellowstone, only as part of reductions undertaken to limit herd size. "Park personnel and cooperating researchers from the U.S. Fish and Wildlife Service have recognized that brucellosis control and/or eradication is not necessary or desirable to accomplish basic park purposes," Bill Barmore explained in a 1968 internal report. "The park has been involved only because of pressure from another federal agency (and ultimately pressure from state and local interests) and perhaps because of the necessity of maintaining an 'image' of interagency cooperation within the federal establishment." Barmore noted that the USDA and state agriculture agencies "firmly expect to eradicate brucellosis from livestock—hopefully by 1975," and that "they will employ all legal and technological methods at their disposal to accomplish this goal on schedule." He recommended that, instead of trying to give the impression that park staff supported eradication in bison, Yellowstone should request to be exempted from the Park Service eradication program.[11]

Barmore claimed that park staff were "operating according to directives from the Regional and Washington offices" to cooperate with the U.S. Department of Agriculture in eradicating brucellosis from park bison herds. But that would have meant live trapping, testing, calf vaccination, and removal of brucellosis reactors, and no such measures had been taken in the park during the last two years "because no bison herd reduction has been necessary." Yellowstone managers believed that a test-and-slaughter program for brucellosis would be "never ending," because the bison would become conditioned to helicopters and it would be impossible to capture every bison in the park year after year until they were certain that all animals carrying the bacterium had been eliminated. "Should we mess with the herd," Barmore asked, "if we cannot be assured of completely eradicating brucellosis when we already know that there need be little or no chance of spreading brucellosis to cattle surrounding the park?"[12]

Yellowstone managers answered "no." In the Natural Resources Management Plan then in effect, the only objective pertaining to bison was "Allow ungulate populations the opportunity to achieve a dynamic balance with their environment by eliminating artificial controls to the greatest extent possible." According to the Annual Wildlife Report for 1969–70, recent studies indicated that the Pelican Valley herd, which then numbered about 200, was "in a state of balance with its habitat." However, the second item listed under "Research Needs" read: "Effects of brucellosis on bison and degree to which they can transmit this disease to other animals." It was one of many of the park's research needs that went unmet that year and in subsequent years.

A resolution passed at the 1971 annual meeting of the Livestock Conservation Association called on the National Park Service to "immediately cooperate" in "testing the Yellowstone Park Bison herd until it is free of Brucellosis."[13] That this would require slaughtering Yellowstone bison until the herd was free of brucellosis went unstated. Similar resolutions were passed at the 1971 conventions of the Wyoming Stockgrowers Association and the United States Animal Health Association.[14] Such petitions did not fall on entirely deaf ears at the Department of the Interior, but they were heard by largely unsympathetic and not always informed ones. "As you may be aware, the normal methods of brucellosis transmission are through sexual contact and nursing," a mistaken Park Service official responded to the Wyoming Stockgrowers. "Activities of this nature between bison and cattle are normally discouraged."

At about the same time, the Park Service's Washington office issued a statement on brucellosis eradication assuring any concerned members of the public that no bison were permitted to move within ten miles of the Yellowstone boundary and that "individual animals that cannot be driven back into the heart of the bison range will be dispatched."[15] As soon as she saw the statement, Meagher notified the Washington office that no such ten-mile limit existed and that the park's east boundary area was customary summer range for some bison.[16]

In March 1972 the Montana Board of Livestock voted unanimously in favor of a motion to "go on record as supporting all and every effort to eradicate brucellosis from the Yellowstone National Park bison herd." That same month, at the request of Wyoming senator Clifford Hansen, Superintendent Anderson invited Fulton Jameson, president of the Wyoming Livestock and Sanitary Board, to a meeting on the park's "brucellosis control" program. Jameson was accompanied by 24 agriculture officials and representatives from the livestock industry in the tristate area. Anderson opened the meeting by describing the agreements that had been worked out with the three state fish and game departments, under which any bison that moved into certain areas near the park boundary would be killed. Park staff believed this program would "reduce the possibility of transmission to livestock to zero" and result in the removal of two or three bison a year on average.[17]

However, the livestock delegation was not interested in boundary control or eliminating a few bison; they wanted brucellosis eradication and they wanted it now. A USDA veterinarian presented their three-step plan: capture and test as many bison as possible, slaughter all the reactors, and hold the nonreactors captive for a year or two until all the noncaptured bison had been located and shot. Anderson objected that this would result in killing at least 80 percent of the bison population, including the entire Pelican Valley and Mary Mountain herds, which they had no means of holding captive. "This seemed to make no impression," Anderson reported afterward to the Park Service director, George Hartzog. "We were also unable to gain any appreciation for the fact that the slaughter of most of the park's bison, including all the scattered single bulls, would eliminate the chance for the public to see bison for a very long time." The livestock delegation was probably also unimpressed by Anderson's belief that "everything presently known points to the particular brucellosis strain in Yellowstone's wild bison being natural, and not causing disease conditions or abortions." Anderson wrote to Hartzog, "We are apprehensive that their proposal would ultimately end up with the complete slaughter of all bison, as occurred on the Crow Indian Reservation after attempts to eradicate brucellosis from the free-ranging population failed."[18]

"Yellowstone's Bison Periled by Effort to Curb Disease," read the New York Times headline, because "the cattlemen want a brucellosis-free U.S. by 1976." Mary Meagher, "who lives six months of each year in a rude, remote cabin, fetching water from a creek," was said to believe that hunting down and shooting all the bison that escaped entrapment would require several years and that "meanwhile the animals held within pens would degenerate into little more than domestic stock."[19]

The Park Service informed the Wyoming Livestock and Sanitary Board that "present research suggests that population numbers of the future will not affect the likelihood of bison leaving the park." (The winter count was then about 840.) "All indications are that although some increase is expected, the population segments will fluctuate naturally between upper and lower levels—increase will not be a constant process. . . . The affinities of the herd groups for specific areas preclude mass movements beyond park boundaries."[20] The forecast of the American Veterinary Medical Association was equally rose tinted, but with a view of a different horizon. In January 1973 the association announced that "the program to eradicate brucellosis from domestic livestock in the United States is rapidly reaching its final stages" and that "methods and expertise to test the [Yellowstone] bison and to remove those found to be infected are available, and the program could be completed without disturbing the ecology of the Park."[21] Meagher's prediction to the National Parks and Conservation Association turned out to be more accurate. "We are still far from reaching an understanding about the Yellowstone bison with the U.S. Department of Agriculture."[22]

When Erin Tarpein, a concerned citizen of Palmyra, Missouri, wrote to inquire about the brucellosis controversy, the USDA's Animal and Plant Health Inspection Service assured her that eradication in Yellowstone bison was "feasible and practicable," while Park Service chief scientist Robert Linn informed her, "It is impossible to eradicate a disease organism with as many niches to reside in as Brucella abortus has—unless one would consider eradicating life from Planet Earth, which seems to me an unacceptable alternative."[23]

Increasing Range and Resistance

Yellowstone managers continued to see no reason or opportunity to test any bison for brucellosis, because they saw no reason to capture bison for herd reductions. Natural regulation seemed to be working. In February 1973 Meagher reported that research conducted during the last decade "clearly indicates" that population control was unnecessary in the Pelican herd, and "strongly suggests" that it would be unnecessary in the other two herds.[24] Although winter feeding had been justified until the 1950s because of the presumably inadequate winter range, Meagher saw it as the cause of rather than the solution to the bison emigration problem because it created an artificially large population. Historically, some bison groups that summered inside the park had regularly wintered outside, but these groups were "long gone," and their winter ranges outside the park were no longer available, "which precludes reestablishment of groups that habitually move outside the park boundaries."[25] Reestablishment was also deterred by the boundary control program, under which park rangers shot three bulls in 1974. The following year the park issued an "Information Paper" on Yellowstone bison that made no reference to brucellosis or boundary control. "Yellowstone bison are wild, free-ranging, and unrestricted by boundary fences, subject to minimal interference by man," Meagher wrote. "The population numbers over 1,000 at present; they will probably increase somewhat in the future."[26]

The next winter was harsh, and Lamar Valley was covered with six inches of ice after several arctic storms were interspersed with thaws. Bison generally become more sedentary during the winter, living on stored fat and reducing movement to reduce energy expenditure. But they do move sporadically, as if they calculate the energy that would be required to burrow through the ice and snow to reach the forage beneath them, versus the energy required to travel to a place with more accessible forage. In January eight bison that left the park near Gardiner were killed by Montana state personnel in accordance with the boundary control program. By mid-February another 84 bison were heading in the same direction. Park managers regarded the large 1976 bison migration as "unlikely to recur again soon"; so they decided to try to keep the animals alive by preventing them from leaving the park.[27] Fences were installed along the Yellowstone River and hazing by foot, horseback, snowmobile, and helicopter kept the animals in the park for six weeks until they began moving back up into the Lamar Valley.

To discourage bison from leaving the park during the winter of 1976–77, this helicopter was herding bison across the Yellowstone River.

At the time, the 1976 exodus was written off as a rare event attributable to the "extremely adverse winter foraging conditions," but in subsequent winters, when conditions were less adverse, the bison continued to expand their range down the Yellowstone River. The bison also became more resistant to hazing, and baiting with hay and scattering charcoal on snow to melt it did not keep them in the park. The bison's affinity for certain winter ranges was apparently overwhelmed by their propensity to stick together in a large group. Although bison had survived many harsh winters in the park's interior by dispersing to small pockets of forage, Meagher found that bison are less apt to break their social bonds than are elk. If possible, the very gregarious bison will travel to a place where sufficient forage enables them to remain together.[28]

The park rangers' authority to shoot bison to prevent them from crossing the boundary was rescinded by the Department of the Interior in 1978 because of negative publicity, leaving the problem and negative publicity to be dealt with by the state of Montana. As for eradicating brucellosis, Yellowstone managers were able to largely ignore the demands of agriculture officials and, depending on one's point of view, stick to their principles

Yellowstone bison population, 1967–1980

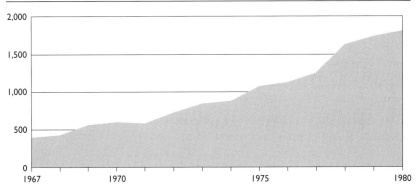

or stick their heads in the sand until more bison began leaving the park in the late 1980s.

The Bison Containment Policy

The winters from 1980 to 1987 were generally below average in severity, and the first three passed with no bison removed at the boundary. By the winter of 1982–83 fewer bison were on the Yellowstone River trail, but more were using the road that leads from Tower Junction into Mammoth Hot Springs and north to the park boundary, sometimes covering 20 miles in a day.[29] Hazing by helicopter was attempted again in 1984 to herd bison back into the park, but it frightened livestock on private land, resulting in damage to fences and complaints from ranchers. Superintendent Bob Barbee described the situation as "something of a stalemate: pressure for eradication comes up periodically, and we reiterate our commitment to boundary control as a means to achieve their real goal, which is not necessarily eradication but is a guaranteed protection precluding transmission to livestock from Yellowstone bison."[30] Barbee may have underestimated the goal of the livestock interests, but the Park Service could no longer say that only minimal boundary control would be needed. During the winter of 1984–85 Montana state personnel killed 88 bison outside the park boundary.

No one was satisfied with this solution to the problem. Speaking for The Fund for Animals, Cleveland Amory still hoped a fence could be built to keep bison in the park, even though extensive fencing was not feasible because it would impede the seasonal migrations of thousands of other ungulates—elk, mule deer, bighorn sheep, and pronghorn. A Park Service briefing statement issued in 1985, when the winter count was about 2,300, could offer no assurances: "It is difficult to predict whether increasing numbers of bison will approach and cross park boundaries. NPS biologists believe the park's bison population to be at or near equilibrium with its environment." Mary Meagher concluded that the solution to the problem of exiting bison was to shoot those that had seen better winter days outside the park. "What we need to do is to remove the knowledge by removing the animals."[31]

Such a remedy would not prevent the animals from regaining the knowledge as they had in the past. That issue was addressed by Valerius Geist, a bison expert from the University of Calgary, when he and Dale Lott of the University of California were invited to make a trip to Yellowstone and render their opinion. After his visit in January 1986, Geist said he believed the "most acceptable" solution would be to eliminate all of the bison that had "developed the habit" of heading to the north boundary. He realized that would include all of the bison that were in the Gardner River valley that January, as well as those in Mammoth Hot Springs and on Blacktail Plateau. When that was done, he would block any movement of bison along the road by using cattle guards and other barriers and "systematically cull, year in and year out, all bison that bypass the barriers and enter the Blacktail Flats so as to prevent a new colonization pulse."[32] But such an undertaking, even if it were feasible, would deny the bison a significant part of their customary range in the park.

The USDA's Animal and Plant Health Inspection Service told the director of the National Park Service, "We are ready to cooperate with the NPS in testing the bio-bullet [vaccine] delivery system on bison. . . . All that is needed is for the NPS to provide the test bison so that bio-bullet penetration and other studies can proceed."[33] But the Park Service wasn't ready to offer some of the unique Yellowstone bison as test cases, and more than 18 years would pass before vaccination of some Yellowstone bison began. Despite the deficiencies of the boundary control program, when the Park Service issued its environmental assessment of bison management options in 1986, the preferred alternative called for continued efforts to keep bison in the park with minimal environmental disruption.[34] Experiments were conducted with slightly more disruptive methods, including 145 meters of fencing, rubber bullets, tin-can rattles, cracker shells, sirens, flashing lights, and tape-recorded wolf howls. The results showed that such techniques could temporarily deter some bison or shift them to other exit points, but bison movements out of the park continued, and the risk of injury to those trying to haze them increased.[35]

Fat and Healthy Hunting Trophies

In the 1930s a Yellowstone biologist had estimated that the forage on the northern range could support 245 bison and about 7,200 elk.[36] By 1988 the count for the thriving Lamar bison herd had reached 868, and the northern elk herd numbered more than 19,000 despite annual hunting seasons. The northern range's carrying capacity had apparently been underestimated, or at least misconstrued. But given the Park Service's refusal to remove bison before they left the park, the alternative preferred by the Montana legislature was to restore wild bison to the state list of big game. The Montana Department of Fish, Wildlife and Parks regarded the change as an unwanted shifting of responsibility for surplus bison from the Park Service to itself, but hunters lobbied hard for the measure. Even on short notice, more than 3,000 applicants paid $5 to enter the random drawing. When bison crossed the boundary, applicants whose names were drawn would have 36 hours to arrive at the designated site with their $200 license fee ($1,000 for non-Montanans) and one day to shoot a bison under the supervision of a state game warden.

Before the first hunt began, The Fund for Animals sued the Park Service for "wanton, cruel, inhumane destruction of an element of Plaintiff's national heritage." The Park Service was "allowing" bison to cross the boundary while "knowing full well that such animals would become the target" of people with guns.[37] The Gallatin Wildlife Association, a hunting group, responded to fellow Montanans' concern that "buffalo hunting will not look good on TV," with this reassurance: "Hunting of all kinds viewed close-up on TV does not look good. If hunting should attract TV attention we expect that after a shot or two the TV broadcasters will lose interest and put us back on our regular diet—the murder, violence, and rape of people." As for the objection that "buffalo are not game animals, they don't run from you," the association argued, "Whoever talks about animals running from you must have forgotten why most hunters like to hunt on opening day of the season, a time when animals do not run away from you, at least not as fast as on the second day."[38]

The Fund for Animals' lawsuit was dismissed and the hunt proceeded as planned in 1985. The 98 participants in the first three years of the program were 100 percent successful, fueling some doubts as to whether the activity was either hunting or sport. All of the bison killed by hunters were "healthy, even fat," Superintendent Barbee pointed out in 1987. "Migrant bison are no hungrier, no less well nourished than any other wild bison; they simply wish to move."[39]

A hunting season for bison may have reduced the risk of brucellosis transmission to cattle, but it did nothing to eradicate the bacteria. Mary Meagher advised Barbee that although the risk appeared low, "given the right circumstances we should accept that transmission could occur." She told him that Don Davis of the University of Texas expected that an oral brucellosis vaccine would be ready in less than 10 years, and cautioned:

> Eradication of brucellosis in the Yellowstone bison would have tremendous ecological consequences, not all of which can be foreseen. These could include higher bison population levels, great disruption of food chain relationships, conditioned avoidance behavior, etc. We cannot prove it is a native organism, nor can the proponents of eradication prove it is not. As a biologist, my thought is to continue to view it as a native from our particular perspective and mandate, while acknowledging proof is not possible.[40]

As director of the National Park Service, William Penn Mott expressed this view when he responded to a letter of concern about brucellosis from U.S. senator Steven Symms of Idaho. The Park Service's responsibility to future generations "extends to disease organisms such as those causing brucellosis and rabies, when these organisms are a natural component of the park ecosystems we are mandated to protect," Mott explained. "While we are supportive of efforts to keep *brucella* in the park, we are not supportive of efforts to eliminate the organism from the park unless it is demonstrated that *brucella* is not a natural component of the ecosystem."[41]

In the winter of 1981–82 a conjunctivitis epidemic caused temporary blindness in most of the 500 bighorn sheep in the northern herd. The herd was monitored more closely than usual, but no attempt was made to arrest the infection, which led to the death of about 300 bighorn sheep. The chlamydial disease is rarely fatal in livestock because they can be treated for it and they can be protected from falling off cliffs or walking onto roads. But since there was no evidence that the organism had been artificially introduced in Yellowstone, the bighorn epidemic was considered a "natural event" and allowed to play itself out despite some outrage from the public.[42]

Despite brucellosis the Yellowstone bison population continued to increase. In March 1989 nearly all the estimated 900 bison in the Lamar herd were approaching the boundary. Fearing a large exodus, Montana officials asked the Park Service to set a minimum herd size to be preserved. After considering "the known history of the herd, their demonstrated ability to recover from low numbers, ecological relationships, public viewing opportunities, and aesthetics," the Park Service arrived at 200. The Montana Fish and Game Commission agreed not to let hunting reduce the herd below that minimum except in case of "an immediate threat that brucellosis will be spread to domestic livestock."[43] Despite this interagency cooperation, that year's hunt became a debacle as 569 bison were killed, many of them shot at close range by hunters who were filmed at close range by the news media. Protesters stood in front of the rifles and poked hunters with ski poles. It did not look good on TV. The hunt was deemed a fiasco not only for the state's image but also as a means of boundary control. The mayhem may have dispersed some bison further from the park than they otherwise would have gone.[44]

In the spring of 1989 the Montana Department of Livestock required brucellosis testing for 810 cattle in 18 herds that were considered to have been "at risk of habitual association with Yellowstone bison" since the preceding September. No reactors were found, but the state veterinarian, Donald Ferlicka, sent the National Park Service a tort claim—a bill for $11,137 for expenses related to the testing, mostly staff time and travel. The Park Service determined that it was under no obligation to pay, because "bison are native animals maintained in the wild in a free-roaming condition" and the Park Service has no legal jurisdiction over, or liability for, bison outside the park.[45] At its annual convention that year the United States Animal Health Association passed a resolution that Ferlicka sponsored: "Whereas, Yellowstone Park managers view the propagation of this disease condition as innocuous or even desirable, . . . therefore be it resolved that the Brucellosis Committee supports the requirement of Federal agencies in custody of wildlife to compensate livestock owners and other aggrieved entities for actual expenses and losses brought about by transmissible diseases from such wildlife."

The Domino Theory of Bison Colonization

In assessing the failure of boundary control efforts during the 1980s, Meagher believed that the "gregariousness" of bison had been the most important factor, rather than the tripling of the population or the availability of forage.[46] Once the bison found extensive winter range beyond the Lamar Valley, they began moving sooner and remaining there longer than they had before, regardless of population size and winter conditions. And the bison herd that had previously been referred to as the "fenced herd," the "tame herd," the "so-called tame herd," the "main herd," and then the "Lamar Valley herd," now became more accurately known as the "northern herd."

The bison in Yellowstone are often referred to as three herds based on their primary wintering areas, but they do intermingle, especially during the summer. After the Lamar herd became free ranging in the 1920s, it began following the spring green-up in late May to higher elevations, moving 10 to 25 miles from the valley floor to the lower slopes of the Absaroka Mountains where its summer range overlapped that of the Pelican Valley herd. The herds divided again when snow sent them down to different winter ranges. Bison in the third herd, which has its primary summer range in Hayden Valley, often crossed the Mary Mountain divide to Firehole Valley, where less snow accumulates in the winter. But the increasing size and range of all three herds in the 1980s resulted in what Meagher has called a "domino effect." Even in relatively mild winters the herd that had previously toughed it out in Pelican Valley began moving west to lower range in Hayden Valley, which may have pushed the Mary Mountain herd out of Hayden Valley to the Firehole earlier in the winter, and pushed bison from the Firehole to extend their winter range further west and north.[47] Although bulls had occasionally ventured northward before, a mixed group was seen at Madison Junction for the first time in the winter of 1982. This movement became an annual occurrence, and eventually bison groups from the park interior were traveling all the way to the park's north boundary.

By the early 1990s bison distribution in the summer was also shifting. Instead of crossing the Mirror Plateau to mingle with the northern herd, approaching the park's east boundary by early August, an increasing portion of the Pelican herd was remaining in Hayden Valley and interbreeding with the Mary Mountain herd. Consequently, the bison in Yellowstone are now

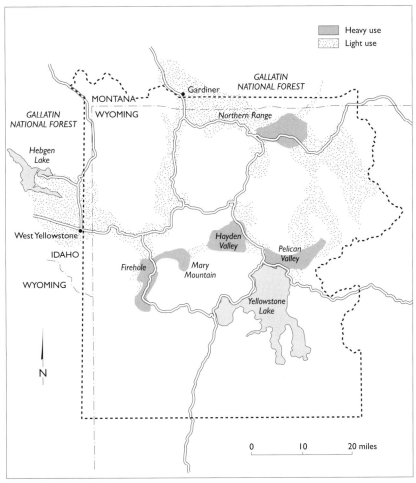

Yellowstone winter bison ranges, 1970–2000. Adapted from Steven Craig Hess, "Aerial Survey Methodology for Bison Population Estimation in YNP" (M.S. thesis, Montana State University, Bozeman, April 2002).

sometimes referred to as just two herds: the northern herd and the "central" or "interior" herd. At the beginning of the 1994 rut, 2,775 bison were counted in Hayden Valley, a near doubling since 1981.[48] These population increases and shifts have caused environmental changes in Hayden Valley— more bison trails, wallows, rubbed trees. According to a paper Meagher coauthored in 1994, "The park is not experiencing overgrazing in the range management sense because the bison are free-ranging and they follow high quality forage during the growing season as it changes spatially across the Yellowstone landscape."[49] But the same paper went on to refer to "loss of functional winter range" as a result of the bison mowing traditional winter range in Hayden Valley before winter began—a loss that would reduce the range's winter carrying capacity. Six years later, after retiring from employment with the federal government, Meagher coauthored a report that cited possible evidence of "habitat degradation" in Hayden Valley and some thermal areas where a forage decline as a result of soil compacting may have been caused by the presence of more bison for more of the year.[50]

If tourists are prohibited from walking on the travertine terraces and fragile thermal crusts, think what a one-ton bison can do. In 1953 Superintendent Rogers referred to the bison's impact on thermal features as "the determining factor" in the decision to reduce the herd in the Firehole area.[51] But concern about bison damage to thermal areas seemed to end along with bison culling in the 1960s. Under a policy of minimal human interference, whatever native wildlife does to natural features in the park is itself natural and therefore acceptable, unless you believe that there is something unnaturally large about the park's bison population and, therefore, its impacts on the landscape. Meagher acknowledged that she had only "indirect" evidence that bison were causing habitat degradation.[52] Others would argue that the fact that certain areas of Yellowstone look different now than they did in the past doesn't mean they have become "degraded."

The changes in bison distribution or habitat that have occurred may be regarded as the natural consequences of population growth and the herds' expansion into more areas of winter range, but Meagher has her doubts. Unlike the movement of the northern herd into Montana, which Meagher regarded as the "reestablishment of historic movement," the situation at the park's west boundary was different because the bison would have to travel more than 35 or 40 miles to find "suitable winter habitat."[53] In 1985, after bison from the park interior did start heading west in winter, Meagher concluded that "the whole emigration-colonization behavior" must have been "greatly influenced by human use."[54] She believed that by using roads groomed for snowmobiles instead of breaking their own trail through the snow, the bison got better mileage and access to more forage, resulting in lower winter mortality and larger and more dispersed herds. "Speaking purely as a biologist," Meagher said in August 1996, "I would shut down the human-caused system change, which is the winter roads, and I would go in and kill a lot of bison, because that would hasten reversing the changes we have caused."[55]

When Nature Conducts the Experiment

As the term "natural regulation" came into general use, it took on a new meaning. Instead of an ecological concept based on factors that affect population size, "natural regulation" became understood as a policy in which park managers no longer managed the wildlife because they were letting nature take its course. However, even if winter road grooming were not a factor, few people would argue that the bison or elk in Yellowstone could be allowed to exist without any human-imposed control on population size. Yellowstone managers have regarded natural regulation as an ideal rather than a realistic goal, and that has been especially true for ungulates on the north side of the park, where the topography extends their winter range beyond the park's boundary. Although the number of elk removed by hunters depends partly on the density of elk outside the park, it is also affected by changes in hunting regulations and in the population density of competent hunters. The number of elk taken from the northern herd by hunters in a year has ranged from 500 to 4,500 since the 1980s.

The growth in the northern elk herd until the 1990s cast more doubt on the idea that the range was overgrazed, but the growth was made possible in part by a substantial increase in the winter range available to elk.[56] More than 10,000 acres of winter range were purchased through a cooperative federal, state, and private effort that constituted a significant shift of land from livestock to wildlife grazing, and hunting regulations were revised to encourage elk to reestablish migratory routes outside the park.[57] But overall, most of the Yellowstone elk, bison, and deer herds increased during the 1980s, possibly responding to the same favorable weather conditions that prevailed on the northern range. Yellowstone's policy of natural regulation was initially described as an "experimental" program for elk and bison based on the expectation that over a period of years, these species' birth and death rates would adjust to the available winter food, resulting in "a stable equilibrium" between the animals and their habitat.[58] However, the fluctuations in the elk population during the 1970s and 1980s were larger than most natural regulation proponents expected. For people who wanted quantitative data and replicable results, evidence of any balance or stability was lacking. When nature conducts the experiment, there is no control group, and only one set of data points is generated each year. The difficulties of analyzing the results are similar to those of determining whether global warming is occurring and, if so, whether certain human activities are contributing to it.[59]

Although nature was increasingly perceived as a state of continuous, often random appearing change, ecologists were still drawn to terms that suggested some orderliness to natural processes, some method to the madness. Perhaps there was at least a "dynamic equilibrium" in the northern elk herd, a balance that shifts over time in response to factors such as winter severity, predator abundance, and hunting pressure.[60] But whatever terms ecologists used to describe it, many livestock interests still thought the northern range was overgrazed. "It is clearly apparent to anyone with even the most basic range management or ecology background" that the park's forage is "suffering greatly under the current and past ungulate grazing pressures," the Montana Stockgrowers Association observed in 1998.[61]

That conclusion was not clearly apparent to a panel of eight representatives from the National Academy of Sciences who prepared a report on the northern range in 2000 at the request of the U.S. House Committee on Appropriations. They looked at an analysis of data collected during more than 160 aerial surveys from 1970 to 1997 indicating that the area used as bison winter range nearly tripled as the population grew more than eightfold. From 1969 to 1981 the northern bison herd grew faster than any other ungulate herd in the park, an average of 16 percent a year. No significant correlation was found between winter severity and the size of ungulate populations from 1968 to 1988, which could mean that population densities were below the carrying capacity of the range during that period. More specifically, the bison population density (the number of bison per acre of range used) increased along with population size until about 1981, but then leveled off; the bison's range continued to increase while the rate of population growth declined to 6 percent a year on average.[62] Although the panel found no sign that the Yellowstone bison population had peaked because of the range's carrying capacity, it saw the declining growth rate as possible evidence of natural regulation, with fewer bison being born or more bison dying as part of the population was forced into poor habitat.[63]

Aside from boundary removals, winterkill is the only significant control on the number of bison in Yellowstone, and the population does not seem to have achieved an equilibrium, dynamic or otherwise, either because natural regulation does not produce one or because the population has not been allowed to reach a size at which it would be limited by natural regulation.[64] But the bison's lack of balance in Yellowstone no longer seems remarkable in a scientific world that has largely abandoned equilibriums in favor of concepts that entail ongoing disturbance and unpredictability— "chaotic dynamics," "nonequilibrium fluctuations," "long-term disequilibrium and flux." Attempts to maintain a steady state in an ecosystem are now disparaged as artificial and even detrimental to plants and animals that have evolved to take advantage of fluctuations. In these shifting terms of engagement, historians find evidence of a tendency to see in nature a mirror image of the prevailing view of human society: where once it was thought to be predictably stable and hierarchical, with everyone destined to fill a certain station in life, now it is seen as fraught with constant change, competition, and unpredictable events in which the people best able to adapt to these conditions are the most successful.[65]

For ecosystems it is now accepted that "carrying capacity" may fluctuate considerably from year to year and favor different species at different periods. These fluctuations can put a rancher out of business, but in a landscape without production goals they do not necessarily indicate that something is wrong with the system. This has been demonstrated by the consequences of naturally caused fire in Yellowstone; its sporadic occurrence over the centuries has kept the landscape in constant flux. Likewise, a symmetrical predator-prey relationship is at most a temporary situation even in the absence of human intervention. Humans could therefore be regarded as just one of many sources of disturbance that keep nature in a state of upheaval. But for national parks like Yellowstone, the official policy since 1988 has been to allow "natural processes" to evolve while "minimally influenced by human actions."[66] That means that instead of trying to maintain a presumed "balance" of animal populations, park managers try to make it possible for ecological processes rather than human activities to be the primary factor in determining the abundance and distribution of species present in the park at any given time.

South of Yellowstone

In keeping with the trend toward more natural conditions for park wildlife, the 16 captive bison in Grand Teton National Park were allowed to become free roaming and freely multiplying in 1969 after they tested brucellosis free. These bison, known as the Jackson herd, soon discovered the adjacent National Elk Refuge, where thousands of elk are fed during the winter. Five bison were killed in 1984 for goring horses on the refuge, but the refuge staff began feeding the bison to keep them from interfering with the elk. When culling to control herd size began in 1989, most of the slaughtered bison tested positive for exposure to *Brucella abortus*. Either the herd hadn't actually been brucellosis free in 1969, or it became reinfected by mingling with elk on the refuge. Brucellosis was already prevalent there because the concentration of animals promotes transmission of the disease.[67]

A 1987 plan to use hunting to limit the herd to 50 bison, reducing it by nearly half, collapsed in the face of public opposition and was replaced by a plan to limit the herd to 110 bison, which was scuttled in 1991, when a lawsuit by animal rights activists alleged that the herd limit had no scientific basis.[68] The herd continued to increase, reaching 215 in 1994, when a new plan was drafted that proposed limiting the herd to 200 bison, which had been determined to be the maximum number that could be supported year-round on the range in Grand Teton National Park. But the herd had grown to nearly 400 bison when the plan was completed in 1997, so it called for limiting the herd to 400 with the help of hunting on the National Elk Refuge. That plan also succumbed to a legal defeat when The Fund for Animals charged that winter feeding on the refuge had artificially increased the herd size, and that it was not "fair chase" to hunt bison that associated humans with feeding. The judge ruled that no bison could be killed on the refuge or in Grand Teton National Park for purposes of population control until an environmental impact statement was completed for the bison and elk feeding programs.

The Wyoming Game and Fish Department has continued to conduct an annual hunt near the refuge in Bridger-Teton National Forest, but too few bison go there for the hunt to control the herd size. By 2004, when completion of the EIS was thought to be still a year away, the herd was estimated to number 800. Most of the Jackson bison herd leave the refuge when winter feeding ends, but as they travel north through Grand Teton, they may calve where cattle arrive in early June. Livestock owners who had used the area before the park's boundaries were expanded in 1950 were granted grazing allotments in the park as a concession, but by 2004 all but one of these 29 leases had been relinquished. Ranchers were less concerned about the bison that had been sent from Yellowstone decades ago than about the reintroduced wolves that had begun dispersing from there.

North of Montana

Like Yellowstone and Grand Teton, Wood Buffalo National Park has free-roaming bison that carry *Brucella abortus* across its boundary, evoking a similar range of reactions among Canadians. But the situations are in some ways very different: at Wood Buffalo bison are the only significantly affected species, about one-third of the bison are also infected by tuberculosis, disease-free bison herds are considered at risk of being infected, and the population began to decline after culling ended in the late 1960s. A large drop occurred in 1974, when 3,000 bison drowned after falling through the ice of a flooded river, but tuberculosis and brucellosis are believed to have contributed to lower rates of reproduction and higher mortality. Another possible factor was the 1968 construction of a hydroelectric dam outside the park that reduced periodic flooding and affected the forage available to bison.[69]

Since the 1960s, bison in the Wood Buffalo area have also undergone periodic outbreaks of anthrax, which may be endemic to the area. The disease is transmitted by spores that can survive in certain soils, vegetation, and water for decades. Animals that consume or inhale the spores often die within days, and the disease can be fatal to humans if untreated. Nearly 28,000 vaccinations against anthrax were delivered in Wood Buffalo during intermittent roundups from 1965 to 1977. Thousands of bison were herded nearly 40 miles to a corral, resulting in separation of calves from cows, loss of calves by trampling, goring by bulls, and stress-related abortions. About 1,100 bison are believed to have died of anthrax and 600 from injuries resulting from capture and restraint for vaccination, and even in the most "successful" year of this expensive program, only one-third of the herd was immunized.[70]

Because of the brucellosis in its wildlife, greater Yellowstone has been referred to as "the last reservoir" of the disease that could prevent the United States from achieving brucellosis-free status for its livestock for international trade purposes.[71] Canada has declared its cattle brucellosis free since 1985, but livestock grazing has increased near the park, and four free-roaming, disease-free bison herds have been established outside it. Efforts to further expand these herds have been stymied by the presence of infected bison at the center of the wood buffalo's historic range. The park was specifically created to preserve wild bison, and it still has more bison that it does human visitors in a year.

Tribal groups in Canada have objected to their lack of influence over what they regard as both a cultural and economic resource, but Canada's First Nations have gained more clout in determining bison management policy than have their counterparts in the United States. Bison that leave Wood Buffalo National Park may be hunted, and other wildlife may be hunted both inside and outside the park by "Treaty Indians" and certain other groups who depended on wildlife for subsistence when the park was established.[72] The number of Canadians who participate in subsistence hunting and trapping has declined, but bison are still important as a direct form of sustenance, and as the primary source of food for the wolves, which would compete more with hunters for other game if the bison population were reduced.

To evaluate alternatives for Wood Buffalo, a task force with representatives from the government agencies responsible for agriculture, the environment, and public health began meeting in 1986. Most of the task force favored slaughtering the herds and reintroducing disease-free bison as the simplest and least expensive option.[73] In 1989 the Federal Environmental Assessment Review Office appointed a Northern Diseased Bison Panel that considered the findings of the task force, held public hearings, heard testimony by experts, and accepted proposals from interest groups and government agencies. It was similar to the process followed for environmental impact statements under the National Environmental Protection Act in the United States, and similar differences of opinion prevailed in Canada as to the threat posed to other species and to the bison themselves.

However, in contrast to the U.S. situation, the consequences of disease transmission in Canada are considered so grave that any degree of risk is unacceptable to both the livestock industry and some wildlife officials, especially those involved in the Wood Bison Recovery Plan. The wood bison is legally protected in some jurisdictions of Canada as a "threatened" or "endangered" subspecies that is distinct from the far more numerous plains bison. Although the bison in Wood Buffalo National Park are generally referred to as wood bison, those native to the area were outnumbered by and interbred with plains bison that were brought to the park in the 1920s. The bison in the Wood Buffalo area are therefore considered hybrids and are not legally protected outside the park, but they are still regarded as the largest free-roaming bison population in the world, at least by those who do not regard the Yellowstone bison as truly free roaming.

Like the government agencies in greater Yellowstone, the Northern Diseased Bison Panel found that no method of managing the risk would be infallible, the cost of maintaining vigilance would be high, mass immunization of free-ranging bison was not yet feasible, and a test-and-slaughter program was appropriate only for smaller herds because of the unreliability of the blood test. Even if methods to immunize bison against brucellosis and tuberculosis were available, they would require that animals be rounded up and maintained in captivity for long periods, resulting in "an unacceptable level of injury and death." However, the panel concurred with the task force and recommended the ultimate level of death—killing all bison in the Wood Buffalo area and replacing them with bison from the newly established herds.[74]

Even though Canada's department of agriculture offered to fund the $20 million program, pressure from conservation and aboriginal groups put the plan on hold. The Canadian Nature Federation claimed that the panel had failed to provide sufficient justification for the slaughter and that it had overstated the risks and understated the possible consequences for the ecosystem. The staff of Wood Buffalo National Park issued an unofficial denunciation of the government's role in developing a plan that depicted the bison as threatening the future of all bison in northern Canada as well as the health of cattle and humans. "On the contrary, visual evidence of the disease is rare," claimed the manifesto, as if visual evidence were what mattered. "The bison are magnificent animals that continue to thrill all park visitors. If allowed to go ahead, the slaughter would set a precedent which threatens the ecological integrity of all national parks."[75]

The First Nations also objected to slaughtering the entire herd and to labeling the bison of Wood Buffalo National Park as biologically and genetically "contaminated." Rather than a scientific assessment, they argued that such ideas were "at the heart of racism." They had no confidence in government promises that bison hunting would be restored within 10 years, and they suspected that the real motivation for the slaughter was that the "white government" wanted to make the land available for grazing leases and the lumber industry.[76] According to the guidelines for management of free-roaming bison recommended by the Fort Smith Buffalo Users Group, "Buffalo are sacred to aboriginal people. Any attempt to eradicate the population is a crime against Nature and the Creator of all life. Aboriginal people who understand and are dependent on bison should be their primary stewards during research and management." The chiefs of the Treaty Eight tribes of Alberta, British Columbia, Saskatchewan, and the Northwest Territories promised to support the recommendations of a committee appointed to determine the bison's fate if most of the members were aboriginal.

The chiefs' proposal was eventually accepted, and after 18 months of intense deliberations, the 17-member board produced a report which found that "because of significant gaps in its understanding of the epidemiology of the two diseases, other fundamental aspects of the ecosystem, and the potential effects of management actions," a three-year, $18 million research program should be undertaken as the basis for designing a bison management plan.[77] Although the research has not yet resulted in any management action, many of the aboriginal representatives were ready to support a slaughter-and-replacement program by 2001, either because the dwindling bison herd had meant a dwindling harvest for hunters outside the park or because the tribes hoped to benefit economically by contracting with the government to carry out the slaughter.[78]

However, while many people were becoming convinced that the bison of Wood Buffalo would die out slowly if they were not killed quickly, the population estimate began to swell. By 2002 it had reached more than 4,000, an increase attributed to both improved survey techniques and an actual growth in the population since the late 1990s, possibly related to a decline in the wolf population. But for the bison of Wood Buffalo, it may be a no-win situation: if their number declines, so does the constituency that believes they are worth trying to save; but if their number increases, so does the risk that they may transmit disease to uninfected bison and cattle herds.

A lack of consensus about the facts of brucellosis in wild bison and about the practicality of ways to deal with it has also hampered interagency negotiations over the bison in and around Yellowstone. But whereas slaughter plans remain on hold in Canada as research continues, the agencies responsible for land, wildlife, and livestock management in greater Yellowstone committed themselves to the eradication of brucellosis in wildlife while the necessary research was yet to be started.

PART THREE

BRUCELLOSIS IN WONDERLAND

Few visitors realize how many wild animals make this wonderland their home, how severe is the struggle for existence during the long winter and deep snows, or how great are the hardships and sufferings of the men whose duty it is to protect the wild creatures against predatory man. . . .

That the buffalo cannot increase, but are doomed to extermination in the park can be readily understood by anyone visiting them in their winter habitat. Struggling in unbelievable depths of snow for the scant and little nourishing grass which they find when they finally reach the ground, or staying for days on some windswept hillside, bleak and so bare that it would not furnish a day's nourishment for a goat, then plunging through immense drifts of snow. . . .

The superior strength, endurance and stamina of the wild buffalo made it desirable to obtain some of this strain of blood for the fenced herd. If full grown ones could not be captured, the calves might offer some chance for success. . . .

My conscience had pricked me considerably about this robbing a mother of her young, but their happy condition in their new environment and a look into their future tended to remove this feeling. They are now the property of Uncle Sam and as long as life shall last they will be provided for.

—Peter Holt, describing his 1903 expedition to
capture bison calves in Yellowstone National Park

Bison in winter near Castle Geyser. Courtesy of Jeff Henry.

CHAPTER 8

Outward Bound

After finding a milk cow to nurse the two wild calves he had captured in Pelican Valley in 1903, Peter Holt reported, "They were so pleased after their feed that they danced around in their stall with joy, then lay down, and grunting with satisfaction, went to sleep. We had no further worry about their future."[1] Both calves did live to maturity with the fenced herd, which was mixing with the wild herd by the 1920s. But with their "superior strength, endurance and stamina" as well as better protection from poachers, Yellowstone's last small band of wild bison survived their winters in the park and slowly increased in number. They were headed for a comeback even without help from the imported bison. But the life-sustaining milk given to the bison calves may have been the source of much worry in the future, the reason for so much bison slaughter and controversy decades later. Like Mrs. O'Leary's cow, which was blamed for starting the great Chicago fire of 1871 by kicking a lantern over in her shed, that cow at Yellowstone Lake might have been the one that spread brucellosis to the park's bison.

When brucellosis eradication programs began in the United States in the 1930s, nearly half of the tested cattle herds showed evidence of the disease.[2] However, the odds are against that particular cow having introduced it to Yellowstone bison, partly because she was not the only cow in the park. In 1903 more free-ranging cattle than bison could be found in Yellowstone. Because transport of food was difficult, hotels in the park were permitted to have livestock, and neighboring ranchers grazed their cattle illegally in the park until at least the early 1920s.[3] All four of the wild calves that were transferred to the fenced herd by 1909 were nourished on milk from domestic cows, but transmission by males is rare, and only one of the captured calves was female.[4]

When the Greater Yellowstone Interagency Brucellosis Committee held a symposium in Jackson, Wyoming, in September 2002, no one mentioned that a century had passed since Yellowstone began managing bison as livestock, a practice that had been phased out by the 1960s but that some people thought should be reinstated. Some speakers did note that eight years had passed since the committee first met in 1994, and eight years remained for achievement of their ultimate goal: "Plan for the elimination of *Brucella abortus* from the Greater Yellowstone Area by 2010." Did that mean they expected to eliminate brucellosis by 2010 or, as some committee members thought more reasonable, that by 2010 they would come up with a plan to eliminate brucellosis? The confusion made it an appropriate goal for "this wonderland" that Holt described. Yellowstone's mysterious geysers and luridly colored hot springs inspired the sobriquet in the park's early days, after Lewis Carroll's 1866 book about Alice, and a Mad Hatter logic has often prevailed in a place where the bison were fed so they would survive the winter at the same time that bison were killed because the herd was thought too large for the range to support.

Along with sharing a piece of the pie known as the Greater Yellowstone Area, the states of Wyoming, Idaho, and Montana share the goal of maintaining a "brucellosis-free" status in the eyes of the U.S. Department of Agriculture and other states. Ranchers in brucellosis-free states are exempt from testing requirements when they sell their animals to someone in another state. States are designated brucellosis free when no infection is found in their domestic livestock for 12 consecutive months. In 2002 all states were classified brucellosis free except Texas and Missouri, which had a total of three infected cattle herds that year. However, neither Wyoming, Montana, nor Idaho was truly without brucellosis because each state also shared in greater Yellowstone's infected wildlife.

About half of the Yellowstone bison whose blood has been tested have been seropositive, indicating they have been exposed to *Brucella abortus*, but only about half of the seropositive bison were infected by the bacteria. The only way to determine whether an animal is infected is by examining the lymph nodes, mammary glands, and reproductive tissue, and that can only be done after the animal is dead. Elk that may be infected with brucellosis wander outside the park in far larger numbers without incurring the same hostility, but this is a Wonderland where things do not have to make perfect sense, and at times the governor of Montana has seemed on verge of ordering "Off with their heads!" when it could be either the bison or Park Service officials whose demise is sought. Bison and elk were not created equal in the eyes of hunters and their support groups, and elk are more hospitably received even though the only cases of undulant fever in greater Yellowstone in the last 20 years have been two hunters who gutted their elk. The risk to humans from contact with an infected animal can be eliminated by following some basic precautions when butchering it.

The state of Montana has rationalized combining intolerance for bison with a welcome mat for elk by citing the low seropositive rate of elk on the northern range—less than 3 percent.[5] Elk on the northern range have outnumbered bison by as much as 20 to 1, which might negate the effect of their lower seropositive rate, but unless they are concentrated on feed-grounds, elk cows tend to seclude themselves during calving and were therefore considered less likely to spread the disease. Montana state veteri-narian Clarence Siroky once dismissed the idea that any wildlife other than bison could transmit the disease to cattle. "Somebody has yet to prove if the other animals are a problem," he said in 1995.[6] That nobody had proved wild bison were a problem was apparently beside the point. But with more than 100,000 elk in greater Yellowstone, and a much higher seroprevalence in elk south of Montana, surely not even the most ambitious livestock regulator or politician could expect to eradicate *Brucella abortus* by 2010. Or could they?

Born to Roam

"It is exceedingly desirable that a wide swathe should be cut along the entire boundary line wherever timber exists," Major John Pitcher proposed in 1903, when he wanted to simplify law enforcement in the park by making the perimeter obvious.[7] That goal was not met, and most people came to appreciate that a conspicuous boundary would be inappropriate for wildlife that made no distinction between inside and outside the park, between lesser and greater Yellowstone. But for human beings the distinc-tion continued to be of utmost importance. Bison are most likely to leave the park during the winter and early spring, usually along routes that take them into Montana. Siroky referred to these bison as "wayward" and a *New York Times* headline called them "errant," both suggesting that the

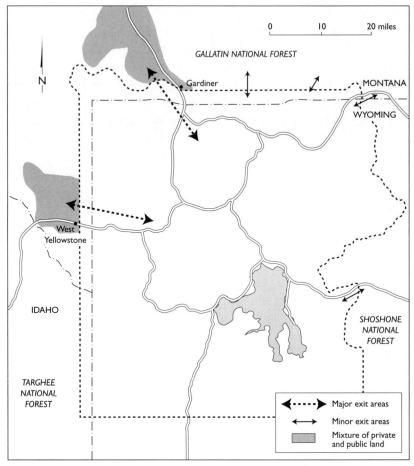

Marked areas show where most bison have exited the park in recent decades. In addition, a small number have crossed the park's southern boundary into Wyoming and west into Idaho.

bison were delinquent or had gone astray. However, as Yellowstone historian Paul Schullery has pointed out, "they are not crossing lines but following them, as they make their way from one portion of a range to another. They are either reestablishing or pioneering lines of migration between seasonal food sources."[8]

Nearly all of the land outside the park's Montana boundary is on Gallatin National Forest, where bison are permitted in certain areas not used for grazing allotments. This includes the Eagle Creek–Bear Creek area, which covers about 23,000 acres along the park's north boundary and sometimes accommodates more than 100 bison during the winter. The higher-altitude Absaroka-Beartooth Wilderness has been used by fewer bison and usually only during the summer. Bison are more inclined to travel north along the Yellowstone River, where they cross private land and national forest grazing allotments. Publishing magnate Malcolm Forbes offered his 12,000-acre Royal Teton Ranch to the Forest Service in 1980 for $6.5 million, but the deal fell apart, and the property was sold to the Church Universal and Triumphant. The church's headquarters and several thousand members moved to the ranch from California, espousing vegetarianism and believing that group prayer was "the most powerful force in the universe."[9] They prayed to keep the 1988 fires that engulfed much of the Yellowstone area from reaching the ranch, but they lost patience with bison from the park that were breaking through fences, and the Montana Department of Livestock killed hundreds of them at the church's request. The situation is similar west of the park: the areas where bison are permitted have rugged terrain and deep snow in the winter, and the bison prefer to go where they are not allowed.

It is no coincidence that the most popular bison routes intersect human communities, which were drawn to the same valley corridors that wildlife had long occupied. Even without brucellosis, tolerance for bison would be limited in these areas of Montana, where about 2,500 people reside. Bison are more destructive of private property than are elk, and more likely to cause human injuries. But the reason that nearly 4,000 wild bison have paid the ultimate penalty for their winter trespasses since 1985 is ostensibly that about 2,000 domestic cows and their calves are present within 10 miles of the park boundary, most of them only in the summer. Bison that cross the park's east boundary onto the Shoshone National Forest are in Wyoming, which permits up to 15 bison bulls where cattle are not present. Deep snow usually deters bison cows and calves from going there in the winter, but if more than 15 bulls or any bison cows are found in that area from July through January, bison hunting applicants are called off a waiting list. The largest bison harvest on the Shoshone National Forest in a single year was 17 in 1996. Occasionally a few bison have crossed the park's west boundary onto the Targhee National Forest in Idaho, where they have been shot by state personnel.

Because bison are born to roam, they may leave the park regardless of population size. In the spring of 1911, when fewer than 200 bison resided in the park, four bulls traveled 43 miles across the boundary before the U.S. Cavalry was sent to drive them back.[10] Since then, the number of bison crossing the north boundary has varied widely from year to year, depending partly but unpredictably on population size and weather. In the west boundary area, which usually has deeper snow and less suitable winter range, migration appears to have become a springtime routine for some bison from the park interior. In a more perfect world designed by the National Park Service, the Yellowstone bison would be treated as a large game animal like elk, with all of the rights and risks attending thereto, including the possibility of disease without medical care and hunting used to control the population outside the park. However, in a system where brucellosis eradication is the order of the day and the Park Service has no jurisdiction over animals that leave Yellowstone, park managers could exert little influence. Montana held all the cards except the Queen of Public Opinion, who is generally opposed to killing photogenic animals on public land but is often trumped by the Jack of Livestock. Television coverage of bloody and writhing bison that ran in front of inept riflemen brought an end to Montana's bison "hunts" after a few years in the 1980s, but efforts to promote tourist boycotts of the state had no apparent effect. Montana's treatment of bison that leave Yellowstone has sometimes been presented as a states' rights issue in which mismanaged wildlife from a national park is invading Montana and jeopardizing the livelihood of hardworking ranchers. "We are innocent neighbors of a park service that has not taken responsibility for its wildlife," Governor Marc Racicot protested in a letter to the *New York Times* in 1996.[11]

Cattle at Home on the Range

Although agriculture has declined as a source of income in Montana since the 1960s, most Montanans believe that agriculture and the businesses it supports are essential to maintain their heritage and way of life.[12] Nearly half of Montanans live in rural areas as compared to one-quarter nationally, and the population of Billings, the state's largest city, is only 89,000. Agriculture accounts for about one-third of the state's labor income, and cattle outnumber people in most counties. Several hundred cattle are kept north of the park year-round by feeding them hay during the winter, but most cattle in the Yellowstone area are present only from May to October. These summer residents spend the winter at their home base elsewhere in Montana or Idaho, sometimes more than 200 miles away, where less snow accumulates and less feed is needed to stay warm. Trucking the cattle back and forth can be economical, especially for those that use public grazing allotments. The federal charge for one "animal unit month" (the cost for grazing a cow and a calf for a month) is $1.43, compared to an average of more than $12 for leasing private land.

As with other controversies in the Yellowstone area — wolves, grizzly bears, snowmobiles, coal bed methane mines — for many people the brucellosis debate is not really about brucellosis but about land use and who controls it. In a 1996 letter used to respond to complaints about Montana's bison policy, Governor Racicot explained:

> The State of Montana simply wants Yellowstone National Park to manage its bison the way every other bison and cattle owner in America manages livestock — eradicate diseases, limit numbers to available forage and be a good neighbor. . . . In a South Dakota state park, for example, every year bison are rounded up and auctioned to landowners and others. We would welcome the opportunity for YNP bison to be rounded up and auctioned.[13]

That same year, a Wyoming rancher referred to his state's possible loss of brucellosis-free status because of wild bison as "just another nail in the coffin of cow-calf operations in Jackson Hole — a nail that will be reused in the coffin of private open space in Jackson Hole."[14] Some people think that wildlife advocates use the bison as a poster child to beg for expansion of national parks. This siege mentality was expressed by the Idaho state veterinarian, Bob Hillman, in a speech to the Livestock Conservation Institute.

> In the current [Clinton] administration, extreme environmental and animals rights groups have strong friends and allies who are attempting

to impose the agenda of these groups on the rest of the country. These groups desire to eliminate ranching, timbering and mining from all public lands of the West. They want these lands dedicated to uncontrolled wildlife populations and to be their playground. . . .

Neither is it acceptable for the Department of Interior to confiscate more private or forest lands for utilization by bison. These proposals do not solve the problem, they only prolong and expand the problem. . . . We could easily lose the battle and in fact are very near to losing it.[15]

Neither private land nor national forest has ever been "confiscated" for use by Yellowstone bison. Under the Gallatin National Forest Plan set forth in 1987, the priority for areas near Yellowstone National Park is to provide habitat for "all indigenous wildlife species and for increasing populations of big game animals."[16] Political scientist Craig Allin therefore used the term "militant minority" to refer not to extreme environmentalists but to Yellowstone's local economic interests. They often prevail against the Park Service because "they care passionately, they work hard, their interests are easy to conceptualize and to quantify," Allin explains. "These are precisely the characteristics rewarded in our political system." He describes the park's national constituents, in contrast, as "a vast and far-flung tribe, not nearly so well informed. As absentee landlords, they assume that Park Service experts are in charge and that nature is being served. They are a silent majority, only partially represented by the national environmental lobby, and that is a poor recipe for political success."[17]

It is easy to paint the ranchers as caring only about their bottom line while the environmentalists are motivated by loftier ideals, but the real picture is hardly that black-and-white. The disdain that farmers, ranchers, and loggers sometimes express for both armchair environmentalists and practicing tree huggers does not spring solely from their bank accounts. People who make their living off the land may believe that they know and love nature more profoundly than environmentalists do. And in a way, they are right. As Evan Eisenberg pointed out in *The Ecology of Eden*, "The backpacker loves nature chastely; the farmer wants to get a child upon her."[18] But the process of impregnation, however lovingly carried out, entails the domestication of nature, the intrusion of civilization, and a loss of the wildness that the backpacker cherishes.

Threats and Sanctions

Hillman also claimed that the Department of the Interior was "in violation of the USDA rules and program standards" because the National Park Service was "allowing brucellosis-infected wildlife to cross state boundaries and expose other animals to brucellosis."[19] This was incorrect. The U.S. Department of Agriculture has no rules pertaining to wildlife in national parks, and it could not deprive Montana of its brucellosis-free status because of wild bison that leave Yellowstone.

However, six state veterinarians sent letters in 1994 threatening to place sanctions on Montana cattle unless Yellowstone bison that left the park were killed. Much like the others, the letter from Washington began, "Today it has come to my attention that the state of Montana is no longer depopulating all the stray, brucellosis-infected bison which migrate into Montana from Yellowstone National Park." It concluded, "Unless you can immediately supply me with the assurance that such information is not correct, I must remove Montana from our list of exempted free states effective today."[20] One explanation for the similar letters is that Montana state veterinarian Siroky asked his colleagues to send them to justify Montana's killing the bison. In the same vein, although the Animal and Plant Health Inspection Service (APHIS) of the USDA appeared to issue Montana a warning, it later backed off and claimed that Siroky had asked it to threaten to downgrade Montana from its brucellosis-free status. The Montana Department of Livestock "wanted cover to deal with bison in the way they saw fit," explained Patrick Collins, director of APHIS legislative and public affairs.[21]

In January 1995 Montana sued the U.S. Departments of the Interior and Agriculture, claiming that the bison management policy carried out by the former would make it impossible to maintain the brucellosis-free status granted by the latter. In March the Western States Livestock Health Association passed a resolution urging APHIS to downgrade the brucellosis status of any state in which infected bison were allowed to roam. The four states that imposed sanctions on Montana cattle that year soon lifted them, but not before some ranchers had to test cows so they could be transported out of state. By requiring tests for interstate cattle shipments, a state veterinarian can impose on another state essentially the same penalty that would be incurred if APHIS revoked the state's brucellosis-free status. Montana made no effort to seek enforcement of laws intended to protect interstate commerce from unfair state-imposed sanctions. But it was the threat of sanctions and the warning from APHIS that the Montana Department of Livestock used to persuade the state legislature to grant it authority over wild bison, transferring this responsibility from the Department of Fish, Wildlife and Parks. This reversed what happened in 1908, when the state of Montana declared free-roaming bison to be wild animals in order to prevent Michel Pablo from claiming as livestock the bison he could not round up on the Flathead Reservation.

In May 1995 U.S. senator Conrad Burns of Montana introduced a bill that would require testing every bison in Yellowstone, neutering or destroying all seropositive bison, quarantining the remainder for up to several years, and keeping the herd at 500 below the "optimum" size as determined by "a team of independent range scientists."[22] The bill did not go anywhere, but rather than challenge Montana's allegations about conflicting federal policies or clarify APHIS's lack of authority over wildlife, the U.S. Departments of the Interior and Agriculture reached a court settlement with Montana. They agreed to prepare an interim plan to be followed while work continued on the environmental impact statement (EIS) for long-term bison management that had begun in 1990. Under the National Environmental Policy Act of 1969, federal agencies must complete an EIS to analyze potential impacts before undertaking a program that could "significantly affect the quality of the human environment." Yellowstone superintendent Michael Finley may have wanted to turn down the settlement with Montana, but Park Service director Roger Kennedy instructed him otherwise.[23] The Department of the Interior wanted Yellowstone to be a good neighbor.

The Montana Department of Livestock and Dead Bison

The interim plan agreed to in 1996 was the first plan in 30 years that called for the Park Service to cull Yellowstone bison. The Park Service built a facility with holding pens, pastures, and chutes two miles inside the north boundary near Stephens Creek where park employees could corral exiting bison and send them to slaughter. Bison that left the park near West Yellowstone were to be captured and tested by the Montana Department of Livestock, which would send seropositive bison and pregnant females (determined by vaginal probing) to slaughter. Because cattle were not present in the winter on private land near West Yellowstone, bison that tested seronegative there would be released with "an official metal ear tag and an unobtrusive visual marking." Montana could shoot any bison found outside the park that could not be captured, except in certain areas of the Gallatin National Forest not used by cattle.

The Sierra Club Legal Defense Fund sued the Park Service in September, charging that to trap bison in the park would be a violation of the National Park Service Organic Act. On December 19, as Yellowstone's most severe winter in more than 50 years was getting under way, the judge denied the plaintiff's motion for an injunction to prevent captures at Stephens Creek. An accumulation of snow ranging from two to five feet was followed by a partial thaw, rain, and then extreme cold, freezing a thick crust of ice that was impenetrable by foraging bison, estimated to number 3,500 that winter. The Park Service tried to haze bison heading north back into the park, but the large number near the boundary made that impossible, and capture operations began.

By January 17 a total of 569 bison had been killed. To reduce the losses, the Park Service began using the facility at Stephens Creek to test bison and hold those that were seronegative. Outside West Yellowstone heavy snow prevented use of one of the two capture facilities, and the park's good neighbor shot almost three times as many bison as were tested. The Montana Department of Livestock (DOL) claimed it could not tell the marked, tested animals from the unmarked, untested animals. To remedy this, Siroky announced that they would start using "high visibility bangle ear markers." To wildlife advocates the use of such conspicuous livestock tags was demeaning to wild bison and symbolized the mindset they were fighting.

On January 28 Yellowstone chief ranger Dan Sholly wrote to Siroky, "We would view the use of bangle tags as a violation of the Interim Plan." He also objected to how bison were being received outside the park's boundary:

Often during DOL bison shooting operations, after the first well-aimed shot is fired, the shooting area becomes a free fire zone. Reportedly, most animals are being wounded multiple times, including numerous rump and gut shots with the idea apparently being to get as many animals down as possible. This shooting strategy, if in fact true, is not only inhumane, but with so much activity and chaos during the shoot would explain why your shooters are not recognizing marked animals.[24]

Montana Department of Livestock employees shooting bison that have left the park, 1997. Courtesy of Yellowstone National Park.

On January 29 APHIS confirmed that Montana could suspend the shooting of bison on public land without jeopardizing its brucellosis-free status. Demonstrating the irrelevance of APHIS to its concerns, the state rejected the proposal. Governor Racicot referred to the animals as "America's bison" as a way of diffusing responsibility for what was happening, but the American government had no power to compel Montana to stop killing them. Yellowstone managers "make us out to be the bad guys," Siroky said, "but they are allowing animals to be controlled by starvation and disease. That's despicable." Describing the state's method for preventing brucellosis transmission from wild bison to cattle, Siroky said, "It's horrible; I detest it, but it has to be done, even though the risk may be small."[25]

Park employees also detested what they were doing and hoped that public opinion would rescue them, that media coverage of the bison butchering would embolden a higher authority to shut down the operation. During the confinement and shipment of bison to slaughterhouses, some were fatally gored or trampled; some had their horns broken off or their eyes gouged out when animals panicked. Some park employees wore black tape across the bison emblem on their badges. This symbol of mourning is ordinarily reserved for fellow employees who die in the line of duty, but some people felt the bison were dying on the job. When a rambunctious

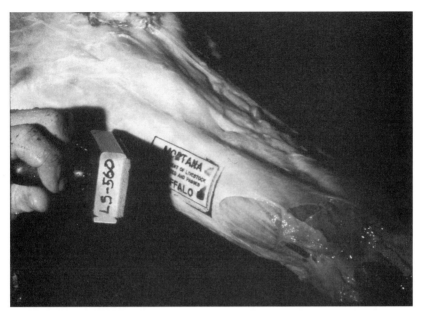

Once the leg of a wild bison in Yellowstone that fell under the jurisdiction of the Montana Department of Livestock after it crossed the park boundary, 1997. Courtesy of Yellowstone National Park.

bull broke the squeeze chute at the Stephens Creek corral, some of the employees assigned to manage the captive bison were inwardly applauding. If they could not take pride in what they were doing, they could feel proud to work in a place that once contained such a magnificent animal.

On February 6 Yellowstone announced that bison shipments from Stephens Creek would resume because the capture facility was full and efforts to haze the remaining exhausted animals into the park were causing starvation. Montana would not permit the 147 seronegative bison in the corrals to be sent anywhere in the state but to a slaughterhouse, and APHIS rules prevented their being sent across state lines to an Indian reservation until after a quarantine period that could last for years. Referring to these bison as "political hostages," Superintendent Finley said, "A lot of people around the country are rightfully questioning why we are doing this. They feel that the Park Service has lost its way. . . . We are participating in something that is totally unpalatable to the American people, and it's something we are not convinced that science justifies."[26]

Claiming the Bison Heritage

Among those dismayed by the slaughter was the InterTribal Bison Coopera-tive (ITBC), whose goal is to restore bison to millions of acres of Indian land. In 1994 the tribes received 335 bison from Yellowstone, but only in exchange for butchering them after the animals had been shot outside the park. Some tribes welcomed the meat, but the ITBC declined to participate the following year. "Because it was being done wrong, you were missing the connection," an Assiniboin said in explaining the difficult decision. "You are treating them just like a cow. . . . When the whites exterminated the herds, they didn't just take our grocery store. They annihilated our church."[27]

Gloria Wells-Norlin, a member of the Little Shell Band of Chippewas, was harassed by both white and Indian activists for helping the Montana Department of Livestock butcher the carcasses and locate suitable recipients for them. To dress, skin, and quarter a bison carcass takes two people about two hours, but she felt she was making the best of a bad situation, con-tributing her time and money to the cause. "For us, it was a very spiritual thing," said Wells-Norlin. "We always gave prayer. We always chose one that was pointing east. We always gave thanks." Other Indians were not grateful. "That's a cruel, cruel attack on our people to give our children murdered animals," said a member of the Crow-Santee tribe who wanted live bison, not carcasses, to be shipped to Indian reservations.[28]

On February 12, 1997, the tribal chairman of the Fort Peck Assiniboins and Sioux was permitted to address a joint session of the Montana legisla-ture. "Those of our ancestors that survived the 19th century found sanctuary on reservations. In 1894, the last wild buffalo herd left in the United States found sanctuary in Yellowstone Park," explained Caleb Shield. "I speak for all Montana Indian Nations when I say that the slaughter of this wild herd must stop. Our cultures are different on this issue. Under our religion, buffalo are respected. They are good medicine. Their skulls and hides adorn our most sacred lodges. We still dance, sing, and pray to them."[29] Dancing to a different tune, Governor Racicot responded caustically to complaints about his state's treatment of wild bison. "It seems preposterous to us that policy paralysis of these federal agencies has created an over-population of diseased bison overgrazing a national park to the extent they seek to leave their alleged sanctuary. And Montana is called inhumane."[30] Of the 147 bison that survived the brucellosis test at Stephens Creek with seronegative results, 35 were trucked to a research lab in Idaho to test vaccines.

Lakota Sioux Chief Joseph Chasing Horse and Arvol Looking Horse at the National Day of Prayer for the Buffalo in Yellowstone, March 6, 1997. Courtesy of Yellowstone National Park.

As the death toll of bison passed 1,000, a large group of American Indians and others in mourning gathered near the bison confined at Stephens Creek. They shared a pipe and prayers to release the spirit of the bison that had been killed. They heard the blast when eight more bison were shot a mile away. Rosalie Little Thunder, a Lakota Sioux from South Dakota, arrived at the scene to find men gutting the carcasses. "It was like a murder in the church parking lot during the service," Little Thunder said. "It was shocking, the disrespect they showed the buffalo."[31]

The turnout for the bison auction at C&P Packing in Livingston was more than twice as large as for the prayer service. The best hides and heads went for $160 each. "We bought three buffalo hides so each of our boys would have a park bison rug. It's our heritage," explained one native Montanan. The state received $185,000 from the sale of wild bison products in 1997, partially offsetting the $245,000 that Montana spent removing wild bison that year. But publicity about ill-gotten gains ended the practice. Since then, all carcasses have gone to tribal members and nonprofit organizations.

"I see this winter as a gift," said Mary Meagher, the native Montanan who had been studying bison in Yellowstone for three decades. "What is happening this winter is essential to the long-term welfare of the bison in Yellowstone. It will have removed a lot of the animals that know where they want to go." She rejected brucellosis as a valid reason for killing bison and doubted the disease could be eliminated from wildlife. But she believed the Yellowstone bison population was twice what it would be without roads groomed for snowmobiles—roads that make it easier for bison to travel to find winter forage. "The drop in numbers is exactly what the system needs."[32]

The media coverage crested on March 23 at a public meeting in Gardiner, whose winter population of 851 was briefly augmented by Montana's governor, two U.S. senators, and the U.S. secretary of agriculture. Michael Pablo, chairman of the Montana-Wyoming Tribal Leaders Council and descendant of bison rancher Michel Pablo, protested that the tribes' request for a seat at the table for the interagency bison management plan had been ignored and that Department of Livestock officials laughed when participants at the vigil asked to pray over the dead bison.

"We are not some primal band of neanderthals running around making sure every living animal is being put in the cross hairs," Governor Racicot said in his state's defense. "We can't go into the park and do what we choose, and we can't do what we choose outside of the park either." Superintendent Finley was permitted a two-minute response. The Bison Action Group, which had referred to state veterinarian Siroky as "the Eichmann of Yellowstone" and which some people regarded as a primal band of Neanderthals, made an uninvited response. One of the activists rushed into the room with a painted face and a bucket of rotting bison guts aimed at Racicot. An aide caught her by the arm and the offal spilled onto the table, spattering the politicians who had a seat at it.

Leaving the Bison Action Group out of the picture, Yellowstone's chief scientist, John Varley, described the feud as "a struggle between the park and agribusiness and we're losing badly."[33] At a meeting of the Montana Farm Forum, the audience applauded when Senator Burns described Michael Finley as "this jughead we've got running Yellowstone Park."[34] Naturalist Doug Peacock noted that the federal and state agencies all claimed to be "caught in the middle—a most improbable and cowardly axiom of ethical geometry."[35] What had seemed equally improbable was how many bison would get caught in the middle, between the privations of

In January 1997 bison that approached the park's north boundary near Gardiner, Montana, were herded into a corral. Until their release in early April, 112 bison were allowed to remain there, but nearly 700 were sent to the slaughterhouse. Courtesy of Yellowstone National Park.

winter in Yellowstone and the forage to be found somewhere out there, north of the park in Paradise Valley, bison habitat of epochs gone by. Nearly all 865 bison counted in the northern herd in early winter may have tried to leave the park. About 250 of them succeeded, remaining where they were allowed on the Gallatin National Forest east of the Yellowstone River. Those bison, and the 112 seronegative bison released from the Stephens Creek corrals in early April, may have been the only ones on the northern range that spring. But a total of 725 bison were removed near the park's north boundary, indicating that hundreds must have also traveled from the park's interior. Some of the bison that were tested and tagged near West Yellowstone showed up later at Stephens Creek, 30 miles away as the crow flies, and more than twice as far in bison miles. Perhaps the commotion around West Yellowstone impelled some bison to head north.

By the end of the winter, 1,084 bison had been removed at the boundary, including some that had tested seronegative and many that had not been tested at all. Most were in good condition when they tried to leave the park, but some of the bison that were unable or unwilling to leave found little to eat. An estimated 374 bison did not survive the poor diet or other natural hardships of winter, leaving about 1,900 bison in the park when spring arrived. At Canyon Village a bull bison whose ancestors had faced down dire wolves was reduced to eating the brooms and welcome mats at tourist cabins. What kind of wild bison would Yellowstone be left with?

"Man wants to see nature and evolution as separate from human activities," Mark Kurlansky wrote in his book about cod, "the fish that changed the world." But as a "ferocious predator," man is part of nature and evolution. "If species cannot survive because man kills them, something more adaptable will take their place. Nature, the ultimate pragmatist, doggedly searches for something that works. But as the cockroach demonstrates, what works best in nature does not always appeal to us.[36]

CHAPTER 9

A Disagreeable Agreement

Wildlife advocates who hoped that the government officials negotiating a bison plan for the future would be haunted by bison ghosts of winters past were disappointed. "When you compromise, you end up with a less than desirable document," Superintendent Finley explained after the draft EIS was released in 1998. "If I were making the decision unilaterally, I would do it differently—I would have bison ranging freely outside Yellowstone on national forest lands."[1] The "preferred" alternative chosen by the inter-agency team was too similar to the existing plan to be desirable to anyone, but that was to be expected. The agencies had to compromise on some-thing, and they ended up largely where they began. The Park Service could have let Montana do as it wished with bison that crossed the boundary, and watched with clenched fists as hundreds of bison were sent to slaughter. Instead it chose to participate in a program that would haze, capture, test, and vaccinate or slaughter some bison in order to obtain visiting rights for a limited number of bison in a limited area outside the park.

The interagency team agreed that the overall purpose of the EIS was "to maintain a wild, free-ranging population of bison and address the risk of brucellosis transmission to protect the economic interest and viability of the livestock industry in the state of Montana." A "wild, free-ranging popu-lation of bison" was defined as one that is "not routinely handled by humans and can move without restrictions within specific geographic areas." The risk of brucellosis transmission from wild bison to cattle was not defined except to acknowledge that it was "low." Because many wildlife advocates

regarded the risk as negligible and gave priority to minimizing the interference with bison, none of the proposed alternatives squared with their idea
of free-roaming animals. "If they were free-roaming buffalo, they would be
coming up the Tongue River to our reservation by now," said Ernie Robinson
of the Northern Cheyenne Tribal Council, which wanted to help some
Yellowstone bison make the trip to southeastern Montana.[2]

Some dissenters submitted their own alternatives. The most widely
supported, "The Citizens' Plan to Save Yellowstone Buffalo," was endorsed
by 17 organizations, including the Greater Yellowstone Coalition, Montana
Audubon Society, Wilderness Society, and InterTribal Bison Cooperative.
Unlike the EIS team's preferred alternative, which set a population target
of 1,700 to 2,500, the Citizens' Plan would not capture or kill bison for the
sake of reducing the possibility of brucellosis transmission. The plan warned
that by interfering with the "epic cycle" in which bison "struggle through
icy snowpacks to find those places where they can survive until spring," the
interagency alternative would "drive a stake through the heart of one of
America's greatest conservation success stories." As for hazing, either attempts
to keep bison in Yellowstone were a dangerous waste of effort and the bison
would leave the park anyway, or techniques would be developed that did
keep the bison in the park, which would increase the winterkill and alter the
population dynamics of bison and other wildlife. The Citizens' Plan would
allow wild bison on all public land outside the park, increase their winter
range through land purchase or conservation easements, control herd size,
if necessary, by permitting hunting outside the park and relocating bison to
Indian reservations or other public land, and create incentives that "encourage
landowners to change their grazing practices" in ways that would reduce
the possibility of disease transmission.[3]

A common refrain among bison advocates is that wildlife should be
given preference on national forest surrounding the park, especially given
the small number of cattle that use it. It does seem worth considering
whether the millions of tax dollars used to prevent Yellowstone bison from
transmitting brucellosis to livestock could be spent with less risk and blood-
shed by buying out the livestock owners. But those 2,000 cow-calf pairs that
are present within 10 miles of the park's boundary are only the front line in
Montana livestock's battle against wild bison. Even in a world without
brucellosis, a line must be drawn somewhere; the question is where and
how it will be enforced for an animal population that has no significant
predator. For wildlife advocates, the park boundary is the wrong place to

draw the line, because it too severely limits the bison's natural winter range and migration routes.

A Plan to Save Greater Yellowstone Livestock

For some people all seven of the EIS alternatives were too hard on wild bison; for others they were all too soft. When a preliminary draft was circulated among the participating agencies in 1995, the USDA complained that it dealt "only tangentially" with brucellosis even though "we have enough knowledge to eradicate brucellosis from the GYA at this time."[4] After a draft had been agreed on for public distribution, the participating agencies could not publicly criticize the results, but the United States Animal Health Association (USAHA) could. USAHA described itself as "the oldest and most prestigious animal health–oriented national organization in the United States," but the health of livestock is its driving concern.[5] Its members include about 1,400 state and federal animal health officials, veterinarians, and livestock producers, and for many years its brucellosis committee took a zero-tolerance stance toward brucellosis in Yellowstone. "We're still totally disgusted with the progress that is being made in dealing with the disease," said J. Lee Alley, Alabama's state veterinarian and the committee chair in 1998. "If I were in President Clinton's position, I'd say USDA has authority for all animal diseases in the country and it ought to be extended to wildlife."[6]

Idaho state veterinarian Bob Hillman was on the USAHA task force that prepared a report explaining why none of the EIS alternatives were acceptable. The "preferred" alternative would leave "an unacceptably high estimated seroprevalence rate as late as the year 2011 (23–28%)." Even Alternative 6, "Aggressive Brucellosis Control within Yellowstone National Park through Vaccination," was not aggressive enough, because it would allow seronegative bison outside the park during the cattle off-season and because there was "no scientifically defensible criteria for delaying phase 2 for 10 years." In phase 2, seven facilities would be constructed in the park for a capture-test-and-slaughter program after vaccination stabilized the rate of infection, which was projected to take ten years.[7]

The EIS alternatives were designed to cover a 15-year period, and they all included some level of vaccination when a safe and effective vaccine became available. To be considered safe, a vaccine could cause short-term "adverse clinical effects, such as listlessness, anorexia, depression, and arthritis" as long as it did not increase the likelihood that the animal would die or be preyed upon. Efficacy would be evaluated in terms of the vaccine's ability to prevent infection and fetal loss. The two existing vaccines, strains 19 and RB51, did not provide total protection for cattle and were of uncertain value for bison. Vaccination of bison in the park would require additional capture facilities or a means of remote delivery. The shortcoming of the air gun used to vaccinate elk on Wyoming feedlots was its short range for an animal with a thick hide. In research on captive bison, marksmen had to be within 20 meters to achieve penetration on at least 80 percent of the shots; safe delivery to unconfined wild bison was expected to require a ballistic system that achieved reasonably accurate penetration from 50 to 75 meters.[8]

Although research on RB51 had already demonstrated that "no adverse effects on lemmings were observed," studies were under way to make sure that vaccinating wild bison would do no harm to other species that might come into contact with the vaccine if a biobullet went astray, or with the bison's afterbirth or carcass.[9] These concerns about animal welfare were not obstacles to vaccinating wild bison for the United States Animal Health Association, which advocated proceeding forthwith to round up the bison and stick it to them. Under USAHA's plan as many bison as possible would be captured and vaccinated annually, using a reduced dose until more was known about its consequences. After five years all bison would be tested, and the seropositive bison w ould be slaughtered. Seronegative bison would be confined for a quarantine period that could last more than four years, depending on the animal's age and sex. In addition, while some wildlife advocates wanted to reduce winter road grooming because it may facilitate bison migration, the USAHA plan called for plowing more roads in order to access the new "capture facilities."[10] A slaughterhouse by any other name would smell as sweet, but the odor would be less noticeable to park visitors in the winter.

Livestock officials like to point out that test-and-slaughter programs were used to eliminate brucellosis in the bison herds at Custer State Park, Wind Cave National Park, and Wichita Mountains National Wildlife Refuge. For wildlife advocates, those examples only reveal the absurdity of attempting a test-and-slaughter program in Yellowstone. Those bison herds were much smaller than Yellowstone's and confined to much smaller areas. They were already accustomed to being periodically rounded up in specially designed corrals, and bison that could not be managed that way were shot. Bison at those parks were not wild and free ranging in the way Yellowstone bison were meant to be.

Yes, We Have No Eradication Plan

The USAHA plan, which called for vaccinating Yellowstone bison until the herds were brucellosis free, stated that to ensure they remained that way, the disease would also have to be eliminated from elk. It did not propose how to do that, but it listed failure to address the problem of brucellosis in elk as one of the EIS's 21 "deficiencies." The EIS required the participating agencies only to "commit to the eventual elimination of brucellosis in bison and other wildlife." It did not specify how or when.

When brucellosis was first detected in the northern elk herd in the 1930s, the seropositive rate was thought to be more than 20 percent, and that was attributed to the herd's congregating in Lamar Valley when bison were fed there. The current low seroprevalance of the northern elk herd could be a vestige of that initial infection or the result of later contact with bison or with elk that use the Wyoming feedgrounds. Hunters and others who do not want to see the northern elk tampered with in the name of brucellosis eradication have argued that if the disease were eliminated from bison and from elk using the feedgrounds, it would eventually disappear from the northern elk. Despite the thousands of elk that were shipped from Yellowstone to start or augment other herds until the 1960s, there is no evidence that they spread brucellosis, which did appear in some bison herds to which Yellowstone bison were transferred.

However, because the elk could theoretically reinfect a cleaned-up bison herd in Yellowstone, a 1998 study by the National Research Council advised that any vaccination program for bison must be accompanied by "a concomitant program" for elk. The authors acknowledged that vaccinating a sufficient portion of the elk population would be difficult because of its wide distribution and the high seroprevalence on Wyoming feedlots. They believed that if vaccination were combined with a test-and-slaughter program, brucellosis might be eradicated in greater Yellowstone, but how long this would take would depend on the effectiveness of the vaccine, the slaughter rate, and whether wildlife populations were reduced despite public opposition. They also noted, "It might prove impossible for various reasons to eliminate brucellosis from bison and elk in the GYA, so the best that could be achieved would be risk control."[11]

Although the agencies participating in the EIS pledged a commitment to the "eventual" elimination of brucellosis in bison and other wildlife, what the EIS offered was seven alternatives for managing the risk of transmission from bison to cattle. The alternatives covered a spectrum of bison management intensity, from "Minimal Management" to "Aggressive Brucellosis Control," and the "preferred" alternative was a compromise between them. Two-thirds of the 67,000 responses received during the public comment period supported the Citizens' Plan, whose sponsors actively enlisted members of their organizations to send in their votes. In general, the comments showed an overwhelming preference for restricting where cattle could graze rather than where wild bison could go. The closest EIS alternative was "Minimal Management," which was also the "environmentally preferred alternative" as defined by the National Environmental Policy Act—that is, it "causes the least damage to the biological and physical environment and best protects, preserves and enhances historic, cultural and natural resources." It would eliminate the test-and-slaughter program and acquire more land for bison winter range.

EIS regulations required the interagency team to respond to all comments received on the draft EIS and to consider them when preparing the final EIS. The team was not obliged to revise its chosen alternative to better conform to public opinion, to choose the environmentally preferred alternative, or to come up with a brucellosis eradication plan. However, it did modify the preferred alternative somewhat, even though doing so caused a rift with the state of Montana.

Degrees of Separation

A less intensive approach to bison management was supported by both public opinion and new research on the viability of *Brucella abortus* when shed in the greater Yellowstone environment. Although the bacterium often uses abortion to spread its progeny to other host animals, ecologist Dale Lott has compared this to "launching a raft of colonists into unknown ocean currents with a week's food and hoping they make a favorable landfall before they starve."[12] Bison have been observed sniffing and licking the placenta expelled when a cow aborts or gives birth, but the bacteria die if they do not reach a hospitable environment in which to reproduce. Ongoing research has found that when deliberately infected bison fetuses are placed in protected sites in the Yellowstone area in February (when

Technicians dressed to handle hazardous materials place brucellosis-infected cattle fetuses in cages in 2001 to study how long the bacteria survive in the Yellowstone environment. Courtesy of Montana Fish, Wildlife and Parks.

abortion could occur), the *Brucella abortus* remained viable for about 80 days; when the fetus was set out in mid-May (when birth is likely to occur), the bacteria survived for no more than 20 days.[13] With this in mind, the federal agencies revised the EIS preferred alternative to emphasize "spatial and temporal separation" of bison and cattle and increase the bison population target to 3,000. Bison that could not be hazed into the park would be captured and tested, with the seropositive animals sent to slaughter. Inside the north boundary, which abuts the Royal Teton Ranch west of Gardiner, the Park Service could hold up to 125 seronegative bison in the corral at Stephens Creek. Outside the west boundary, up to 100 bison that tested seronegative or could not be captured but were considered "low risk" would be allowed to remain in a designated zone outside the park until May 15. "Low risk" bison could include any bison that had not recently calved or aborted and were therefore unlikely to cause "environmental contamination."[14] Any bison in the north or west zones in excess of these numbers could be shot or sent to slaughter regardless of test results.

Montana's 1995 lawsuit had been premised on the idea that APHIS and the National Park Service had contradictory brucellosis policies. However, now that those agencies had come to an agreement, Montana refused to accept it. "Whatever conclusions the federal agencies unilaterally draw will not be binding on the state of Montana," Governor Racicot said.[15] Montana stuck to its guns in the belief that there was no such thing as "low risk" untested bison. The federal agencies were unwilling to surrender the "low risk" untested bison to Montana, because they wanted to counter the widespread view that the proposed plan would result in the continued "unnecessary" killing of bison. More than half of the bison that had been killed since 1996 were in the "low risk" category, and all of those removed in the West Yellowstone area had been taken before April, even though cattle were not scheduled to be in the area until June. But Arnold Gertonson, who replaced Siroky as state veterinarian in 1997, protested that allowing bison to remain outside the park would constitute a "de facto expansion" of the park's borders, an expansion not perceived when elk left the park.[16]

The killing of bison bulls outside the park when no cattle are present has brought Montana livestock officials the scorn of some wildlife advocates. However, even if the risk of their transmitting brucellosis to cattle is "vanishingly small," as the National Research Council concluded, more conspicuous is the possibility that where a few bulls go, many cows may eventually follow. Although the evidence is only circumstantial, it makes sense that a band of cows and calves would be less likely to risk going where no bison has gone before. If the bulls return in the spring from their annual foray yonder and a matriarchal cow takes note that they appear well fed, the next year she may follow the scent trail they have left and lead her band to the promised land. In that case Wyoming's policy of allowing up to 15 bulls outside the park's east boundary each year may be drawing some bison cows to their death. Killing the bulls would more likely prevent mixed bison groups from trying to recolonize areas outside the park.

Because the EIS was part of the lawsuit settlement, the court appointed a mediator to resolve the state's differences with the federal agencies, and the mediation led to a slightly modified version of the plan that the federal agencies had proposed. Vaccination of bison captured at the boundary could begin as soon as the safety of a vaccine had been established, even if its efficacy had not. Since the safety of RB51 for use in calves had already been demonstrated, it was expected that calf vaccination could begin immediately at the boundary. In return, Montana would allow up to 100 untested bison in the management zone around West Yellowstone after a remote vaccination program had begun in the park interior, and an additional 100 untested bison in the management zone north of the park after a cattle lease expired on the Royal Teton Ranch in 2002.

While Yellowstone managers flinched at accusations that the Park Service had been uncooperative in working with the state of Montana, they were more bothered by objections from wildlife advocates that they had caved in to political pressure by agreeing to the interagency plan. Continuing the effort begun by Mary Meagher, Park Service employees such as John Varley and Wayne Brewster had spent more than a decade trying to keep the bison from being treated like livestock. They believed they had fought the good fight since the lawsuits began in the 1980s, beat their head against the hard wall of Montana's obstinacy in order to obtain some concessions, and arrived at what was the best of all possible bison management plans in an imperfect world that happened to contain the Montana livestock industry.

Sound Science and Unfounded Fears

The EIS for bison management in Yellowstone and Montana called for selecting a preferred alternative "based on factual information." The Greater Yellowstone Interagency Brucellosis Committee (GYIBC) seeks to "base brucellosis-related management recommendations and decisions on sound science." The National Wildlife Federation and the InterTribal Bison Cooperative said that "the Yellowstone bison population should be managed scientifically." Everyone agrees on the value of science but not on the facts themselves, which helps explain why completing the EIS took ten years. The GYIBC continues to disagree about the feasibility of eliminating the disease and the efficacy of various remedies. Were there facts that could justify spending millions of dollars a year to protect several thousand cattle from a risk of brucellosis that is too small to measure? Was there a scientific basis for expecting that brucellosis could be eliminated from greater Yellowstone by 2010?

While in political battles people may assume that God is on their side, in environmental controversies, it is science that people put their faith in, attributing opposing views to ignorance, self-interest, or emotion. The Fund for Animals described the EIS as "scientifically fraudulent" and declared that "the state of Montana is willing to sacrifice national treasures to the misguided passions of the livestock industry."[17] The Defenders of Wildlife objected that many of the management actions proposed in the EIS were not "scientifically justifiable"; they were "based on unfounded fears and are promoted as necessary by biased parties which have no real interest in maintaining the free-roaming nature of Yellowstone's bison."[18] But participants at six town meetings held by the Montana Stockgrowers Association in 2001 were told that it was the environmentalists who were the radical fringe. "One of the principles that we've observed in the terrorist attacks in New York City and Washington, D.C. is that when you get right down to it, a very small number of well-organized and committed people can have a huge effect. And the same principles are true of Montana and the nation's environmental wars."[19] The association's president, Bill Garrison, said, "For many years the State of Montana has been caught between managing the very real brucellosis disease risk in a science-based manner, and fighting opponents—even within the federal government— who attempted to play on emotions and rhetoric."[20]

In *Alice in Wonderland* terms, drafting the interagency plan involved considerable "Reeling and Writhing," and some of the numbers it contains seem to have been derived from the Mock Turtle's "different branches of Arithmetic: Ambition, Distraction, Uglification, and Derision." Although the more than 2,000 pages of the final EIS contained much scientific data, the most important details in the resulting plan were based on politics as much as biology: how many bison will be allowed outside the park, where they will be permitted to roam and when, whether Montana will reauthorize bison hunting, and whether a quarantine facility will be constructed to hold seronegative bison until they can be certified brucellosis free.

To estimate how the Yellowstone bison would be affected by each alternative, the EIS used a population model constructed in 1990 to project the impact of wolf reintroduction.[21] At that time, when the highest recorded winter bison population was 3,159, the model indicated that from 1,700 to 3,500 bison could live year-round in the park, depending on fluctuations in forage production and winter severity. This was not a prediction of how many bison would stay in the park year-round if they were free to leave, only an estimate as to how many could survive there. Based on its own interpretation of the historical data, the USAHA task force wanted the population limited to 1,800 until "scientifically valid research is conducted by non-partisan range management experts to prove that YNP has the capacity to sustain larger populations."[22]

Using the unfortunate term "population target," which suggested some-thing to be shot at, the interagency plan finally settled on a maximum pre-calving bison population of 3,000. This provision did not limit the popu-lation to 3,000, but if the late winter count found more than 3,000, bison leaving the park could be sent to slaughter without testing. A wildlife count is the number of animals tallied during a visual survey, in this case from a small plane. It differs from a population estimate, which is higher because it combines information about observed animals and assumptions about how many were not seen as a result of factors such as weather and terrain.

Although the target of 3,000 looked like a compromise between the original 2,500 limit that public opinion had found objectionable and the 3,500 maximum the park could theoretically support, the final EIS justified it by referring to a National Research Council finding that bison "show the greatest probability" of moving out of the park when the population is more than 3,000. Because the likelihood of bison leaving the park would be expected to increase as the population grew, this cutoff seemed arbitrary. The National Research Council study acknowledged that population size "did not quite reach statistical significance" as a factor determining bison movement, and noted that even at higher population levels, there was little or no evidence that forage in the park was inadequate.[23] Probability state-ments based on population size are problematic because other factors also affect migration out of the park, and because such calculations are based on relatively short-term experience during a period when the bison popu-lation has undergone substantial shifts in size and distribution. The data used to predict outward migration were also faulty because they were based only on the number of bison removed at the boundary; they did not include bison that submitted to hazing and returned to the park, or bison outside the park that escaped with their lives, including those that migrated to permitted areas of the Gallatin National Forest.

The first year that Yellowstone began the winter with more than 3,000 bison was 1988, which was also a year of severe drought and low forage production. The number of bison leaving the park increased abruptly that winter, and 569 were killed in Montana. By 1990 the bison population had topped 3,000 again, but only 14 were removed at the boundary. In 1994 the bison count reached a new high of 3,551, but that was a mild winter, and few bison seemed to think that 3,500 was as many as the park could support, for only five were removed at the boundary. At the other end of the popu-lation spectrum, the bison count at the start of the 1998–99 winter was

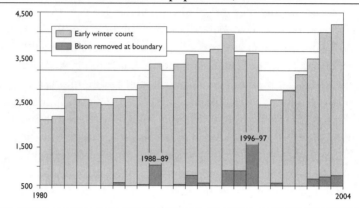

Yellowstone bison population, 1980–2004

The number of bison removed at the boundary each year has not been directly related to the population size. That is because not all of the bison that cross the park boundary are removed, and because the number of bison that cross the boundary each year also depends on factors such as winter conditions.

only 2,239, yet still the state of Montana found 94 to kill outside West Yellowstone.

The use of science to argue in favor of a particular wildlife management goal—to have more bison or fewer bison, to ignore brucellosis or eradicate it—has been a recurrent theme at Yellowstone since the 1930s. Accepted scientific truths are often based on limited data and are therefore subject to change after more data is collected. But the conflict about brucellosis in Yellowstone is not between different scientific views but between people with different attitudes toward wildlife. Human-caused environmental changes will continue to be driven by the prevailing social and political priorities, not by a scientific determination of the value of wildlife or the likelihood of brucellosis transmission. Advances in scientific knowledge can influence public attitudes, but they are only one factor among many.

A Risk Too Small to Measure

In addition to the Citizens' Plan and the plan recommended by the USAHA task force, three other parties submitted their own alternatives. Because all of the dissenters believed their plan would fulfill the purpose of the EIS—to maintain a wild, free-ranging population of bison and address the risk of brucellosis transmission to livestock—the wide variation on how to best achieve that goal demonstrated the extent of discord on the basic issues. Some concerned parties believed that the risk of transmission from bison to cattle was so small that it could be managed by keeping the two species separate, while others thought that bison should not only be kept separate from cattle but tested for the disease and slaughtered if they were seropositive or quarantined if they were seronegative.

Montana state veterinarian Siroky likened the risk of cattle getting brucellosis from Yellowstone bison to the odds of getting struck by lightning and maintained that even though it was remote, any risk was unacceptable because it could have disastrous economic consequences.[24] It was an odd analogy, given that Montana does nothing to protect cattle from lightning even though many such electrical transmissions have occurred, sometimes killing more than a dozen cattle in a single strike. But presumably the economic impact of a rancher losing some cattle to lightning is considered insignificant, whereas brucellosis transmission could affect not only the rancher whose herd became infected but also other ranchers who would have to test their herds to comply with USDA regulations.

Because the interagency team agreed that it was not possible to quantify the risk, they had no means by which to quantify how much effort should be made to reduce it. However, like all environmental impact statements, the EIS for bison management was required to analyze cost-effectiveness. It did this by comparing the cost of implementing each alternative for a 15-year period to the possible economic consequences if other states imposed sanctions or if Montana lost its brucellosis-free status. To be downgraded, a state must either have two infected herds within two years or fail to take adequate remedial action after a single herd is infected. The primary expense that results from loss of brucellosis-free status is not for replacing cattle but for USDA-required testing, which was estimated to cost up to $16.3 million if the entire state were affected.

The National Research Council study concluded that the risk of transmission from bison to cattle was "too small to measure with accuracy," so the EIS concluded that none of the alternatives had any "measurable benefits" in reducing the risk.[25] However, the alternatives' price tags did differ substantially, ranging from $0.8 million to $3.0 million a year for all agencies' expenditures combined, not including the cost of land acquisition, which was part of some alternatives. The least expensive and most cost-effective risk reduction activities were those affecting cattle, including conversion from cow-calf to steer or spayed heifer operations in order to reduce the likelihood of transmission within the herd and eliminate the need for vaccination and testing. Of the possible bison management activities, only the most basic were likely to be cost-effective: monitoring bison to ensure separation from cattle, bison hunting, and shooting bison when they left the park. The EIS noted that even if bison capture, testing, and vaccination cut the seroprevalence in Yellowstone bison in half over the life of the plan, the same reduction in risk could be achieved by reducing the number of cattle at risk by one-half, and that could be less expensively done by modifying national forest grazing allotments.

Consequently, the EIS admitted that none of its alternatives was cost-effective.[26] However, for those not persuaded that the risk called for a test-and-slaughter program in Yellowstone, the state veterinarians were prepared to make the case for national security. At the 2002 symposium, Idaho state veterinarian Bob Hillman mentioned that the Centers for Disease Control and Prevention had listed brucellosis as a possible biological weapon. "In a time when homeland security has become so important," he asked plaintively, "can we not address that problem?"

One could just as well argue that at a time when homeland security had become so important, there were far more critical problems to be addressed than that of brucellosis in Yellowstone wildlife. If the risk of transmission from a Yellowstone bison to cattle can be compared to getting struck by lightning, then the risk of a terrorist cell using *Brucella abortus* from a Yellowstone bison must be comparable to getting struck by an extraterrestrial invader. Even if someone wanted to bother using such a nonlethal weapon, brucellosis-infected cattle are readily available in many developing countries, and there would be easier ways to get your hands on some *Brucella abortus* bacteria than by hijacking a Yellowstone bison.

Why did the interagency team end up without any alternatives that were cost-effective? The final EIS explained that because of the "purpose, need, objectives, and policy restrictions" that were agreed to at the outset, only alternatives that involved intensive bison management were "considered adequate by all agencies." That sounds like saying the ends justify the means. But if the means cannot be cost justified, that could indicate that something is wrong with the objectives that were set. Even though the interagency plan was not intended to be a brucellosis eradication plan, the final EIS admitted that it was the "commit to eliminate brucellosis in wild-life" objective, not the "protect livestock from risk of brucellosis" objective, that precluded cost-effectiveness.[27]

CHAPTER 10

The High Cost of Free Roaming

Like Alice's Wonderland, the Greater Yellowstone Area (GYA) is more an imaginary concept than a precisely defined place in the real world. It is sometimes called the "Greater Yellowstone Ecosystem," which suggests a scientifically arrived-at boundary based on ecological considerations, but the perimeter is subject to the whims of the person drawing it. It may be a wavy line surrounding the patchwork of federal lands concentrated at the intersection of Idaho, Montana, and Wyoming, or a straight line that follows political boundaries. In one often used configuration, greater Yellowstone covers 18 million acres and 20 counties, which makes it slightly larger than West Virginia, but with only one-fifth as many people, or about 370,000. Federal agencies manage about 70 percent of this area, including two national parks, seven national forests, and three national wildlife refuges. However, only in Yellowstone is wildlife entirely under federal jurisdiction. Responsibility for the elk in Grand Teton National Park and the National Elk Refuge is shared with the state of Wyoming. On the national forests, the U.S. Forest Service manages the habitat, but the state government is responsible for managing wildlife populations.

If greater Yellowstone is an oddly shaped pizza pie, in land management terms it may be thought of as one ordered by parties with conflicting tastes. Everyone may agree on the tomato sauce—the lip service paid to preserving an undefined quality of life and scenery—but on little else. For many years, the government agencies with land management responsibilities could each order their portion of the pie the way they wanted it. But as tastes changed and dietary knowledge increased, objections have been raised by those who not only claim a fatal allergy to cheese but fear that the cheese on their neighbor's portion will melt onto their own. The number of parties demanding a voice in the pie's contents has also increased to include the state and federal agencies responsible for regulating the pie's ingredients, as well as taxpayers, who must help pay for the pie even though they may never partake of it.

The Greater Yellowstone Interagency Brucellosis Committee includes representatives from the state and federal agencies that oversee agriculture and wildlife management. The committee agreed that its overall goal was "to protect and sustain the existing free-ranging elk and bison populations in the GYA and protect public interests and the economic viability of the livestock industry in the three states." But the committee has no authority to protect or sustain anything; it has served primarily as a means of keeping agencies with conflicting mandates on speaking terms. In 1996, two years after the committee was established, Wyoming governor Jim Geringer announced that he was "increasingly concerned about the seemingly glacial speed" of its progress. He told his fellow governors in Idaho and Montana that the committee "needs a kick in the pants and a new committed focus on the Goal, Mission, and Objectives."[1] At the 2002 symposium, Geringer again exhorted the troops. "We need to redouble our efforts. We're not working hard enough, we're not working fast enough." But he also expressed confidence that the goal of brucellosis eradication by 2010 could be met, that common ground could be found among the divergent interests, provided it did not include common ground for livestock and bison.

Speeches in a similar vein by other state officials were interspersed with presentations by researchers. Amid judicious waffling—"there's a lot of stochasticity in this data"—was evidence that *Brucella abortus* could not be eliminated from greater Yellowstone by the year 2010 or any other year in the foreseeable future regardless of what means were used. Surely at least two of the bacteria had been present even on Noah's ark. GYIBC members who privately acknowledged the impossibility of the eradication goal were apt to downplay its significance. The U.S. Department of Agriculture has seen many deadlines for brucellosis eradication come and go since the campaign began in 1934. According to APHIS's 2001 "Strategic and Performance Plan," all states were to be brucellosis free by 2003, another goal that was not met. The document also committed APHIS to "make progress toward developing a plan for the eradication of brucellosis from bison and elk in the Greater Yellowstone Area." APHIS did not set a target date for this goal, but it intended to come up with a plan, or at least make progress toward developing one.

Glenn Plumb, who reported on the interagency plan for Yellowstone and Montana at the 2002 symposium, had done his 1991 doctoral thesis on the "foraging ecology of bison and cattle on a northern mixed prairie." However, he was speaking at the symposium not as a wildlife biologist or a representative of the National Park Service but "for the cooperating agencies." That was necessary because of the Park Service's reputation for being uncooperative in the brucellosis eradication effort. However, becoming a team player meant that after years of representing the interests of wild bison, the Park Service no longer had a voice of its own on bison management, or at least not a voice it could use in public. For the new plan to succeed, the Park Service had to speak the party line, even if it was a Mad Hatter's tea party line of occasional incongruity. In the words of the official Record of Decision, the plan called for both "a wild and free-roaming bison popula-tion in Yellowstone National Park" and the need to "capture, test, and pos-sibly hold bison in a facility seen by many persons as inappropriate for managing wildlife in a national park."[2]

The Record of Decision referred to the agreed-on alternative as the "Joint Management Plan," but by the time Plumb spoke at the GYIBC symposium less than two years later, Montana officials were objecting to the use of that name. They felt that "joint" implied "shared responsibility," that their Yellowstone counterparts were not bearing an equal burden in carrying out the most disagreeable parts of the plan, and that the state of Montana still had the lion's share of bison blood on its hands. Plumb did not mention any of this unpleasantness, but his presentation referred to the "Long-Term Interagency Bison Management Plan." Long-term could be a very long time, like a bad marriage in which the partners do not get along but share an abhorrence of the lawsuits that would accompany a divorce. However, in contrast to speakers who emphasized the goal of brucellosis eradication, Plumb stressed that "the Interagency Bison Management Plan is *not* a plan to eradicate brucellosis." He could say that, not because he doubted that this goal could be achieved by 2010, but because that's what the interagency plan stated. Still, if this wasn't a plan to eliminate brucellosis, then what was the plan?

Defining Success

Campaign goals may be set mostly to give people a kick in the pants, to use Governor Geringer's phrase. According to the 1998 study by the National Research Council, "Total eradication of brucellosis as a goal is more a statement of principle than a workable program at present; neither sufficient information nor technical capability is available to implement a brucellosis-eradication program in the GYA."[3] However, the repeated harping on the goal of brucellosis eradication by 2010 can seem alarming because of the possible consequences. As the absence of any progress persists, increasing demands may be made that it's time to bring out the big guns.

"If you don't define eradication as the goal," Geringer stated, "I don't know how you define success." But eradication is not the definition of success for wild bison. Brucellosis they can live with; intensive management could mean eradicating all that makes them wild. And how does one define the "free-ranging bison" that the GYIBC has agreed to sustain? For many people the idea that bison are "free ranging" within the 2.2 million acres of Yellowstone National Park seems freedom enough. The metaphor of the six blind men describing an elephant comes to mind: the different sides to the brucellosis debate are not simply describing different aspects of the same animal; they seem to be describing different animals existing in parallel universes. Everyone may say, "We want to preserve free-ranging bison herds," but for some people this means that no bison should be allowed to leave Yellowstone alive, while for others it means that livestock grazing allotments on the surrounding national forests should be eliminated.

The fervor of the crusade by some ranchers against the Yellowstone bison has sometimes been attributed to their defeat in their biggest battle with the National Park Service, the one that brought wolves back to greater Yellowstone in 1995.[4] But livestock interests have been grumbling about brucellosis in Yellowstone almost since the Park Service helped eliminate wolves from the region six decades ago. Rob Hendry of the Wyoming Stockgrowers Association, who owns a cattle ranch east of greater Yellowstone, began his speech at the 2002 symposium by acknowledging that he was mostly repeating what had been said by other livestock representatives on previous occasions. As it appeared in the proceedings, his text was nearly identical to that of the 1994 symposium, including the statement that the total number of cattle and calves in the 22 counties of the GYA as of

January 1, 1993, was 1,066,000.[5] But as of January 1, 2002, according to USDA data, the total number of cattle and calves in those counties had dropped 16 percent. Real estate in greater Yellowstone was becoming more valuable when occupied by human residents than by livestock.

Other parts of Hendry's text repeated from 1994 suggested that little had changed in the eyes of the livestock industry. "The protective stance toward diseased bison taken by the Gallatin National Forest around West Yellowstone and the nonchalant attitude of Targhee National Forest toward diseased bison migrating through occupied forest cattle allotments around Island Park indicate the true lack of concern for the livestock industry or human health." As in 1994 the text noted, "Many good resource personnel have retired and have been replaced by individuals sympathetic to the preservationist cause."[6] Apparently it was still not possible to be both a good resource person and sympathetic to preservation issues.

Feed the Elk, Kill the Bison

Despite the formation of the GYIBC, the regulatory agencies of Idaho, Montana, and Wyoming were unable to present a united front against their common enemy, the roaming wild bison and its enabler, the National Park Service. They developed lines of attack that appeared contradictory because despite their common boundaries and share in the wildlife of greater Yellowstone, the states have different ways of managing the bison and elk that leave the Park Service's jurisdiction.[7] Less than half of the elk found in Yellowstone and Grand Teton during the summer may remain in those parks all year long. Wyoming has responsibility for about 63,000 elk in greater Yellowstone during the winter and feeds them to help keep them alive until spring. Once upon a time, that many elk may have survived the winter on Wyoming's windswept plains without human assistance, but that was before settlers moved into the foothills and valleys of the Rocky Mountains, through which the elk migrated from higher ranges in the fall. In 1909 Wyoming legislators appropriated $5,000 to feed several thousand elk that were raiding ranchers' haystacks in Jackson Hole. They thought that would be simpler and less expensive than reimbursing ranchers for the pilfered hay as state law required.

Ninety years later, Wyoming was spending $1.5 million to maintain 23 feedlots for up to 25,000 elk from December to March on state, federal, and private land outside Grand Teton National Park. On some feedgrounds more than half of the elk tested have been seropositive, but the only elk killed because of brucellosis have been those removed for research purposes. The presence of this unnaturally large elk population has meant that Wyoming officials cannot join Montana's tirade against the wild bison, or object that 4,000 bison is more than the available habitat can support, or insist that any bison that leave the park should be removed because some have been exposed to brucellosis.

Ranchers who sold hay to the feedgrounds so the elk wouldn't steal it were the first beneficiaries of the program, but it grew over the years with widespread public support. In bureaucratic parlance the large elk herds "provide a variety of non-consumptive and consumptive benefits to local economies throughout western Wyoming."[8] People do not like to see starving elk, and although they are called "elk ghettos" by their detractors, the feedgrounds help keep elk away from cattle and keep more elk alive through the winter so that more are available to be shot by hunters the following fall, in what critics refer to as the "Feed 'em, breed 'em, and bleed 'em" approach to elk management.

Elk license fees (up to $38 for residents, $200 for nonresidents) cover only part of the cost of winter feeding, but the Wyoming Game and Fish Department estimated that with the trickle-down effect, each elk killed by a hunter generates $4,000 in economic activity in the state, or a total of $88 million for an annual harvest of 22,000 elk by 57,000 hunters.[9] That is only a small part of all tourism-related revenues in Wyoming, but hunters help extend the tourist season into the fall and spend money important to rural communities where the agricultural economy has declined. Wyoming cattle production has dropped 17 percent since its peak in 1975.

Hunting is also important in Montana, which has responsibility for about 49,000 greater Yellowstone elk each winter. But Montana has never sponsored wildlife feeding and prohibits it on private land. The state has been able to sustain a large elk population without artificial feeding by making adequate winter range available to elk. During the last five decades, more than 160,000 acres north of Yellowstone have been designated as wildlife habitat through the combined efforts of the Rocky Mountain Elk Foundation, National Park Service, U.S. Forest Service, and Montana Fish, Wildlife and Parks. This has been done primarily by purchasing private land, but also through land trades, leasing, and conservation easements.

Idaho straddles the 45-degree meridian that lies halfway between the equator and the north pole and that separates the elk management policies of Montana and Wyoming. It has the shortest boundary with Yellowstone National Park and the smallest share of the greater Yellowstone elk population, generally no more than 6,000 in the winter. By 1990 Idaho had acquired more than 17,000 acres that are "managed exclusively for elk," and the state leases nearly 12,000 acres for that purpose. Idaho elk were considered brucellosis free until 1998, when more than 800 were fed at four sites to deter their foraging on private land. Testing indicated that about a third of these elk were seropositive. The Idaho Game and Fish Department reduced its winter feeding program and adopted a policy to "provide emergency feed for big game animals only during those periods of critical stress," rather than "a sustaining program which would carry larger game populations than the range can normally support."[10] But differing opinions about what constitutes "critical stress" and "normal" game populations have left room for feedgrounds.

In April 2002 brucellosis was detected in seven vaccinated cows in Idaho with "very, very strong evidence that the transmission occurred from elk to cattle in a wild setting," according to Rob Hendry. This met no one's definition of success. To make sure that Idaho did not lose its brucellosis-free designation, State Veterinarian Hillman saw to it that the entire herd of 110 cattle was slaughtered and that 46 other herds in five states were checked for animals that might have shared pasture or had contact with the infected herd. More than 1,000 of these cattle were tested that spring and again the following fall, and all tested seronegative.

The reason that elk were feeding near that cattle herd is that the cattle owner put food out for them every winter. The situation therefore fell short of transmission "in a wild setting," but some wildlife advocates thought that it was better to have elk than bison blamed for transmission from wildlife to cattle, since the elk's larger population and more powerful constituencies would ordain the futility of a livestock-style test-and-slaughter program for wildlife. But this is a wonderland where the cattle owner was compensated by the USDA so that she could buy a new cattle herd. The state of Idaho built a fence to keep elk away from her cattle and hazed elk past the area the following fall "to hopefully reestablish the natural migration down the canyon," and livestock interests used the incident as a smoking gun with which to shoot the wild bison.[11] "This infection points to the fact that vaccination alone will not work," Hendry said. "We will have to use all the known methods of vaccination and test and removal of all infected animals to get free of brucellosis."

Turning a Problem into Its Solution

Some hunters defend feedlots because letting animals starve is immoral and a waste of resources, while other people consider it a waste of resources to feed elk that are destined to become a hunting statistic. Most environmentalists regard feedgrounds as a political compromise of no benefit to wild elk. Even if they did not serve as incubators for disease, artificial concentrations of wildlife would be environmentally incorrect because they alter the animals' feeding habits and migratory patterns. They interfere in the process of natural selection, favoring elk who thrive on feedgrounds rather than in the wild, and they habituate elk to the presence of humans, a species sometimes fatally armed with guns or automobiles. But it was the traditional hunter's point of view that led the Wyoming legislature to make an unsuccessful attempt to collect $1.32 million ($4,000 per elk) from the federal government as compensation for the estimated 330 elk that were eliminated in 2002 by greater Yellowstone's reintroduced wolf population.[12]

In the 1970s, after the number of its feedlots peaked at 56, Wyoming sought to get some elk off the dole by eliminating some sites, shortening the winter feeding period, and increasing the quantity and quality of winter range available to elk. However, the primary objectives of Wyoming's feedground program have been to "provide nutritional supplement for wintering elk that frequent elk feedgrounds" and "minimize damage conflicts on adjacent private lands."[13] Minimizing "damage conflicts" meant that snowmobiles and aircraft haze elk away from cattle feeding sites. When this does not work, "special depredation hunting seasons are employed to remove problem animals." Terry Kreeger of the Wyoming Game and Fish Department explained that winter feeding of elk in western Wyoming may never be eliminated "due to biological and political ramifications"—that is, the reduction in elk numbers that it would entail and the prospect that some reduction would occur through starvation. "It will take decades, if ever, to replace all the historical elk winter range lost to human occupation," Kreeger said.[14] Yet the time it would take to replace all the historical winter range that bison have lost has not figured in GYIBC discussions. Minimizing "damage conflicts" with "problem bison" has often meant killing them.

Although Wyoming's feedground elk have received more than 53,000 vaccinations since 1984, the vaccine is widely regarded as a placebo that serves only political purposes, to give the appearance that something is being done about the problem. The U.S. Fish and Wildlife Service barred the state of Wyoming from vaccinating elk on the National Elk Refuge until a change in political climate under the George W. Bush administration led to the settlement of a lawsuit filed by Wyoming. Even those who believe the vaccination program may reduce the rate of abortion acknowledge that it could not eliminate brucellosis from elk. But the rationale seems to be that, given that the feedgrounds are already established, that they are the best way to minimize the risk of transmission to cattle because they help segregate the elk and make it possible to approach thousands of them with a gun that shoots vaccine bullets.

"People in Wyoming would rather live with brucellosis than have less elk," explained Barry Reiswig, manager of the National Elk Refuge, in 1997. "Then we better get off this horse," said John Mundinger of Montana Fish, Wildlife and Parks, referring to the GYIBC intention to eradicate the disease. "I'm ready," replied Reiswig.[15] Seven years later Reiswig was still the refuge manager responsible for overseeing a feeding and vaccination program that he opposed, and was still trying to work from within the system for change. He has described the refuge program of feeding elk and bison as a "giant house of cards on the verge of collapse." If chronic wasting disease, which has become endemic in deer in southeast Wyoming, spread to feedground elk, nothing could be done to halt major population losses.

In December 2003 brucellosis was detected in a vaccinated cattle herd near Pinedale, Wyoming, adjacent to the Muddy Creek feedground, which accommodates up to 600 elk during the winter. In February, after the disease was found in six vaccinated cows that had come from in the Pinedale herd, Wyoming lost its brucellosis-free status. The owner of the Pinedale herd complained that the Wyoming Game and Fish Department had not done enough to prevent the spread of the disease, but he also blamed wolves, which he said were forcing elk into cattle grazing areas.[16] The loss of the state's brucellosis-free status meant that about 330,000 cattle would have to be tested for exposure to brucellosis, with the cost to cattle owners partly subsidized by state and federal funds. In June the testing turned up brucellosis in a vaccinated cow in a herd near Jackson that had grazed near an elk feedground. In October the testing revealed four seropositive cows in a herd that had had contact with the Jackson herd. The owners of the affected herds had most of their cattle slaughtered rather than face the expense of quarantine.[17]

The Buffalo Field Campaign Is Their Shepherd

The EIS for bison management in Montana and Yellowstone contained many projections about the number of bison dead and alive under each alternative, but what would happen after the plan went into effect would depend on the actual behavior of the weather, the bison, and the people responsible for carrying out the plan. On both the northern and western fronts the winter of 2000–01 was relatively quiet. Along the west boundary the Montana Department of Livestock's count of hazed bison was 415, but only 14 were captured. The nine that tested seronegative were released and allowed to remain outside the park until mid-May, five seropositive bison were sent to slaughter, and one was shot because he could be neither captured nor hazed into the park.

In the spring of 2002, however, hundreds of bison headed west out of the park. With the late winter count at more than 3,000, the state of Montana could have sent bison to slaughter without trying to haze them into the park or testing them. However, the Department of Livestock tested 129 bison, sent 66 seropositive bison to slaughter, and released the rest. Then, on April 18, when the number leaving the park was still increasing, 133 bison were sent to slaughter without testing. Three bison were shot outside the park because they could be neither captured nor hazed into the park.

Despite the Department of Livestock's leniency in carrying out the interagency plan, it was the target of the usual jibes in the press and from the Buffalo Field Campaign, an organization that regards the boundary control effort as the wildlife equivalent of ethnic cleansing. Seven members were arrested in March, including a man who had chained himself and 50-gallon barrels filled with concrete to a gate on the road to a capture facility. Four women were charged with disorderly conduct, obstructing a police officer, and resisting arrest after locking themselves together in a state livestock office in Helena.

The Buffalo Field Campaign has used public education and civil disobedience to get its message out since 1997. To cover expenses, feed volunteers, and pay the rent, it relies on many small donations from sympathizers and occasional large contributions from celebrities like Bonnie Raitt and Green-leaning companies like Patagonia. Its headquarters outside West Yellowstone is run like a military camp where alcohol and drugs are forbidden. Buffalo Field Campaign videotape distributed to news media in 1999 showed cowboys from the Montana Department of Livestock on horse-back and snowmobiles driving bison uphill to exhaustion and forcing them to leap barbed-wire fences. Even those not moved by the sight of an injured young bull struggling to stand up as the other bison nudge him from the snow with their heads might suspect that the state wranglers were having a whale of a good time at the bison's expense. "It would be more humane to shoot the animals," declared one animal rights activist, because hazing "uses up energy that they need to survive the winter."[18] But when righteous members of the Buffalo Field Campaign escort bison back into the park through the valley of the shadow of death, they call it shepherding. Armed with cameras to bear witness to atrocities by government employees, these activists try to provide a human shield for the bison in the presence of their enemies.

According to founder Michael Mease, more than 1,700 people from across the United States and several foreign countries have joined the Buffalo Field Campaign for short or long terms of duty, but that number may include many of what the Department of Livestock would consider repeat offenders. While tree sitters in old-growth forests of the Pacific Northwest have come and gone, the Buffalo Field Campaign has sustained one of the longest environmental protests in U.S. history.[19]

It Could Be Ugly

"Two beloved buffalo were sent to the slaughterhouse this morning," the Buffalo Field Campaign reported at its website on December 6, 2002. This was the same day that APHIS met with state and federal officials in Billings to "begin steps to erase brucellosis" from "bison and elk in and around Yellowstone National Park," according to the *Billings Gazette*, overlooking the fact such efforts had begun decades ago.[20] The real story was that APHIS had a burr under its saddle because after all these years greater Yellowstone still did not have a plan to eradicate brucellosis in wildlife; the existing piecemeal efforts were limited to reducing the risk of brucellosis trans-mission. APHIS officials wanted the Department of the Interior to commit to a more aggressive eradication program. Perhaps they thought that with Bush administration appointees at the helm, the Department of the Interior would be more tractable than it had been in the past. Bob Lee, chairman of the Montana Board of Livestock, reminded the group that the presence of brucellosis in greater Yellowstone posed a threat to both the safety of the public and Montana's livestock industry as a potential weapon of bioterrorism.

"We know the destination. The question is: What route do we want to take?" asked Bill Hawks, who headed the USDA's delegation. To support her claim that a different route was needed than the current road map, Valerie Ragan of APHIS said, "I don't know anybody who's really happy with the bison management program." But that was to be expected; bureaucratic compromise is characterized by an absence of happiness. If anyone were really happy with the status quo, someone else would be filing a lawsuit. Instead, the state officials vented their obvious frustration over the lack of progress in eliminating brucellosis from greater Yellowstone wildlife. Jim Logan, the Wyoming state veterinarian, described how he had once castrated a 900-pound boar hog with only the rudimentary tools available, and he called for using the same approach in Yellowstone. "The process would involve lots of squealing and blood—it could be ugly—but we can get the job done with what we have now!" Ragan, who seemed averse to ugliness, said that "technical solutions" developed through scientific research were needed, and she recommended that vaccines specifically developed for bison and elk be used in conjunction with "alternative management strategies" for these animals. "It's pretty obvious that if we're going to do anything to get rid of the disease long-term, we're going to have to make some herd-management adjustments for a time, then we can go back to natural regulation or whatever the park thinks is best." She did not specify which "herd-management adjustments" she had in mind.

"I think the time is finally right to eradicate brucellosis from Yellowstone National Park," Governor Judy Martz told the Montana Stockgrowers Association after the APHIS meeting. "I'm confident that we've finally got an administration at the federal level and a Park Superintendent at Yellowstone who will help us do just that. Thank God for President Bush. . . . In brucellosis, in water rights, in our tax policy and in our budget, we're going to keep fighting for your industry . . . because your industry represents all that is right about Montana."[21] For those doing research on vaccines, the next steps might be clear—enough time and funding may eliminate all disease—but the next steps for interagency cooperation remained hazy. Representatives of the Interior Department declined to be corralled. Yellowstone superintendent Suzanne Lewis dodged by pointing out that representatives of the park's associated tribes were not at the table and, as sovereign governmental entities, their concerns should be part of the decision-making process.

As the winter of 2002–03 wore on, the state of Montana appeared to be rattling its sabers in the brucellosis eradication campaign. "We have substantially more buffalo than Yellowstone National Park has the resources to carry," stated Todd O'Hair, an adviser to Governor Martz, on January 26.[22] "We could see a lot of buffalo come out of the park, and if that's the case, we'll have to take them." The Buffalo Field Campaign saw more volunteers arriving every day, including Randall Mark, who had just been released from jail after a two-month sentence for obstructing bison-hazing operations. "Randall is doing well and expresses his thanks to all who phoned the jail in response to his 38-day hunger strike for vegan food."[23] At a press conference, Governor Martz was asked how she could justify spending millions on killing wild bison when Montana had a budget deficit and "a growing tourist economy dependent on wildlife, not livestock." Martz responded, "If you really care about the buffalo, you will help us to get the Park to control the numbers so they aren't coming out. . . . I don't want to kill even one, or send them to slaughter. I want them vaccinated. . . . It's been nine or ten years we've been asking for that."[24]

On the *New York Times* op-ed page on February 8, former Montana ranch wife Judy Blunt kept alive the misinformation that "half of Yellowstone's bison test positive for brucellosis," when the test only provides evidence that the animals have been exposed to the disease. "Perhaps it's time to set aside sentimental fantasies and face the fact that the eradication of brucellosis in a wild herd will be impossible without invasive actions," she suggested. "Some people imagine we can get rid of 2,000 diseased bison while allowing the other 2,000 to repopulate the park. Dream on."[25] By overwhelming majorities, both houses of the Montana legislature passed a resolution urging the U.S. Departments of Agriculture and the Interior to expedite "alternative brucellosis elimination strategies."[26] The program envisioned by the Montana Stockgrowers Association, for which Representative Pat Wagman sponsored the resolution, would round up and test all Yellowstone bison over a five-year period, slaughter the seropositives, and vaccinate the seronegatives. Wagman noted that by eliminating brucellosis in bison, brucellosis in the region's elk would automatically disappear.[27] Dream on.

In its often nightmarish tone, the Buffalo Field Campaign claimed that the federal government and the state of Montana were already developing a new plan for eradicating brucellosis that would call for "a massive program of capture, test, slaughter, and quarantine for bison, elk, and numerous other wildlife species" in and around the park. "The result would be the end of the Yellowstone bison and elk as free-roaming wild herds."[28] However, despite the posturing by the state of Montana, it was the National Park Service that sent the most bison to slaughter during the next two winters. These were the first bison to be captured in the north boundary zone since the winter of 1996–97. That could be because the winters had been relatively mild, or because the bison that tried to get past the northern border guard that bad, sad winter didn't live to tell their children about that route or didn't have anything good to say about it. A small number of bison had been hazed back into the park at the north boundary each year, and a small number had continued to use winter range where they could roam unmolested on the Gallatin National Forest east of the Yellowstone River.

Then early in 2003 about 80 bison crossed the Yellowstone River over the bridge in Gardiner and went up the Bear Creek drainage of Gallatin National Forest, where they were permitted to be. But most of the bison that left the park that winter remained west of the river, where they were not allowed. On February 26 park rangers on horseback escorted 223 bison loitering around the Gardiner school about ten miles back into the park. On March 2 more than 30 bison were herded into the park after they wandered onto private property north of the boundary. At least two of the cows had crossed the west boundary the previous winter; they still wore the radio collars they had received as participants in a research project on bison movements. Perhaps the ordeal they'd undergone there served as a deterrent from going west again, but which way these bison might have gone in 2004 will never be known. On March 3, as bison were continuing to leave the park, capture operations began at Stephens Creek. Because the late winter bison count was more than 3,000, the animals were killed first and tested for brucellosis later. In all, 231 bison were sent to slaughter over a four-day period in March, and 81,750 pounds of bison meat were sent to food banks, Indian tribes, schools, and other nonprofit organizations.[29]

The Park Service Culls Again

The agreement with Montana did not require the Park Service to send all those bison to slaughter without testing them, but the Park Service did what seemed most sensible. Hazing efforts had become ineffective and unsafe for both the bison and park staff. Hardened layers of snow made it difficult for

Bison in chute at Stephens Creek prior to having blood samples removed for testing, 2003. Courtesy of Yellowstone National Park.

the bison to find food, and they could not be prevented from crossing the boundary at night. Furthermore, little would be gained by holding sero-negative bison in the corral until they could be released later in the spring. Although it provides a larger genetic pool for future bison generations to draw on and insurance in case of a severe winter, under the terms of the interagency plan, a large population makes bison management more difficult and more lethal over the long run. Every bison kept alive at the park boundary in the spring could mean one more that would have to be captured or hazed back into the park the following year—or two more if the animal were pregnant. Both the bison and public reaction would be more easily managed if bison were removed at a steady rate rather than with a huge reduction during a severe winter. However, the removal of untested bison had no more effect on brucellosis in the herd than did bison culling in the 1960s.

When the interagency plan was agreed to, it was anticipated that the Park Service would be able to release up to 100 seronegative bison at Stephens Creek when a grazing lease expired on the Royal Teton Ranch in 2002. The Church Universal and Triumphant, which had fallen on hard times, had accepted $13 million from the U.S. Forest Service in exchange

A bison held in place for
testing at the Stephens Creek
corral, 2004. Courtesy of
Yellowstone National Park.

for nearly half its land and a conservation easement on a portion of the
remainder. These 6,000 acres were expected to provide habitat for wildlife
that would include bison, but after the grazing lease expired, the church
began grazing 105 of its own cows on the land, which prevented the Park
Service from exercising its option to release seronegative bison.

Nearly all of the bison that approached the north boundary in 2003
came from the park interior, not from the northern herd, most of which
remained in the park. The same was true the following year, but more bison
arrived, and the number captured by the Park Service more than doubled.
However, the number of bison that were killed increased only slightly
because the Park Service tested most of the captured bison and detained
198 that were seronegative. That left 207 seropositives and 58 untested
bison to be sent to slaughter. The fenced area at Stephens Creek had been
enlarged to encompass about 100 acres with two simulated creeks, but 200
bison was thought to be the maximum number that could be held there

humanely, assuming that it is humane to confine a wild animal for any length of time. The Buffalo Field Campaign described the testing procedure as "gruesome," with the bison held in place by a clamp over its head and its nose pinched by a metal ring.[30] Most of the bison seemed resigned to mill around the pen with numbered tags on their backs while their test results were checked, but some kicked up dust or noisily butted heads or the metal walls of the chute. To reduce the violence in the pens, mature bulls were sent to slaughter without testing, but cow number 18 was chased around by another cow, who hooked her with a horn and drove her against the wall. Number 18 fled again, now with a large area of red flesh bared where her hide was torn.[31]

Faced with melting snow, new forage, and the impending birth of calves, the Park Service opened the gate on April 8 and reported that "all 198 bison moved rapidly in a southern direction," further into the park.[32] But no one knew if they would be back again the next winter with their yearlings, or if they would be more resistant to capture the next time or more willing to enter a corral where food had been served the year before. If the migration toward the corral became an annual event, it would seem a throwback to the 1940s, when bison arrived at the Buffalo Ranch each winter for feeding.

Yellowstone managers wanted to test captured bison rather than send them all to slaughter as in the previous year, because despite doubts about the efficacy of the RB51 vaccine, they wanted to vaccinate the captured calves and yearlings that tested seronegative. Like the "brucellosis control" efforts in Yellowstone of the 1960s and the vaccination of elk at the feed-grounds, this may be considered a token effort made to placate the livestock interests. To determine if the vaccine were having any effect, at least some of the bison would have to be recaptured and tested again, but there were no plans for that. The vaccinated bison did receive ear tags, but they were not livestock-style bangle tags that would detract from the animals' appearance as wildlife. The markers were too inconspicuous to be seen unless the animal happened to be seen again in a squeeze chute.

To Haze or Not to Haze

In the same two years that the Park Service removed hundreds of bison at the north boundary, the Montana Department of Livestock was hazing with a vengeance at the west boundary. In its news releases, the DOL enumerated its "successful" hazing activities as evidence of the size of the problem. In

May 2004, when the Buffalo Field Campaign placed 278 "headstones" on the state capitol lawn in Helena in memory of the bison that had been killed that winter, a DOL spokeswoman suggested that they should do "1,246 happy faces" for the bison that had been "moved back into the park from the west boundary."

Given their forbearance in not sending those animals to slaughter, DOL personnel felt persecuted by the ceaseless vilification. "You never read, 'The DOL saved 300 buffalo today by hazing them back into the park,'" an employee complained to a reporter, who quoted him in the *Casper Star-Tribune*, where people would read it.[33] But many of those bison had been saved only to return another day for more hazing. When the DOL announced that over 1,600 bison had been "successfully moved back" into the park during the winter of 2002–03, it did not mean that half of the bison in the park had tried to leave; many bison were what the DOL considered repeat offenders, and some were still in the park but got caught in the roundup as exiting bison that had left the park were hazed further in. Despite its apparent effort to avoid having to capture bison, the DOL was still maligned in some circles because of its intolerance of bison outside the park.

DOL personnel sometimes set off explosive cracker rounds next to bison, sending them running in all directions. The profane verbal detonations that some Buffalo Field Campaign members fired at government employees trying to do their job did not further the activists' cause, and in April 2003, a federal judge rejected their lawsuit, which charged that the use of helicopters to haze bison was endangering three pairs of nesting bald eagles.[34] A stillborn bison calf was found outside the park later that month. "I can't imagine that running seven miles is conducive to a healthy birthing process," said a Buffalo Field Campaign member who attributed the death to the stress caused by hazing.[35] Testing of the birth site found viable *Brucella abortus* on the ground, and it was still there in the soil when it was checked again nearly a month later.[36]

However, the presence of the activists and their video cameras had a restraining effect on at least some government employees. In late spring, DOL and Park Service staff worked together to rescue a bison calf that had become stranded while crossing the Madison River. Then they ceased hazing operations early that day, leaving the exhausted calf with its mother and the rest of the bison group outside the park. The DOL captured a total of only 34 bison during the winters of 2002–03 and 2003–04, and not a single potentially bacteria-expelling cow was sent to slaughter or even captured outside the west boundary after February. According to the interagency plan, bison outside the west boundary were to be captured or shot after May 15 to ensure that no "contamination" remained when cattle arrived in June, but in 2003 the DOL kept hazing until the last bison returned to the park and stayed there on June 30. In 2004 the last two bulls outside the park were shot on June 21 after they moved onto private property.

The reason given by the Department of Livestock for its hazing frenzy was that the interagency plan calls for bison to be hazed back into the park if possible, and it was possible, so they were.[37] But the plan also states that if the bison count is more than 3,000, bison may be sent to slaughter without hazing or testing them first. After years of complaining about the need to reduce and vaccinate the park's bison population, Montana's reluctance to take the bulls and cows by the horns seemed so out of character that ulterior motives were suspected. Perhaps the DOL was dragging its feet on moving toward captive and remote bison vaccination, because those steps would, according to the interagency plan, compel Montana to permit up to 100 untested bison in the management zone outside the west boundary.

But at the GYIBC meeting in September 2004, it was the National Park Service that was berated for insufficient diligence. The ostensible reason was the Park Service's opposition to adopting a stronger commitment to brucellosis eradication in the statement of GYIBC objectives. However, that may be like saying that the ostensible reason for killing bison that leave Yellowstone is that some of them are infected with brucellosis. Many people are simply made uncomfortable by forces that seem impervious to their control. While for years the Park Service was chastised for being the "do nothing" agency in regard to brucellosis, now that it was doing something and carrying out the interagency plan—capturing and vaccinating bison, and testing methods of remote vaccination—the Park Service had undermined the state officials' demands for stronger intervention by the USDA. In addition, the discovery of brucellosis in three cattle herds in Wyoming and that state's loss of brucellosis-free status, for which bison leaving Yellowstone or Grand Teton could not be blamed, had increased the frustration and alarm among officials in all three states. In August, Interior Secretary Gale Norton received a copy of Wyoming governor Dave Freudenthal's letter to President Bush, "a former Governor of a state that faced the same situation" who could "appreciate the difficulties that Wyoming now confronts." Freudenthal attributed his state's livestock woes to "the large reservoir of brucellosis-infected elk and bison in the GYA."

Being mindful of the GYIBC's lofty goal of eliminating brucellosis from the GYA by 2010, I respectfully ask that you work with the Departments of Interior and Agriculture to ensure that this objective remains a federal priority. . . . By giving USDA-APHIS the tools and wherewithal to finish the task, we might not be too far from meeting our mutual goal of eradicating the disease. Implied in my optimism is the notion that all federal land management agencies, including the National Park Service . . . will be willing partners.[38]

The beneficent-sounding "Animal Health Protection Act," which the U.S. Congress passed in 2002 to increase the USDA's authority to manage livestock diseases and counter possible food contamination by terrorists, has been seen by some wildlife advocates as a Trojan horse that agriculture officials could use to round up Yellowstone bison for a test-and-slaughter program.[39] Although Robert Frost, former president of the United States Animal Health Association, did not share that goal, he acknowledged that some people at the USDA "would like nothing better than to bring the Park Service to its knees."[40]

Fetal Monitoring and Disappearance

In his letter to President Bush, Freudenthal explained the need for more federal funds for "livestock and wildlife vaccine research, wildlife management, testing and monitoring." In the interest of research, the interagency plan for Montana and Yellowstone encouraged bison to go forth and multiply by allowing some pregnant bison that were captured to live. In the past, pregnant bison were automatically sent to slaughter even if they tested seronegative, because pregnancy can awaken a latent infection. But in the spring of 2002 seronegative cows captured outside the west boundary were checked for pregnancy, and the death sentence of 18 was commuted in exchange for their participation in a research experiment. Each of the cows was equipped with a radio collar and a vaginal transmitter that was designed to be expelled when the calf was born, so that the researchers could determine when and where calving occurred and examine the birth site for bacteria.

The radio collar was used to track the cows almost daily until mid-June, and several times a week during the summer. Two of the bison wore Global Positioning System collars from which hourly location data could be downloaded to a computer via satellite, making it possible to determine how often and where the animals left and reentered the park. To ascertain pregnancy, the researchers used the low-tech and fallible method of inserting a gloved arm into the cow. Blood tests done after the cows were released indicated that two were actually seropositive and another was not actually pregnant. Of the 17 pregnant bison, 15 gave birth to viable calves without evidence of infected afterbirths. The two seropositive cows expelled transmitters but were not observed with calves, indicating that the pregnancies were probably aborted.[41]

In addition to permitting some bison to live that would otherwise be killed, using the vaginal transmitters enabled wildlife biologists to learn more about bison pregnancy. But this kind of intensive monitoring takes the "free" out of "free-roaming" in more ways than one. Although the brucellosis controversy has brought bad publicity to both the state of Montana and the National Park Service, it finally opened the federal spigot for funding bison management and research. For years Yellowstone managers had been requesting a budget increase so that they could monitor bison movements and brucellosis. In 1999 the park still had the equivalent of only one full-time wildlife biologist responsible for bison. Starting in 2001, when its annual congressional appropriation for ongoing operations was $25 million, Yellowstone received the $1.2 million supplement it requested to carry out its responsibilities under the new interagency bison management plan, and soon the park had the equivalent of seven full-time bison staff, plus the park rangers who help out when necessary with hazing and other boundary control operations. This was in addition to the amount spent on bison management by the state of Montana and APHIS, a total of about $3.5 million in 2003, and funding for academic and government scientists who are studying brucellosis in wild bison and ways to eradicate it, including a study to "evaluate the wound site characteristics of biobullets on bison."[42]

A research project suitably titled for Wonderland, the "Fetal Disappearance Study," was designed to find out how long aborted bison fetuses remain in the Yellowstone environment before disappearing as a result of scavenging and decomposition, and "how far a potentially infected fetus may be moved." During 11 weeks of the calving season in 2002 and 2003, about 70 disease-free bison fetuses from commercial herds were "deployed" at sites inside and outside the park boundary "where bison are known to egress." Data were collected by trained observers with binoculars and spotting scopes positioned 50 meters away, motion-sensitive radio transmitters, and motion-sensitive cameras. One-third of the fetuses in this experiment were moved at least two-tenths of a mile, and one was moved more than two miles, perhaps by a scavenger that wished to hoard the meat for itself or its kin. Most of the fetuses were scavenged in less than 16 days.[43] Although wildlife other than ungulates that consume the bacteria may become infected, they are considered "end hosts" that have no reasonable means of trans-mitting the disease to other animals.

The Fatal Attraction of Research Data

Even when money doesn't corrupt, it can affect priorities. Wildlife managers like to think of themselves as steadfast protectors of the nation's wildlife, and they generally are, although unlike the Humane Society, their primary mission is to protect the long-term welfare of species, not individual animals. But wildlife managers also have human instincts for adapting to oppor-tunities for professional achievement. As planned, the 15-year bison program for Yellowstone and Montana is one of the largest, most ambitious wildlife management efforts ever undertaken. The official justification that accom-panied Yellowstone's request for a budget increase described the program as a "globally precedent-setting operation." It calls for eventually quaran-tining some bison for years and developing the technology needed to remotely vaccinate as many calves and yearlings as possible each year.

As the human population grows and natural resources decline, pressure increases for human control over ecological processes, leading to what ecologists Crawford Holling and Gary Meffe call "the pathology of natural resource management."[44] Efforts to create a more stable and predictable environment reduce the range of natural variation in an ecosystem, including its biodiversity, which in turn reduces the system's resilience in the face of human-caused or other disturbances. The millions of dollars spent annually to put out forest fires and apply pesticides have created the conditions under which more dangerous fires and resistant pests have flourished. "Planet Management has become the dominant world view among scientists and policy-makers," Evan Eisenberg believes.

The finicky eye of God has been replaced with remote-sensing satellites that tell us, without moralizing, just where we stand. . . . What worries me about the Managers is that they like managing: they have trouble keeping

To learn how long aborted bison calves may remain a possible source of brucellosis exposure before they decompose or are consumed by scavengers, bison fetuses obtained from commercial herds were placed near the park boundary and monitored by human observers at a distance and by motion-sensitive cameras up close. Courtesy of Montana Fish, Wildlife and Parks.

their hands off. Their attitude toward nature is roughly that of aeronautic engineers who have been given a chance to examine a captured enemy aircraft. They want to learn how it works and how to fly it.[45]

In 2004, 22 Yellowstone bison were wearing radio collars so managers can learn more about where they go and when they go there, but that is a trifle compared to the intensively monitored wolf population. Thirty percent of the wolves whose territory lies at least partly within Yellowstone are briefly captured so that they may be equipped with radio collars. The routine tracking of such a large portion of a "free-roaming" wolf population flies in the face of most concepts of wildlife and seems downright un-American. If wild animals do not live free or die, living by their wits instead of under the long arm of radio frequencies, pitting their wiles against those of the rancher, the hunter, and others who have something to gain by seeing them dead, then what is the point? Doug Smith, head of the wolf management office at Yellowstone, acknowledges that this monitoring is done not only because wolves can cause problems outside the park but also

The targeted area on the carcass of a bison yearling at a Montana ranch is marked for practicing rifle-propelled vaccination, 2003. Courtesy of Yellowstone National Park.

A park employee practices shooting at a bison at a Montana ranch in 2003 with the kind of biodegradable bullet that can be used to inject a vaccine. Courtesy of Yellowstone National Park.

because the opportunity to learn more about wolves, to collect more data, is too good to pass up.

The results of this human tendency can be seen in all areas of endeavor, and Yellowstone may be no more exempt from it in the future than it was in 1877, when Superintendent Norris wanted to capture the wild bison and domesticate them, or than the grasslands of North America were when the Indians burned them to improve the bison hunting. Even the most kindly brain surgeon who believes that he must first "do no harm" may be attracted by the opportunity to push the edge of what is scientifically possible. And once a hospital has invested in the latest technology and promoted itself as being on the forefront of brain surgery advances, the momentum created by the concentration of expertise may result in its being applied even in situations where it does not improve the patient's quality of life. The U.S. Geological Survey planned to spend more than $500,000 to "net gun" 60 bison a year in the park for three years in order to collect blood samples that would help determine whether the bison that had been sent to slaughter were genetically a random sample of those that remained in the park. But the project was called off after four bison died during capture operations in the first two days. According to a report by those monitoring the study, two of the bison, goaded to flee by the proximity of the helicopter, were "going too fast" when the nets were dropped, "flipping them and breaking their necks."[46]

A Benefit Too Elusive to Capture

When park managers renounced wildlife culling in the 1960s in favor of natural regulation, the origin of the brucellosis that infected bison and elk was still a matter of debate. In retrospect, the belief that the bacteria causing brucellosis in Yellowstone wildlife might be native to the area seems to reflect wishful rather than scientific thinking, but it persisted for many years as a possibility. The absence of *Brucella abortus* in the New World until it arrived in Old World livestock cannot be proven absolutely. However, the lack of archeological and historical evidence of brucellosis in wildlife or undulant fever in American Indians eventually led to a consensus that the bacteria had come from Europe. Mary Meagher's 1994 publication, "On the Origin of Brucellosis in Bison of Yellowstone National Park," documented the reasons why she had come to accept its nonnative source.[47]

Although this made brucellosis in wildlife more difficult for park managers to discount, it provided a new rationale for wildlife advocates opposed to drastic measures. If livestock had caused the problem, it seemed unfair to penalize Yellowstone bison by slaughtering them, especially since the disease had no long-term effect on the bison population. However, livestock officials turned this reasoning on its head. According to Valerie Ragan of APHIS, it is precisely because brucellosis is a foreign disease that we would have to dedicate ourselves to eliminating it in Yellowstone bison even if they did not pose a threat to livestock. As a veterinarian Ragan speaks compassionately of the infected bison she has seen with abscesses on their testicles.

To a wildlife biologist, however compassionate, disease-causing bacteria may be regarded as a kind of predator, a process by which the fittest are selected; it is not necessarily something to be eradicated. As a nonnative invader, *Brucella abortus* is unwelcome in the park, but Yellowstone has many nonnative plants and animals and cannot launch a crusade against them all. Park managers must choose their battles, figure out what can realistically be accomplished with the means at hand and minimal collateral damage to the environment, and target the aliens that are most threatening to native species—the knapweed that is displacing native grasses, for example, and the lake trout that prey on the native cutthroat trout. But in the case of neither knapweed nor lake trout do park managers have expectations of eradication in the foreseeable future, only of reducing the impact of the invasion. After years of intensive gill netting in Yellowstone Lake, progress appears to have been made in reducing the lake trout population, but now the native cutthroat trout is being assaulted by whirling disease, to which lake trout seem immune.

The European parasite that causes whirling disease, *Myxobolus cerebralis*, has infected hundreds of streams in the United States, including some of Montana's most prized trout streams. No remedy is known—the parasite is too tiny to be caught in a gill net, and there are too many hundreds of thousands of fish in Yellowstone to vaccinate, even if a safe and effective vaccine were found. But without an immediate solution to the problem, John Varley, a Yellowstone manager and an avid fisherman, is philosophical about the loss and optimistic that the range of natural variation in the Yellowstone ecosystem will enable some native trout to survive. Some of the park's waters are likely to be too cold to suit *Myxobolus cerebralis*, and some native fish are likely to outmaneuver it, perhaps by changing their spawning schedule.

So if some Yellowstone bison have irritated testicles, that may be a relatively minor nuisance in the grand scheme of things. These bison are tough; they were built to last. That's what makes wildlife special, what makes it wild; these animals deal with life in the raw in a way that most people have become removed from. The brucellosis eradication campaign was launched in the 1930s because people were getting undulant fever from drinking raw milk and because the government was looking for an excuse to pay ranchers for reducing their herds during a period of drought and economic depression. Neither of these rationales pertain any more. Few diseases can be managed for zero risk, even those that are fatal to humans. The only contagious disease to have been eliminated in the last century is smallpox, whose easily identified blisters made it possible to quickly quarantine the victim and immunize those who had been exposed. Commenting on the long campaign to eradicate polio, Atul Guwande of the Harvard School of Public Health noted that even if it succeeds,

> it is entirely possible that more lives would be saved in the future if the money were spent on, say, building proper sewage systems or improving basic health services. More and more money is spent chasing the few hundred cases that keep popping up. Stopping the very last case of polio might cost as much as two hundred million dollars. No cost-benefit calculus will tell us whether all that money is well spent.[48]

Rabies poses a far greater risk to human health than does brucellosis, but no one has called for a national campaign to try to eradicate it; instead, the risk is managed to minimize the consequences. Brucellosis continues to be a health issue for livestock, but most of the costs associated with it result from the eradication program requirements. We can use scientific research to predict how long *Brucella abortus* remains viable on the ground after it has been shed by a bison, and economic analysis to predict whether the expense of vaccinating wild bison is likely to save livestock owners money over the long run, but neither science nor economics can tell us whether allowing wild bison to roam outside Yellowstone National Park is more valuable than reducing the risk of brucellosis transmission, property damage, and human injury.

It is sometimes said that brucellosis in Yellowstone bison is not about science; it's about grass and which animals get to eat it and who gets to decide which animals eat it. Although differing opinions about land use cannot be ignored, any effort to determine whether the right tack is being taken in regard to brucellosis in Yellowstone bison must consider the question of proportion, of whether the financial and environmental costs involved can be justified in terms of the benefits received. Using the methods at hand to eliminate brucellosis from Yellowstone wildlife could have unintended and undesirable consequences, as Alice discovered when she solved the problem of getting through a door much smaller than herself by swallowing the unknown contents of a bottle labeled *"Drink me."*

PART FOUR

LIVING IN THE MODERN WORLD

Men who have been engaged in cutting ice for the hotels . . . report seeing one fine buffalo between the Upper and Lower Basins, where he took to the road just ahead of their horses, keeping in sight and being sometimes only fifty yards off for half a mile, until he turned off on another road. He did not appear much alarmed, considering probably that he had a perfect right to the use of the Government roads, and preferred traveling them to the rough work in the timber.

—Thomas Elwood Hofer,
"Winter in the Park," *Field and Stream* (1888)

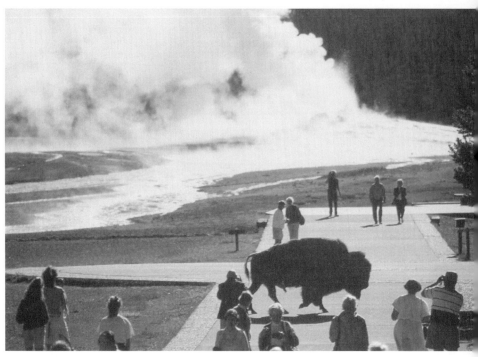

A lone bull distracts tourists who have come to see Old Faithful. Courtesy of Jeff Henry.

CHAPTER 11

Confronting People and Predators

Bears have been the most lethal animal in Yellowstone for humans, causing five known deaths in the park's history, and encounters with grizzly and black bears resulted in an average of 45 human injuries a year during the 1960s.[1] But the number of "problem" bears declined after the park began enforcing rules against bear feeding and other incitements to bear violence. As the bison population grew to exceed that of bears in the 1970s, bison caused more human injuries than any other animal in the park. A study of park records from 1980 to 1999 found that bison had charged and made contact with humans 79 times.[2] In 61 of the incidents an injury was reported, compared with 24 injuries caused by bears during the same period. Not all of these injuries were inflicted directly by the animal; some occurred when the person fell while trying to flee. All but one of the bison-caused injuries occurred in developed areas or along roads, where people are apt to assume they are safe from the perils of the wilderness. This contrasts with bear-inflicted injuries; nearly all of them have occurred in backcountry areas during the last 25 years.

The bison's rap sheet is bad, partly because people tend to think of bison not as wild animals but a kind of cattle, an impression reinforced by the bison's usually impassive behavior and the fact that most bison herds in the United States today *are* a kind of livestock. People often expect wildlife to either flee or become aggressive if approached too closely, when in fact both responses are those of a frightened animal and do not necessarily indicate wildness.[3]

During the 1990s, 41 reports were made of incidents in which bison charged and made contact with humans. In those cases where an estimate was attempted, the average distance between the bison and the person when the bison charged was 28 feet. In 11 cases the bison tossed the person in the air with his horns; one man flipped while being hurled 15 feet and landed in a tree. A photographer trying for the best angle was lying on the ground when he was trampled by a bison who then sat on him. The most common injury was a puncture wound to the thigh from a bison's horn. Four people were knocked to the ground by a bison without being injured. The persons attacked were about equally divided between males and females and included small children.

In 10 of the 41 cases, the person was either trying to photograph or be photographed with the bison just before the charge occurred. In two cases, people were throwing sticks or stones at the animal; in another, a woman was reportedly trying to feed grass to a bison. But some incidents were surprise attacks in which the people were either unaware of the bison's presence or had no reason to think that the bison was aware of theirs—a woman exiting a building who did not see the bison behind a fire escape, a woman in a telephone booth (the bison butted the booth), a family at a picnic table 100 yards from a wallowing bison. In three cases the bison warmed up by butting trees first, but otherwise the bison gave little or no warning that an assault was imminent.

Immediately after the charge, the bison usually moved away and began grazing as if nothing had happened, but in three cases the bison stood over his fallen conquest for a minute or two, and sometimes the bison briefly engaged in tree thrashing, snorting, foot stomping, or rolling on the ground as if to vent excess exasperation. In one case the bison butted a woman back to the ground when she tried to get up. During an unusually long encounter that lasted about an hour, a bison charged a snowmobile and chased it four times for distances of up to 50 yards. In another case a bison charged but stopped short of making contact with a group of backcountry skiers. In only one of the reports that specified gender was the charging animal said to be a cow. She had a newborn calf nearby when she charged a jogger, who dove into the dirt, where the bison struck her on the head and back with her hooves.

Bison are known to have been responsible for two human deaths in the park's history—both of them men who approached a bison in pursuit of a photograph, one in 1971 and the other in 1983. In 1984 Gladys Hoffman from Waco, Texas, was charged by a bison in the Bridge Bay Campground after reluctantly complying with her brother's request to move closer to the animal as she posed for a photo. The bison gored the 67-year-old woman below her rib cage and again in her buttocks, throwing her about 15 feet and leaving her with fractures to her ribs, back, and wrist. She later claimed she was 65 feet from the bison when it charged; a witness said she had been no more than 15 feet away. In the human form of charging, Hoffman charged the Department of the Interior with negligence in failing to provide adequate warning of the danger, sued for $100,000, and then three days later asked that $200,000 be awarded to her husband for loss of consortium.[4]

The following summer, as the Hoffman case was working its way through the legal system, a park ranger shot a bison responsible for two goring incidents at the Bridge Bay Campground. As her physical and emotional distress continued, Hoffman raised her claim to $1.5 million, but a U.S. district court ruled against her in June 1987. The Park Service tried aversive conditioning that year to move bison away from developed areas. The "thumper gun" used on bears sometimes had little or no effect on bison, but five bulls stayed away after two treatments with a tractor and a shotgun filled with birdshot. Later that summer, after 25 visitors had been charged by bison, a dog trainer was authorized to use a border collie to try to herd a bison away from Fishing Bridge. According to the ranger log, "Procedure went well, bison was moved as planned and collie was not injured."[5]

When Wolves Prey on Bison

They follow in the wake of the buffalo in bands of several hundreds, waiting an opportunity to strangle some small calf or mired grown animal. When hard pressed by hunger they will attack a full-sized cow or bull and by dint of great perseverance torment and tire the animal to death.
—Edward Denig, describing North American wolves
in the nineteenth century[6]

The extinction of larger predators such as the dire wolf and the saber-toothed tiger left the gray wolf as the bison's most significant foe until humans became numerous enough and suitably armed to affect bison numbers. The appearance and behavior of bison in Yellowstone today may therefore have been shaped partly by wolves that trailed them thousands of years before the park was established. The bison may have evolved into a smaller, more agile animal with shorter horns in order to be fleeter of foot or better able to defend itself as part of a closely bunched herd. The six-foot horn spread and large appetite of a *Bison latifrons* would have required it to keep its distance from similarly attired bison, and the herd that stays together is less likely to be preyed on together.

Wolves subsist almost entirely on meat, either animals they kill or ones that die from another cause. By evolving a social organization that supported hunting in packs, wolves were able to expand their food options, prey on larger animals, and better compete for carcasses against other scavengers. Wolves usually kill large animals by biting the hind legs until the animal cannot run or defend itself, but bison are the wolf's most difficult prey. They can outdistance wolves on most terrain, galloping at 30 miles per hour for at least half a mile and continuing to run for another 10 miles without resting.[7] Dale Guthrie has described a herd of running bison as "a windmill of powerful hoofs too formidable for an easy bite by wolves";[8] but a running calf may offer an easier bite than a stationary calf whose mother is using her horns to ward off an attack. Therefore, running is not necessarily the bison's best defense or the most fuel-efficient strategy. A bison may use up to ten times as much energy running as standing still, and that may be more fuel than the animal consumes in a day.[9]

Wolves can attain speeds of up to 35 miles an hour, but only for short sprints; to get a bison, they must sometimes slowly wear down a herd until they can overcome an animal weakened by illness, injury, or age. If the wolves drive them onto a frozen surface where the bison lose their footing, or into crusted snow in which their sharp hooves sink, bison may be overtaken by the large-pawed wolves. Although the adult bison in a herd often defend a calf, cows may abandon their own calves and run rather than risk injury themselves. But even a calf can come at a high price for a pack of wolves. In Canada six wolves were observed in pursuit of a six-month-old calf for eight miles before they could stop it.[10] In encounters between wolves and bison observed in Yellowstone, predation occurs more often when bison run than when they stand their ground.[11] A running herd may expose its vulnerable members, or it could be that the bison that don't flee in a panic are those that are more capable of defending themselves.

But the bison's confrontational strategy is likely to fail against human hunters. The confidence of a bison herd in its ability to defend itself and its reluctance to waste energy running meant that Indians could often approach within arrow range by disguising themselves in wolf skins. As large-scale bison hunting became more widespread in the nineteenth century, so too did reports of wolf abundance. Hunters helped the wolf packs to thrive; often taking only the bison's tongue or hide, they left behind much for the wolves. Sometimes the wolves became so bloated that the Indians could run them down on horseback, kill them with arrows, and sell their pelts to traders.[12] On his 1805 expedition with William Clark, Meriwether Lewis saw such wolves at an Indian buffalo jump on the banks of the Missouri River.

> Today we passed the remains of a vast many mangled carcasses of Buffalow which had been driven over a precipice of 120 feet by the Indians and perished; the water had washed away a part of this immence pile of slaughter and still there remained the fragments of at least a hundred carcases they created a most horrid stench. . . . we saw a great many wolves in the neighbourhood of these mangled carcases they were fat and extreemly gentle.[13]

Wolves Return to Yellowstone

By the 1870s large wolf packs were fast disappearing with the bison on which they had fattened, as settlers sought to eliminate a threat to livestock and a competitor for big game. When wildlife protection improved in Yellowstone after the turn of the century, wolf numbers rebounded until a major extermination campaign began in 1914. Wolves and coyotes were shot, trapped, and poisoned to reduce complaints from Yellowstone's neighbors that the park was a breeding ground for livestock slayers. Park managers also hoped that removing these "bad" animals would increase the elk, deer, and bison herds—the "good" animals that visitors wanted to see. By the 1930s, attitudes were shifting and predator control had become incompatible with the prevailing view of national parks as nature preserves, but by then the sighting of a wolf pack in Yellowstone was little more than an occasional rumor.

In the 1980s, after wolves were designated an endangered species and became an animal that visitors wanted to see, a campaign was launched to return them to Yellowstone. People debated how much wolves would reduce the ungulate herds and whether that would be good or bad. Hunters were most concerned about the impact on elk, whose large number would make them the wolf's primary food. But even though wolves might rarely succeed in preying on bison, their presence could affect bison movement and distribution. In Wood Buffalo National Park about 90 bison set in motion by a pack of eight wolves were reported to have traveled more than 50 miles in less than 24 hours. The bison had continued to move even though the wolves stopped after only a short distance to feed on the calf they had brought down.[14]

Yellowstone received 31 wolves sent from Canada in 1995 and 1996, and a litter of ten orphaned pups from northern Montana was released in the park in 1997. As defined by the U.S. Fish and Wildlife Service, wolf recovery for the Yellowstone area required having at least ten packs that each produced litters for three consecutive years. That goal was met in 2002. The following year 301 wolves were counted in the Yellowstone area, and 19 packs produced litters, more than half of them with territories mostly outside Yellowstone and Grand Teton national parks.[15] The wolf restoration goal has also been met in Idaho and northern Montana, which means that the wolf can be delisted as an endangered species in the Rocky Mountains when those two states and Wyoming agree to acceptable plans for taking over wolf management outside Yellowstone. Delisting will loosen restrictions on the circumstances under which wolves can be killed, a change impatiently awaited by many ranchers and hunters. The overall trend in the size of the northern elk herd has been downward since 1988, and the ratio of elk calves to cows has declined more recently.[16] This hasn't halted criticism of Yellowstone management for allowing the northern range to become overgrazed, but it has fueled objections to the wolf reintroduction program.

The role of wolf predation in the elk population decline is difficult to measure because the population size is also affected by weather and hunting, but the effect of a much smaller amount of wolf predation on bison has so far been negligible. Although some of the wolves released in Yellowstone came from an area of British Columbia where they may have preyed on bison, the others would have to learn from experience. None of the bison in Yellowstone had any experience in fending off wolves, but they will have little opportunity to gain it if the wolves can survive on carcasses and more easily obtained prey.

Wolves are known to have brought down 80 bison in the park from 1997 through 2003; additional bison kills may have gone undetected. The number of bison killed by wolves each year increased, but the 22 documented bison kills in 2003 were still only 6 percent of all documented wolf predation in the park that year. Predation on elk is less labor-intensive and risky for wolves. "I have seen 10 wolves hanging off a 2,000-pound bull bison," says Doug Smith, Yellowstone wolf biologist. Two of the wolves were briefly airborne, one was kicked, and the other was launched by a bison horn. The nine-hour assault ended with fresh meat for the pack, but one of the wolves did not live to eat it, and two others were badly injured.[17]

In 57 interactions between wolves and bison documented in the park, the wolves approached the bison with no attempt at concealment, and whether an attack took place depended on the bison's behavior. In 43 of the interactions, including 12 with lone bison, the bison stood their ground rather than flee. In most of the encounters with multiple bison, the bison grouped tightly and faced the wolves. If the bison did not run, the wolves soon lost interest, presumably because they sensed the bison were able to defend themselves. In some situations where wolves in Yellowstone have been observed trying to prey upon a healthy bison plunging through deep snow, when the targeted animal reached solid ground and turned and faced the wolves, the wolves backed off.

In at least four of the 14 cases where bison ran, the wolves succeeded in killing a bison. In March of 1999, when 14 wolves from the Crystal Creek pack took on 55 bison in Pelican Valley, the assault lasted nine and a half hours. The wolves chased the bison from areas of no snow to areas with snow up to two meters deep, where the entire pack attacked the bison and eventually killed an adult female. Less than two weeks later in the same area, the same wolf pack succeeded in separating a bison cow and yearling from the rest of their herd. The wolves killed the yearling and ignored the cow, who ignored them, standing motionless five meters away during the assault.

Most of the bison predation documented in Yellowstone has occurred in late winter in areas like Pelican Valley where elk are absent or scarce at that time of year. Although one pack has been observed leaving the Pelican Valley after the elk migrate out, Smith thinks they have figured out that if they return in March, some of the bison in Pelican Valley will be weak and ready to die without putting up much of a fight.

A lone wolf is unlikely to approach a bison herd, but in March of 1999 a wolf attacked a bison calf in Gibbon Meadows with the help of four coyotes. Other bison were nearby, but if the calf's mother was around, she was not making her presence known. Wolf encounters with coyotes in Yellowstone often result in coyote deaths, but this time it was the bison calf that died. Sometimes coyotes will harass a lone wolf, but these coyotes lay down at a respectful distance to hope for leftovers as the wolf fed on the carcass.[18]

Part of a Well-Balanced Bear Diet

For bears the bad news about wolf reintroduction in Yellowstone may have been offset by the good news. Wolves are thought to have killed two grizzly bear cubs in 2001, and they have probably killed other bear cubs without anyone noticing. Wolves have also been able to kill at least one adult male black bear that appeared to be healthy. However, what wolves take from the bear population by preying on it, they may give back in the form of the carcasses they provide. When meat is plentiful, wolves may leave behind enough on a carcass to be of value to a bear, and if a bear finds wolves feeding on a carcass, the bear often prevails. In one case a grizzly bear was observed holding 24 frustrated wolves at bay while it fed.

Bears require a more diverse diet than do wolves, and bison make up a small but important part of it. Because grizzly bears are listed as a threatened species, their eating habits have been monitored far more closely than those of black bears. Ungulates, cutthroat trout, cutworm moths, and whitebark pine seeds are the best sources of energy available to grizzly bears in the Yellowstone area, but each is limited in distribution and varies in abundance by season and year. In years when one of their primary foods is in short supply, grizzly bears are more likely to approach humans in search of food and are therefore more likely to come to an untimely end. A study done prior to wolf reintroduction estimated that each Yellowstone grizzly bear consumes 5 to 14 ungulates per year. However, less than 5 percent of the bison meat that grizzlies consume was obtained from animals they killed; the rest was from carrion. Bison constituted only about 8 percent of the ungulate meat available to grizzly bears, but 24 percent of the ungulate meat that the bears ate.[19] That's probably because smaller carcasses are more likely to be consumed before they are found by a grizzly bear, and the bison's tough hide makes scavenging from them difficult for smaller animals. The return of wolves to Yellowstone has meant that ungulate carcasses have become available to bears more evenly throughout the year, rather than being concentrated in late winter and early spring, when bison and elk are most likely to die for other reasons.

Grizzly bears can sprint up to 45 miles an hour, but not for an hour at a time, and they can rarely outrun a healthy adult ungulate. They do, however, take an unknown number of elk and bison calves, and some grizzly bears can take advantage of elk and bison bulls that have weakened or died as a result of fighting with their own kind during the rut. A single male bison carcass provided food for 23 grizzly bears that were observed helping themselves from the buffet over a period of days in the fall of 1968.[20] Evidence as to why grizzly bears must be cautious in preying upon bison was found in June 1951, when a park ranger found a dead grizzly sow in the Lamar Valley. Her carcass was bruised and bloodied, all the ribs on one side appeared broken, and her belly was punctured by two holes that could have been made by the horns of a young bison. Near the carcass were several patches of bison hair and numerous bison hoof prints, and it was concluded that a bison had probably killed the grizzly.[21]

In one case a grizzly bear got into a tug-of-war over a bison calf with some wolves before the calf was dead. This protracted struggle was witnessed in March 2000 in Pelican Valley by researchers Dan MacNulty and Nathan Varley.[22] The preceding day they had watched as five adult wolves from Mollie's pack had made three unsuccessful attacks on a group of 59 bison. A grizzly bear had appeared running near the wolves, and two other grizzlies were seen in the vicinity. The next day most of the bison fled when the wolves approached, but nine bulls and one 11-month-old calf remained behind. This was an unusual configuration, as male calves usually remain in mixed groups with their mothers until they are two or three years old.

The wolves tried for six hours to get the calf, twice attacking while the bison were running single file through deep snow, and other times lunging at the bison while they stood together on a thermal feature. In four of the attacks, the wolves were able to grab the calf and inflict visible damage to the rump and flanks, but the calf was defended by one or more of the bulls and the wolves retreated. Between the attacks, which lasted from 2 to 11 minutes, the wolves and bison rested, remaining within sight of each other. In addition to the two people watching through a spotting scope from six kilometers away, three grizzly bears observed the fracas from close up. When one grizzly bear rushed the wounded calf where it was surrounded by the nine resting bulls, the bulls stood up and closed around the calf, and the grizzly retreated. Unlike wolves, adult bears do not cooperate in bringing down prey; it's every bear for himself.

As the last two bulls left the site late in the afternoon, the wounded calf trailed after them, moving with difficulty through the snow. When the wolves grabbed the calf, the bulls kept going, but one of the grizzly bears approached. Three of the wolves released the calf and charged the grizzly. The grizzly fled but soon returned and pulled the calf from the wolves and began to feed on it. The wolves gave up the fight, and several of them rested a short distance away. But then the nine bull bison reappeared, which seemed to cause the grizzly bear to lose its appetite, and the wolves repossessed the carcass after the grizzly left. The bulls ran past the carcass, but this only temporarily displaced the wolves, some of which chased the bison. With the bison gone, the grizzly returned for the carcass. The bear was still feeding on it at nightfall, and the same or another grizzly was seen feeding on it early the next morning. Three wolves slept nearby. Their efforts may not have gone entirely unrewarded, for examination of the site afterward suggested that the calf had been torn into several pieces during the tussle and the wolves may have fed on part of it.

Although neither the wolves' nor the bison's role in its recovery can be quantified, the grizzly bear population in greater Yellowstone was estimated to have reached about 600 in 2004, and plans are under way to delist it as a threatened species.

Changing Influences on Food for Wildlife

John Craighead, one of Yellowstone's most renowned bear researchers, opposed closing the park dumps to bears in the late 1960s because he believed that the garbage provided nutritional food that helped keep bears in the park and out of trouble. He also disputed the idea that the bears' use of the dumps, which he elegantly referred to as "ecocenters," was deviant behavior resulting from the proximity of humans. Instead, he equated the congregating of bears at refuse piles with the days when bears were "eco-logically associated" with the enormous bison herds that roamed the Great Plains.[23] Like the wolves, grizzlies took advantage of large-scale bison die-offs, whether the result of spring floods, winter storms, or human predation.

Although the open dumps are gone now, roadkills continue to provide a significant source of food for carnivores in the park. More Yellowstone bison have been killed by motor vehicles than by wolves in recent years. Of course there are far more motor vehicles than wolves in the park, but unlike wolves, drivers have nothing to gain by hitting a bison; yet they killed 123 over a seven-year period without even trying.[24] As a percentage of their total population, far more bison have died as a result of road accidents in the park than have elk. This is presumably because elk are more skittish and likely to stay away from moving vehicles. When park staff learn that a dead animal is lying on or near the road, they move the carcass some distance away so that the scavengers attracted to it, and tourists drawn by the scavengers, do not become roadkill themselves.

While roadkills provide an arguably unnatural source of food for wildlife, at least the food itself is more natural than were the doughnuts once tossed to bears from cars, and the bison fatality rate has not affected the population as a whole. It is not the vehicles but the roads themselves that some people think are leading bison to their Waterloo by providing an easy way to reach greener pastures in winter.

CHAPTER 12

Winter Range for Snowmobiles

The local Chamber of Commerce, at first quiescent at the novelty of a hinterland officially labeled as wild, tasted its first blood of tourist money. It then wants more, wilderness or no wilderness. The jeep and the airplane, creatures of the ever mounting pressure from humanity, thus eliminate the opportunity for isolation in nature. . . . Mechanized recreation already has seized nine-tenths of the woods and mountains; a decent respect for minorities should dedicate the other tenth to wilderness.
—Aldo Leopold, *A Sand County Almanac,* 1949[1]

The park headquarters are located in Mammoth Hot Springs because the north side of the park was the most easily reached in 1872, and it continues to offer the most reliable access in winter because it receives the least snow. Since 1940 the road through the park from the north entrance to Cooke City, beyond the northeast entrance, has been plowed to keep it open for cars. Local chambers of commerce repeatedly petitioned to have all 275 miles of park road plowed to increase tourism, but the Park Service declined the chore. Yellowstone managers cited the lack of funds for winter operations and the deep snow canyons that plowing would create in the park interior, altering the movement of wildlife and endangering the movement of cars.

Some people visited Yellowstone during the winter anyway, driving on the plowed road and using snowshoes or skis to penetrate further into the

Bison usually assume they have right-of-way, and in crossing this park road groomed for snowmobilers, they were given it (2001). Courtesy of Yellowstone National Park.

park. In freezing temperatures the park's hot spots emit fantastical billows of steam, and the geysers become cloaked in dazzling ramparts of ice. Wildlife is more easily spotted against a snowy backdrop, and during winter the animals are more likely to be drawn to thermal areas. The stolid bison, their shaggy heads and shoulders shrouded in snow and ice, appear even more archaic and mysterious than usual.

Human ingenuity inevitably came up with ways for more people to enjoy these sights with less effort. In 1955 visitors began making the trip in snowcoaches, ten-passenger vehicles that move on tractor-style treads. Snowmobiles made their first appearance in the park in 1963, when only about 3,000 winter visitors came to Yellowstone by all means of conveyance. Despite the park's closed hotels and gas stations and the absence of warming huts or groomed trails, snowmobiling quickly became popular and was the main reason that winter visitation quadrupled in the next four years. However, local businesses were still agitating to get the roads plowed for wheeled vehicles. At U.S. Senate hearings on the issue in 1968, the only opposition to road plowing for environmental reasons came from the Wildlife Management Institute in Washington, D.C. "Winter is the extreme period of physiological stress for wildlife, and both the direct and indirect harassment of the animals by humans could be harmful," it stated.[2] The Park Service remained chiefly concerned about visitor safety and financial constraints, and it compromised with business interests by grooming the roads to make oversnow travel safer and more comfortable. But as more visitors were coming into the park in the winter, more bison were leaving.

Good Grooming and Other Questionable Practices

When the first large exodus occurred during the winter of 1975–76, most of the bison followed the Yellowstone River into Gardiner, but it was also the first time that more than a few bison were seen traveling the plowed road into town.[3] Within seven years, as unsuccessful efforts were made to keep bison from leaving by either route, the road became the bison route of choice. However, it was thought that using plowed roads on the northern range was unlikely to provide the bison with "any meaningful energy savings."[4] It was in the park interior, where much more snow accumulates, that groomed roads were suspected of boosting the bison population and migrations since 1980. It was during the relatively snowless February of that year, when 332 bison were tallied in Pelican Valley, that mixed groups were first seen on the groomed road near Mary Bay, heading away from their traditional winter range. By the mid-1980s many bison from Pelican Valley were taking the road all the way to Hayden Valley in the winter.[5] If road grooming enabled the bison to cover longer distances and find more forage in winter, the theory went, bison would be more likely to survive the winter, produce a large crop of calves in the spring, and try to expand their range beyond the park boundary.

The ten-year lag between 1971, when formal road grooming began, and the period when significant bison range expansion occurred could be attributed to the animal's "behavioral inertia," according to the National Research Council, which looked at the data in its study of brucellosis in greater Yellowstone. However, the council found that grooming had not had any "substantial influence" on the population size, and noted that by the early 1980s the population had reached a density that could have pushed bison into new habitat even without groomed roads.[6] Therefore, attributing the bison population increase to the use of groomed roads might be reversing cause and effect.

Bison can also be seen walking along the road during the summer, and they can be seen there more often now that there are more bison, but this does not necessarily mean that the warm pavement has increased the size of the population or induced them to undertake longer summer expeditions. After all, which came first—the bison or the roads? Much of the road system in Yellowstone has been designed to follow the easiest topographical gradient and river corridors and provide access to thermal areas. Bison could have been drawn to these routes for similar reasons long before they were bulldozed for roads. But they don't always use the most obvious route. Instead of following the road to the west boundary, bison have crossed the frigid Madison River in February, climbed its steep bank, and headed north of West Yellowstone on a winding route through deep snow.

Despite uncertainty about the effect of groomed roads, the Park Service initially joined the chorus that found in them a reason why more bison were leaving the park and why there were more bison to leave. In December 1994 a Park Service briefing statement explained that because of the weather and the approximately 4,000 bison in Yellowstone, "it is anticipated that hundreds of bison may exit the park into Montana in search of food. These numbers may be inflated to double natural levels because the snow-packed roads for winter use provide energy-saving travel corridors for bison."

But in May 1997, at the end of the winter in which more than 1,000 bison were killed outside the park, the Park Service's admission about the possible role of groomed roads became grounds for a lawsuit. The Fund for Animals wanted all road grooming in Yellowstone to cease unless "scientific evidence" showed that it did not harm wildlife. The animal rights activists did not care that an end to road grooming would curtail access by snowcoaches, skiers, and snowshoers, as well as by snowmobiles. They objected that Yellowstone's winter use policy was "turning a national park into a national playground."[7] This derisively meant term was routinely used in statements issued by The Fund for Animals, whose members were perhaps unaware that the phrase "pleasuring-ground" appeared in the legislation that established the park in 1872. The word "playground" had been used approvingly by Theodore Roosevelt when extolling Yellowstone in days gone by, before the park became a place where the geysers and wildlife were supposed to carry on with minimal interference from humans.

This bison near Giant Geyser shows how the animals usually use their heads rather than their feet to dig below the snow for forage. Courtesy of Yellowstone National Park.

Blue Haze and Purple Rage

Wildlife may react to the proximity of humans with apparent indifference, curiosity, or a "flush," which in wildlife biology is "an immediate, short-term behavioral response to disturbance that includes flight or running from a perceived threat."[8] But even when no response is visible, the animal's heart rate may increase, which may use up more energy and affect the animal's ability to survive, especially during winter, when the animal may be just barely getting by. Not only does forage tend to be less nutritious in winter, snow increases the energy required to obtain it and makes escape more difficult from predators, snowmobiles, and other disturbances.[9]

Lawsuits tend to be an expensive and energy-consuming disturbance, but Yellowstone staff were concerned about the blue haze of snowmobiles, and many were glad to see the park's winter use policies challenged. Park rules required snowmobilers to remain on the groomed roads and adhere to a 35-mile-per-hour speed limit, but the park rangers were hard-pressed to keep hotdoggers from tearing off the roads and into the underbrush. The adverse effects of snowmobile-polluted snow on wildlife and surface water had been reported as far back as 1973, and visitor snowmobile use had ended in Glacier, Lassen, Sequoia–Kings Canyon, and Yosemite national parks. In 1983 national park regulations were amended to prohibit snowmobiles except where their use is "consistent with the park's natural, cultural, scenic and aesthetic values, safety considerations, and park management objectives, and will not disturb wildlife or damage park resources," an exception loose enough to drive thousands of snowmobiles through at Yellowstone and Grand Teton.[10]

At the National Park Service website, "snowmobiling" does not appear between "snow skiing" and "swimming" on the menu of 13 activities to be enjoyed at national parks. But it is allowed on designated routes in seven other parks—Acadia, Crater Lake, Mount Rainier, Olympic, Rocky Mountain, Theodore Roosevelt, and Zion—where the level of use and perceived impacts have been small. Only the off-road snowmobiling allowed in parts of Voyageurs and Denali has stirred a controversy that comes anywhere close to that in the more heavily visited Yellowstone. By the winter of 1997–98 Yellowstone was receiving more than 120,000 winter visitors, nearly half of them arriving on snowmobiles through West Yellowstone, which proclaimed itself "Snowmobiling Capital of the World."

"Without snowmobiling, this town would be nothing," claimed Glen Loomis, West Yellowstone's mayor and owner of a snowmobile store.[11] This sentiment in local communities would have made snowmobiles politically difficult for Yellowstone managers to take on without the spur of a lawsuit. In a settlement approved by the court in October 1997, the Park Service agreed to pay The Fund for Animals' legal bills, prepare an environmental impact statement for winter use in Yellowstone and Grand Teton national parks, and consider leaving a road segment ungroomed and untraveled by humans in order to assess the effects on bison and other wildlife.

The settlement infuriated tourism promoters. "By caving in to a radical group such as The Fund for Animals, the Park Service has unnecessarily placed a lot of small businesses and the families that rely on them in jeopardy," objected U.S. senator Conrad Burns of Montana. "I'm beyond upset, I'm purple with rage," declared Viki Eggers, director of the West Yellowstone Chamber of Commerce.[12] Eggers, who grew up in West Yellowstone, could remember the lean, presnowmobile winters when fathers "every day got up and packed their lunches and went down to Earsel's gas station and played cribbage because there wasn't any work."[13] But winter tourism in West Yellowstone is not dependent on snowmobiling in the park.

Although the park's thermal features and wildlife are an attraction, the adjacent national forests have 500 miles of snowmobile trails.

The Park Service deferred closing any road segments for experimental purposes because "further research [on the roads when not closed] was necessary before closing a road would provide useful research informa-tion."[14] Perhaps it was just behavioral inertia on the part of the Park Service, but The Fund for Animals believed the decision "had nothing to do with science and everything to do with placating certain Congresspersons."[15]

The Road to Ruin?

Although the lawsuit did not curtail road grooming, it did encourage researchers to walk hundreds of miles observing bison winter travel in Yellowstone. Two biologists from Montana State University, Dan Bjornlie and Bob Garrott, found that bison travel both on and off the road from Old Faithful to Norris was lowest during the snowmobile season and then peaked in April, after plowing began and melting snow began to expose small and widely scattered foraging patches. Based on data collected during the winters of 1997–98 and 1998–99, most bison winter travel occurred on trails pre-viously broken by bison, along stream banks, or through geothermal areas, so only a small portion of it required the animals to move snow.[16] Bjornlie observed groups of bison taking turns to break a trail when necessary through deep snow, sometimes forging a path parallel to the road. The winter popula-tion shift from the park's center to the Firehole and Madison drainages was largely accomplished on a trail over Mary Mountain that became cordoned by shoulder-deep snow as the bison maintained it without any help from the Park Service. Once across Mary Mountain, bison heading further west were most likely to use the road in places where the constricted topography offered little choice, as in the canyons of the Madison and Firehole rivers.

More than half of the 145 bison groups observed on the road during this study responded to approaching snowmobiles by running, changing direc-tion, or exiting into the snow berm. This suggested that any energy saved by using groomed roads might be expended by bison in responding to oversnow vehicles. However, Bjornlie and Garrott's conclusion that "grooming roads during winter does not have a major influence on bison ecology" was dismissed as "flawed" by The Fund for Animals because the data covered only the two relatively mild winters that followed the major bison popu-lation reduction in 1997.[17]

Yellowstone staff were also collecting information on bison use of groomed roads. By 2004 they had seven winters' worth of data but no evidence that conflicted with Bjornlie and Garrott's findings, and no winter of bison movement like that of 1996–97.[18] The ideal experiment—one that compares a control group that is identical to a test group except for the factor being tested—is rarely feasible when studying wild animals. An unequivocal answer as to whether groomed roads were affecting Yellowstone bison distribution and survival would require monitoring their movements and mortality during two winters that were the same—the same fall bison count, the same forage availability and snow conditions, the same pressure from wolves—except that in one winter some or all of the roads were not groomed. The impossibility of controlling the variables was one reason the Park Service had not closed a road segment for research purposes.

Even if the lure of the open road did provide an initial boost to bison establishing new winter routes and ranges, many wildlife biologists believe that halting road grooming now would be like closing the barn door after the bison have escaped. Given the influence of behavioral inertia, the bison would probably continue to use these routes to winter forage whether they were groomed or not. As Mary Meagher and Valerius Geist agreed in the 1980s when they proposed eliminating all bison that left the park, the only way to remove this knowledge from the population would be to remove the bison.

The War against Tourism

Although the sight of slaughtered bison outside Yellowstone may have launched the first thousand pages of environmental analysis of winter recreation, it did not drive the resulting winter use policy for Yellowstone and Grand Teton national parks. Arrived at in the waning days of the Clinton administration, the chosen alternative called for phasing out snowmobiles in three years, but the primary motivation was to improve the quality of life for people rather than for bison. Assistant Secretary of the Interior Don Barry described snowmobiles as "dirty house guests who have over-stayed their welcome in all National Parks."[19] The 60 percent of Yellowstone winter visitors who used them were willing to tolerate the noise and fumes, but most of the other 40 percent saw themselves as a besieged minority who would remain a minority as long as snowmobiles were allowed. The reputation Yellowstone had gained as a magnet for "sled-heads" meant that an unknown number of "slat-rats" and other potential winter guests were staying away. Instead of wolves howling in the distance, winter visitors were likely to hear the snarling of an approaching pack of snowmobiles.

While environmental groups saw the decision to phase out snowmobiles as a major victory, The Fund for Animals objected that park roads would still be groomed for use by snowcoaches. Instead of welcoming the reduction in oversnow vehicles in the park, The Fund claimed this would increase use of the groomed roads by bison, a situation they considered more alarming than harassment by snowmobiles. In support of their position, The Fund referred to "evidence collected by Dr. Mary Meagher, the world's foremost authority on Yellowstone bison," that the groomed roads had "resulted in an unnatural increase in the bison population size" and "facilitated bison emigration."[20] But the well-funded snowmobile groups were even more upset, and now it was their turn to sue the Park Service. "The war on tourism that has been launched by so-called 'environmental groups' is destined to destroy the economy of this region and perhaps all of Montana if we continue to pussy-foot around the issues," stated Viki Eggers, who began working for the BlueRibbon Coalition, a nonprofit group based in Pocatello, Idaho, that champions "responsible multiple-use" of public land. "I cannot stand quietly by and allow my friends and neighbors to be destroyed. We are at war, and I'm headed for the trenches to do my part."[21]

The International Snowmobile Manufacturers Association charged that the Park Service had made decisions "contradictory to evidence," failed to "properly interpret and implement the parks' purpose," and discriminated against disabled visitors. The Park Service was advised by its legal counsel that it could prevail in court, and Yellowstone managers were willing to defend the snowmobile ban, but they were overruled by their superiors in Washington, now in the first flush of the Bush administration with Gale Norton as secretary of the interior. While denying the allegations, the Park Service agreed to a settlement under which a supplemental environmental impact statement would be prepared in order to "solicit more public comment and consider any new or updated substantive information not available at the time of the earlier decision, especially as it related to new snowmobile technology."[22] So the snowmobile phaseout was suspended while the Park Service spent $2.4 million to complete another round of studies for which the conclusion appeared foregone. As stated in a Park Service meeting agenda, the agency's "internal objective" for the supplemental EIS was "to determine under what terms and conditions snowmobiling will continue" in Yellowstone and Grand Teton, not whether it should continue at all.[23]

Negative Interactions

By the time the supplemental EIS was completed in February 2003, reams of information about snowmobile technology had been presented, including comparisons of two-stroke and four-stroke engines, air quality studies, and a "draft supplemental technical report on noise." The document also included new research on how winter recreation affects wildlife, but the focus was more on the question of wildlife harassment than on how groomed roads may affect the Yellowstone bison. Asked to provide written accounts of the wildlife-vehicle interactions they observed, nine park rangers reported that the most common problem was snowmobilers who tried to pass through groups of bison, often causing the animals to bolt down the road, along which they were "herded" by snowmobilers until the bison were pushed off the roadway, often into deep snow.[24]

During the winter of 2001–02, park staff recorded more than 7,000 observations of snowmobiles and 18,000 of bison visible from the groomed road from West Yellowstone to Old Faithful. Most of the bison were more than 60 meters from the road, but more than 500 events were documented in which humans interacted with wildlife, usually bison.[25] Of the 886 bison observed in the presence of snowmobiles, 42 percent appeared agitated (kicking, running away, charging, or jumping the snow berm) and 19 percent showed a smaller reaction (remaining in a state of alert attention to the snowmobiles, walking away, or getting up if resting); the others showed little or no reaction.

One way to check for stress that does not depend on visible evidence is to measure the glucocorticoid (GC) levels in the animal's fecal samples. As in humans, when an animal perceives a threat, the adrenal gland releases a spurt of adrenaline and GCs, preparing the body to fight or flee. If this stress response is repeated or prolonged, it can cause fatigue, hypertension, and gastric ulcers. Research in Yellowstone has found some correlation between the presence of snowmobiles and GC levels in elk, but not in bison. In addition to collecting 473 bison fecal samples to analyze for her master's thesis, Amanda Hardy observed that skiers, snowshoers, and other off-trail human activity evoked stronger visible reactions in bison and elk than did on-trail or on-road activity, probably because the appearance of humans off-trail was more unexpected and sporadic. Elk tended to be further from roads, but both bison and elk seemed to become habituated to on-road activity as traffic increased during the season.[26] Wild animals that become accustomed to humans and their vehicles are less likely to react to them. That may sound like a good thing, especially for humans trying to take photographs, but because habituation alters the survival instincts of a wild animal, Park Service policies are generally designed to prevent habituation from occurring. Furthermore, the lack of response may reflect the animal's weakening condition and the difficulty of reacting in deepening snow rather than habituation.

For Mary Meagher, however, the critical issue was still how bison are affected by groomed roads, not the vehicles on them, and she submitted a report stating her case to the committee preparing the supplemental EIS. The evidence suggested to her that the shift of the Pelican Valley bison to Hayden Valley during the winter may have prompted some bison there to move further west into the Firehole area, which may have bumped some of those bison further north to Madison Junction and, by the 1990s, sometimes pushed bison all the way to the park's north boundary. She called this "the domino effect," but in the scenario she described, the dominoes weren't just falling over, they were sliding a long distance into lower winter ranges, and "wild bison are disappearing as a wintering population from the Pelican country."[27] In a late winter survey in 2000, only 24 bison were counted in mixed groups in Pelican Valley (not counting lone bulls), scarcely more than the all-time recorded low of 22 in 1902, when they were the only bison in the entire park. However, that could represent just a short-term fluctuation rather than a long-term trend. More recently, even though the presence of wolves has provided a reason for bison to leave Pelican Valley in the winter, several hundred bison were counted there in March of 2003 and 2004.[28]

In 1946 a group of 38 bison from Pelican Valley drowned in the ice-covered Yellowstone River, apparently while traveling toward Hayden Valley through three feet of snow.[29] That may be considered evidence either that bison were heading west even before the roads were groomed or that, before groomed roads, bison were more likely to die in the attempt. The supplemental EIS described the relationship between changes in the bison population and their use of groomed roads as "disputable and under study."[30] Meagher warned that even though the data do not show "a clear cause-and-effect relationship," the potential consequences of road grooming were too grave to ignore. "The future for bison looks bleak." She alluded to the likelihood that the number of bison trying to leave the park would continue to increase and that many would be killed as a result.

> I cannot say how many bison will persist, nor their distribution. I can be certain that the population will decrease over time, and distribution likely will continue to change also. Although I find it difficult to think that the population could be exterminated entirely, they are at risk. . . . I conclude that the National Park Service as the responsible agency stands a good chance of completing what the bison poachers were not able to do at the turn of the century in the Pelican country.[31]

The BlueRibbon Coalition saw the same Yellowstone bison as lying in clover. "With groomed trails to help conserve precious body fat and energy stores, the bison population is thriving in Yellowstone these days. Oddly, The Fund For Animals and other environmental extremists seem to see this boon to winter survival as a bad thing." The coalition applauded a presumed decline in "wintertime deaths by slow, painful starvation," perhaps believing that bison, if given the choice, would prefer the trip to the slaughterhouse that may await them at the end of the groomed road to West Yellowstone.[32] But even if there were a cause-and-effect relationship between groomed roads and the park's thriving bison population, in wildlife management terms there is no such thing as a beneficial human impact. If more bison survive the winter in Yellowstone because of groomed roads, or in the National Elk Refuge because of the feeding program, that would mean that the population is unnaturally large for its habitat, and no good could come of that.

Caring Capacity

The supplemental EIS concluded that ending snowmobile use in Yellowstone and Grand Teton would result in "the lowest levels of impacts to air quality, water quality, natural soundscapes, and wildlife" and "the widest range of beneficial uses of the environment without degradation and risk of health or safety."[33] But no one was surprised when the "preferred alternative" chosen by the Park Service continued snowmobile use with some new restrictions. The number of snowmobiles permitted to enter Yellowstone would be limited to 950 a day. The daily average for the preceding decade was 765 snowmobiles, but on peak holidays and weekends the number sometimes exceeded 1,200.

Although the new winter use plan was not made over the dead bodies of bison, its rationale bore some striking similarities to that of the bison management plan for Yellowstone and Montana. Both plans have to do with boundary control and risk management. Rather than eradicate brucellosis, the bison plan was intended to manage the risk of possible brucellosis transmission. Instead of eliminating snowmobiles, the winter use plan was intended to manage the risk that they will adversely affect the park environment and visitor satisfaction. The difference is that if bison leave the park when their population exceeds the established threshold, they may be killed, whereas if snowmobilers enter the park in excess of the permitted threshold, they will just be evicted and subject to a fine or brief confinement.

While both plans set forth widely accepted goals for protecting park resources and local economic interests, opinions in both cases diverged on how to achieve the goals, and the result was a plan that was neither the "environmentally preferred" plan nor the plan most supported by the public. Instead, it was a plan far more expensive to administer, with a cost out of proportion to the potential impact of brucellosis transmission or a snowmobile phaseout. Both plans are expensive because they are complicated and labor-intensive and require technological advances and long-term monitoring. And both plans became complicated because of exhaustive efforts by the Park Service to use what leverage it had to obtain whatever concessions it could. Instead of simply allowing no bison outside Yellowstone or no snowmobiles into it, a few hundred bison would eventually be allowed outside the park, and more than 900 snowmobiles a day would be allowed into it, but the bison/snowmobilers and their impacts would be intensively studied, and steps would be taken to reduce the impacts. For bison this involved three kinds of management zones, capture and testing at the boundary, and vaccinations. For snowmobilers it meant making reservations in advance and using cleaner, quieter machines and licensed guides. To monitor winter use, the park was divided into nine management zones, each of which would permit a different level of visitor impacts, ranging from none to a lot, and assessment of wildlife impacts would continue.

Both plans also called for an assessment of the park's "carrying capacity" — for bison in one case, and snowmobiles in the other. After this number is determined, the official tolerance level—for bison outside the park or snow-mobiles in the park—could be adjusted accordingly. For winter use, "the carrying capacity would be determined by defining the desired future condition for park resources and visitor experiences." Progress in establishing a carrying capacity for bison has been nil since the bison management plan was adopted in December 2000; setting a carrying capacity for snowmobilers could be even more difficult. The American public has widely divergent views on the "desired" experience for winter visitation in Yellowstone, and it would be necessary to consider the opinions of the people who do visit Yellowstone in the winter—most of whom are satisfied with the experience; otherwise they wouldn't come—as well as the disgruntled people who don't come and the people who may never come to the park but care about how it is managed. How should the balance be struck between wilderness and civilization in Yellowstone?

The Merchants of Zoom

Ed Klim, manager of the International Snowmobile Manufacturers Association, described most of the comments on the supplemental EIS as "e-mail based, engine-generated letters, with virtually no original meaning or thought" submitted by "the Green Community."[34] However, unlike the bison management plan, which evoked a wait-and-see reaction from environmental and animal rights groups, the U-turn performed in the winter use plan triggered immediate legal challenges that have left the future of the snowmobile in Yellowstone as uncertain as that of bison outside it. The Fund for Animals sued again, taking the opportunity to restate its case against thoughtless, engine-generated oversnow travel, but Klim remained optimistic. "We are hopeful that the court will see this lawsuit for what it is and dismiss it as an affront on the American public," he said. "We hope to be joined by others who will help shine a bright light on these devious efforts concocted by truly fringe elements of the environmental movement."[35] The Greater Yellowstone Coalition and the Sierra Club were among the plain-tiffs in a lawsuit to reinstate the snowmobile phaseout but continue to allow road grooming and snowcoaches in the park.

On December 15, 2003, several days after the Department of the Interior issued its final rules for the new winter use plan and the day before the snowmobiling season was scheduled to begin in Yellowstone, U.S. district judge Emmet Sullivan in Washington, D.C., threw out the plan. Sullivan derided the plan as a "politically driven" change in course for which no good reason had been given.[36] The effect of Sullivan's decision was to reinstate the snowmobile phaseout and send Wyoming state officials running to U.S. district judge Clarence Brimmer in Cheyenne, Wyoming, to reopen the lawsuit that had led to the new winter use plan. On February 11 Brimmer issued a temporary restraining order setting aside the snowmobile phaseout pending further appeals. While Judge Sullivan had concluded that the National Park Service "is bound by a conservation mandate and that mandate trumps all other considerations," Judge Brimmer believed that "public interest is served by protecting the business owners and concessionaires."[37]

Secretary Norton construed Brimmer's ruling as a decision that "deferred to the experts in the National Park Service to create a temporary winter-use plan that offers a unique and enjoyable visitor experience and protects park resources,"[38] by which she meant that snowmobiling was to be allowed. Judge Sullivan, who was unimpressed by the Park Service's expertise, threatened to hold Interior Department officials in contempt of court for violating his order. He also criticized their failure to explain why they had not studied the impact of a winter road closure on wildlife, or considered a winter use plan that would eliminate road grooming. The EIS had stated that "it is unknown if and to what extent beneficial effects [of road grooming] outweigh negative effects on bison movement," and Sullivan believed that such a disclosure "screams out for further study." He therefore ordered the federal government to reexamine how road grooming affects bison and other wildlife in Yellowstone.[39]

While the future of snowmobiles in the park remained uncertain and largely beyond their control in the spring of 2004, the experts in Yellowstone welcomed the news that Cormack Gates from the University of Calgary had accepted their invitation to conduct a study that would address the screams about road grooming. A respected Canadian wildlife expert who is familiar with the ways of bison but removed from the politics of Yellowstone, Gates is expected to submit a report in 2005 with his recommendations for winter bison management in the park and, perhaps inevitably in the world of science, "priority areas requiring further research."[40]

CHAPTER 13

Hunted Again

There are many reasons that make the bison a tremendous animal to hunt. Once your bull is on the ground and you have successfully driven the rest of the herd away, your senses will eventually calm down and you will begin to understand all of them.
—Frank Medicine Wolf Springer, 2003[1]

In its 1998 report on brucellosis in greater Yellowstone, the National Research Council described as "optimistic" the idea that winterkill and other natural factors would eliminate the need for human control of bison outside the park if winter road grooming ceased.[2] Even if someday brucellosis is no longer sufficient reason for killing bison that cross the boundary, the state of Montana would still have to do something to keep bison from expanding their range and recolonizing backyards in Livingston. The "civilized" option would be the same as that of the 1930s: to ship surplus bison to willing buyers, or to public or tribal land where the animals might become more like livestock. The "wilderness" option, or at least the one that is arguably more "natural," would manage wild bison in the same way as elk, which generally means tolerance on public land and control of population size and distribution through hunting.

When Montana officials escorted licensed hunters to bison outside the park boundary in the 1980s, it was a public relations blunder that used paying volunteers to carry out a grisly chore that state employees would otherwise have done. It wasn't the sports channel that showed men in plaid shirts repeatedly shooting stationary beasts that toppled over, got up, and then fell again, blood staining the snow. But some people believed that a "fair chase" bison hunt was possible outside the park, and in 2003 Montana legislators passed a bill to reauthorize bison hunting on public land.

The Sheer Excitement

Bison are shot by hunters elsewhere in North America on both public and private land to cull herds and provide revenue. "You will love the hospitality, the camaraderie, the sheer excitement of going back in time to hunt a legendary animal in a magnificent setting in east central North Dakota," promises the Bison Ranch at Coteau Ridge.[3] "Capture a part of the American West and experience the same thrill as frontiersmen and Sioux warriors did over a century ago during your own personal buffalo hunt," offers the Sanders Ranch of South Dakota.

"These massive Lords of the Prairie are amazingly quick and agile!" exults John Morningsky Ray on the Thousand Hills Bison Ranch in Colorado. "When you combine their power with a fiery temper, they command every hunter's respect, making for a majestic trophy and memorable hunt. They are truly fine trophy bulls, each one selected for his size, cape, horn length and base diameter." At Thousand Hills, trophy bulls are usually located from four-wheel drives or horseback, then stalked on foot. "Stalks require dedication, intelligence and skill," warns Morningsky Ray. "Having hunted Peary Island caribou and musk ox on Victoria Island in the Arctic Circle, I believe this to be a more difficult hunt. Once you see your bull and the huge territory he has available, you'll see that his chances at escaping are pretty good. A startled buffalo can settle into a gentle lope that can go on for hours." However, the $4,000 fee includes the services of a guide who makes sure that no client goes home empty-handed.[4]

After Ted Turner purchased the 113,500-acre Flying D Ranch in Montana in 1989 and stocked it with several thousand bison, he began letting about ten people a year hunt a trophy. This may have been primarily a way to reduce an excess of cantankerous bulls on the property, but hunting options at the ranch expanded as the number of bison removed each year increased to several hundred. Instead of a one-day guided trophy bull hunt on the full expanse of the ranch for $3,500, starting in 2001, you could "harvest" a bison cow for $650 or a mature but nontrophy bull for $1,500. A "harvest" means shooting your choice of the bison that have been moved into a 160-acre pasture, where the average shot is taken from 75 to 100 yards.

"In spite of what the bleeding hearts would like to think, meat doesn't just magically appear on the grocery store shelf, and this offers you the opportunity to harvest your own meat, right in the same country where they were born and lived," explains Bill O'Connell of Cowboy Heaven Consulting, which books hunters and harvesters on the Flying D. They're not selling the steak; they're selling the sizzle, the natural virility, and the snort of a free-ranging bison, or at least a bison that was free ranging until it was driven into the harvest pasture. One year Cowboy Heaven tried offering an unguided hunt to provide a lower-cost option in which hunters had to locate and retrieve the buffalo themselves, but it was more trouble than it was worth. "There's just too much potential for woundings [of buffalo, instead of receiving lethal shots] and stampedes and folks getting lost and no end of problems," said O'Connell.[5]

After watching the harvest of her chosen bison at the Flying D, a customer commented, "The rest of the herd does not seem alarmed by this process. The scent of blood elicits curiosity rather than fear."[6] This reaction was also noted by some nineteenth-century bison hunters, but it is not always so. When a bison is shot within a herd at some ranches, vehicles are immediately driven around the fallen animal to keep it from being gored by the others. The Thousand Hills Bison Ranch does only "release and catch" hunts, in which the bull is released away from the herd at an undisclosed location. "I believe this is a much more sporting hunt than shooting an animal in the herd," says Morningsky Ray. A lone bull "can cover a great deal of territory in a short period" and is wary without the protection of the herd. "Our guides do not know the where or when of your bull's release, so everyone is truly hunting and there are a lot of places to hide on 62,000 acres. All of these factors make for an exciting hunt!"

Bison Hunting on Public Land

Alaska was the bison's first home in the Western Hemisphere, and bison were once the most numerous large mammal there. But several hundred years ago when they were still plentiful on the Great Plains, bison were gone from Alaska. Native hunting and habitat changes have been suggested as likely factors in the extinction. The bison's potential range in Alaska is considered limited now, but the state used surplus from the National Bison

Range to reestablish four herds with a total population of about 850. Alaskans pay only $10 to hunt a bison, but with about 50 applicants for each permit issued, the chances of winning the bison lottery are small. Alaska's Farewell herd is located in a remote area without road access. Most of the hunters arrive there by plane during the September hunt and by snowmobile in March, and only slightly more than half of those who have made the venture have gained a bison.[7]

In South Dakota most of the surplus bison at Custer State Park are auctioned live, but some hunting permits are sold each fall. Using a euphemism typical of the livestock business, the Custer State Park hunt is "our management tool to rotate the oldest breeding bulls out of the herd." Unlike baseball pitchers who have been benched, however, these bulls can never be rotated back in again. Similar to hunts on private ranches, this is considered a "canned" hunt because anyone who pays the price of admission is guaranteed a bison. The hunter seeks his prey in a vehicle driven by a park guide who indicates which locations can be accessed to collect the carcass and which animals can be taken. The bulls selected for this form of removal are typically one-ton ten-year-olds that leave the mixed herd after the summer rut to forage by themselves or in small groups. Despite the $4,000 fee the ten permits issued every year easily find buyers.[8]

In 2003 Custer State Park also began offering a "non-trophy" hunt, in which a young bull could be taken for $1,500 or a cow for $1,000. Custer State Park is financially self-supporting, and the addition of the nontrophy hunt was probably motivated more by finances than by a desire to give more people a chance to kill a bison. With a glut of bison meat on the market, the amount that Custer received from its annual live auction had dropped. A two-year-old bull went for an average of $515 in 2002, less than a quarter of the price fetched at the market peak a few years before. It's just one of those quirks of human nature that some people will pay more for a bison they must kill than one that is still alive.

The Arizona Game and Fish Department is responsible for bison in two wildlife areas that are managed "to provide viewing opportunities as well as recreation for sport hunters."[9] Whether anyone has viewed or hunted bison as a native species in Arizona in recent millennia is a matter of debate, but several hundred descendants of the herd imported by Buffalo Jones in 1905 remain in the state. After Grand Canyon National Park declined the offer, the state of Arizona adopted the bison in 1926 and released them on the House Rock Valley Wildlife Area, adjacent to the park. Part of the herd was sent to the Raymond Ranch Wildlife Area in 1945. The size of both herds has been limited through hunting. At the Raymond Ranch a state employee accompanies each hunter to assure that an animal of the correct age and gender is taken. In the more rugged conditions of the 65,000-acre House Rock Valley, where the bison tend to be wary of humans and more difficult to find, hunters are on their own, but they are required to attend an extensive orientation session that covers gender and age identification.

Utah also offers a different kind of bison hunt for each of its two herds on public land. One herd was started in 1893, when several ranchers brought 12 bison to Antelope Island in Great Salt Lake on a barge. By 1987 the state had acquired the entire 28,000-acre island and the bison, and it now keeps the herd size at about 550. Income is generated by admission tickets to the annual roundup, a bison auction, and hunting permits for a mature bull ($1,105 for residents, $2,605 for nonresidents). Compared to the raucous roundup with its bucking Bronco drivers, the bison hunt is a sedate undertaking. A park employee is assigned to escort each permit holder around the island and point out eligible animals. According to the Utah Animal Rights Coalition, "the hunter merely drives their car up to the herd, gets out of the car (an unnecessary step), and shoots point blank one of the animals."[10] The most difficult part is what to do with the bull once you've brought him down, but 402 people entered the lottery for six permits in 2002.

Hunting the free-roaming descendants of the Yellowstone bison relocated to Utah's Henry Mountains is more difficult because the bison tend to occupy areas not easily accessed by road, but the permits are less than half as expensive and in greater demand. In 2002 nearly 4,500 people entered the drawing for 42 permits to keep the herd size at about 400. At first, hunters were allowed to take either a bull or cow, making it the kind of hunt that is the easiest to administer, produces the highest success rate, and is most popular with hunters. The problem with "hunter's choice," however, is that if they have a choice, hunters usually choose a bull, preferably a larger, older bull. In the case of the Henry Mountains herd, this made it impossible to maintain the desired herd size without distorting the gender and age distribution.[11] Because the Utah Department of Fish and Game wants the herd to have at least one bull for every two cows, some hunts are now designated "cow only." Applicants whose names are drawn are required to attend a three-hour orientation session that covers bison gender and age identification, bullet placement, and carcass handling, but then they are on their own. Only 14 of the first 249 bison killed in cow-only hunts turned out, on closer examination, to be bulls. To encourage hunters to confess their sins of misrecognition, they are allowed to keep the meat if they report the illicit kill to an enforcement officer. Heads and hides are confiscated to discourage intentional mistakes.

The Wyoming Game and Fish Department has offered bison hunting in two areas. South of Yellowstone, during the suspension of bison hunting on the National Elk Refuge, the small number of bison from the Jackson herd that wander onto Bridger-Teton National Forest have been fair game for those with permits. Bison that cross Yellowstone's east boundary onto the Shoshone National Forest are also removed by hunters when the number exceeds the state's tolerance limit of 15 bulls and no cows in this area. In anticipation of the return of large-scale bison hunting on the National Elk Refuge to reduce the Jackson herd, the requirement that hunters attend a two-hour orientation program to learn about shot placement and demonstrate shooting proficiency was dropped in 2004 despite animal rights groups' objections that accurate shot placement is essential to ensure a quick kill and reduce the animal's suffering.

Fair Chase

In 1933 conservationist Aldo Leopold described "physical combat between men and beasts" as an inherent part of subsistence living, "but the hunting instinct, the love of weapons, the zest in their skillful use, did not disappear with their displacement by economic substitutes."[12] However, empathy for the hunter's instincts has largely disappeared as fewer people hunt for either subsistence or sport. In its successful effort to halt bison hunts on the National Elk Refuge, The Fund for Animals contended that killing bison in a herd whose size was inflated by winter feeding was bad management and that hunting bison that had learned to trust the hands that fed them was not fair chase. "The Jackson Hole bison are accustomed to the click of a camera, not the crack of a rifle," said Michael Markarian, The Fund's executive director. "Shooting these docile creatures is about as sporting as shooting a parked car."[13] State game officials do not use the word "docile" to describe the Jackson bison herd, which is known for bullying elk at the feed lines, but the bison may be more habituated to humans than they would be if they had to fend for themselves during the winter.

Markarian claimed that the more than 2,000 Wyoming residents who applied for bison permits were "all but proof that Wyoming hunters are among the most unethical and unsporting in the nation."[14] For those opposed to all hunting of animals, the concept of "ethical hunting" may seem an oxymoron. But some hunting practices are considered more unethical than others, and Fund members have sought to reduce what they regard as the most egregious practices, such as canned hunts and animal baiting. They make their case partly by appealing to the hunter's self-interest. Since most people do not hunt and are offended by cruelty to animals, if hunters do not clean up their own act, they risk having their act brought to an end, as happened with bison hunting in Montana in 1991.

Jim Posewitz, who was working for the Montana Department of Fish, Wildlife and Parks in the 1980s, criticized how that hunt was conducted and went on to write a book, *Beyond Fair Chase: The Ethics and Tradition of Hunting*. He disapproves of game farms and other "hunts" in which a paying customer is guaranteed an animal to shoot. "Fair chase by definition means hunting animals that are free-ranging." The "hook and bullet" magazines are a major distraction in the crusade for ethical hunting, as their lifeblood is advertising gadgets intended to help the hunter bag the biggest beast with the least effort. In 1993 Posewitz founded an organization dedicated to hunter education, and he is trying to promote a different message. For him the concept of fair chase means that the balance of power between the hunter and the hunted is such that the animals can generally avoid being taken and the hunter only occasionally succeeds.[15]

Standards for a fair chase are analogous to sports rules that restrict the type of equipment that may be used in order to prevent a player from gaining an unfair advantage. But as the title of Posewitz's book suggests, "ethical hunting" may be seen as more than just fair chase and good sportsmanship. Unlike baseball, hunting is a life-and-death matter, and for many people that changes everything. Whether a hunter's behavior is ethical is a subjective judgment that may be influenced by religious beliefs or cultural background. A hunter may be considered "sportsmanlike" because he gives his prey a sporting chance, yet be regarded as "unethical" because he flings the carcass into the back of a pickup and parades it through town with no respect for the animal's dignity.

"Hunting for sport is an improvement over hunting for food," Aldo Leopold wrote, "in that there has been added to the test of skill an ethical code, which the hunter formulates for himself, and must live up to without the moral support of bystanders."[16] But for some American Indians, hunting for food requires an ethical code, and the very idea of hunting for sport is a blasphemy. The InterTribal Bison Cooperative objected that the hunting provisions in the interagency bison management plan reflected a "Euro-centric" view that associates difficulty of killing an animal with fairness and a belief that merely shooting the animal is unacceptable. "The important distinction to Indian people is not between hunt and shoot, but between taking an animal's life with or without respect."[17] Hunting practices that many people regard as "unsportsmanlike" because the animal has no chance would be considered "fair" by some Indians if the necessary reverence for the animal were shown.

Using what is killed is another essential part of ethical hunting, according to the Posewitz code, in which the hunter "cares for harvested game in a respectful manner, leaving no waste." Field dressing helps prevent "spoiling edible parts," and "surplus parts" such as the entrails "should be thoughtfully returned to the earth."[18] From a purely ecological perspective, nature wastes nothing: a decaying carcass in its native habitat provides nutrition for other living things and does not require human assistance in order to become useful. However, for some people the ethics of hunting depend partly on whether it puts meat on the table that would otherwise come from a factory farm where animals are pumped up with hormones and treated like products on an assembly line. As Posewitz says, "Efficient is ethical: the ethical choice is to sustain one's needs with the least system impact."[19]

Bison Hunting in Montana Revisited

In its environmental impact statement on bison management, Montana said that complying with the national brucellosis eradication effort and preventing damage to private property "preclude the ability to regulate bison using traditional recreational hunting."[20] Three years later Montana legislators passed a bill to reauthorize bison hunting on public land despite fierce opposition from within their own ranks and from a variety of local and national interest groups. Some legislators objected that re-igniting the bison hunting controversy was imprudent in a state whose economy had become dependent on tourism. Animal rights groups such as the Humane Society of America and People for the Ethical Treatment of Animals (PETA) objected for the usual reasons having to do with the presumed docility and habituation of the Yellowstone bison, even though they are not fed by humans.

Some legislators scoffed at such opposition. "I don't think we should kowtow to these PETA people," said a member of Montana's House of

Representatives. "They don't share the same values as the average Montanan."[21] Another house member argued that "it's not fair to say that Joe Average in the state can't hunt bison, but someone who can pay Ted Turner can hunt bison."[22] Many Montanans, average or not, opposed bison hunting outside Yellowstone because a fair chase hunt seemed impossible. Yellowstone bison that cross the park boundary "have absolutely no reason to fear people, let alone lead them on a fair chase," opined the *Helena Independent Record.*

> Licenses to shoot a bison would cost $100 for residents and $1,000 for non-residents. Licenses for the state to shoot itself in the foot would be free. . . . It's hard to see how it could be otherwise. Letting Yellowstone bison range far into the countryside in order to provide some semblance of a fair hunt would defeat the whole idea of preventing the spread of brucellosis to cattle. Trying to explain that hunting is a strong tradition in Montana and that bison are just another species of game would be like arguing that puppies are just another kind of food.[23]

Montana Fish, Wildlife and Parks (MFWP) sought to allay fears of a return to the maligned bison hunts of the 1980s by emphasizing that hunters would have to track the animals on foot, away from roads and without the escort services of state officials. Nonetheless, the legislation was opposed by hunting organizations such as the Montana Wildlife Federation, which wanted authority for all wild bison management in the state to revert from the Department of Livestock back to MFWP. "This bad legislation is based on an eradication and intolerance mentality that merely shifts the burden to unsuspecting Montana hunters," said Glenn Hockett, president of the Gallatin Wildlife Association, although the hunters were obviously suspicious. "We fear the time-honored Montana tradition of fair chase public hunting and the privileges we enjoy in this regard will be severely tested and eroded in the national spotlight."[24] Another hunter put it more bluntly. "The bill takes guns out of Department of Livestock hands and has sportsmen do the dirty work. Before any hunting of Yellowstone buffalo is contemplated, the herd must be permitted to be free-roaming, like all other wildlife."[25]

But hunting the Yellowstone buffalo was contemplated, and a bison hunting bill was signed by the governor in May 2003. Although the bill was presented to the legislature as a way to reduce the risk of brucellosis transmission to cattle, the Montana Department of Livestock dismissed such notions.[26] The number of bison removed through hunting would be too small to lessen the need for other forms of boundary control, and the hunt would take place in the winter, when the only bison likely to be outside the park were those least likely to transmit brucellosis—some old bulls, Yellowstone's trophies, the survivors.

MFWP's goal for a new, improved bison hunt was aimed beyond brucellosis and greater Yellowstone to a change in the bison's image. Pat Flowers, an MFWP supervisor, saw an opportunity to "reframe" bison in Montana as wildlife "rather than just a disease vector."[27] By starting on a small scale and winning over potential hunters and the public at large, the department hopes to increase support for bison reintroduction and hunting in other locations. "Sportsmen have not made the commitment to bison populations that they have to every other large indigenous herbivore in North America," according to the MFWP draft environmental assessment of bison hunting. A "fair chase" public hunt "in a highly visible area such as southern Montana would undoubtedly spur interest by sportsmen in establishing additional wild bison populations" and would support the government programs needed to sustain them.[28]

"When sportsmen are invested in a species and species management program, they bring a voice of reason to the table," explained Kurt Alt of MFWP, suggesting that the voice of reason may have been missing from the state's bison management deliberations. "Throughout the history of North American conservation and restoration, sportsmen have always been a critical part in resolving those issues."[29] MFWP's environmental assessment therefore "reframed" the issue by reverting to the nineteenth-century view of bison as uncivilized animals that hunters could help keep in line. Among the "primary benefits" of establishing a hunt for bison outside the park would be the "removal of persistent problem animals," that is, those most dangerously wild and resistant to hazing. "Bison are capable of transmitting brucellosis to livestock, injuring livestock, destroying fences and stackyards, removing forage (in fields and hay stacks) reserved for livestock, and may even threaten humans. Hunters can reduce all of these problems by removing specific offending animals." Impervious to the resentment of many hunters, the environmental assessment pointed out that government personnel currently "perform this service" at taxpayer expense, even though "recreational hunters would willingly pay" to do it. And even though specific offensive animals were to be targeted, fair chase "will be insured by defining large hunting areas (including areas where bison can move to escape hunting pressure), by limiting numbers of hunters in the field, and by prohibiting hunting from vehicles." MFWP acknowledged that "each hunter will have to make a personal decision on the ethics of shooting an animal that may not flee when approached by a human."[30]

However, in the fall of 2004, MFWP reduced the hunting area to avoid conflict with hazing activities and cut the number of licenses to be issued from 25 to 10. More than 8,000 people paid $3 to enter the drawing, but just before it was to be held, the hunt was postponed until November 2005. Montana's newly installed governor, Brian Schweitzer, said he wanted to deter criticism of the state by enlarging the area in which bison could disperse from the park so as to permit a fair chase. But the prospect of bad publicity did not prevent Schweitzer, a cattle rancher, from also suggesting that all the bison in the park be captured and tested, so that the seropositive bison could be slaughtered and the seronegative put in quarantine facilities. That was not intended to be a fair chase.

Bison Learn to Be Wary

The Eagle Creek area of Gallatin National Forest is the only place adjacent to the park where bison are tolerated and have gone in significant numbers in some winters. The presence of hunters there might reduce bison use of this range and push the animals down toward the Yellowstone River, where they may be shot by the Department of Livestock. However, a fair chase hunt, at least as some would define it, is possible. Maybe not right away; maybe the bison as well as the state of Montana would have some learning to do, but it could happen. There is some truth to images of bison in the nineteenth century being mowed down like so many bowling pins, but that was largely on the open plains where herds numbered in the thousands and a bison's best protection was to stand behind another bison or hope for a gutter ball. As the size of the herds dwindled and bison became more wary and sought cover in more difficult terrain, hunting them became increasingly difficult.

When the first bison hunt in Utah's Henry Mountains was held in 1950, the bison were relatively easy to find and kill, but they quickly learned to become distrustful of people during the hunting season. The Utah Division of Wildlife Resources maintains that now it really is "a hunt," as opposed to "a shoot."[31] The Henry Mountains bison are descendents of Yellowstone bison, and there is no reason to think they are inherently any shrewder than the bison now in Yellowstone. With nearly 90 percent of the bison hunters in the Henry Mountains getting a bison, it seems to fall short of a fair chase in which the hunter only occasionally succeeds, but sometimes the principles of fair chase are overtaken by a herd reduction goal. It's been estimated that the 650,000-acre range in the Henry Mountains can support 1,000 large herbivores, but 600 of them are cattle with signed leases for grazing allotments from the Bureau of Land Management.

In Arizona some people would like to make bison hunting easier in the House Rock Wildlife Area in order to reduce a herd that has increased to about 150. In 2001, when the roads were especially snow jammed, only 13 of 54 hunters assigned to the area adjacent to Grand Canyon National Park succeeded in getting a bison, and it took them more than five days on average to do so.[32] As in Yellowstone, the House Rock bison are inclined to move to higher elevations in the summer, which has taken some of them across the boundary to the Grand Canyon's North Rim. Bison may prefer the forage there or the sanctuary from hunters, and an increasing number began remaining there in the fall, when the hunting season begins at House Rock. This has created a controversy in which the Park Service and state roles are reversed from those in Montana. Arizona's Game and Fish Department values the bison for their "recreational viewing opportunities" and as big game that bring in $40,000 a year in hunting fees, while the Park Service objects that the bison create mud wallows, defecate in ponds, crush grasses, and trample archeological sites. Even if evidence were found that bison were once native to the North Rim, the Park Service has had the animals tested genetically to prove that, as descendants of Buffalo Jones's hybrid herd, they are part cattle and therefore not deserving of a place in a national park.[33] This means that whereas bison in Montana are hazed into the park so they do not have to be killed, Park Service employees in Grand Canyon haze bison out of the park so that they may be hunted.

Grand Canyon has witnessed a great effort to restore the California condor, another Pleistocene species whose range once extended across North America. Every six months the "free-flying" and charismatic condors are captured to be tested and sometimes painfully treated for lead poisoning. The condor once fueled its nine-foot wing span by scavenging the carcasses of large species that have become extinct or much harder to come by, and the remains they do find may be laced with lead bullets. For want of enough naturally occurring dead mammoths and bison, humans provide carcasses at feeding sites in Arizona and California for the 84 condors living "in the wild."[34]

PART FIVE

PUSHING THE BOUNDARIES

Here all the wild creatures of the old days are being preserved, and their overflow into the surrounding country means that the people of the surrounding country, so long as they see that the laws are observed by all, will be able to insure to themselves and to their children and to their children's children much of the old time pleasures of the hardy life of the wilderness.

— President Theodore Roosevelt, at the dedication of the entrance arch to Yellowstone National Park, April 24, 1903

These bison outside Roosevelt Arch in March 2003 will probably be hazed back into the park several times before the increasing migration makes their capture necessary. Courtesy of Yellowstone National Park.

CHAPTER 14

Indians at the Crossroads

When a journalist tried to flatter Ted Turner about all the carnivores that have been welcomed back to his Flying D Ranch in Montana, the owner of 30,000 bison in six states bristled. "We don't have any grizzly bears! We don't have any Indians!" Perhaps that didn't sound quite right to the man who owns the tomahawk-emblazoned Atlanta Braves, for he added, "We have Indians visit!"[1]

The same may be said of Yellowstone National Park. It has cougars, coyotes, wolves, lynx, and even grizzly bears, but no Indians hunting the bison, only a few who are employed at the park and those who are visitors. And most Indians who come to Yellowstone don't consider themselves tourists, but people with a special claim on the land. It is the white people who are the visitors to the park, to this continent. Seven tribes claim treaty rights to park land, and some Indians cite provisions of the Fort Laramie Treaty of 1851 the way other Americans cite the Second Amendment for the right to bear arms. In their treaties Indians gave up land in exchange for promises that the Supreme Court has held created a "trust responsibility" which obliges the United States to protect the safety and well-being of the tribes.[2] Some Indians believe that their well-being depends on that of the bison in Yellowstone.

"The Yellowstone area is like a crossroads of many different Indian nations who have come here from many different directions, for food, for plants," explained Tony Incashola of the Confederated Salish and Kootenai Tribes at a Yellowstone National Park tribal consultation meeting in 2002. "It's something we were given, something we were born with, something that was passed down from generation to generation. . . . as I drive back to my reservation, and I see the development happening all over, the sadness that I feel is that those areas that were sacred to people are disappearing. You have to go to certain areas, like Yellowstone Park." Sometimes the Indians' claim on Yellowstone gets caught behind their sense of privacy about their traditional practices. "This is our aboriginal territory," an Eastern Shoshone told a group of Yellowstone staff. "This is where we come to collect, this is where we come to for our spirituality. We have vision quests all over this place. I know you don't know nothing about it, because we're not going to tell you."[3]

The Associated Tribes of Yellowstone

By the time Yellowstone was established as a national park in 1872, nearly all of the land within and adjacent to its boundaries had been taken from tribal control, but some tribes believe their treaties entitle them to continue to hunt there. The 1868 treaty with the Eastern Shoshones and Bannocks, for example, granted them "the right to hunt on the unoccupied lands of the United States so long as game may be found thereon."[4] Consequently, the current claims of Indians upon the park and its bison are as debatable as the question of whether Yellowstone's backcountry may be considered "unoccupied." In June 1992 two years after drafting of the EIS for bison management had begun, the Park Service notified eight tribes of this fact in order to "help ensure that the proposed project will not negatively impact ethnographic resources with a cultural affinity to members of your tribe."[5] Although some tribes maintained that treaty rights entitled them to participate in drafting the EIS, their request was not granted because the Indians were not considered to have any authority for making decisions about the Yellowstone bison.

However, in 1996 Yellowstone National Park managers began holding "government-to-government" consultations with representatives from six Indian tribes twice a year. As at other national parks, any federally recognized tribe that so wishes can become officially "associated" with Yellowstone by explaining its traditional ties to the area. By 2003 Yellowstone's list of associated tribes had grown to 26, from the Comanche tribe of Oklahoma to the Confederated Tribes of the Colville Reservation in Washington. Bison have been the major topic of discussion at Yellowstone tribal consultations, but other issues have also been raised. National parks typically waive entrance fees for members of their associated tribes, and Yellowstone came under pressure to do likewise. "We're fighting to get a fee waived just to come in to see our ancestral land," said Darrin Old Coyote of the Crows. "We do not come as tourists. We come to be part of nature, part of the earth, part of this life. We like coming to be close to the animals that mean so much to us, to our culture. Coming here is refreshing, gives us good thoughts, good minds."[6]

Yellowstone managers, whose minds may have benefited from their living in the park, granted a fee waiver to the tribes in 1998, but the Indians were required to obtain the written "sanction" of their tribal chair to show that they were coming to the park to "conduct religious or traditional activities."[7] The Indians objected that this letter, which was not required at other national parks, was an intrusive inconvenience, and it did not help Indians who were traveling through the park on their way to someplace else, like the Indians who used to pass through on their way to the buffalo hunting grounds to the east. The requirement for a letter was dropped in 2001. Tribal requests for exemptions from rules that prohibit removing natural artifacts from the park for religious, medicinal, or any purpose other than an approved research project have been turned down, but changing the policy remains under consideration.

The tensest issue at the meetings has been the tribes' frustration over the nature of the "government-to-government consultations." For Indians who see themselves as representing sovereign nations, consultation means "sitting there talking with the tribal council and with the people from D.C."—the president or the secretary of the interior. "Where are the policy makers? We should be talking to them face to face," said Michael Dann, representing the Shoshone-Bannock tribes. "When your people came to us and wanted some of this stuff that we had and regulated us, put us in the Black Hills, put us in Wyoming, put us up in the mountains, put my people on flat land, put these guys way out here, they regulated us. It was done by treaty. And I don't know if you people really recognize treaties. . . . And it was done by the big agencies. They're the ones that regulated us, not you, not the park agencies."[8]

Aside from the burden of history and the lack of faith in treaties, the Indians' discontent sprang from the lack of weight being given to their views. Instead of being consulted about bison management in Yellowstone, they felt they were merely being informed about decisions that had already been made. The Nez Percé have been involved in salmon recovery in the Columbia River and in wolf restoration in Idaho, and some Indians believed the tribes should have a significant role in preventing the "senseless destruction" of Yellowstone bison by government agencies.[9]

"Some environmentalists want to let them all roam until they die of old age," said Mike Fox, who is fish and wildlife director at the Fort Belknap Reservation. "No, that's not what the Creator put them here for. Humans have to be part of the management. In the old days, we didn't call it management. We called it survival. . . . Dealing with these animals, you know that at some point you're gonna have a surplus if you don't use them as they're meant to be used."[10] About 3,700 members of the Gros Ventre and Assiniboin tribes live on the Fort Belknap Reservation in Montana along with 400 bison, the descendants of 12 that came from the National Bison Range in 1974. By Fox's reckoning, about one-third of the Indians on the reservation have retained their tribal culture, one-third have some ties to it, and one-third are completely removed from it. Cattle ranchers usually fall into the last group, and they are the ones most likely to oppose or at least question efforts to restore the role of bison in tribal life. But having bison to use in tribal gatherings has meant that the tribe gathers more often now for traditional events. The ritual of the Sun Dance was revived, with a bison supplying meat, rattles, hides for drum heads, and the bleached skull that serves as an altar in the ceremony.[11]

During the public comment period that followed release of the draft EIS in 1998, the Fort Belknap Community Council submitted its own plan, which was designed to "preserve the bison as a wild, free-ranging species and reaffirm the trust relationship between the bison and Indian tribes." Unlike the alternative proposed by the EIS, the Fort Belknap plan would halt lethal removal of bison by government agencies. Instead, bison would have priority over cattle on all public land outside the park. Any bison deemed "excess" would be captured and tested for brucellosis; seropositive animals would be turned over to an Indian tribe for ceremonial harvest, and seronegative animals would be kept on the Fort Belknap Reservation for the necessary quarantine period, after which they would be distributed to other tribes.

Other tribes that submitted comments on the draft EIS agreed that the designated alternative was overkill, but differed on the best course of action. Some Indians object to vaccinating bison as a matter of principle. The Fort Belknap bison herd was not vaccinated, because of "fears of altering the spirit or the character" of the animal. "We use the buffalo blood to heal cancer," said Eagle Hunter. "Once you contaminate that, what good would it do?"[12] Some Indians supported "Plan B," an alternative submitted by environmentalists who were more focused on preserving Yellowstone bison as wild animals. Under Plan B the bison population size would be controlled by hunting outside the park, and brucellosis would be addressed by vaccinating the bison when an effective vaccine and remote delivery method were available. Only tribal members would be permitted to participate in the hunt, but no bison would be captured, so no live bison would be available for distribution to tribes.

A Blood Sacrifice for the Buffalo

Another objection to the draft EIS was the past tense used in some references to the Indian tribes, such as "Bison were critical to the indigenous cultures of North America."[13] Many Indians still regard the bison as both a cultural and natural resource, or consider the distinction between cultural and natural resources to be artificial, a peculiar notion of the white man. Although many Indians share with deep ecologists a nonhierarchical, egalitarian view of animal life, the idea that the Creator put the bison on Earth for human use is at odds with the perspective of environmentalists who believe that plants and animals have a value independent of how humans use or relate to them. According to Mark Heckert of the InterTribal Bison Cooperative (ITBC), most Indians don't "demarcate one area as inviolable wilderness and another as an area to clear-cut. It's all to be honored as sacred, and it all has potential for use."[14]

Indians have tried to use the regulations of the prevailing cultural bureaucracy to their advantage, however. The ITBC claimed that the Yellowstone bison qualified for protection under the National Historic Preservation Act, which would impose certain requirements on government agencies in managing the animal. "While there may be no precedent for designating wildlife as an historic resource and object under the NHPA, the present circumstances are unique." The eligibility criteria set forth in the federal regulations include "objects that possess integrity of location, . . . feeling and association and that are associated with events that have made a significant contribution to the broad patterns of our history." The ITBC also argued that its members' "sacred companion, the buffalo" was eligible for protection under the American Indian Religious Freedom Act, which requires government agencies to "consider and evaluate the potential effects of any proposed action to those resources of cultural and religious importance to Indian people."[15]

The view of the buffalo as sacred was exemplified by Indians who responded to its plight by conducting a traditional ceremony instead of submitting comments to the EIS team. In February 1999, 40 Indians left Rapid City, South Dakota, on foot, horseback, and in pickup trucks for a 500-mile procession to Yellowstone. Some Lakota on the Standing Rock Reservation came up with the idea as a way to raise public awareness of the buffalo's importance to their culture. In the Lakota language the buffalo is called *tatanka*, which means "he who owns us." Three weeks later, when the Indians reached the park's north entrance, their number had swelled to 100. Park staff and other local residents provided food and accommodations for them, and Chief Joseph Chasing Horse explained why they had come. "Many tribes of indigenous people have survived because the buffalo gave us our food, shelter, clothing, even our spirituality. This journey we make was made by my ancestors for ten thousands of years, according to the ancestral routes of the buffalo."

The Indians were joined by an equal number of white people as they gathered at the park entrance near the Roosevelt Arch for the ceremony. Rosalie Little Thunder sat on a rock holding the spiritual bundle that had been carried from Rapid City. A song was sung for the children present, who were said to embody the future. Park superintendent Mike Finley, who perhaps embodied the present, offered a greeting. "We welcome you to Yellowstone and, more importantly, we welcome you home." Old Indian songs were sung, and elders from the Nez Perce and Tuscarora nations spoke. For the ritual climax of the ceremony, riders on horseback positioned themselves around the group as a show of strength against the cameras present, which were required to keep their eyes shut.

"Long ago, the buffalo gave his blood for us. Today, we give our blood for him," Chasing Horse proclaimed. Gary Silk, a Lakota, stripped to his waist and stood in the wind that whipped through the large stone arch as he was handed a sacred pipe. Some people who felt blown outside their mental comfort zone thought it best to avert their eyes and leave the ceremony. Burning sage smoldered in a cast-iron skillet. Silk cupped his hands in the smoke and moved them over his body to cleanse it. Tyler Medicine Horse mixed a reddish-brown paint and drew a circle with a vertical line through it on Silk's back below each scapula. Then he used a surgical lancet to make two cuts near each circle. Blood trickled down Silk's back. A bald eagle flew slowly overhead and the crowd murmured. Medicine Horse pushed a wooden rod through the incisions on each side of Silk's back. To each rod was tied a leather cord, and to the cord were attached two buffalo skulls. As the Indians sang and drummed and blew whistles made of eagle bone, a Gros Ventre elder carried the smoking sage, and Silk danced slowly around the gathering, dragging the skulls behind him. He stopped at each quadrant of the compass to extend his arms toward the sky and sing a prayer. Many people wept. After circling the group seven times, Silk stopped and two children sat on the skulls. Silk's horse was brought to him and he took hold of the tail. With a whoop, someone slapped the horse and when the animal pulled away, Silk was jerked forward and the rods were torn from his flesh. Medicine Horse applied a powder scraped from the inside of a buffalo horn onto Silk's wounds to stop the bleeding.

Rosalie Little Thunder and several men came forward to make their own flesh offerings for the buffalo. A teenager who rolled up her sleeves was given the sacred pipe to hold, and Medicine Horse opened a fresh lancet and cut four lines on each of her shoulders as she stood without flinching. The ceremony ended when the pipe was touched to the shoulders of everyone in the crowd as a gesture of unity. More people wanted to make flesh offerings, and they were accommodated that night when the Indians gathered for dinner at the Gardiner school, where about 30 people waited in line for Medicine Horse to cut them. Chasing Horse said he hoped that in the future Indians would be allowed to hunt buffalo in the park.

Buffalo Are Us

Many of the white people who were moved by the ceremony stumbled into the cultural chasm it lay bare. How could the same Indians who decried the slaughter of buffalo outside the park want to hunt them in the park? The Indians' regard for the buffalo as family was difficult for many people to grasp, including most white people who would not consider eating their relatives. According to the traditional belief of many Indians, the universe is pervaded by a spirit that resides in certain topographical features, artifacts, and living things, and one's relationships with them should be governed by expectations and obligations similar to those felt toward one's family and allies.[16] Some Indians regard buffalo as members of their extended family because they see the relationship as a reciprocal one. According to Winona

LaDuke, a member of the Anishinabes, many Indians regard the historic buffalo slaughter as "the time when the buffalo relatives, the older brothers, stood up and took the killing intended for the younger brothers, the Native peoples."[17]

The sacrifice made in ritual dances through fasting, thirst, and inflicted pain may reflect the Indians' desire to return something of themselves to nature.[18] Some Indians speak of a time long ago when it was the buffalo who ate man. As told by Arvol Looking Horse, a Lakota whose family has been keeper of a sacred buffalo pipe for 19 generations, a race was held between the two-legged creatures and the four-legged creatures, the winners to eat the losers.[19] The magpie and the hawk won the race for man. A council was held, and the buffalo came forward, offering his body for cere-monies and his spirit to strengthen man's spirit. In return, the Lakota said they would honor the buffalo by calling themselves the buffalo people. "We and the buffalo are one," said Looking Horse. "I humbly ask all nations to respect our way of life, because in our prophecies, if there is no buffalo, then life as we know it will cease to exist."[20]

The sacred status accorded the buffalo by some Indians has been com-pared to the Christian belief in Holy Communion, a ceremony in which the body and blood of Christ are, depending on one's faith, symbolically or literally consumed by participants. This analogy demonstrates how religious practices that are routinely accepted in one culture may seem outlandish to another, but it may cast more smoke than light on the Indians' relation to the buffalo. Generalizations about Indian attitudes toward the buffalo, even when referring only to tribes whose traditions revere the animal, are difficult to make. Some Indians pray to the buffalo for help and use buffalo imagery or parts of the buffalo to cure the sick, and some say that they "worship" the buffalo.[21] But this does not necessarily mean that they regard the buffalo in Yellowstone or anywhere else as deities. The buffalo has admirable traits that Indians can emulate — its strength and endurance, its facing into the wind in a storm, its presumed loyalty to its family. Whether the buffalo also has supernatural powers depends on which Indian you ask.

For Indians and non-Indians alike, perceptions about brucellosis in the Yellowstone bison may be colored by feelings about the animal. Park Service biologists were once inclined to think that brucellosis in Yellow-stone was caused by a native organism rather than the mundane bacteria known in cattle, or that it might at least behave very differently in Yellowstone bison, which could explain the apparent infrequency of abortions.[22] After more research, wildlife biologists came to accept the idea that Yellowstone bison acquired brucellosis from cattle and that although the disease may manifest itself somewhat differently in bison, the rate of abortion in Yellowstone bison is probably no lower than in a cattle herd that has been infected for many years and built up some immunity to the disease.[23]

Some Indians, however, continue to view brucellosis in bison in a way that reflects their veneration for the animal. When he comes to tribal consultations, Haman Wise of the Eastern Shoshones feels obliged to explain "the part nobody understands" to Yellowstone managers:

> You really don't know why the buffalo leaves, do you? The buffalo leaves the park because they have to eat that certain food, that certain medicine plant. . . . The cows that we have now are so dumb they don't know how to take care of themselves. They have to have human hands take care of them through the winter and give them shots, keep them alive. You don't have to do that with the buffalo, because he knows what kind of plants to eat to take care of his own body. . . . That's why you don't see very much aborting in buffalo.[24]

The October 2002 consultation was the first to be hosted by an associated tribe instead of Yellowstone. Assistant Superintendent Frank Walker and three other Yellowstone employees went to Pierre, South Dakota, for the meeting, and it was probably the first time since Superintendent Norris went to the Indians to tell them to stay out of the park in 1881 that an official Yellowstone delegation went to the Indians for any reason. Two tribal representatives at the meeting mentioned the same kind of remedy for brucellosis as had Haman Wise. "The disease that you are talking about, mother nature will provide the medicine. It sprouts from the ground, so they eat it and they get well," offered Al Grassrope of the Lower Brule Sioux, who maintain a herd of about 140 bison. Louis Golus, manager of the Yankton Sioux's herd of 80 bison, said, "It seems like the buffalo know which plants to eat if they are sick or if something is wrong with them. I don't know if the Park Service would introduce these plants."

"Thank you very much, Louis," said Walker, who was chairing the meeting. But no one from the Park Service pressed to learn more about the wondrous plants known to the Indian consultants.

Buffalo Return to Indian Country

The Flandreau-Santee Sioux of Nebraska, who started their herd in 1995 with 24 bison from Wind Cave National Park, now have about 68 bison. "We never had a buffalo herd and we pretty much got it under control now that we got a lot of the bulls taken out," explained tribal member Jean Paul Roy. "We do buffalo kills probably four times a year. We have a ceremony, a song, and we take them down in a spiritual way like the ancestors used to. We recently started implementing that, instead of just gunning them down and taking the meat home."[25]

The draft EIS noted that the InterTribal Bison Cooperative had proposed "transporting surplus bison from Yellowstone to tribal reservations where they would join bison already on ranches." The National Wildlife Federation, which has supported the ITBC's goal of setting up a quarantine program for Yellowstone bison, objected to that statement. "Tribes manage their bison as wildlife and do not 'ranch' their bison."[26] Most of the herds managed by ITBC tribes are primarily for "cultural and aesthetic purposes," and the ITBC encourages minimal management and traditional killing ceremonies instead of just gunning the bison down. "Rounded up and worked just like cattle through corral systems, then put in feedlots and finished on grain, and the genetic selection to produce bigger animals—it's offensive to the animal and very damaging to the species," says Fred DuBray of the ITBC. "That's all part of domestication and commercialization. For us, respect for the animal is the bottom line rather than profit." The ITBC discourages tribes from accepting the meat, heads, and hides from Yellowstone bison that have been slaughtered. "I know there's people who could use the meat," DuBray says, "but it's too easy for the officials to claim they're doing these tribes a favor."

In the final EIS the text was revised to read, "Bison were and still remain critical to the indigenous cultures of North America," but the reference to bison ranching on Indian reservations remained for reasons the National Wildlife Federation should understand. Tribal bison herds may get lots of respect, and they may not be milked for a revenue flow, but they are more like livestock than wildlife. The Ho-Chunk nation, formerly known as the Wisconsin Winnebago tribe, refers to the facilities for its 150 bison as the "Bison Ranch," where "tour groups enjoy the scenery, bison, and resident prairie dogs, while being informed of the agricultural practices used at the site in the context of Ho-Chunk history and culture."[27] The Ho-Chunks do strive for "complete organic farming" in order to "ensure the health of the bison and the balance of nature." Bison feed and hay are grown without pesticides or artificial fertilizer, and the animals are rarely given antibiotics or other medications. Eight years after the herd was started in 1993, budget cuts nearly resulted in its sale. Some tribal members argued that it was more important to "feed our people than to feed the buffalo" and that bison meat could be purchased for less than the cost of running the Bison Ranch. But others hoped to expand the herd to 1,000 so that it could be economically viable, to add bison meat to the menus of the tribe's three casinos, and to someday have 2,000 "free-roaming" bison on the Kickapoo Valley Nature Reserve, which the tribe manages jointly with the state of Wisconsin.[28]

Since the ITBC was established in 1990, its membership has grown to 53 tribes in states from Michigan to Alaska. But most of the 35 tribal herds have less than 100 bison and are on limited ranges where they must receive supplemental feed part of the year and are subjected to occasional roundups. The Cheyenne River Sioux, who have gone the farthest of any tribe to take the ranch out of bison ranching, have the largest tribal herd—about 2,500 bison on 30,000 acres of native grass in South Dakota. In November 2003 the tribe received some direct descendants of Yellowstone bison when an animal welfare group, In Defense of Animals, raised $25,000 to transport 105 surplus bison from Catalina Island to the Cheyenne River Sioux and the Standing Rock Sioux, whose reservation is in North Dakota.

Tribal member DuBray hopes to eventually double the herd's size, but it must compete for land on the 2.8 million–acre reservation with Indian cattle ranchers, many of whom will tolerate the bison only if they are enclosed by barbed wire fences and kept away from the range where the cattle feed. Some bison are killed each year for traditional use, and others produce revenue through the sale of meat and hunting permits. "We want to develop our herd as large as possible, but not just to sell meat," said DuBray. "Actually, it would be ideal if we get to the point where we don't sell any meat at all, but instead provide a healthy diet to the people to eat. By selling meat now we are helping to sustain the herd financially."[29]

Most ITBC member tribes are in dire need of jobs and revenue. Nearly all the residents of the Cheyenne River Sioux reservation have incomes below the federal poverty line. But their traditional relationship with the buffalo makes it difficult for some Indians to look on the animal as a cash cow. "The commercial production of buffalo is a hard sell in Indian Country," said Louis LaRose, a member of the Winnebago tribe and director of the Northern Plains Bison Education Network, a group of ten tribal colleges that teach bison management skills. "There's a difference between producing bison for the spiritual and cultural needs of a tribe and producing bison for a commercial market."[30]

Along with providing technical assistance to its members, the ITBC wants to develop a distribution plan that will provide "a fair market price to Tribal buffalo producers and also a healthy source of food to the people who have the greatest need." Diabetes and heart disease are much more common on the reservation than off, as is the belief that buffalo meat can play a significant role in addressing health problems. "Many years ago when we ate buffalo, we had no diabetes, we had no heart disease, we were strong, we were survivors in the coldest days of the winter, just like the buffalo when the north wind comes in," said Robert Chasing Hawk of the Cheyenne River Sioux. "That's how strong we were, until the white man came and wanted us to be a white man." In addition to having less fat and cholesterol than beef or chicken, research suggests that bison raised on native grass may be healthier because its "ratio of Omega-3 to Omega-6 fatty acids" has been linked to lower rates of heart disease, learning disabilities, and cancer.[31]

"We don't want these buffalo to look at," explained Ernie Robinson of the Northern Cheyenne reservation, where one out of seven members has diabetes. "I want to eat them. I want my people to eat them so we can be healthy. . . . Cows are killing us. They're killing you guys, too. But genetically, the science of it is that the tribal people have not had time for their metabolism to adjust to the foods that are on the market, so we need to stay a little closer to the earth."[32]

The modern bison is not venerated by all Indians whose ancestors depended on the animal. In 1983 a traditional buffalo-calling ceremony was held at the Fort Berthold Reservation in North Dakota for the first time in a century, to celebrate the first transfer of surplus bison from Theodore Roosevelt National Park. But Bud Mason, chairman of the Three Affiliated Tribes (Arikara, Hidatsa, and Mandan) at Fort Berthold, regarded the bison as only a distant cousin of their ancestors and thought it was too late to save what once was. "The bison we have now are already domesticated to a limited degree," he said in 1998, when the herd size was kept at about 235 by selling the surplus at public auction. "We deal with bison on a commercial basis."[33]

In April 2004 tribal elders and government officials were investigating charges of negligence in the bison operations at Fort Berthold for the second year in a row. Some tribal members alleged that many bison in the herd of 600 had been mistreated, the local veterinarian found bison carcasses left to rot, and the bison staff were accused of spending most of the day watching movies. "If they can't adequately take care of them, we should send [the bison] home," said one tribal councilman, referring to Theodore Roosevelt National Park.[34]

Self-Determination

Of the 26 tribal organizations associated with Yellowstone, 15 have bison. The Eastern Shoshones of Wyoming do not have a herd, because white ranchers and agriculture officials aren't the only people who distrust wild bison. In 1994 Grand Teton National Park wanted to give 14 bison to the tribe, and the Jackson Hole Conservation Alliance was going to help the Indians construct a fence. "But we had a problem on our reservation," explained Haman Wise. "We have too many cattle people. Most of our council was cattlemen, and they just threw out the idea. They wouldn't let it happen because they was afraid of brucellosis."

The Confederated Salish and Kootenai Tribes are without bison on the Flathead Reservation, where until 1907 the largest remaining bison herd roamed freely. This was the herd that had to be dispersed when the U.S. government gave 160-acre allotments to each Indian family and sold the remaining land to the general public, leaving the Indians outnumbered four to one on their reservation. President Theodore Roosevelt set aside 18,000 acres of the reservation for the National Bison Range in 1908, but the bison purchased for it were entrusted to the U.S. government. In 1994, when the National Bison Range employed no Indians and did not even mention them in the information provided at the visitors center, the tribes began negotiating with the Department of the Interior for a contract to manage the National Bison Range.[35] The tribes' case is based on the Indian Self-Determination Act Amendments of 1994, which provide that self-governing tribes are eligible to manage certain federal properties, or specific operations on them, if they can demonstrate that the property has "special geographic, historical, or cultural significance" to them.[36]

The Interior Department has proposed that the U.S. government would continue to own, and have ultimate management authority over, the National

Bison Range, but would contract with the Salish and Kootenai tribes to carry out most of the chores, including weed control, wildlife management, facility maintenance, and visitor services. Negotiations have been slow as the tribes have pressed for more control and faced vehement opposition from those who think that national wildlife refuges should remain staffed by federal employees. Since 1994 the list of properties deemed eligible for tribal management has grown to include 41 national wildlife refuges and 34 units administered by the National Park Service, but not Yellowstone, at least not yet.

"I've managed a herd of 400 head of buffalo for the past seven years, so I know a little about how the critters operate," wrote Mike Fox of the Fort Belknap reservation in the comments he submitted for the draft EIS. "The Park Service's stance that that's a natural system down there just isn't true. If you want a natural system, you would have to capture, quarantine, and relocate the Indians back into the park."[37] George Catlin's idea in the 1830s for a park that would preserve "the native Indian . . . amid the fleeting herds of elks and buffaloes" was dismissed by historian Aubrey Haines in 1977 as impractical: "Such an environment would be unstable because man was included among the exhibits."[38] But the possibility of an Indian presence in the park is not so easily rejected today, when volatility is an accepted part of natural environments. Even parks like Yellowstone that were established because of their natural wonders have come under pressure to make known the areas' human past, both Indian and non-Indian. This trend is consistent with the increasing recognition that even so-called "wilderness" areas have human histories worthy of study.

To have Indians hunting in Yellowstone again is not a goal of the ITBC, but members have said they would like to see subsistence hunting resumed "as a tribal treaty and sovereign right."[39] Support for such views comes from ecologists who believe that the Yellowstone bison population has grown unnaturally large because it is not curtailed by aboriginal hunting. "Native Americans were the ultimate keystone predator and their absence has completely changed the Yellowstone Ecosystem until today it is little more than an ecological slum, and we have a bison overpopulation problem that never existed in the past," stated ecologist Charles Kay in 1997. He is an adherent of the "aboriginal overkill" theory, according to which prehistoric cultures were responsible for the extinction of many large mammals in North America and on other continents. "I suggest that we simply permit Native Americans to hunt bison in the park."[40]

Aside from the fact that there would be nothing simple about letting Indians hunt in the park, this view assumes that Indian impacts on the North American landscape are inherently "natural" while those of other ethnic groups are not. Kay also assumes that "your goal is to mimic the processes that were structuring the ecosystem before Europeans got here."[41] The "primary goal" recommended by the panel of scientists and conservationists who prepared the 1963 Leopold Report on wildlife management in the national parks was in fact that "the biotic associations within each park be maintained, or where necessary recreated, as nearly as possible in the condition that prevailed when the area was first visited by white man."[42] However, the report made no reference to the existence of Indians prior to the arrival of white men, and it appears reasonable to assume that, like most wildlife managers at that time, the panel was largely heedless of their influence.

Ecologist Mark Boyce has countered that even if Kay's "implausible hypothesis" about Indian impacts could be substantiated, it would be irrelevant. "Understanding the history of exploitation of natural resources by humans is interesting, but it has no bearing on how we should manage resources in the future. Just because previous generations of humans decimated wildlife populations and altered natural ecosystems does not provide justification for doing so today."[43] For many people Indians are "native" to the land in a way that other ethnic groups are not, but most people have also accepted the evidence that everyone living in the Western Hemisphere has ancestors who came from someplace else at some point.

Bison Hunting in Indian Country

Kay's reference to the Indian hunter as a "keystone predator" suggests that they had more in common with wild carnivores than with Euro-American hunters, which some Indians may consider a compliment. But it may be argued that tribal societies all over the world have controlled nature to benefit themselves as much as they were able to, and that the changes that have occurred in North America since European colonization differ in extent rather than kind, being the result of population increase and technological advances, not cultural differences.[44] The Indians have not spurned the use of new techniques to make their lives easier. The Nez Perce were able to kill more animals and feed a larger population by switching from the atlatl to the bow and arrow about 3,000 years ago and adopting the horse in the 1830s. For the contemporary but traditional-minded Nez Perce, hunting still involves prayer and the most effective equipment available, the rifle and four-wheel drive.[45]

When Indians refer to their own hunting practices as "natural" in contrast to Euro-American methods of killing wildlife, they are often referring to the ways of killing, not the means. In commenting on how Yellowstone bison were being managed at the park boundary in 1997, a Salish from the Flathead Reservation said, "Although the park claims it is managing for natural regulation, it is not natural to shoot buffalo in the winter. It is necessary to harvest animals when they are in good condition. Salish people typically did not hunt buffalo during the winter and buffalo were left to survive the harsh winters in peace." Members of the Shoshone-Bannock tribe from the Fort Hall Reservation in Idaho were also opposed to hunting bison after they had lost significant weight when they came out of the park in the winter.[46] "That's the time the animals should be at rest," said Haman Wise of the Eastern Shoshone. "They should have a rest period someplace to revise their spirituality."[47]

However deeply felt, these declarations must be regarded as statements of principle rather than fact, similar to Euro-American ideals about preventing cruelty to animals. The Indians did hunt buffalo in the winter when they were hungry, or because they preferred fresh meat to dried pemmican, or because that is when the buffalo were wearing their warmest robes. "We were swimming in abundance," Father Nicolas Point, a French missionary traveling with a band of Salish, wrote in his journal for January 22, 1842. "Each hunter, on this day, killed three and four cows." Several weeks later, after kneeling "to invoke the help of their patron," the same Indians killed 150 bison south of present-day Missoula, Montana.[48] Today, bison on tribal lands may be hunted or otherwise killed during the winter. What matters about these Indians' beliefs is not their historical accuracy or consistency but the assumption that hunting done under certain conditions is part of the natural regulation of an animal species.

None of the seven Indian representatives in the Montana legislature voted in favor of the 2003 bill that allows the department of Fish, Wildlife and Parks to reinstate a hunting season for bison that leave Yellowstone National Park. Aside from the fact that many Indians would prefer to have bison that leave the park relocated to tribal lands, some believe that Indians should be entitled to do any bison hunting that takes place outside the park, and some are opposed to sport hunting as a matter of principle. "This shows no respect or reverence for the animal spirit," said a member of the

Confederated Salish and Kootenai Tribes, which collect hunting and fishing fees on the Flathead Reservation. He was concerned not about commercializing a natural resource but about "what people feel about what they are doing and how they utilize the resource."[49] The definition of "sport" therefore lies with the holder of the gun, and many of those whom Indians may disdain as "sport hunters" believe they have great respect for the animal they are pursuing.

The Fund for Animals does not actively campaign against subsistence hunting, but from its perspective, which tries to be the animal's perspective, the result is the same whether you're killed by an Indian, a white sport hunter, or a poacher.[50] From the traditional Indian perspective, however, the animals do know and care whether they are being killed with respect. The six tribes that sell permits for bison hunting on their reservations either do not have qualms about sport hunting or set them aside because of financial considerations. At the Cheyenne River Reservation, which maintains a goal of "culturally appropriate and spiritually responsible economic development," bids for bison hunting permits for nonmembers start at $2,000. If you make a winning bid, you're entitled to a two-day hunt with Indian guides who will drive you to within stalking distance of the bull you're guaranteed to get, retrieve the carcass for you, and assist in the field dressing. But you can leave your bow and arrow at home; out of consideration for the bison, you must use at least a .30 caliber gun and your guide may intervene if you cannot bring the animal down in two shots.[51]

Some Plead for Quarantine

In 1994 the ITBC proposed relocating seronegative bison captured at the park boundary to the Choctaw Nation of Oklahoma for the required quarantine period until the animals could be distributed to other tribes.[52] But rules set by the Animal and Plant Health Inspection Service (APHIS) of the USDA did not allow animals from an infected herd to cross state lines until they completed their quarantine period. APHIS was willing to overlook the fact that Yellowstone bison frequently crossed state lines without leaving the park, perhaps because APHIS did not consider the bison under its jurisdiction until they were captured and could be regarded as livestock instead of wildlife.

In 1997 the ITBC proposed quarantining seronegative bison from Yellowstone at the Fort Belknap Reservation in Montana. But APHIS rules did not

Although these Indians took care of the carcasses of bison shot outside the park by the Montana Department of Livestock in 1997 in order to receive the meat, head, and hides, other Indians declined the offer because they objected to the slaughter. Courtesy of Yellowstone National Park.

allow animals from an infected herd to be sent anywhere in a designated brucellosis-free state except to a slaughterhouse. The Park Service argued that Yellowstone was an unsuitable location for a quarantine facility, leaving APHIS in the awkward position of forbidding quarantined bison elsewhere in Montana while acknowledging the presence of unquarantined bison from an infected herd that wandered outside the park. More difficult to overlook was the presence of broad support from both wildlife advocates and livestock supporters for sending "surplus" bison from Yellowstone to Indian tribal lands. Disagreement persisted about what constitutes surplus bison and what type of quarantine would be necessary, and bison that survived the long confinement may no longer be considered wildlife, but even some people who consider a quarantine facility inappropriate or cruel for wild bison regard it as preferable to sending the animals to slaughter.

The Citizens' Plan, which the ITBC endorsed, agreed to the use of a quarantine facility if it had several large pastures of at least 320 acres to allow bison to forage on natural vegetation, and if it were not located in or adjacent to the park or in any other place where it might impair wildlife migrations or winter range. Mike Fox of the ITBC sought even higher standards. "We're talking about four or five thousand acres where you would have ready access to those animals for periodic testing, but they won't be standing ankle deep in their own waste. We're not stuck on the idea of it being on an Indian reservation, just somewhere where the animals are basically treated with respect, and that's all we're asking."[53] Sometimes Indian support for a quarantine facility appears driven by the priority they place on keeping Yellowstone bison alive, even if it meant they were no longer the wild animals the Indians' ancestors once knew and respected. In other cases the priority simply appears to be obtaining bison for Indians. "Our whole purpose is to try to get buffalo restored to our tribal lands," said Fred DuBray during a meeting with Montana governor Judy Martz in 2003.[54]

By the time the bison management EIS was completed in 2000, APHIS had changed its rules to permit a quarantine facility in Montana that meets certain specifications, but quarantining bison that leave the park remained a complicated and expensive prospect. Bison could be bought for tribal lands from private ranchers for far less, but it wouldn't be the same for Indians who regard the Yellowstone bison as special, as survivors like themselves.

CHAPTER 15

A New Buffalo Nation

Many Indian Tribes and Native Americans believe that the plight of the Yellowstone herd is inextricably tied to their own survival. They believe that respect for the Yellowstone bison and the defense of the bison's inherent right to prosper in the Yellowstone ecosystem are intertwined with Native American prophecies that portend the return of the Buffalo Nation.
—InterTribal Bison Cooperative, 1998[1]

If quantity were quality, the Indians' prospects for survival would appear promising. In the summer of 2004, bison may have been more numerous in Yellowstone than at any time in recorded or unrecorded history. They are more numerous in the United States than they have been since the 1870s, and indeed, so are the Indians, whose numbers have increased about 20 percent in eastern Montana, and in the Dakotas and Nebraska. That is in contrast to the region's shrinking white population. The rural counties of the Great Plains, where the population has declined by about one-third since the 1920s, along with the topsoil and economic health, have been confronted with the possibility of reverting to a "buffalo commons," a new take on the old concept of manifest destiny. For some people the changes suggest that Euro-American agricultural settlement of the Great Plains may have been only an accident of history, or an experiment that didn't work out in the long run because periods of drought came too often and lasted too long. An area equal to the size of the original Louisiana Purchase, nearly

900,000 square miles, is now so sparsely populated that it meets the nineteenth-century Census Bureau definition of frontier, with no more than six people per square mile.[2]

Cattle seem slightly lost on the Great Plains, and more than a little clumsy to wildlife biologist and former cattle rancher Dan O'Brien. "They have always been a sort of ungulate tourist, and in ranching them I felt a little like a tour guide who spends his life translating menus and pointing out the rest rooms." The bison that O'Brien now raises on 1,700 acres in South Dakota are at home on the range, having had eons of coevolution to develop a symbiotic relationship with the native vegetation on which they graze. "They were a product of this country, selected not by men to conform to human logic but by the elements of this land to meet pressures beyond our experience," says O'Brien.[3]

However, about half of the 30,000 bison in North America in 1970 were being raised commercially, selected by men and women to sell for meat or breeding stock. Since then, the population has grown to more than 300,000, and nearly all of the expansion has been in commercial herds that respond to human financial pressures. This is another chapter in the story of the bison's comeback, but it twists the plot in a different direction. Quantity is not necessarily quality in assessing the return of the bison as a wild animal on the North American landscape. One of his tribal elders told Fred DuBray, "If you're going to bring these buffalo back, first you have to ask the buffalo if they want to come back." DuBray doubts they'd want to "if they have to stand around in a feed lot for the rest of their life."[4]

The Indian's sense of identification with the buffalo extends to how they are treated as livestock. The weaning of calves and removal of their horns to make them less aggressive is equated with how Indian children had their braids cut off when they were sent away to boarding schools until the 1960s. "You take the young calves away, wean them, keep them separated from the older bunch, they never get to learn what it is to be a buffalo," said DuBray. "That's what happened with Indian people, they put them in boarding schools to break the culture, take them away from it and force another way of life. But they forgot about the genetics . . . that's still there in Indian people, the genetic part of it, that's been put there for thousands and thousands of years, that couldn't be taken away by government policy."[5]

But the genetics are altered when Indians marry non-Indians and when buffalo are bred like livestock. Ecologist Dale Lott believes that in the twenty-first century, bison may be eliminated by domestication instead of by slaughter. He points to what happened to the wild cattle known as aurochs thousands of years ago: humans selected animals for breeding that grew faster and were easier to control, that produced the most meat and milk, even though they were less able to survive without human assistance. Lott suggests that instead of having bled to death at the end of a spear, the last wild aurochs may have mated with its domesticated relatives and been "bred to death."[6] A domesticated form of the water buffalo of India (*Bubalus arnee*) has been introduced throughout tropical Asia as a source of milk, meat, and labor. It has become different enough from the wild water buffalo for zoologists to consider it a different species (*Bubalus bubalis*) or at least a different subspecies. Although an estimated 4,000 water buffalo live in the wild, zoologists are uncertain how many, if any, are actually *Bubalus arnee*, a humpless animal larger than the bison. Some are domesticated water buffalo that have become feral, and others may be a form of *Bubalus arnee* that has bred with the domesticated water buffalo.[7]

Domestic Violence

Although the domesticated water buffalo has taken on a variety of shapes and sizes as a result of the different purposes for which the animal is used, livestock management is not conducive to maintaining genetic diversity. Domestic species tend to have smaller brains and less keen senses than their wild ancestors had, because intelligence and acute senses were no longer selected for as necessary to escape from predators.[8] The goal of commercial ranching is generally to maximize calf production and the efficiency of converting feed to meat. This calls for a high cow-to-bull sex ratio in a herd, which reduces the need for a bull to compete for a particular cow and the possibility that a cow will reject a particular bull. As any woman at a singles' bar knows, when there are few bulls, the immediately receptive cows are more likely to mate than those playing hard to get in order to test their suitor's fitness. And as at a singles' bar, the profit motive can lead to high population density and selection against animals that are stressed by crowding or so resistant to confinement that they injure themselves or others trying to escape. Selective breeding for docility produces an animal more vulnerable to predation, but the defensiveness that animals need to keep their distance from predators in the wild is a nuisance to a rancher. Even a calf's attachment to its mother is inconvenient if it makes her less likely to breed again.[9]

Ranchers care about environmental issues, too, but the bison industry has been described as "speeding along a road paved by the cattle industry," and that means increasing production by modifying the animal's environment as well as the animal: growth hormones, early weaning, dehorning, and feeding animals on grain instead of grass.[10] Roaming animals use up calories and time that could be spent making more meat and milk if they were sedentary and fed in one place. Supplemental feed is generally less expensive than supplemental land and fencing. Grain feeding also enables bison to reach market size sooner and with a greater consistency in meat quality than if they eat only grass.

The National Bison Association promotes commercial bison ranching partly by promoting the health and environmental advantages of bison meat over beef. Bison ranchers realize that those advantages will be lost if their industry becomes too much like cattle ranching. But an article on "the future of the bison industry" in the trade association's magazine warned:

History dictates that they should be roaming free on large pastures, with little or no human intervention. That's what the public wants to see. In reality, some things have to change if we are going to include the bison in production agriculture. There will be animals in feedlots and in small pastures. There will be bison that can be hand-fed, or even ridden. This is the hard truth and there is little we can do to change it. . . . Even though the bison is a good animal naturally, there will always be undesirable characteristics that need to be eliminated from a breeding herd.[11]

The National Bison Association also believes that "bison are not a domestic animal and require different handling than cattle."[12] The second part of that statement is indisputable, but the accuracy of the first part depends on what is meant by "domestic." Narrowly defined, "domesticated" animals are those that have been selectively bred to eliminate undesirable traits, and that is what happens on most bison ranches. The term "domesticated" may also apply to an animal population in which genetic changes occur as a result of adaptation to captivity or artificial feeding. Some traits that would be disadvantageous in the wild become advantageous in a captive environment and are therefore more likely to be reproduced in subsequent generations even without selective breeding.[13]

However, an animal's tameness or habituation to humans is not evidence of domestication. Depending on the wild animal, habituation may occur within days or years of proximity to humans, or not at all, and it does not require captivity. Domestication inevitably occurs after captivity has altered the species genetically. But how long does that take? Were the 21 bison purchased from ranchers for Yellowstone in 1902 already genetically altered by domestication? Probably not, but it's an uncertain boundary.

O'Brien is trying to restore native grasses to his bison range and minimize the domestication effect.

We have gone to great lengths to get inspection of our meat where we can kill the buffalo in the field. What we do is let the animals grow to two years old and then we go out and try to randomly select our group for slaughter and we shoot them right there, right out of the herd, the same herd they've been with their whole life. There's no ramming them into trucks and trailers and hauling them off to a slaughter plant where they're killed full of adrenaline and fear. They just lay down and go back to the ground that they've lived on their whole lives.

O'Brien regards this as "a distasteful part of the job," but he likes to believe, "the same way that my Lakota friends believe, that if you do these sorts of things with honor, that the buffalo does not take offense."[14]

Ted Turner also wants to have his bison wild and eat them too. The mission of Turner Enterprises, Inc., is "to manage Turner lands in an eco-nomically sustainable and ecologically sensitive manner while promoting the conservation of native species." In Turner's own more blunt terms, "If you really want to bring something back, make it pay." When he bought bison that had tags in their ears, he had the tags removed. "The managers say they can't tell them apart without tags, and I tell them to get to know them by their first names."[15]

Bison for Park Visitors, Hunters, and Habitat Restoration

People's understanding of the bison as a wild animal has been confused by the growth of commercial herds and by the fact that most noncommercial herds use some livestock management practices. Some herds on public land are managed more intensively and with less honor than those of maverick ranchers like Dan O'Brien and Ted Turner. In his 1995 plea, *Bring Back the Buffalo! A Sustainable Future for America's Great Plains,* Ernest Callenbach saw no contradiction in writing about "wild bison" that are periodically corralled. "Today's wild bison, such as those on the National Bison Range in Montana, can be herded by expert riders into enclosures for annual culling and vaccination, though a few recalcitrant bulls always elude the herders."[16]

All bison herds in the United States are limited in size and space to some extent, and all have been subjected to some form of human control that can affect the gene pool. In most herds more animals are removed by humans than by other forms of mortality, and few herds are culled in a random way that does not interfere with natural selection. Even in herds on public land, animals may be chosen for culling because of their age, sex, failure to reproduce, small size, or other physical anomalies. Herd managers may also maintain a high cow-to-bull ratio in order to maximize the number of bison available for sale or hunting and minimize the injuries inflicted by bulls confined within a pasture.

Custer State Park in South Dakota takes pride in being the only park in the country that is financially self-sufficient, but this is possible because the bison is used as a profit center. Herd management sounds more like an assembly line than wildlife biology: "Marketing opportunities dictate that adjustments to total herd grazing demand be done the fall prior to the upcoming growing season, thus requiring that a production prediction for the upcoming growing season be made. We make that prediction using a two-year moving mean of precipitation as a percentage of normal, and then adjusting our normal production estimates for forages park-wide by that percentage."[17] Custer State Park staff rotate about 1,100 bison among fenced pastures to prevent overgrazing and each pregnant cow receives a daily pound of "32% protein cake" for 60 days prior to her expected delivery date. Calves are weaned by the end of January "to keep the productivity of 3+ year cows at the 90% level." (In Yellowstone about 70 percent of the sexually mature cows calve each year.)[18] The herd is rounded up annually to select animals to be auctioned and bulls to be shot by hunters.[19] As little as possible is left to chance, or to nature.

If Custer State Park seems to be part of the bison industry, it recognizes that it is also in the tourism business. The headline on its Internet site offers "Buffalo Roundup Vacation Packages" to watch the entire herd "stampede over the hilltop" and into the corrals. "Each fall the wild west returns to Custer State Park during the annual Buffalo Roundup," the park advertises, as if the Wild West were epitomized by corralling bison rather than simply slaughtering them where they stood or ran. But Horace Albright may be applauding from his grave; at least some parks still know how to stage a buffalo stampede.

In Alaska the primary motivation for establishing four bison herds on public land was not to restore a wild animal to its native habitat or to promote tourism, but to give sport hunters something else to shoot at. The herds are treated like a crop to be harvested, and each has a target size ranging from 50 to 360. The Delta herd is managed "for maximum productivity" with a ratio of three bulls for each ten cows. To reduce bison foraging on adjacent private land and keep the animals on the 90,000-acre Delta Junction Bison Range, the Alaska Department of Fish and Game "enhanced" the habitat by clearing 2,800 acres and planting it with nonnative grasses. About 500 acres are fertilized every year and "noxious plants" are evicted. The native bluejoint reedgrass (*Calamagrostis canadensis*) is considered "a major threat to successful bison forage management" because it responds poorly to repeat grazing in the same season.[20]

With entirely different priorities, The Nature Conservancy has herds on eight preserves not for the sake of the bison or the people who want to see, buy, or shoot them, but for the sake of native plants. By 2006 its largest herd is expected to reach a summertime goal of 2,600 bison on 24,800 acres of the Tallgrass Prairie Preserve in Oklahoma, where the bison is "one of the primal forces on which the success of this entire venture depends." However, the projected acreage for bison has been reduced in order to increase the land available for the herd of more than 5,000 cattle, as part of the Conservancy's effort to "export conservation-friendly cattle grazing models to the ranching industry."[21] The use of cattle as part of "natural area management" is as incongruous to some people as hunting on snowmobiles is to others, but "natural" must be considered a matter of degree.

Nature provides the 30 to 50 pounds of forage a bison consumes each day at the Tallgrass Prairie Preserve, but bulls are sold at age six or seven because "after this they tend to become more aggressive and dangerous." Cows are sold at age 10 to 12, before their sale value drops and because older cows are "less physically fit for withstanding the rigors of roundup." Tallgrass Prairie supporters not equipped to withstand the rigors of bison ownership may "adopt" an animal for $40 a year. "You will receive a handsome adoption certificate, suitable for framing, complete with your name along with the name and photo of your bison." You'll also have the satisfaction of knowing that you are "playing a vital role in restoring and preserving one of the last great expanses of tallgrass prairie."[22] The Nature Conservancy does not claim that you are helping to preserve the wild bison.

The Yellowstone Bison Gene Pool

Yellowstone bison are often photographed but rarely named, and they are the only herd in the United States that is not currently subject to at least one of these human interventions: supplemental watering or feeding or artificially enhanced forage; confinement by fences; periodic roundups for branding, tagging, or inoculations; hunting or other means of culling based on the animal's age, sex, or other criteria. "Systematic culling for desired characteristics reduces genetic variety," points out zoologist Jim Shaw of Oklahoma State University. "Herds should be culled randomly. We should keep aggressive cows, disfigured bulls. Above all, we shouldn't breed for pretty."[23]

Although it has not been bred for pretty, the Yellowstone bison population is partly the product of current and past human activities in and outside the park, including hunting, the introduction of bison from captive herds, brucellosis, and efforts to reduce the risk of bison transmitting the disease to cattle. The consequences of past human influences on bison in Yellowstone could not be eliminated even if we knew exactly what they were and the goal had widespread support, but decisions are being made about which current human influences are acceptable or at least unavoidable. The impacts of most concern are those that could affect a herd's demographic or genetic structure, because they could have the most profound long-term implications. Some people believe that grooming the roads for winter use could do that; others are more concerned that a brucellosis or boundary control program could reduce the genetic diversity of the herd.

For her Ph.D. dissertation, Natalie Halbert analyzed DNA samples from ten of the largest bison herds on federal land in order to assess the genetic diversity within each herd and among the herds. Although nearly all of the 488 bison from Yellowstone that were tested had been removed at the boundary and therefore may not have been genetically random, Halbert found that Yellowstone and Wind Cave national parks had the highest levels of genetic variation of the herds. The Yellowstone sample, like most of the others, had some alleles (pairs of genes) that were not found in any of the other samples, which indicates the population may be genetically distinctive.[24]

Since periodic culling to limit herd size ended in 1966, human-caused mortality in Yellowstone bison has been exceeded by other causes of death, but it has not been negligible. At a symposium in 1997, wildlife consultant Craig Knowles claimed that because the boundary control program largely confines bison to the park, the result is a "non-random harvest strategy" with "heavy selective pressure against migratory animals."[25] There is no harvest strategy for Yellowstone bison in the sense of a plan to remove a certain number of animals meeting certain criteria from the population each year. But if a large number of bison were frequently removed year after year and the genetic makeup or demographics of those bison were consistently different from those of the population overall, this could affect the herd's gene pool and behavior. Although mature bulls are the most likely bison to leave the park throughout the year, the large groups that move toward the boundary in late winter and early spring have been mostly cows and calves, probably because pregnant and lactating cows are the most motivated to find forage then. The bison removed at the boundary have therefore been disproportionately female, a practice which, if continued on a large scale over the long run, could affect the sex ratio and social relations within the herd.

In addition to population demographics, boundary removals could also affect the herd's genetic diversity. The Buffalo Field Campaign has used this concern as an argument against the "clear cutting" of bison at the boundary.[26] To support their case, they cite remarks made at a 1998 meeting of the Greater Yellowstone Interagency Brucellosis Committee (GYIBC) by Joe Templeton, a geneticist at Texas A&M University. He said that "the so-called random shooting at the Montana borders is actually eliminating or depleting entire maternal lineages; therefore this action will cause an irreversible crippling of the gene pool. . . . It would be a travesty to have people look back and say we were idiots for not understanding the gene pool. Bison have developed a natural resistance genetically as long as they have enough to eat, limited stress and are not consumed by other disease."

Templeton and other researchers at Texas A&M found that about 20 percent of cattle do not become infected when exposed to virulent *Brucella abortus*, and they identified a gene that controls this natural resistance.[27] An analogous gene has not yet been found in Yellowstone bison samples. Some bison that carry antibodies for brucellosis and test seropositive are infected, while other seropositive bison are not infected; no genetic basis for this difference has been established. Even if heredity played no role in brucellosis, however, boundary removals could theoretically discriminate against traits that do have a genetic basis. Most bison populations in the United States are periodically rounded up the way the Lamar herd used to be in Yellowstone, and bison whose behavior makes them too dangerous or too much of a nuisance may be shot. According to the National Research Council study, this management practice "has the consequence of some artificial selection for domestication because wildness and intractability, salient traits of wild bison, are disfavored." The authors believed that these are important traits to retain in Yellowstone bison, because it is "one of the few herds where it is feasible to maintain natural behavior."[28]

It may also be argued that bison prone to leaving the park have salient traits worth retaining in the name of "natural behavior." Sending boundary-crossing bison to slaughter does not appear to mimic the natural selection process by which the least fit bison do not pass on their genes to the next generation, nor even that by which unwary elk are removed by hunters outside the park. Instead, the bison removed from Yellowstone's gene pool might seem to be among the most fit—those most capable of winter travel, most resistant to being hazed, and most determined to find forage. They sound like the bison you'd want on your team when choosing sides for survival. But bison are more like sheep than volleyball players. Historical accounts describe thousands of bison drowning because they followed other drowning bison onto thin ice.[29]

Within a bison herd at any given time, smaller groups are evident, but what prompts some bison to band together, mix with other groups, or break into smaller groups is not well understood, and what has been documented is based largely on observation, not genetics. A calf may remain with its mother until she gives birth again, but some researchers believe that cow-calf pairs are not necessarily closer genetically to the rest of the group they are in at the moment than they are to other bison in the herd.[30] Others believe that bison, especially those not subject to livestock management practices, assemble in matriarchal groups that are likely to include several generations of related females, leaving the bulls responsible for the genetic mixing between extended bison families.[31]

It may take only one dominant cow determined to head for lower elevation range and others will follow, perhaps regardless of their fitness for the undertaking or how closely they are related to that cow. It is not known why some bison leave the park and others do not. But some of the people most familiar with Yellowstone bison ecology see no reason to think there

Bison in Yellowstone often travel in matriarchal groups with a bison cow leading the way. Courtesy of Yellowstone National Park.

is anything special about these bison, or anything likely to be genetically nonrandom about removing several hundred that cross the boundary.[32] According to this view, because of the mixing of bison among herds within the park, and because all of the bison are descendants of a relatively small number, removing the small portion of the population that happens to cross the boundary is unlikely to affect the genetic diversity of the herd overall.

Joe Templeton, who received funding from the Department of the Interior for a four-year research project to better understand the Yellowstone bison gene pool, has distanced himself from his 1998 statement. He believes that nonrandom removal of genetic groups could be occurring, but until more research is done, "no one knows" the effect of current management of the Yellowstone bison on the genetic structure of the herd.[33] Glenn Plumb, the supervisory wildlife biologist at Yellowstone, suggests that in terms of its effect on the herd, removing several hundred bison that cross the boundary may be no different than when the Indians drove several hundred bison over a cliff.

Some Indians would argue that it's not the same thing at all, because there's no "respect" in the boundary removals. Yellowstone managers have invited the park's associated tribes to have representatives present at the Stephens

At the 100th anniversary celebration for the Roosevelt Arch at the park's north entrance, the Buffalo Field Campaign made a silent protest (August 25, 2003). Courtesy of Greg Gordon, Buffalo Field Campaign.

Creek corral when bison are sent to slaughter, to conduct the rituals they think necessary to release the spirit of the buffalo and pray for its safe journey to the spirit world. People who sought employment with the Park Service because they value wildlife endure the chore of confining bison and sending them to slaughter, only because there is no politically viable alternative at present, and they would welcome a ceremony that would make what they were doing seem more respectable.

American Traditions

On August 25, 2003, a crowd of 1,000 gathered at the park entrance in Gardiner, Montana, to celebrate the 100th anniversary of the Roosevelt Arch with the pomp of a military band, a color guard, and the presence of Theodore Roosevelt IV. The arch over the entrance road bears the inscription "FOR THE BENEFIT AND ENJOYMENT OF THE PEOPLE," and it became known as the Roosevelt Arch because President Theodore Roosevelt was present at its unveiling in 1903. When Yellowstone superintendent

Suzanne Lewis stepped to the podium a century later, a large banner was unfurled on the hillside behind her, "Buffalo Slaughter, an American Tradition," as members of the Buffalo Field Campaign donned their buffalo masks.

If greater Yellowstone is to be part of a new Buffalo Nation, it's a nation in which the remaining cattle ranchers will not go gently into the night. The National Wildlife Federation successfully sued the Forest Service for failing to do an environmental analysis before reissuing a permit to the Munns family for a grazing allotment on Horse Butte, west of the park. The federation also obtained a $120,000 donation to move the Munns's cattle to an allotment in Idaho in April 2003. The Forest Service would retire the grazing allotment on Horse Butte, but the 10,000-acre peninsula that juts into Hebgen Lake would still be out-of-bounds for wild bison. About 80 percent of Horse Butte is national forest, and it offers a natural enclosure at the end of a bison migration corridor from the park, but for the state of Montana, it was a natural place to set up a trap to capture the animals.

"There are too many of them," 70-year-old Delas Munns had said of the bison four years before, when there were fewer of them. "They ought to have an open season on them." Munns and his five brothers had trucked their livestock from Rexburg, Idaho, to Horse Butte since 1961, and they still own 720 acres there. But when Munns said "I feel like they're trying to run me out," he was talking not about bison, but about environmentalists. "Restrictions of this kind, restrictions of that kind—and someday this world is going to go hungry."[34]

It is the restrictions placed on hungry buffalo that have riled the 60 members of the Horse Butte Neighbors of Buffalo (HOBNOB), who claim to represent a majority of their small community. "We residents welcome these shaggy icons of the wild West, including many pregnant buffalo who choose Horse Butte as a place to give birth," wrote Liz Kearney in the *Bozeman Chronicle*.[35] But if greater Yellowstone is to be part of a new Buffalo Nation, it's a nation in which technical solutions are enticing. According to a newsletter issued by the GYIBC, "Permanent sterilization, surgical or chemical, is a disease management strategy that could be used to virtually eliminate the possibility of transmission of brucellosis between animals."

Veterinarian Jack Rhyan's 2002 presentation entitled "Contraception: A Possible Means of Decreasing Transmission of Brucellosis in Bison" skimmed over the associated decrease in bison calves and focused on the existing methods of contraception and their drawbacks for use in wildlife.

Vaccines that prevent conception produced only short-term sterility unless boostered annually; the use of an IUD or hormonal implant that would last for several years required "minor surgery," and a female ungulate that does not conceive during an estrus cycle may come into estrus again. Vaccinated white-tailed deer "continued to exhibit sexual activity into February." The consequences of a bison rut that lasted into the winter at Yellowstone would not be pretty. Or as Rhyan put it, a prolonged breeding season "may be deleterious to winter survival of dominant bulls and vaccinated cows." On the other hand, a contraceptive that prevented some bison cows from coming into estrus at all would also complicate life for the bulls.[36]

The following year, the Animal and Plant Health Inspection Service (APHIS) leased 400 acres of land north of the park and brought in 20 bison cows from a commercial herd in order to test contraceptive vaccines. Rhyan, who is in charge of the research, refers to the possible use of birth control in Yellowstone bison as "just another tool in the tool box." But it is an expensive tool with no immediate application. The initial contraception experiment was fruitless, the bull purchased to mate with the 20 cows having failed to impregnate even the unvaccinated control group.

Save the Children

To concerned Indians the idea of birth control for bison is ludicrous; they want more bison, not fewer. But Rhyan has worked with Keith Aune of Montana Fish, Wildlife and Parks to develop a plan that would save some bison calves from an early death at the park boundary. The proposal they presented to the state of Montana, APHIS, and the National Park Service in 2004 was for a "feasibility study of bison quarantine procedures," but it may as well have been entitled "a captive breeding program for Yellowstone bison."[37] Because brucellosis frequently manifests itself during calving, the quarantined female participants must reproduce in order to determine whether they are really seronegative, but the focus of the effort, however unintentional, appeared to be on calf production. Although it would do nothing to eliminate brucellosis in Yellowstone wildlife, these scientists advocate the use of a quarantine program both to reduce "population pressures" that contribute to bison migration from the park and to establish new bison herds on public or tribal lands.

The proposed project could begin in 2005 with up to 100 calves that are captured at the boundary and test seronegative. Although a smaller number of calves could be used, 100 is considered preferable for purposes of obtaining statistically meaningful results from the research. The calves would be taken from January to April before their first birthday and moved to the APHIS facility north of the park that was previously used for the contraception research. They would be divided into two groups, and after a year's confinement in a "three pasture rotation system," the bison would be retested. If any bison test positive, they would be slaughtered, and the remaining bison in that group would have to restart the quarantine period. Regardless of the test results, about half of the bison would be euthanized after the first year in order to obtain tissue cultures that can be used to help determine whether even quarantined young seronegative bison may carry latent *Brucella abortus*. The survivors would be moved further north to a 400-acre site in a state-owned wildlife management area. The bison would receive supplemental feeding to maintain them on a "high nutritional plane" so that as many as possible would be ready to breed as two-year-olds. "Breeding will be carefully monitored and mating will be constructed to maximize genetic diversity"; bulls will be separated from cows during calving; and "pregnancy and calving progress will be monitored with vaginal implants and intense observation."

Two groups of up to 100 captured calves would be put through this regimen over a four-to-five-year period to determine whether it was adequate to ensure that the resulting bison were brucellosis free. Bison in groups that continued to test seronegative and "demonstrate one successful calving" would be available for release to public or tribal lands where the females would continue to be isolated and intensely monitored through at least a second calving. The program would be expensive—an estimated $2.4 million, not including the cost of bison confinement and monitoring after release. That comes to $13,111 per calf, according to the proposal, assuming a high rate of seronegative calf production from the quarantined group. "However, the reward of conserving unique genetics, the benefits of alleviating social conflict, and the expense of managing an unregulated population of bison in the GYA must be weighed against this cost."

In other words, in order to spread the ecological wealth of the wild Yellowstone bison, some of them must become a captive, closely managed animal for as long as it takes to ensure the quarantine process is working. Aune has embraced rather than downplayed the paradox; he sees the quarantine facility as a way to repeat the "success story" of Yellowstone's Buffalo Ranch. Like Peter Holt, who captured two bison calves from the wild herd to improve the prospects of the fenced herd in 1903, those involved in the new buffalo ranch may feel some qualms about separating 200 calves from their mothers and holding them captive, but they believe it will be for the best in the long run.

CHAPTER 16

Thinking Outside the Box

A Latin word for wilderness, vastitas, hints at a crucial quality: a small wilderness is no wilderness at all. The more wilderness we preserve, the less we have to manage. We would need to do less managing of wilderness if we managed the human landscape better. But this runs counter to all our habits. In general, we find it easier to manage wilderness than to manage our own affairs.
                                    —Evan Eisenberg, *The Ecology of Eden* (1998)[1]

The idea of the American wilderness as a place free of human influence may have become tarnished, but wilderness by anyone's definition still does not fit well in a box. The line between a large zoo and a small nature preserve becomes blurred when "free-roaming" animals are tagged, tracked, and provided with matchmaking services. Historian William Cronon has pointed out the contradiction inherent in a wilderness that survives "only by the most vigilant and self-conscious management of the ecosystems that sustain it."[2] People responsible for managing the boxes who think they are collaborating with nature may be deluding themselves. "Few humans can do creative work with the boss looking over their shoulder, correcting each dubious move," says Eisenberg. "In this regard, human and nonhuman nature are very much alike."[3]

But it's only natural for humans to collaborate with nature by managing it—that's what humans were born to do; they manage things. As philosopher

Holmes Rolston has pointed out, "insisting on being part of everything, even wilderness," distinguishes the human species "because nothing else on earth so insists."[4] The difficulty lies in understanding the limits of our ability to control natural processes, and to predict whether the results of interventions made in places like Yellowstone will be desirable in the long run and will reduce the need for future interventions. Backfires and prescription burns that have been set with the best intentions of protecting a community or improving forest health have sometimes gone horribly wrong.

The list of plants and animals that have disappeared as a result of human actions will not include the wild bison anytime soon, but that is both because of and despite human actions taken in the name of preservation since Yellowstone National Park was established. The bison has survived as part of the Eurasian and North American landscapes for millions of years by adapting to changes in its environment, human caused and otherwise, and it will have to continue to do so. That is the essential paradox of human involvement in wildlife preservation: we try to preserve what must change by protecting the biological diversity that enables a species and its habitat to adapt to change.[5]

"Yellowstone provides superb summer habitat for bison," says Park Service wildlife biologist Glenn Plumb, who believes that even if they were free to leave in the winter, most bison would return to summer ranges in the park, as the elk do.[6] As for whether it's natural for the park to be accommodating 4,000 bison in the summer—well, that depends on what you mean by "natural." We can and do distinguish between the results of human activities and those of the honey bee, but English does not provide a good word to differentiate them. Instead, we refer to honey as "natural" and saccharin as "artificial," as if it were not inevitable that the human species would devise a low-calorie substitute.

Even if 4,000 bison were present in the area at some point in the distant past when there were no human influences whatsoever, that would tell us nothing about how many bison should be there today. Perhaps the large bison population in Yellowstone now *is* a result of human influences, of the fact that the roads are groomed in the winter or that bison are killed by humans only at the park boundary, but that doesn't necessarily make it the wrong number of bison in Yellowstone at this moment in time.

The bison itself has always been a paradox, the only large wild animal in North America that has been preserved mostly in captivity.[7] But given the manifest destiny of Euro-American settlement, it was inevitable that the animal whose evolution was most affected by landscape-level ecological changes would become the wildlife species most subject to the constraints of human management. Whatever idealism motivated Peter Holt when he captured those wild bison calves in 1903, the primary impetus behind Yellowstone's Buffalo Ranch was a desire for park visitors to be able to see bison, a whole big herd of them, even if it meant keeping them behind a fence. Since then, the Park Service may have become dedicated to minimizing human interference with wildlife in the face of pressure to do otherwise, but bison management in Yellowstone is still driven by politics rather than a scientific consensus about what is ecologically necessary or appropriate.

Any controversy that arouses people's emotions will be decided by politics rather than the best facts science has to offer. Of course a decision to interfere in the lives of wild animals should be supported by compelling evidence and a consensus of experts that the intervention is necessary. We can hope for a well-informed public and better-informed politicians so that decisions are based on something more than the heat of the moment. But what appeared to be compelling evidence and consensus were present for some of the Park Service's most regretted intrusions, including the extirpation of wolves and the severe culling of elk and bison.[8]

Although advances in scientific knowledge can change public views and political pressures, a free society also works the other way around: the desire for a particular outcome can generate the science needed to support it. As the teaching of evolution became more acceptable in schools, people who believed in a literal Biblical account of creation found scientific evidence for it. People who favor an aggressive effort to eliminate brucellosis in Yellowstone bison can find the science to support their view, and so can those who prefer a live-and-let-live approach. The way bison live in their Yellowstone box has been affected not only by past and current human activities in and around the park but also by our beliefs about the animal— its scarcity or surplus, its docility or dangerousness. As a national park, Yellowstone was born of a Euro-American belief in both its untouched nature and its inevitable improvement through the human touch—constructing roads; feeding and protecting some species, killing off others; channeling the hot springs into swimming pools. Over the years, an appreciation for untouched nature grew, but so did the recognition that such a thing cannot exist in the presence of humans.

Mending the Social Fabric

When Yellowstone biologist Rick Wallen was quoted in the press saying, "We're trying to push the boundaries to allow bison to resemble a wildlife species,"[9] those opposed to federal land management may have considered it evidence of the Park Service's expansionist aims. But Wallen's goal, like that of other wildlife managers in greater Yellowstone, is conceptual as much as geographic; it's about pushing the mental boundaries that have preserved the bison as an icon rather than a wild animal. Wallen believes that even greater Yellowstone is no longer big enough to accommodate bison without some population control by humans, but we can increase the size of the mental box in which the Yellowstone bison have been placed for so long, so that they are perceived and treated more like the wild animals that they are.

Like many historians, Dan Flores takes the long view on the question of what we're doing when we try to preserve or restore nature. "After much hard thought, I have decided that I simply don't care if the image of America that we hold in our heads does not really deserve to be called wild," he says. "Acknowledging that what I value springs not so much from God as from evolutionary history, with humanity's hand firmly on the tiller for several thousand years, should not diminish the luster."[10] How firmly we've guided the tiller may be disputed, given the forces of nature that remain beyond our control. We're rocking the boat and we've got a lot of oars in the water, but the waves are large and the consensus on which way to go is always shifting. We still cannot prevent the climate from whipping up a lethal storm, or a wildland fire from destroying thousands of homes, or bison from leaving Yellowstone National Park. Flores's premise is irrefutable, however. Our attitudes toward nature cannot be detached from cultural ideals. Even the deep ecology belief that plants and animals have a value independent of how we use or appreciate them springs from a certain human understanding of the world.[11] To value the bison as part of our cultural heritage does not in any way detract from its importance as part of a wildlife community that helps keep the native grasses mowed, the nutrients recycled, and the predators and scavengers fed.

The history of Euro-Americans' relationship with the bison vividly illustrates the phases of their relationship with the North American environment: discovery, exploitation, and budding conservation, which has led some people to regard human culture as the enemy.[12] Also growing, however, has been an awareness that wilderness is not the opposite of civilization, but something that civilization needs for its own full flowering. "We humans, dominant though we are, want to be a part of something bigger," says Rolston, "and this we can only do by sometimes drawing back . . . by recognizing the otherness of wildness."[13]

For Yellowstone superintendent Suzanne Lewis, following a period in which Mike Finley chose a politically bumpy but righteous road, her job is about avoiding stridency and "building relationships," which she makes sound much nicer and more noble than playing politics. Lewis sees her role in the bison management controversy as one of developing trust with the state of Montana and other parties whose priorities differ from those of the National Park Service, moving gradually toward a time when the bison will not be discriminated against outside the park. As described by its former president Bob Frost, the 108-year-old United States Animal Health Association has also shifted its emphasis to becoming part of something bigger, to "bringing and keeping people at the table" rather than berating them in the campaign against brucellosis.[14] Although Frost, a California llama breeder, credits USAHA's change in attitude toward wildlife to "a new generation of state veterinarians," he has been an important catalyst, heading the organization in 2003, the same year that both the National Park Service and the U.S. Department of Homeland Security became members.

"The problem is not biological; it's a social and ethical problem," says wildlife manager Glenn Plumb. "I'm not worried about the future of the Yellowstone bison, but about the future of the park I'm leaving to my children, and about what the controversy does to the social fabric."[15] The InterTribal Bison Cooperative looks to the bison as a source of healing for its communities instead of fearing it may tear them apart. The cooperative would like to see free-roaming bison back on the Great Plains, but its priority is to restore a cultural relationship with the bison, not an ecosystem. Member tribes welcome bison to their lands not as the wild animal their ancestors knew but as a species that must be managed within the box to which each tribe is limited. "I believe that the greatest threat to the survival of American Indians—more than the wars, the disease, the poverty, the discrimination, and the pervasive indifference that have defined their existence from the time of European occupation—is the removal of the spiritual matrix of traditional life, the theft of the sacred," says Kiowa author

N. Scott Momaday, who has set up the Buffalo Trust to help preserve the Indians' cultural heritage and return it to them.[16]

At its January 2004 meeting the Greater Yellowstone Interagency Brucellosis Committee agreed to move forward on granting a nonvoting membership to the InterTribal Bison Cooperative. Wyoming rancher Rob Hendry said of the time that the GYIBC had spent debating the issue, "I can see it is already having an effect of slowing the process down," by which he meant the process of getting something done about eliminating brucellosis in greater Yellowstone wildlife, a goal toward which he felt no progress had been made at all. "We've done a lot of studies, but has the incidence of elk and bison brucellosis gone down? Do we have an elimination plan?" While addressing brucellosis in livestock may be a problem of biology, in wildlife it's about building relationships and shared cultural values in greater Yellowstone; it's about finding a place at the table for the Indians.

The Enigma Factor

The oldest human record of bison may be in the Ardèche valley of southern France. Using a bumpy cave wall illuminated by fire about 31,000 years ago, an artist gave substance and splendor to the enormous, hump-backed animal that became known as the steppe bison. Some of the paintings created by Paleolithic people show bison pierced with spears, the prey of human hunters, and some are precise enough to provide clues about bison evolution. But their purpose appears to have been spiritual rather than documentary or decorative, for they are often tucked in dark caves. To see some murals, one must navigate through a half mile of winding, stalactite-spiked passages. One theory is that such cave paintings were devoted to the unseen powers that control the movement of game, and the magic that can carry the hunter's spear to its target.[17] Without the spiritual strength derived from their art, their hunting rituals, and their amulets worn to ward off evil forces, people felt helpless against the vagaries of nature.

To be considered effective in medical terms, a vaccine does not have to ward off the evil *Brucella abortus* 100 percent of the time; it only has to be shown that a test group of bison that received the vaccine were less likely than a control group of unvaccinated bison to become infected after being exposed to the bacteria. Steve Olsen's research on Strain RB51 at the USDA National Animal Diseases Center in Ames, Iowa, indicates that he may have come up with such a vaccine that will survive transmission in a biobullet.

Developing a pneumatic rifle that could safely and accurately deliver a biobullet 50 meters to its target on a wild bison would also be an impressive human achievement, and it could be useful in other situations involving wildlife health or contraception. But the bison field crew at Yellowstone has been working on a method that depends less on new technology than on understanding what drives the bison's movements.

By spending many hours with bison in different parts of the park and conducting "mock vaccination approaches" with small groups of bison, Rick Wallen's crew is learning when, where, and how the bison are most approachable and most likely to ignore getting pinched on the backside by a biobullet, how to get close enough to minimize the possibility of shooting the wrong bison, or the right bison in the wrong place. In traveling from one foraging area to another, bison usually move slowly, often in single file, as if lining up the children for the vaccinations that might be delivered by someone standing nearby. Wallen thinks it is possible to collaborate with the bison in getting them to take their medicine.

"Field data collected," according to the 2001 progress report, "includes multiple sets of independent variables: topography, weather, wind speed and direction, direction of approach (in relation to the wind), precipitation type, number of humans present and habitat type." The crew members used a starter pistol to simulate the noise of the pneumatic rifle. "Although crews analyzed many parameters that might affect bison behavior, it was not possible to analyze the synergy of these and other parameters, such as presence of predators of which the bison were aware but not the crew. No pattern for predicting bison behavior *a priori* could be determined with any certainty."[18] Despite the effort to make it all sound terrifically scientific, the enigma factor seemed well suited to vaccinations in Wonderland.

A catch-as-catch-can vaccination program on free-roaming Yellowstone bison may be regarded as just another political tool, its effect on the presence of brucellosis in Yellowstone bison may be too slight to justify the large effort that is being invested in it, and getting bison accustomed to wildlife biologists in the park shooting biobullets may confound efforts to get bison outside of the park wary of people and running from hunters. But it is only natural for wildlife biologists to want to see if they can get the art and science of remote vaccine delivery to work, to try to make progress toward a long-term biological and political goal of brucellosis eradication in Yellowstone wildlife by compromising on a cultural goal of minimizing interference with wildlife.

The current period of Americans' relationship with wilderness may be seen as one in which the line between natural and cultural is becoming as blurred for many white people as it has traditionally been for many Indians.[19] Yet for every scholar who has concluded that a national park is nothing more than a large cultural construct that mirrors changing fashions in nature lore, there is someone wild at heart who knows that wildlife is something that Disneyland cannot replicate. "We need a vast world," says philosopher Mary Midgley, "and it must be a world that does not need us; a world constantly capable of surprising us, a world we did not program, since only such a world is the proper object of wonder."[20]

If a bison bellows in Pelican Valley when no one is there to hear him, does he still make a sound? Yes, of course, and we can hope that many other bison are there listening. But we can only imagine that sound and what it means to be a wild bison by using our human intellect, by looking through the scrim of beliefs about the animal that have been passed down through the ages. Now we are armed with something called science instead of religion when we try to make sense of and control nature. The electric lights installed in a limestone cave make it easier to see the pigments daubed long ago to represent a vanished form of bison, but they can get in the way of understanding the unseen powers that inspired the artist and led the animals to their extinction. Although scientific knowledge has enabled us to influence nature far more profoundly than our Paleolithic ancestors could, it would be futile to ignore the magic that still exists, the wonder and awe that are still an important part of our own response to life's mysteries.

Notes

Much of the information in this book pertaining specifically to the history of bison in Yellowstone was found in the Yellowstone National Park Archives (YNPA) and the park's library (YNPL) in Gardiner, Montana. Except where otherwise indicated, statements from Yellowstone superintendents are from the annual report for the year noted in the text. Much of the information pertaining to Yellowstone bison management since 1980 can be found in the three volumes of the final environmental impact statement entitled *Bison Management for the State of Montana and Yellowstone National Park*, August 2000 (cited below as the Interagency Bison Management EIS), and in the Record of Decision for the Final EIS (December 20, 2000). *Brucellosis in the Greater Yellowstone Area*, a report prepared by Norman F. Cheville and Dale R. McCullough for the National Resources Council (Washington, D.C.: National Academy of Sciences, 1998), is another important source. Many of the newspaper articles published since 1995 can be found on the Internet, including those from the *Billings Gazette*, the *Bozeman Chronicle*, *High Country News*, and the *New York Times*.

Introduction

1. Roderick Nash, *Wilderness and the American Mind*, 4th ed. (New Haven: Yale University Press, 1982), 2.

2. "Protection of Buffalo," *Congressional Record*, 43rd Congress, 1st session, 10 March 1874, 2107.

3. Nash, *Wilderness and the American Mind*, xiv.

4. Theodore Roosevelt, *Outdoor Pastimes of an American Hunter* (New York: Arno, 1905), 310–13.

5. Holmes Rolston, III, *Conserving Natural Value* (New York: Columbia University Press, 1994), 131.

6. Mary Meagher, "Yellowstone Bison," Information Paper no. 1, Yellowstone National Park, January 1975, YNPA.

7. Scott McMillion, "First Bison of Season Slain after Hazing Fails," *Bozeman Chronicle*, 29 November 2001.

Chapter I. Coming to America

1. Larry Barsness, *Heads, Hides and Horns: The Complete Buffalo Book* (Fort Worth: Texas Christian University Press, 1985), 163.

2. The major source for the summary of bison evolution provided in this chapter is the work of R. Dale Guthrie, *Frozen Fauna of the Mammoth Steppe: The Story of Blue Babe* (Chicago: University of Chicago Press, 1990); and Guthrie, "Bison and Man in North America," *Canadian Journal of Anthropology* 1 (1980): 55–73.

3. George C. Frison, "The Foothills-Mountains and the Open Plains: The Dichotomy in Paleoindian Subsistence Strategies between the Two Ecosystems," in *Ice Age Hunters of the Rockies*, ed. D. Stanford and J. S. Day (Niwot: University Press of Colorado, 1992), 323–42.

4. Kenneth P. Cannon, "Caldera Unrest, Lake Levels, and Archeology: The View from Yellowstone Lake," *Park Science* 15, no. 3 (1995): 28–31.

5. John Alroy, "A Multispecies Overkill Simulation of the End: Pleistocene Megafaunal Mass Extinction," *Science* 292, no. 5523 (2001): 1893–97.

6. James Willard Schultz (Apikuni), *Blackfeet and Buffalo: Memories of Life among the Indians* (Norman: University of Oklahoma Press, 1962), 311.

7. John W. Fisher and Tom E. Roll, "Ecological Relationships between Bison and Native Americans during Late Prehistory and the Early Historic Period," in *Proceedings of the International Symposium on Bison Ecology and Management*, ed. Lynn R. Irby and James R. Knight (Bozeman: Montana State University, 1998), 283–302.

Chapter 2. A Removable Resource

1. National Park Service, *Yellowstone's Northern Range: Complexity and Change in a Wildland Ecosystem* (Yellowstone National Park: National Park Service, 1997), 29.

2. Rexford Daubenmire, "The Western Limits of the Range of American Bison," *Ecology* 66, no. 2 (1985): 622–24; Charles Kay, "Aboriginal Overkill: The Role of Native Americans in Structuring Western Ecosystems," *Human Nature* 5, no. 4 (1994): 359–98; Michael Yochim, "Aboriginal Overkill Overstated: Errors in Charles Kay's Hypothesis," *Human Nature* 12, no. 2 (2001): 141–67.

3. Mark Daniel Barringer, *Selling Yellowstone: Capitalism and the Construction of Nature* (Lawrence: University Press of Kansas, 2002), 9.

4. Shepard Krech, III, *The Ecological Indian: Myth and History* (New York: W. W. Norton, 1999), 99.

5. National Park Service, *Yellowstone's Northern Range*, 29.

6. Paul Schullery and Lee Whittlesey, "Greater Yellowstone Bison Distribution and Abundance in the Early Historical Period," Yellowstone Center for Resources, National Park Service, draft 30 May 2003.

7. Joseph Campbell, *The Masks of God: Primitive Mythology* (New York: Viking Press, 1959), 283–86.

8. Peter Nabokov and Lawrence Loendorf, *American Indians and Yellowstone National Park: A Documentary Overview* (Yellowstone National Park: National Park Service, 2002), 89.

9. Mary Meagher and Douglas Houston, *Yellowstone and the Biology of Time: Photographs across a Century* (Norman: University of Oklahoma Press, 1998), 248.

10. Joel C. Janetski, *Indians in Yellowstone National Park*, rev. ed. (Salt Lake City: University of Utah Press, 2002), 37–39.

11. Osborne Russell, *Journal of a Trapper* (Lincoln: University of Nebraska Press, 1965), 36.

12. Aubrey Haines, "The Bannock Indian Trail," *Archaeology of Montana* 4, no. 1 (1962): 1–8.

13. George Catlin, *North American Indians* (1841; repr., Edinburgh: John Grant, 1926), 1:27, 143.

14. William M. Denevan, "The Pristine Myth," in *The Great New Wilderness Debate*, ed. J. B. Caldicott and M. P. Nelson (Athens: University of Georgia Press, 1998), 425.

15. Thomas Haynes, "Bison Hunting in the Yellowstone River Drainage, 1800–1884," in *International Symposium on Bison Ecology*, 303–11.

16. Krech, *Ecological Indian*, 123–49.

17. Rod Preece, *Animals and Nature: Cultural Myths, Cultural Realities* (Vancouver: University of British Columbia Press, 1999), 234.

18. Elizabeth Atwood Lawrence, "The Symbolic Role of Animals in the Plains Indian Sun Dance," *Journal of Human-Animal Studies* 1, no. 1 (1993), http://www.psyeta.org/sa/sa1.1/lawrence.html.

19. John C. Ewers, *The Horse in Blackfoot Culture* (Washington, D.C.: Smithsonian Institution Press, 1969), 134.

20. Larry Barsness, *The Bison in Art: A Graphic Chronicle of the American Bison* (Fort Worth: Amon Carter Museum of Western Art, 1977), 6–7.

21. Schultz, *Blackfeet and Buffalo*, 317.

22. William Farr, "'When We Were First Paid': The Blackfeet Treaty, the Western Tribes and the Creation of the Common Hunting Ground, 1855," *Great Plains Quarterly* 21, no.2 (2001): 131–54.

23. Andrew Isenberg, *The Destruction of the Bison: An Environmental History, 1750–1920* (Boston: Cambridge University Press, 2000), 112.

24. John F. Finnerty, *War-Path and Bivouac* (Lincoln: University of Nebraska Press, 1966), 121.

25. Richard I. Dodge, *The Plains of the Great West and Their Inhabitants* (New York: G. P. Putnam's, 1877), 26.

26. William T. Hornaday, "The Extermination of the American Bison, with a Sketch of its Discovery and Life History," in *Report of the National Museum, 1886–'87* (Washington, D.C.: Government Printing Office, 1889), 469.

27. John James Audubon, "Missouri River Journals," in *Audubon and His Journals,* ed. Maria R. Audubon and Elliot Coues (New York: Charles Scribner's Sons, 1897), 2:131.

28. Edward Harris, *Up the Missouri with Audubon: The Journal of Edward Harris,* ed. John Francis McDermott (Norman: University of Oklahoma Press, 1951), 149.

29. Isenberg, *Destruction of the Bison,* 131.

30. E. Douglas Branch, *The Hunting of the Buffalo* (1929; repr. Lincoln: University of Nebraska Press, 1997), 153.

Chapter 3. A Park Is Born

1. Aubrey Haines, *Yellowstone National Park: Its Exploration and Establishment* (Washington, D.C.: Government Printing Office, 1974), 59.

2. Nabokov and Loendorf, *Indians and Yellowstone,* 102.

3. Catlin, *North American Indians,* 294.

4. Alfred Runte, "Yellowstone: It's Useless, So Why Not a Park?" *National Parks and Conservation Magazine* 46 (1972), 4–7.

5. Katharine Seelye, "Yellowstone Bison Thrive, but Success Breeds Peril," *New York Times,* 26 January 2003, sec. 1, 16.

6. Mark David Spence, *Dispossessing the Wilderness: Indian Removal and the Making of the National Parks* (New York: Oxford University Press, 1999), 49.

7. Ibid., 32.

8. Janetski, *Indians in Yellowstone National Park,* 86.

9. Nabokov and Loendorf, *Indians and Yellowstone,* 186.

10. William Ludlow, *Report of a Reconnaissance from Carroll, Montana Territory, on the Upper Missouri to the Yellowstone National Park, and Return Made in the Summer of 1875* (Washington, D.C.: Government Printing Office, 1876).

11. Janetski, *Indians in Yellowstone National Park,* 74–81.

12. Patrick Henry Conger, *Report of the Superintendent of the Yellowstone National Park to the Secretary of the Interior, 1883* (Washington, D.C.: Government Printing Office, 1883), 5.

13. George Bird Grinnell, "Their Last Refuge," *Forest and Stream: A Weekly Journal of Outdoor Life,* 14 December 1882, 382.

14. Columbus Delano, *Annual Report of the Secretary of the Interior, 1873,* 42nd Congress, 1st session, H. exdoc. 1 (Serial 1560), 5.

15. Valerius Geist, *Buffalo Nation: History and Legend of the North American Bison* (Stillwater, Minn.: Voyageur Press, 1996), 83.

16. For details about the political debate over buffalo protection, see Hornaday, "Extermination of the American Bison," 518–19; Branch, *Hunting of the Buffalo,* 176–84; and Isenberg, *Destruction of the Bison,* 150–56.

17. Dan Flores, *Natural West: Environmental History in the Great Plains and Rocky Mountains* (Norman: University of Oklahoma Press, 2001), 52–53.

18. Wayne Gard, *The Great Buffalo Hunt* (Lincoln: University of Nebraska Press, 1968), 270.

19. Tom McHugh, *The Time of the Buffalo* (New York: Knopf, 1972), 286.

20. Chris J. Magoc, *Yellowstone: The Creation and Selling of an American Landscape, 1870–1903* (Albuquerque: University of New Mexico Press, 1999), 155.

21. Theodore Roosevelt, *Works*, Memorial Edition, ed. Hermann Hagedorn (New York: Charles Scribner's Sons, 1923), xviii.

22. Grinnell, "Their Last Refuge," 382.

23. Nabokov and Loendorf, *Indians and Yellowstone*, 54.

24. Aubrey Haines, *The Yellowstone Story* (Boulder, Colo.: Yellowstone Library and Museum Association in cooperation with Colorado Associated University Press, 1977), 2:58.

25. Grinnell, "Their Last Refuge," 382.

26. Secretary of the Interior Henry Teller to Superintendent Patrick Conger, 15 January 1883, YNPA.

27. "An Important Park Order," *Forest and Stream* 19, no. 25 (1883): 481.

28. H. Duane Hampton, *How the U.S. Cavalry Saved Our National Parks* (Bloomington: Indiana University Press, 1971), 61.

29. Nash, *Wilderness and the American Mind*, 114–15.

30. Ibid., 115.

31. George Wingate, *Through the Yellowstone Park on Horseback* (New York: O. Judd Co., 1886), 36.

32. Karl Jacoby, *Crimes against Nature: Squatters, Poachers, Thieves and the Hidden History of American Conservation* (Berkeley and Los Angeles: University of California Press, 2001), 89.

33. Arnold Hague, "Mr. Hague on the Park," *Forest and Stream* 26, no. 5 (1886): 26.

34. "A Case for Prompt Action," *Forest and Stream* 32, no. 12 (1889): 233.

35. Harris to Murdock Deckson and Company of Toronto, 24 August 1888, YNPA.

36. David Dary, *The Buffalo Book* (New York: Avon Books, 1974), 131.

37. "A Case for Prompt Action," 234.

38. William T. Hornaday, "The Passing of the Buffalo," *The Cosmopolitan* 4, no. 2 (1887): 85.

39. Hornaday, "Extermination of the American Bison," 532–35.

40. "Buffalo Types," *Forest and Stream* 34, no. 2 (1890): 24.

41. Hornaday, "Passing of the Buffalo," 82.

42. McHugh, *Time of the Buffalo*, 294.

43. George Bird Grinnell, "American Bison in 1924," in *Hunting and Conservation*, ed. George Bird Grinnell and Charles Sheldon (New Haven: Yale University Press, 1925), 356–411.

44. Henry Inman, *Buffalo Jones' Forty Years of Adventure* (Topeka: Crane and Company, 1899), 222.

45. Barsness, *Heads, Hides and Horns*, 146–47.

46. Multiple accounts for the origin of the Pablo-Allard herd, based on oral histories, can be found in Robert Bigart, ed., *"I Will Be Meat for My Salish:" The Montana Writers Project and the Buffalo of the Flathead Indian Reservation* (Pablo, Mont.: Salish Kootenai College, 2001).

47. "The Yellowstone Park Report," *Forest and Stream* 39, no. 15 (1892): 309.

48. Jacoby, *Crimes against Nature*, 100.

49. The original account of Howell's capture is found in Emerson Hough, "Yellowstone Park Game Exploration," *Forest and Stream* 42, no. 18 (1894): 377–78.

50. "A Premium on Crime," *Forest and Stream* 42, no. 12 (1894): 243.

51. Jacoby, *Crimes against Nature*, 127.

52. Anderson to Secretary Hoke Smith, 24 May 1894, YNPA.

53. "Killing Park Buffalo," *Forest and Stream* 45, no. 23 (1895): 494.

54. Dan Beard, "In a Wild Animal Republic," *Recreation* 15 (December 1901): 417–23.

55. Jacoby, *Crimes against Nature*, 127, 132.

56. James R. Walker, *Lakota Society*, ed. Raymond J. DeMallie (Lincoln: University of Nebraska Press, 1982), 153.

57. Captain W. E. Wilder to Waters, 29 March 1899, YNPA.

58. Secretary Hitchcock to Captain Wilder, 15 April 1899, YNPA.

59. Nabokov and Loendorf, *Indians and Yellowstone*, 62.

60. W. F. Scott to Superintendent Young, 24 August 1907, YNPA.

61. Captain R. Bigford to Major Benson, 17 June 1908, YNPA.

Chapter 4. Not Just Another Buffalo

1. Clyde Jones et al., "Revised Checklist of North American Mammals North of Mexico," Occas. Paper no. 173 (Lubbock: Museum of Texas Tech University, 1997), 1–19.

2. Don E. Wilson and DeeAnn M. Reeder, *Mammal Species of the World: A Taxonomic and Geographic Reference*, 2nd ed. (Washington, D.C.: Smithsonian Institution Press, 1993), 288–99.

3. Wingate, *Through the Yellowstone Park on Horseback*, 211.

4. Mary Meagher, *The Bison of Yellowstone National Park*, Scientific Monographs 1, no. 161 (Washington, D.C.: Government Printing Office, 1973), 13–29.

5. Mary Meagher, "Yellowstone's Free-Ranging Bison," *Naturalist* 36, no. 3 (1985): 20–26.

6. Norman F. Cheville et al., *Brucellosis in the Greater Yellowstone Area* (Washington, D.C.: National Academy Press, 1998), 116. For a Canadian view, see C. C. Gates, T. Chowns, and H. Reynolds, "Wood Buffalo at the Crossroads," in *Buffalo*, ed. J. E. Foster, D. Harrison, and I. S. MacLaren (Edmonton: University of Alberta Press, 1992), 140–41.

7. Mott to U.S. Senator Steven Symms [1987], YNPA.

8. Paul Schullery, *Searching for Yellowstone: Ecology and Wonder in the Last Wilderness* (Boston: Houghton Mifflin, 1997), 121.

9. Aubrey L. Haines, *Yellowstone Place Names: Mirrors of History* (Niwot: University Press of Colorado, 1996), 224–26.

10. Greg Wilson and Curtis Strobeck, "Genetic Variation among Wood and Plains Bison Populations," *Genome* 42 (1999): 483–96; Wilson and Strobeck, "Microsatellite Analysis of Genetic Variation in Wood and Plains Bison," in *International Symposium on Bison Ecology and Management*, 180–91.

11. Cormack Gates et al., "National Recovery Plan for the Wood Bison," National Recovery Plan no. 21 (Ottawa: Recovery of Nationally Endangered Wildlife, 2001), 25, 29.

12. Mark Derr, "Genetically, Bison Don't Measure Up to Frontier Ancestors," *New York Times*, 23 April 2002.

13. Francis Haines, *The Buffalo: The Story of American Bison and Their Hunters from Prehistoric Times to the Present* (Norman: University of Oklahoma Press, 1995), 215.

14. Karen E. Chambers, "Using Genetic Data in the Management of Bison Herds," in *International Symposium on Bison Ecology and Management*, 151–57.

Chapter 5. For the Great National Playground

1. Grinnell, "Their Last Refuge," 382–83.

2. Jack London, *The Call of the Wild* (1903; repr. New York: Heritage Press, 1960), 57.

3. Roderick Nash, introduction to *The Call of the Wild (1900–1916)*, ed. Roderick Nash (New York: George Braziller, 1970), 1–13.

4. John Muir, "The American Forests," *Atlantic Monthly* 80 (August 1897): 146.

5. William T. Hornaday, *Our Vanishing Wildlife: Its Extermination and Preservation* (New York: New York Zoological Society, 1913), 335.

6. Donald Worster, *Nature's Economy: A History of Ecological Ideas* (Cambridge: Cambridge University Press, 1985), 2.

7. Mark Daniel Barringer, *Selling Yellowstone: Capitalism and the Construction of Nature* (Lawrence: University Press of Kansas, 2002), 18.

8. Francis Jennings, *The Invasion of America: Indians, Colonialism, and the Cant of Conquest* (Chapel Hill: University of North Carolina Press, 1975), 15–31.

9. Aldo Starker Leopold et al., *Wildlife Management in the National Parks* (Washington, D.C.: Advisory Board on Wildlife Management, 1963), 3.

10. Hampton, *How the U.S. Cavalry Saved Our National Parks*, 166.

11. Langley to the Secretary of the Interior, 6 February 1902, quoted in U.S. Senate, *American Bison in the U.S. and Canada*, 57th Congress, 1st session, S. 445 (Washington, D.C.: Government Printing Office, 1902), 1.

12. "The Courtenay Buffalo Case," *Forest and Stream* 46, no. 5 (1896), 95.

13. Jones to Secretary Hoke Smith, 9 June 1896, YNPA.

14. Jones to Thomas Ryan, First Asst. Secretary of the Interior, 26 April 1897, quoted in Inman, *Buffalo Jones*, 264–65.

15. Ibid., 265.

16. "Snap Shots," *Forest and Stream* 48, no. 19 (1897): 361.

17. Jacoby, *Crimes against Nature*, 109.

18. Barsness, *Heads, Hides and Horns*, 155.

19. Peter Holt, "Catching Buffalo Calves," Part I, *Forest and Stream* 75, no. 12 (1910): 448.

20. U.S. Senate, *American Bison in the U.S. and Canada*, 1.

21. Pitcher to Hitchcock, 14 February 1902, YNPA.

22. "Herd of Buffaloes Will Be Preserved," *Washington Republic*, 6 July 1902, YNPA.

23. Pitcher to Dick Rock, 10 February 1902, YNPA.

24. Nolie Mumey, *Rocky Mountain Dick* (Denver: Range Press, 1953), 73–76.

25. Haines, *Yellowstone Story*, 2:457.

26. Barsness, *Heads, Hides and Horns*, 156.

27. Jones to Pitcher, January 19, 1903, YNPA.

28. The account of this expedition comes from Peter Holt, "Catching Buffalo Calves," Part I, *Forest and Stream* 75, no. 12 (1910): 448–50, and Part II, 75, no. 13 (1910): 488–90.

29. Jones's account appeared in the *New York Independent* on 7 June 1906, 29.

30. Melville W. Miller, Acting Secretary, to Acting Superintendent, 20 June 1903; Thos. Ryan, Acting Secretary, to Acting Superintendent, 10 July 1903, YNPA.

31. Jones to Roosevelt, 2 June 1903, YNPL vertical files.

32. Holt, "Catching Buffalo Calves," Part I, 448.

33. Paul Schullery, "Buffalo Jones and the Bison Herd in Yellowstone: Another Look," *Montana The Magazine of Western History* 26, no. 3 (1976): 40–51.

34. Paul Reddin, *Wild West Shows* (Urbana: University of Illinois Press, 1999), 1–26.

35. Ibid., 53–85.

36. Michael Wallis, *The Real Wild West: The 101 Ranch and the Creation of the American West* (New York: St. Martin's Press, 1999), 290–92.

37. McHugh, *Time of the Buffalo*, 299.

38. George Bird Grinnell, "Pleading for the Buffalo," *New York Times*, 1905, reprinted in *Forest and Stream* 65, no. 1 (1905): 27.

39. Isenberg, *Destruction of the Bison*, 168.

40. Ibid., 183.

41. W. A. Bartlett, "The Pablo-Allard Herd: Origin," in Bigart, *"I Will Be Meat for My Salish,"* 69–98.

42. Janet Foster, *Working for Wildlife: The Beginning of Preservation in Canada* (Toronto: University of Toronto Press, 1998), 66–72.

43. Morton J. Elrod, "The Flathead Buffalo Range: A Report to the American Bison Society of an Inspection of the Flathead Indian Reservation, Montana, for the Purpose of Selecting a Suitable Location for a National Buffalo Range," in *Annual Report of the American Bison Society, 1905–1907* (n.p.: American Bison Society, 1908), 15–46.

44. Dary, *Buffalo Book*, 238.

45. Isenberg, *Destruction of the Bison*, 166.

46. William Hornaday, "Report of the President on the Founding of the Montana National Bison Herd," in *Second Annual Report of the American Bison Society, 1908–1909* (n.p.: American Bison Society, 1910), 9–15.

47. Isenberg, *Destruction of the Bison*, 192.

48. Hornaday, *Our Vanishing Wildlife*, 333–36.

49. Barsness, *Heads, Hides and Horns*, 168.

50. Fred M. Dille, "The Niobrara Reservation," in *Sixth Annual Report of the American Bison Society* (New York: American Bison Society, 1913), 37.

51. Franklin Hooper, "President's Annual Report," in *Seventh Annual Report of the American Bison Society* (New York: American Bison Society, 1914), 9.

52. Victor H. Cahalane, "Restoration of Wild Bison," in *Transactions of the Ninth North American Wildlife Conference* (Washington, D.C.: American Wildlife Institute, 1944), 9:135–43.

53. Brett to the Secretary of the Interior, 30 September 1916, YNPA.

54. Norman F. Cheville et al., *Brucellosis in the Greater Yellowstone Area* (Washington, D.C.: National Academy of Sciences, 1998), 34.

55. E. A. Tunnicliff and H. Marsh, "Bang's Disease in Bison and Elk in the Yellowstone National Park and on the National Bison Range," *Journal of the American Veterinary Medical Association* 86 (1935): 745–52.

56. Granville H. Frye and Bob Hillman, "National Cooperative Brucellosis Eradication Program," in *Brucellosis, Bison, Elk and Cattle in the Greater Yellowstone Area: Defining the Problem, Exploring Solutions*, ed. E. Tom Thorne et al. (Cheyenne: Wyoming Game and Fish Department, 1997), 79–85.

57. James A. Pritchard, *Preserving Yellowstone's Natural Conditions: Science and the Perception of Nature* (Lincoln: University of Nebraska Press, 1999), 57.

58. Horace M. Albright and Frank J. Taylor, *"Oh Ranger!": A Book about the National Parks* (Stanford: Stanford University Press, 1928), 76–79.

59. Horace M. Albright, "Yellowstone's 'Thundering Herd': Our Greatest National Bison Herd," January 1925, YNPL vertical files.

60. Isenberg, *Destruction of the Bison*, 184.

61. Richard West Sellars, *Preserving Nature in the National Parks: A History* (New Haven: Yale University Press, 1997), 76.

62. "A Buffalo Stampede," *New York Times*, 2 March 1925, 20.

63. Richard A. Bartlett, *A Wilderness Besieged* (Tucson: University of Arizona Press, 1985), 292.

64. Albright, "Yellowstone's 'Thundering Herd.'"

65. Ludwig Carbyn and David Watson, "Translocation of Plains Bison to Wood Buffalo National Park: Economic and Conservation Implications," in *Large Mammal Restoration: Ecological and Sociological Challenges in the 21st Century*, ed. David S. Maehr, Reed F. Noss, and Jeffrey L. Larkin (Washington, D.C.: Island Press, 2001), 189–204.

Chapter 6. Under More Natural Conditions

1. George Baggley, "Suggested Plan of Management for the Yellowstone Buffalo Herd," 17 January 1934, YNPA.

2. William Rush, "Final Report on Elk Study, Northern Yellowstone Herd," 1932, YNPL vertical files.

3. Baggley, "Plan of Management for the Buffalo Herd."

4. R. Gerald Wright, *Wildlife Research and Management in the National Parks* (Urbana: University of Illinois Press, 1991), 14.

5. George M. Wright and Ben H. Thompson, *Wildlife Management in the National Parks*, Fauna Series no. 2 (Washington, D.C.: Government Printing Office, 1934), 59.

6. Curtis Skinner, "Shuffling Off the Buffalo," *(National Park Service) Courier*, December 1978, 15.

7. Frank Ernest Hill, "Back to the Indian Goes the Buffalo," *New York Times Magazine*, 26 May 1935, 10.

8. Wright and Thompson, *Wildlife Management*, 59.

9. National Park Service, *Yellowstone's Northern Range*, 7.

10. Haines, *Yellowstone Story*, 2:461.

11. Wayne B. Alcorn, "History of the Bison in Yellowstone Park," Supp. 1942–1951, YNPL vertical files, 1.

12. Rudolph Grimm, "Northern Yellowstone Winter Range Studies," *Journal of Wildlife Management* 3, no. 4 (1939): 295–306.

13. Michael B. Coughenour and Francis J. Singer, "History of the Concept of Overgrazing in Yellowstone," in *Effects of Grazing by Wild Ungulates in Yellowstone National Park*, ed. Francis J. Singer, Yellowstone National Park Technical Report, 1996, 1–12.

14. Daniel B. Beard, "Bison Management in Yellowstone National Park," U.S. Fish and Wildlife Service, 10 December 1940, YNPL vertical files.

15. Pritchard, *Preserving Yellowstone's Natural Conditions*, 179.

16. Alcorn, "History of the Bison in Yellowstone Park," 3.

17. Victor H. Cahalane, "Buffalo: Wild or Tame?" *American Forests*, unpaginated reprint, American Forestry Association, Washington, D.C., October 1944, YNPL vertical files.

18. Alcorn, "History of the Bison in Yellowstone Park," 2.

19. Cahalane, "Buffalo: Wild or Tame?"

20. Pritchard, *Preserving Yellowstone's Natural Conditions*, 179.

21. Horace M. Albright, "Our National Parks as Wild Life Sanctuaries," *American Forests and Forest Life* 35 (August 1929): 536.

22. Horace M. Albright, "The Bison of Yellowstone National Park," *The Backlog: A Bulletin of the Campfire Club*, October 1944, 7–11.

23. Ibid.

24. Victor Cahalane, "Buffalo Go Wild," *Natural History* 53, no. 4 (1944): 148–55.

25. Pritchard, *Preserving Yellowstone's Natural Conditions*, 179–81.

26. Sellars, *Preserving Nature in the National Parks*, 158.

27. Erling R. Quortrup, "A Report on Brucellosis Investigations, Yellowstone National Park, December 1 to 20, 1944," YNPL vertical files.

28. Cahalane, "Restoration of Wild Bison," 140.

29. Quortrup, "A Report on Brucellosis Investigations," 10–26.

30. Rogers to Regional Director, 8 April 1947, YNPA.

31. Alcorn, "History of the Bison in Yellowstone Park," 2.

32. Skinner, "Shuffling Off the Buffalo."

33. Rudolph L. Grimm, "History of the Bison in Yellowstone Park," Supplement 1948. The 62 refers to the testing of 146 bison in 1941 by four different veterinarians; in his report, Coburn included only the data on the 36 bison he tested in 1941, in which he found 30.5 percent reactors and suspects (Don R. Coburn, "Special Report," 1948, YNPA).

34. Interagency Bison Management EIS, 1:288, 381.

35. Dr. B. N. Carle, National Institutes of Health, to A. L. Nelson, Fish and Wildlife Service, 14 November 1949, YNPA.

36. Cheville et al., *Brucellosis in the Greater Yellowstone Area*, 90.

37. William J. Barmore, "Bison and Brucellosis in Yellowstone National Park: A Problem Analysis," 1968, internal report, YNPL vertical files, 28.

38. National Park Service Assistant Director Howard Baker to Regional Director, Midwest, 22 July 1964, YNPA; 1964–65 Bison and Habitat Management Plan for Yellowstone National Park, November 1964, YNPA.

39. Robert Howe to Chief Park Ranger Wayne Howe, memorandum, 12 May 1965, YNPA.

40. Mary Meagher, "Evaluation of Boundary Control for Bison of Yellowstone National Park," *Wildlife Society Bulletin* 17, no. 1 (1989): 15–19.

41. Elizabeth S. Williams, Steven L. Cain, and Donald S. Davis, "Brucellosis: The Disease in Bison," in *Brucellosis, Bison, Elk and Cattle in the Greater Yellowstone Area*, 7–19.

42. Kendall L. Nelson, *Status and Habits of the American Buffalo in the Henry Mountain Area of Utah*, Publication 65-2 (Utah State Department of Fish and Game, April 1, 1965).

43. Dirk Van Vuren and M. P. Bray, "Population Dynamics of Bison in the Henry Mountains, Utah, *Journal of Mammalogy* 67, no. 3 (1986): 503–11.

44. Michael J. Gilsdorf, "Brucellosis in Bison—Case Studies," in *International Symposium on Bison Ecology*, 1–10.

45. Ed Struzik, "The Rise and Fall of Wood Buffalo National Park," *Borealis* 3, no. 2 (1995): 11–25.

46. Wright, *Wildlife Research and Management in the National Parks*, 76.

47. Pritchard, *Preserving Yellowstone's Natural Conditions*, 179.

48. Cahalane to Director Conrad Wirth, 19 May 1961, as published under the heading "Public Hunting in the National Parks," in *Atlantic Naturalist* 16, no. 3 (1961): 191–92.

49. "Wildlife Management Background Information," 4 December 1964, YNPA. Slightly different data are contained in "Final Reduction Report 1961–62, Northern Yellowstone Elk Herd," undated, prepared by Robert E. Howe, YNPA.

50. Pritchard, *Preserving Yellowstone's Natural Conditions*, 203.

51. "Wildlife Management Background Information."

52. Leopold et al., *Wildlife Management in the National Parks*, 10.

53. Pritchard, *Preserving Yellowstone's Natural Conditions*, 221–23.

Chapter 7. The Imbalance of Nature

1. S. T. A. Pickett and Richard S. Ostfeld. "The Shifting Paradigm in Ecology," in *A New Century for Natural Resources Management*, ed. Richard L. Knight and Sarah F. Bates (Washington, D.C.: Island Press, 1995), 261–78.

2. Charles S. Elton, *Animal Ecology and Evolution* (Oxford, England: Clarendon Press, 1930), 17.

3. Frank Egerton, "Changing Concepts of the Balance of Nature," *Quarterly Review of Biology* 48 (1973): 322–50.

4. Absaroka Wildlife Conservation Committee, minutes of meeting, 21–22 September 1946, YNPA.

5. "Brucellosis and the Yellowstone Bison," 1967, YNPA. Some of the same statements also appear in Mary Meagher's *Bison of Yellowstone National Park*.

6. Committee on Ungulate Management in Yellowstone National Park, National Research Council, *Ecological Dynamics on Yellowstone's Northern Range* (Washington, D.C.: National Academy Press, 2002), 84.

7. Glen F. Cole, "An Ecological Rationale for the Natural or Artificial Regulation of Native Ungulates in Parks," *Transactions of the North American Wildlife and Natural Resources Conference* 36 (1971): 417–25.

8. Ibid., 419.

9. Yellowstone National Park, "Guidelines for the Management of Ungulates in Yellowstone National Park," Information Paper no. 8, 7 December 1967, YNPA.

10. Acting Assistant Deputy Secretary Layton to L. H. Bull, Secretary-Treasurer, National Association of State Departments of Agriculture, 4 December 1968, YNPA. The letter appears to be based on the 1967 policy statement drafted by Yellowstone staff, "Brucellosis and the Yellowstone Bison," cited in note 5.

11. Barmore, "Bison and Brucellosis in Yellowstone National Park," 8–10.

12. Ibid., 13.

13. Paul Zillman, President, Livestock Conservation Institute (LCI), to Thruston Morton, Secretary of the Interior, 25 May 1971, YNPA.

14. Dean E. Flagg, Chairman, Brucellosis Committee, United States Animal Health Association, to U.S. Representative John Melcher, 8 November 1971, YNPA; Harold Moss, President, Gallatin Dairy Herd Improvement Association, to U.S. Representative Richard Shoup, 6 April 1972, YNPA.

15. Acting Associate Director Ernest Allen Connally to Congressman Teno Roncalio, 3 November 1971, YNPA.

16. Meagher to Chief, Branch of Wildlife Management, National Park Service Washington Office, 12 July 1971, YNPA.

17. National Park Service, "A Boundary Control Program for Yellowstone Bison," 1972, YNPA.

18. Anderson to Hartzog, memorandum on "Bison-Brucellosis Meeting," 21 March 1972, YNPA.

19. Homer Bigart, "Yellowstone's Bison Periled by Effort to Curb Disease," *New York Times*, 19 September 1972, 35.

20. Linn to Dr. N. R. Swanson, Executive Officer, Wyoming Livestock and Sanitary Board, 3 October 1972, YNPA.

21. D. A. Price, Executive Vice President, American Veterinary Medical Association, to Senator James A. McClure, 29 January 1973, YNPA.

22. Meagher to John W. Grady, IV, National Parks and Conservation Association, 5 January 1973, YNPA.

23. Donald Miller, Director, Program Development and Application, Animal and Plant Health Inspection Service, U.S. Department of Agriculture, to Tarpein, 2 March 1973, YNPA; Linn to Tarpein, 30 March 1973, YNPA.

24. Mary Meagher, "Brucellosis in Yellowstone Bison—The Controversy," Information Paper no. 14 (Rev.), Yellowstone National Park, February 1973, YNPA.

25. Mary Meagher, "Yellowstone's Bison, A Unique Wild Heritage," *National Parks and Conservation Magazine: The Environmental Journal*, May 1974, 9–14.

26. Meagher, "Yellowstone Bison."

27. Mary Meagher, "Evaluation of Boundary Control for Bison," 15–19.

28. Mary Meagher, "Yellowstone's Free-Ranging Bison."

29. Mary Meagher, "Range Expansion by Bison of Yellowstone National Park," *Journal of Mammalogy* 70, no. 3 (1989): 670–75.

30. Barbee to Regional Director, Rocky Mountain Region, 22 October 1985, YNPA.

31. Jim Robbins, "Bison Hunt Is Over but Debate Lives," *New York Times*, undated clipping, YNPA.

32. Valerius Geist, "Evaluation of the Boundary Control Programme for Bison," undated, following onsite visit on 24 January 1986, YNPA.

33. Bert Hawkins, Administrator, APHIS, to Denis Galvin, Acting NPS Director, 3 June 1986, YNPA.

34. Yellowstone National Park, Draft Environmental Assessment, Bison Management Program, 1986, YNPA.

35. E. Tom Thorne, Mary Meagher, and Robert Hillman, "Brucellosis in Free-Ranging Bison: Three Perspectives," in *The Greater Yellowstone Ecosystem*, 275–87.

36. Rudolph Grimm, "Northern Yellowstone Winter Range Studies," *Journal of Wildlife Management* 3, no. 4 (1939): 295–306.

37. Paul Schullery, "Drawing the Lines in Yellowstone: The American Bison as Symbol and Scourge," *Orion Nature Quarterly* 5, no. 4 (1986): 33–45.

38. Gallatin Wildlife Association Report, undated, attached to letter dated 14 January 1985, YNPA.

39. Robert D. Barbee, "Bison Confound All the Attempts to Fence Them In," *Rocky Mountain News*, 1 February 1987.

40. Meagher to Barbee, 9 October 1987, YNPA.

41. Mott to U.S. Senator Steven Symms [1987], YNPA.

42. M. Meagher, W. J. Quinn, and L. Stackhouse, "Chlamydial-Caused Infectious Keratoconjunctivitis in Bighorn Sheep of Yellowstone National Park," *Journal of Wildlife Diseases* 28, no. 2 (1992): 171–76.

43. Ron Aasheim, "Montana's Bison: A Management Dilemma," *Montana Outdoors* 20, no. 6 (1989): 27–29.

44. Thorne, Meagher, and Hillman, "Brucellosis in Free-Ranging Bison," 282.

45. Ferlicka to James Ridenour, National Park Service Director, 15 June 1989, YNPA; F. Eugene Hester, Associate Director, National Park Service, to U.S. Representative Ron Marlenee, 24 July 1989, YNPA.

46. Thorne, Meager, and Hillman, "Brucellosis in Free-Ranging Bison," 281.

47. Mary Meagher, "Recent Changes in Yellowstone Bison Numbers and Distribution," in *International Symposium on Bison Ecology*, 107–112.

48. Mark L. Taper, Mary Meagher, and Christopher L. Jerde, *The Phenology of Space: Spatial Aspects of Bison Density Dependence in Yellowstone National Park*, Final Report (Bozeman, Mont.: U.S. Geological Survey, Biological Research Division, 2000).

49. Meagher et al., "Bison in the Greater Yellowstone Area: Status, Distribution and Management," in *Brucellosis, Bison, Elk, and Cattle in the Greater Yellowstone Area*, 50.

50. Taper, Meagher, and Jerde, *The Phenology of Space*, 18, 54.

51. Rogers to National Park Service Regional Director, 31 December 1953, YNPA.

52. Taper, Meagher, and Jerde, *The Phenology of Space*, 18.

53. Stu Coleman, memorandum to files about meeting that Superintendent Barbee held with Meagher, other park personnel, and officials from the Montana Department of Fish, Wildlife and Parks, 5 November 1987, YNPA.

54. Meagher, "Yellowstone's Free-Ranging Bison," 26.

55. Mary Meagher, "The Biology of Time: Looking at Landscape Changes through a Photo Series," *Yellowstone Science* 5, no. 2 (1997): 12–18.

56. Francis J. Singer and Jack E. Norland, "Niche Relationships within a Guild of Ungulate Species in Yellowstone National Park, Wyoming, following Release from Artificial Controls," *Canadian Journal of Zoology* 72 (1994): 1383–94.

57. National Park Service, *Yellowstone's Northern Range*, 70.

58. Francis J. Singer et al., "Thunder on the Yellowstone Revisited: An Assessment of Management of Native Ungulates by Natural Regulation, 1968–1993," *Wildlife Society Bulletin* 26, no. 3 (1998): 375–90.

59. Cheville et al., *Brucellosis in the Greater Yellowstone Area*, 120.

60. National Research Council, *Ecological Dynamics on Yellowstone's Northern Range*, 131.

61. National Park Service, "Draft Environmental Impact Statement for the Inter-agency Bison Management Plan for the State of Montana and Yellowstone National Park," 1998, 370.

62. Taper, Meagher, and Jerde, *The Phenology of Space*, 19.

63. National Research Council, *Ecological Dynamics on Yellowstone's Northern Range*, 72–76.

64. Dan E. Huff and John D. Varley, "Natural Regulation in Yellowstone National Park's Northern Range," *Ecological Applications* 9, no. 1 (1999): 17–29.

65. Worster, *Nature's Economy*, 305.

66. National Park Service, *Management Policies* (Washington, D.C.: Government Printing Office, 1988).

67. Williams, Cain, and Davis, "Brucellosis: The Disease in Bison," 15.

68. Robert B. Keiter and Peter H. Froelicher, "Bison, Brucellosis, and Law in the Greater Yellowstone Ecosystem," *Land and Water Law Review* (University of Wyoming) 28 (1993): 175.

69. Ludwig N. Carbyn, Nicholas J. Lunn, and Kevin Timoney, "Trends in the Distribution and Abundance of Bison in Wood Buffalo National Park," *Wildlife Society Bulletin* 26, no. 3 (1998): 463–70.

70. Carbyn and Watson, "Translocation of Plains Bison to Wood Buffalo National Park."

71. E. Tom Thorne and Thomas F. T. Linfield, "The Greater Yellowstone Inter-agency Brucellosis Committee: 1994–2003," paper presented at the United States Animal Health Association Annual Meeting, San Diego, 15 October 2003.

72. World Commission on Protected Areas, "Principles, Guidelines and Case Studies: Indigenous and Traditional Peoples and Protected Areas," ed. Javier Beltran, Best Practice Protected Area Guidelines Series no. 4 (2000).

73. Struzik, "The Rise and Fall of Wood Buffalo National Park."

74. Environmental Assessment Panel, "Northern Diseased Bison," Report 35 (Hull, Quebec: Federal Environmental Assessment Review Office, August 1990), 2.

75. Struzik, "The Rise and Fall of Wood Buffalo National Park."

76. Theresa Ferguson and Clayton Burke, "Aboriginal Communities and the Northern Buffalo Controversy," in *Buffalo*, ed. J. E. Foster, D. Harrison, and I. S. MacLaren (Edmonton: University of Alberta Press, 1992), 189–206.

77. Carbyn, Lunn, and Timoney, "Distribution and Abundance of Bison in Wood Buffalo National Park."

78. Lu Carbyn, *The Buffalo Wolf: Predators, Prey and the Politics of Nature* (Washington, D.C.: Smithsonian Books, 2003), 225.

Chapter 8. Outward Bound

1. Holt, "Catching Buffalo Calves," part 2, 490.

2. Granville H. Frye and Bob Hillman, "National Cooperative Brucellosis Eradication Program," in *Brucellosis, Bison, Elk and Cattle in the Greater Yellowstone Area*, 79–85.

3. Lee H. Whittlesey, "Cows All over the Place: The Historic Setting for the Transmission of Brucellosis to Yellowstone Bison by Domestic Cattle," *Wyoming Annals* 66 (Winter 1994–95): 42–57.

4. Mary Meagher and Margaret E. Meyer, "On the Origin of Brucellosis in Bison of Yellowstone National Park," *Conservation Biology* 8, no. 3 (1994): 645–53.

5. Interagency Bison Management EIS, 1:23.

6. Shea Andersen, "Feds Want to Kill Some Yellowstone Bison," *High Country News*, 7 August 1995.

7. John Pitcher, *Annual Report of the Acting Superintendent of the Yellowstone National Park to the Secretary of the Interior, 1903* (Washington, D.C.: Government Printing Office, 1904), 5.

8. Schullery, "Drawing the Lines in Yellowstone," 33–45.

9. Mark Prophet and Elizabeth Prophet, *Science of the Spoken Word* (Corwin Springs, Mont.: Summit University Press, 1986), 1.

10. Lieutenant Colonel Lloyd Brett to Secretary of the Interior, 30 June 1911, YNPA.

11. Marc Racicot, "Montana's Quarrel over Yellowstone Bison Is with Washington," *New York Times*, 7 April 1996, sec. E, 10.

12. Interagency Bison Management EIS, 1:328.

13. Racicot, State of Montana, Office of the Governor, to Sandra Olson of West Fargo, North Dakota, 17 May 1996, YNPA.

14. Bob Lucas, Teton County Rancher, "Conversation," *Caldera* 5, no. 5 (1996): 47.

15. Robert Hillman, "Addressing the Politics of Brucellosis Eradication in Yellowstone," speech at the 1997 LCI Annual Meeting, Columbus, Ohio, 1–3 April 1997.

16. Interagency Bison Management EIS, 1:589.

17. Craig W. Allin, "The Triumph of Politics over Wilderness Science," in *Wilderness Science in a Time of Change*, ed. David N. Cole and Stephen F. McCool (Ogden, Utah: U.S. Forest Service, Rocky Mountain Research Station, 2000), 2:184.

18. Evan Eisenberg, *The Ecology of Eden* (New York: Knopf, 1998), 381.

19. Hillman, "Brucellosis Eradication in Yellowstone."

20. Virginia Ravndal, Guest Opinion, *Bozeman Chronicle*, 30 November 1997.

21. Justin Lowe, "How Montana Asserted Deadly Control over the Yellowstone Bison," *Mother Jones*, 30 June 1998, http://www.motherjones.com/news/feature/1998/06/bison.html (accessed October 2004).

22. U.S. Senate, 104th Congress, 1st session, S. 745, 3 May 1995.

23. Doug Peacock, "The Yellowstone Massacre," *Audubon* 99, no. 3 (1997): 43.

24. Sholly to Siroky, 28 January 1997, YNPA.

25. Michael Satchell, "A Discouraging Word for Buffalo," *US News & World Report*, 30 September 1996, 61–63.

26. Todd Wilkinson, "No Home on the Range," *High Country News,* 17 February 1997.

27. Delmar Bigby, speaking at Yellowstone National Park tribal consultation, 12 August 1998 (transcript available at Yellowstone Center for Resources, Mammoth Hot Springs, Wyoming).

28. Associated Press, "Distribution of Bison Meat Causing Divisions among Indians," *Billings Gazette,* 16 January 1999.

29. Interagency Bison Management EIS, 3:791.

30. Racicot, State of Montana, Office of the Governor, to Gail Richardson of Bozeman, Mont., 17 February 1997, YNPA.

31. Patricia Walsh, "The Slaughter of Bison Reopens Old Wounds," *High Country News,* 9 June 1997.

32. Angus M. Thuermer, Jr., "Bison's Future Unclear," *Jackson Hole News,* 5 March 1997.

33. Satchell, "A Discouraging Word for Buffalo," 61–63.

34. James Brooke, "Yellowstone Bison Herd Cut in Half over Winter," *New York Times,* 13 April 1997, sec. 1, 18.

35. Peacock, "The Yellowstone Massacre," 102.

36. Mark Kurlansky, *Cod: A Biography of the Fish That Changed the World* (New York: Walker and Company, 1997), 204.

Chapter 9. A Disagreeable Agreement

1. Justin Lowe, "How Montana Asserted Deadly Control." Mike Finley left the National Park Service in 2001 to become president of the Turner Foundation, Inc., whose motto is, "Working to protect and restore the natural systems that make life possible."

2. Yellowstone National Park tribal consultation meeting, 1 October 2000.

3. "The Citizens' Plan for Saving the Yellowstone Buffalo," undated brochure, YNPL vertical files.

4. Michael J. Gilsdorf, "Brucellosis in Yellowstone National Park," paper presented to the LCI Annual Meeting, Kansas City, Mo., 4 April 1995.

5. Interagency Bison Management EIS, 3:622.

6. Justin Lowe, "Critics Say APHIS Is Too Cozy with Livestock Producers," *Mother Jones,* 30 June 1998, http://www.motherjones.com/news/feature/1998/06/usaha.html (accessed October 2004).

7. Interagency Bison Management EIS, 3:623–36.

8. Glenn Plumb and Keith Aune, "The Long-Term Interagency Bison Management Plan for Yellowstone National Park and the State of Montana," in *Brucellosis in Elk and Bison in the Greater Yellowstone Area,* 144.

9. Interagency Bison Management EIS, 1:98.

10. Ibid., 3:634–36.

11. Cheville et al., *Brucellosis in the Greater Yellowstone Area,* 8–9.

12. Dale F. Lott, *American Bison: A Natural History* (Berkeley and Los Angeles: University of California Press, 2002), 113.

13. Greater Yellowstone Interagency Brucellosis Committee, 2003 GYIBC Annual Report, 7.

14. Interagency Bison Management EIS, 2:53.

15. Andrea Barnett, "Political War Continues over Bison Herd," *High Country News*, 31 January 2000.

16. Scott McMillion, "Bison Sleek but Suspect," *High Country News*, 11 May 1998.

17. Wilkinson, "No Home on the Range," 9.

18. Interagency Bison Management EIS, 3:186–94.

19. Tom Daubert, "Can We Combat High-Minded Ignorance?" Montana Stockgrowers Association, 1 January 2002, http://www.mtbeef.org/index.php.

20. Montana Stockgrowers Association, "Montana Stockgrowers Association Applauds Cooperative Effort to Resolve Brucellosis Threat," news release, 19 March 2002.

21. Mark S. Boyce, "Wolf Recovery in Yellowstone National Park: A Simulation Model," in *Wolves for Yellowstone? A Report to the United States Congress*, ed. John D. Varley and Wayne G. Brewster (Yellowstone National Park, Wyoming: National Park Service, 1990), 2:3–59.

22. Interagency Bison Management EIS, 3:635.

23. Cheville et al., *Brucellosis in the Greater Yellowstone Area*, 58.

24. Todd Wilkinson, "How Real Is the Brucellosis Threat?" *Audubon* 99, no. 3 (1997): 46.

25. Interagency Bison Management EIS, 1:514.

26. Ibid., 1:550.

27. Ibid., 1:551.

Chapter 10. The High Cost of Free Roaming

1. State of Wyoming, Office of the Governor, "Geringer Welcomes Independent Review Team to Study Brucellosis Issues," news release, 18 March 1997.

2. Record of Decision for the Final EIS, 20 December 2002, 6.

3. Cheville et al., *Brucellosis in the Greater Yellowstone Area*, 7.

4. Wilkinson, "No Home on the Range," 9.

5. Jim Hagenbarth, Dick Raths, and John Eyre, "The Cattle Industries of the Greater Yellowstone Area," in *Brucellosis, Bison, Elk and Cattle in the Greater Yellowstone Area*, 154–60.

6. Robert L. Hendry, "The Cattle Industry of the GYA," in *Brucellosis in Elk and Bison in the Greater Yellowstone Area*, 146–52.

7. Many of the details about state elk management in this section came from the 1994 and 2002 GYIBC symposium proceedings: *Brucellosis, Bison, Elk and Cattle in the Greater Yellowstone Area* and *Brucellosis in Elk and Bison in the Greater Yellowstone Area*.

8. Dean Clause et al., "Brucellosis-Feedground-Habitat Program" in *Brucellosis, Bison, Elk and Cattle in the Greater Yellowstone Area*, 66–79.

9. Data from Wyoming Game and Fish Department, based on 2001 results.

10. Idaho Fish and Game Commission meetings, Moscow, Idaho, 24–26 April 2002 and 17–19 July 2002.

11. GYIBC Executive Committee Meeting, Jackson, Wyo., 23 April 2003.

12. State of Wyoming, Senate Joint Resolution SJ0004, 6 March 2002.

13. Clause et al., "Brucellosis-Feedground-Habitat Program," 88.

14. Terry J. Kreeger, Skip Ladd, and Jim Logan, "Where Do We Go from Here," in *Brucellosis in Elk and Bison in the Greater Yellowstone Area*, 131–35.

15. Dan Neal, "Experts Talk Elk, Brucellosis," *Casper Star-Tribune*, 8 January 1997.

16. Robert W. Black, Associated Press, "Remaining Cattle from Brucellosis Herd Shipped to Slaughter," *Billings Gazette*, 14 January 2004.

17. Jeff Gearino, "Wyo[ming] Looks for Brucellosis Source," *Casper Star Tribune*, 3 August 2004.

18. Rachel Odell, "The Great Bison Chase Continues," *High Country News*, 18 January 1999.

19. Todd Wilkinson, "Yellowstone Bison: To Shoot or Not to Shoot?" *Christian Science Monitor*, 7 April 2004.

20. Becky Bohrer, Associated Press, "Officials Begin Steps to Erase Brucellosis," *Billings Gazette*, 7 December 2002.

21. Excerpt from Martz's speech as it was posted on the State of Montana website on 12 December 2002, http://www.discoveringmontana.com/gov2/css/speeches.asp?ID=40.

22. Seelye, "Yellowstone Bison Thrive."

23. Buffalo Field Campaign, "News from the Field," 2 January 2003, http://www.wildrockies.org/buffalo/update02/010203.html.

24. Buffalo Field Campaign, "News from the Field," 16 January 2003, http://www.wildrockies.org/buffalo/update02/011603.html.

25. Judy Blunt, "When the Buffalo Roam," *New York Times*, 18 February 2003, sec. A, 23.

26. State of Montana, House Joint Resolution HJ0015, 28 June 2004.

27. Buffalo Field Campaign, "News from the Field," 20 March 2003, www.wildrockies.org/buffalo/update02/032003.html.

28. Buffalo Field Campaign, "News from the Field," 13 February 2003, http://www.wildrockies.org/buffalo/update02/021303.html.

29. Scott McMillion, "DoL and Press Put Spin on Buffalo Slaughter," *Bozeman Chronicle*, 12 March 2003.

30. Buffalo Field Campaign, "Park Service Slaughters 260 Wild Buffalo inside Yellowstone, Domesticates Another 198 Captive Wild Buffalo," news release, 18 March 2004.

31. Rebecca Huntington, "No Room to Roam for Bison," *Jackson Hole News and Guide*, 24 March 2004.

32. Yellowstone National Park, "Bison Released from Stephens Creek Facility," news release, 6 April 2004.

33. Nadia White, "It's All a Haze," *Casper Star-Tribune*, 14 March 2004.

34. Associated Press, "Suit against Bison Hazing Rejected," *Billings Gazette*, 2 April 2003.

35. Mike Stark, "Bison Hazed during Calving Season," *Billings Gazette*, 2 May 2003.

36. "Farm Bill Could Mean Killing of Sick Bison in Yellowstone," *New York Times*, 18 April 2002.

37. Karen Cooper, Montana Department of Livestock spokeswoman, personal communication with author (hereafter abbreviated as pers. comm.), 12 June 2003; Arnold Gertonson, Montana state veterinarian, pers. comm., 17 September 2003.

38. State of Wyoming, Office of the Governor, news release, 20 August 2004.

39. Keith Aune, pers. comm., 30 September 2003.

40. Robert Frost, pers. comm., 29 September 2004.

41. Yellowstone Center for Resources, 2003 Annual Report (Mammoth Hot Springs, Wyo.: National Park Service, 2004), 65.

42. Yellowstone Center for Resources, 2002 Annual Report (Mammoth Hot Springs, Wyo.: National Park Service, 2003), 60.

43. Animal and Plant Health Inspection Service, "The Study of Bison Fetal Disappearance Rate," Addendum to the Revised Environmental Assessment and Confirmation of the Finding of No Significant Impact, January 2003.

44. C. S. Holling and Gary K. Meffe, "Command and Control and the Pathology of Natural Resource Management," *Conservation Biology* 10, no. 2 (1997): 328–37.

45. Eisenberg, *Ecology of Eden*, 287. Donald Worster discusses the trend toward ecologists as environmental managers in *Nature's Economy*, 313–14.

46. Greater Yellowstone Interagency Brucellosis Committee, Technical and Information and Education Subcommittee meeting, Bozeman, Mont., 13 January 2004.

47. Meagher and Meyer, "Origin of Brucellosis in Bison of Yellowstone National Park."

48. Atul Guwande, "The Mop-Up," *New Yorker*, 12 January 2004, 34–40.

Chapter 11. Confronting People and Predators

1. Kerry G. Gunther, "Bear Management in Yellowstone National Park," *International Conference of Bear Research and Management* 9, no. 1 (1994): 553.

2. James and Edna Caslick and Laura Bittner, "Aggressive Behavior and Food-Begging by Wildlife in Yellowstone: A Summary of Incidents 1963–99," Yellowstone Center for Resources, March 2000.

3. James Shaw and Mary Meagher, "Bison," in *Ecology and Management of Large Mammals in North America*, ed. S. Demarais and P. R. Krausman (Upper Saddle River, N.J.: Prentice-Hall, 1999), 447–66.

4. Case Incident Record 844128, YNPA.

5. "Bison Incidents 1981–1987," YNPA.

6. Edwin Thompson Denig, *Five Indian Tribes of the Upper Missouri: Sioux, Arickaras, Assiniboines, Crees, Crows*, ed. John Ewers (Norman: University of Oklahoma Press, 1961), 119.

7. McHugh, *Time of the Buffalo*, 171.

8. Guthrie, *Frozen Fauna of the Mammoth Steppe*, 289.

9. Geist, *Buffalo Nation*, 64.

10. McHugh, *Time of the Buffalo*, 227.

11. Except where otherwise indicated, much of the information about Yellowstone wolves in this chapter can be found in Douglas Smith, Rolf Peterson, and Doug Houston, "Yellowstone after Wolves," *Bioscience* 53 (April 2003): 330–40.

12. John C. Jackson, *The Piikani Blackfeet: A Culture under Siege* (Missoula, Mont.: Mountain Press, 2000), 13.

13. Meriwether Clark, *The Journals of the Lewis and Clark Expedition*, ed. Gary E. Moulton (Lincoln: University of Nebraska Press, 2001), 4:216–17.

14. Ludwig N. Carbyn and Timothy Trottier, "Description of Wolf Attacks on Bison Calves in Wood Buffalo National Park," *Arctic* 41, no. 4 (1988): 297–302.

15. U.S. Fish and Wildlife Service, Nez Perce Tribe, National Park Service, and USDA Wildlife Services, "Rocky Mountain Wolf Recovery 2003 Annual Report," ed. T. Meier (Helena: USFWS Ecological Services, 2004), table 2.

16. Northern Yellowstone Cooperative Wildlife Working Group, "2003–2004 Winter Count of Northern Yellowstone Elk," news release, 6 January 2004.

17. Douglas Smith, pers. comm., 5 August 2003.

18. Douglas Smith, Kerry Murphy, and Stan Monger, "Killing of Bison *(Bison bison)* calf, by a wolf *(Canis lupus)*, and four coyotes *(Canis latrans)* in Yellowstone National Park," *Canadian Field-Naturalist* 115, no. 2 (2001): 343–45.

19. David J. Mattson, "Use of Ungulates by Yellowstone Grizzly Bears," *Biological Conservation* 81 (1997): 161–77.

20. John J. Craighead, Jay S. Sumner, and John A. Mitchell, *The Grizzly Bears of Yellowstone: Their Ecology in the Yellowstone Ecosystem, 1959–1992* (Washington D.C.: Island Press, 1995).

21. McHugh, *Time of the Buffalo*, 241.

22. Daniel R. MacNulty, Nathan Varley, and Douglas W. Smith, "Grizzly Bear, *Ursus arctos*, Usurps Bison Calf, *Bison bison*, Captured by Wolves, *Canis lupus*, in Yellowstone National Park," *Canadian Field-Naturalist* 115, no. 3 (2001): 495–98.

23. Craighead, Sumner, and Mitchell, *The Grizzly Bears of Yellowstone*, 32.

24. Data compiled from the annual reports of the Bear Management Office, 1997 to 2003, Yellowstone National Park.

Chapter 12. Winter Range for Snowmobiles

1. Aldo Leopold, *A Sand County Almanac* (1949; repr., New York: Oxford University Press, 1966), 271–72.

2. Michael Yochim, "Snowplanes, Snowcoaches, and Snowmobiles: The Decision to Allow Snowmobiles into Yellowstone National Park," *Annals of Wyoming* 70, no. 3 (1998): 6–23, documents many of the details about the history of winter use included here.

3. Mary Meagher, "Range Expansion by Bison of Yellowstone National Park," *Journal of Mammalogy* 70, no. 3 (1989): 670–75.

4. Interagency Bison Management EIS, 1:36.

5. Mary Meagher, Mark Taper, and Christopher Jerde, "Recent Changes in Population Distribution: The Pelican Bison and the Domino Effect," in *Yellowstone Lake: Hotbed of Chaos or Reservoir of Resilience?* ed. Roger J. Anderson and David Harmon (Yellowstone National Park: Yellowstone Center for Resources; Hancock, Mich.: George Wright Society, 2002), 135–47.

6. Cheville et al., *Brucellosis in the Greater Yellowstone Area*, 68.

7. Richard Woodbury, "Artic Cats and Buffalo," *Time*, 17 March 1997, 62.

8. National Park Service, *Winter Use Plan*, Final Environmental Impact Statement for the Yellowstone and Grand Teton National Parks and John D. Rockefeller, Jr., Memorial Parkway (Lakewood, Colo.: NPS Intermountain Regional Office, 2000), 1:298

9. Harold D. Picton, "Energetic Cost of Displacement to Wildlife by Winter Recreation," in *The Effects of Winter Recreation on Wildlife: A Literature Review and Assessment*, Report to the Greater Yellowstone Coordinating Committee, ed. S. T. Olliff and K. L. Legg (Mammoth Hot Springs, Wyo.: National Park Service, Yellowstone National Park, 1999), 135–44.

10. *The Fund for Animals et al. v. Gale Norton et al.*, memorandum opinion, U.S. District Court of the District of Columbia, 16 December 2003, 18.

11. Woodbury, "Artic Cats and Buffalo."

12. Scott McMillion, "Snowmobiles Remain an Issue," *High Country News*, 27 October 1997.

13. Kurt Repanshek, "Sled Wars: Snowmobile Use in Yellowstone Is under Attack," *Wyoming Wildlife* 62, no. 1 (1998): 8–13.

14. John A. Sacklin et al., "Winter Visitor Use Planning in Yellowstone and Grand Teton National Parks," in *Wilderness Science in a Time of Change*, 4:243–50.

15. "Yellowstone Grooming to Continue," Environmental News Network, 9 April 1999, http://www.enn.com (accessed May 4, 2004).

16. Dan D. Bjornlie and Robert A. Garrott, "Effects of Winter Road Grooming on Bison in Yellowstone National Park," *Journal of Wildlife Management* 65, no. 3 (2001): 560–72.

17. The Fund for Animals, "Response to Record of Decision for the Final EIS and Bison Management Plan," 26 December 2000.

18. Eric Reinertson, Dan Reinhart, and Greg Kurz, "Winter Bison Monitoring, 2001 Annual Report," Yellowstone National Park.

19. Jack Welch, President, BlueRibbon Coalition, "Update: Fund for Animals Lawsuit & Yellowstone SEIS," news release, 4 December 2002.

20. Andrea Lococo, "Statement on the National Park Service's Consideration of Alternative G," The Fund for Animals, 15 March 2000.

21. BlueRibbon Coalition, "Viki Eggers—Headed for the Trenches," news release, 18 September 2000.

22. National Park Service, "Winter Use Plan Supplemental EIS Factsheet," 25 March 2003.

23. National Park Service meeting agenda, 3 June 2003, cited in *The Fund for Animals et al. v. Gale Norton et al.*, 31.

24. National Park Service, *Winter Use Plan*, Final Supplemental Environmental Impact Statement, Yellowstone and Grand Teton National Parks and the John D. Rockefeller, Jr., Memorial Parkway, February 2003, 1:117.

25. R. Jaffe et al., *Final Report: Wildlife Road Survey & Human Interactions on and off Road* (Yellowstone National Park, Wyo.: West District Resource Management, 2002).

26. Scott Creel et al., "Snowmobile Activity and Glucocorticoid Stress Responses in Wolves and Elk," *Conservation Biology* 16, no. 3 (2002): 806; Amanda Hardy, "Bison and Elk Responses to Winter Recreation in Yellowstone National Park" (master's thesis, Montana State University, 2001).

27. National Park Service, *Winter Use Plan*, 3:291.

28. Rick Wallen, pers. comm., 18 May 2004.

29. Yellowstone National Park, Annual Superintendent's Report, 1946, YNPA.

30. National Park Service, *Winter Use Plan*, Final Supplemental EIS, 1:200.

31. Ibid., 3:291.

32. Sharetrails, "Fund for Animals Set to Continue String of Yellowstone Lawsuits," news release, 14 April 1999.

33. National Park Service, *Winter Use Plan*, Final Supplemental EIS, 1:72.

34. Ed Klim, ISMA Yellowstone Information Sheet, 25 November 2002.

35. International Snowmobile Manufacturers Association, "Fringe Environmental Groups Sue to Close Yellowstone National Park," news release, 22 December 2002.

36. *The Fund For Animals et al. v. Gale Norton et al.*, 31.

37. "Endless Litigation Blocks Snowmobile Policy," editorial, *Billings Gazette*, 18 February 2004.

38. Department of the Interior, "Statement of Interior Secretary Gale Norton Regarding District Court Snowmobile Ruling at Yellowstone and Grand Teton National Parks," news release, 11 February 2004.

39. *The Fund For Animals et al. v. Gale Norton et al.*, 37–49.

40. Yellowstone National Park, "Study of How Groomed Roads Influence Bison Movement," news release, 7 June 2004.

Chapter 13. Hunted Again

1. Frank Medicine Wolf Springer, "Buffalo: Hunting the American Legend," ESPN Outdoors (undated), http://espn.go.com/outdoors/hunting/s/h_fea_American_bison02_F.Springer.html (accessed October 2004).

2. Cheville et al., *Brucellosis in the Greater Yellowstone Area*, 69.

3. The Bison Ranch at Coteau Ridge, "A Bison Hunt at the Bison Ranch" (undated), http://www.thebisonranch.com/bisnhunt.html (accessed October 2004).

4. Thousand Hills Bison Ranch, "Trophy Buffalo Hunts" (undated), http://www.thbison.com (accessed October 2004).

5. Bill O'Connell, pers. comm., 11 October 2004.

6. Aleen Kienholz, "Bison Harvest on Flying D Ranch," 20 March 2002, http://www.mnstate.edu/kienholz/bison3.htm.

7. Springer, "Buffalo: Hunting the American Legend."

8. Jackson Whitman and Robert Stephenson, "History and Management of the Farewell Bison Herd, Alaska," in *International Symposium on Bison Ecology*, 267–70.

9. Arizona Game and Fish Department, "Buffalo" (undated), http://www.gf.state.az.us/h_f/game_buffalo.shtml (accessed October 2004).

10. Utah Animal Rights Coalition, "Antelope Island Bison Roundup" (undated), http://www.uarc.com/campaigns/antelope_island/ (accessed October 2004).

11. Ronald Hodson and James Karpowitz, "Utah's Henry Mountains Bison Herd: Management by Hunting," in *International Symposium on Bison Ecology and Management*, 229–32.

12. Aldo Leopold, *Game Management* (New York: Charles Scribner's Sons, 1933), 391.

13. The Fund for Animals, "Fund Condemns Wyoming Bison Hunt," news release, 4 November 1999.

14. Ibid.

15. Jim Posewitz, *Beyond Fair Chase: The Ethics and Tradition of Hunting* (Helena: Falcon Press, 1994), 57.

16. Leopold, *Game Management*, 391.

17. Virginia Ravndal, "A General Description of the Social and Cultural Environment Surrounding the Bison/Brucellosis Issue in the Greater Yellowstone Ecosystem," 6 April 1997, YNPL vertical files, 89. This report was drafted under a contract with the National Park Service. Ravndal interviewed representatives from organizations and government agencies that had an interest in the bison management controversy, and merged comments from the interviews to present a composite perspective for each group. The draft was not circulated among all participants for review nor finalized.

18. Posewitz, *Beyond Fair Chase*, 90–91.

19. Posewitz, pers. comm., 7 July 2003.

20. State of Montana, Final Environmental Impact Statement for the Interagency Bison Management Plan for Montana and Yellowstone National Park, 15 November 2000.

21. Walt Williams, "Bison Hunting Bill on Its Way to Full House," *Bozeman Chronicle*, 2 April 2003.

22. Matt Gouras, "Montana Bison Hunt Recalls Near-Decimation of Species," Associated Press, 4 April 2003.

23. "Bison Hunting a Big Mistake," editorial, *Helena Independent Record*, 3 April 2003.

24. Glenn Hockett, "Governor Urged to Veto Legislation for Bison Hunt," *Billings Gazette*, 21 April 2003.

25. Joe Gutkoski, "Buffalo Are Wildlife; We Should Celebrate, Not Persecute Them," *Bozeman Chronicle*, 21 April 2003.

26. Walt Williams, "Animal Rights Groups Takes Aim at Legislation Creating Bison Hunt," *Bozeman Chronicle*, 14 March 2003.

27. Mark Henckel, "FWP OKs Bison Hunt Unofficially," *Billings Gazette*, 12 September 2003.

28. Montana Department of Fish, Wildlife and Parks (MFWP), Draft Bison Hunting Environmental Assessment, 7 June 2004.

29. Paula Clawson, "Plan Would Allow Up to 25 Bison Harvested a Year," *Livingston Enterprise*, 7 June 2004.

30. MFWP, Draft Bison Hunting Environmental Assessment, 3.

31. Hodson and Karpowitz, "Utah's Henry Mountains Bison Herd," 230.

32. Arizona Game and Fish Commission meeting minutes, 15 March 2002.

33. Anabelle Garay, "Buffalo Roam onto Grand Canyon," *Santa Monica Daily Press*, 10 November 2003.

34. Ann McDermott, "South Rim of the Grand Canyon Saturday July 26, 2003," *Gamble's Tales: The Newsletter of the Sonoran Audubon Society* 5, no. 1 (2003): 5.

Chapter 14. Indians at the Crossroads

1. Jack Hitt, "One Nation, Under Ted," *Outside Magazine* 26, no. 12 (2001): 74.

2. Stephen L. Pevar, *The Rights of Indians and Tribes* (Carbondale: Southern Illinois University Press, 1992), 26.

3. Haman Wise, Yellowstone National Park tribal consultation meeting, 26 April 2000.

4. "Treaty with the Eastern Band Shoshoni and Bannock, 1868," in Nabokov and Loendorf, *American Indians and Yellowstone National Park*, 345.

5. Interagency Bison Management EIS, 1:774.

6. Yellowstone National Park tribal consultation meeting, 25 April 2001.

7. Yellowstone Center for Resources Annual Report, 1998 (Yellowstone National Park, 1999), 15.

8. Yellowstone National Park tribal consultation meeting, 25 April 2001.

9. Brodie Farquhar, "Tribes Offer Alternative to Bison Slaughter," *Casper Star-Tribune*, 6 June 2003, http://www.wildrockies.org/buffalo/press0203/0 60603.html.

10. Ruth A. Rudner, *A Chorus of Buffalo: Reflections on Wildlife Politics and an American Icon* (Short Hills, N.J.: Burford Books, 2000), 106, 114.

11. Richard Manning, "The Buffalo Is Coming Back," *Defenders of Wildlife* (Winter 1995–96), http://www.defenders.org/manning1.html.

12. Yellowstone National Park tribal consultation meeting, 21 May 1999.

13. National Park Service, "Draft Environmental Impact Statement," 1998, xxv.

14. Robert Crum, "Healing the Spirit," *Wildlife Conservation* 100, no. 2 (1997): 36–43.

15. Interagency Bison Management EIS, 3:795.

16. Krech, *Ecological Indian*, 136.

17. Winona LaDuke, *All Our Relations: Native Struggles for Land and Life* (Cambridge, Mass.: South End Press, 1999), 154.

18. Lawrence, "The Symbolic Role of Animals in the Plains Indian Sun Dance."

19. Judith Graham, "For Tribes, Bringing Back Buffalo a Labor of Love," *Chicago Tribune*, 3 November 2002.

20. Winona LaDuke, "Buffalo Nation," *Sierra Magazine* 85, no. 3 (2000): 66.

21. Declaration of Michael Fox for *InterTribal Bison Cooperative v. Bruce Babbitt*, Interagency Bison Management EIS, 2:799.

22. Mary Meagher, "The Department of Agriculture, the Department of the Interior, Brucellosis, and the Farmer," *Bioscience* 32 (1973): 311–12.

23. Cheville et al., *Brucellosis in the Greater Yellowstone Area*, 18.

24. Yellowstone National Park tribal consultation meeting, 25 April 2001.

25. Yellowstone National Park tribal consultation meeting, 25 October 2002.

26. Interagency Bison Management EIS, 2:242.

27. Ho-Chunk Nation, "Bison Prairie I" (undated), http://muscodabison.com/Bison/bison_a.htm (accessed October 2004).

28. John Kozlowitz, "Bison to Stay," Ho-Chunk Nation, 10 July 2001, http://www.muscodabison.com/Bison/Articles/bison_to_stay.htm (accessed October 2004).

29. Mark Matthew, "Don't Fence Me In," *High Country News*, 8 June 1998.

30. David Cournoyer, "Tribes Find a Future in the Past," *High Country News*, 2 August 1999.

31. Fred DuBray, "Buffalo Tracks," *InterTribal Bison Cooperative Newsletter*, April 2003, 2.

32. Yellowstone National Park tribal consultation meeting, 11 October 2000.

33. Matthew, "Don't Fence Me In."

34. Associated Press, "Tribal Elders Recommend They Be Allowed to Monitor Bison," *Grand Forks Herald*, 13 April 2004.

35. Tania Branigan, "Groups Lock Horns over Bison Range," *Washington Post*, 2 September 2003.

36. *Federal Register* 64, no. 44 (1999), 11033.

37. Interagency Bison Management EIS, 3:749.

38. Haines, *Yellowstone Story*, 1:161–62.

39. Tim Wapato, Yellowstone National Park tribal consultation meeting, 6 October 1999.

40. Charles E. Kay, "Bison Myths, 'Natural Regulation,' and Native Hunting: A Solution to the Yellowstone Bison Problem," Gallatin Institute, 9 February 1997, http://www.webcovn.com/gallatin/buffalo/kay.html.

41. Greg Hanscom, "Politics Tangles with Science," *High Country News*, 15 September 1997.

42. Leopold et al., *Wildlife Management in the National Parks*, 3.

43. Mark S. Boyce, "The Importance of Science for Sound Management in National Parks," testimony before the Subcommittee on National Parks and Public Lands, Committee on Resources, U.S. House of Representatives, 27 February 1997.

44. Rod Preece, *Animals and Nature: Cultural Myths, Cultural Realities* (Vancouver: University of British Columbia Press, 1999), 177.

45. Ravndal, "Social and Cultural Environment Surrounding the Bison/Brucellosis Issue," 83.

46. Ibid., 74, 60.

47. Yellowstone National Park tribal consultation meeting, 26 April 2000.

48. Nicolas Point, *Wilderness Kingdom: Indian Life in the Rocky Mountains, 1840–1847*, trans. Joseph P. Donnelly (New York: Holt, Rinehart and Winston, 1967), 153–55.

49. Ravndal, "Social and Cultural Environment Surrounding the Bison/ Brucellosis Issue," 75.

50. Samuel Western, "Fair Game," *E: The Environmental Magazine* 10, no. 4 (July–August 1999), http://www.emagazine.com/july-august_1999.

51. Cheyenne River Sioux, "Buffalo Hunts" (undated), http://www.crstgfp.com/bufhunts.htm (accessed October 2004).

52. Fred DuBray and Mark Heckert, "Perspective of the InterTribal Bison Cooperative on the Yellowstone Bison Management Issue," in *Brucellosis, Bison, Elk and Cattle in the Greater Yellowstone Area*, 178–80.

53. Interagency Bison Management EIS, 3:749.

54. Associated Press, "Bison Group Wants More Say in Management," *Billings Gazette*, 24 July 2003; Associated Press, "Freudenthal Opposes Giving Bison to Tribes," *Billings Gazette*, 17 July 2003.

Chapter 15. A New Buffalo Nation

1. Interagency Bison Management EIS, 3:791.

2. Timothy Egan, "As Others Abandon Plains, Indians and Bison Come Back," *New York Times*, 27 May 2001; Florence Williams, "Plains Sense," *High Country News*, 15 January 2001. The term "buffalo commons," which they describe as a metaphor rather than a prescription for "a change to new uses of land that fell between intensive cultivation and pure wilderness," was first used by Frank and Deborah Popper in 1987. See the Poppers' "The Buffalo Commons: Metaphor as Method," *Geographical Review*, October 1999, 491–510.

3. Dan O'Brien, *Buffalo for the Broken Heart: Restoring Life to a Black Hills Ranch* (New York: Random House, 2001), 14, 25–26, 77.

4. Fred DuBray, "Ethno-Ecological Considerations in Bison Management," in *Proceedings of the Northern Public Bison Herds Symposium*, ed. Ronald E. Walker (Custer, S.D.: Custer State Park, 1993), 398.

5. Ibid., 396.

6. Lott, *American Bison: A Natural History*, 197.

7. Bison, Buffalo and Cattle Taxon Advisory Group of the American Zoo and Museum Association, "Asian Buffalo" (undated), http://www.csew.com/cattletag/ Cattle%20Website/Fact_Sheets/Asian_Buffalo/Asian_Buffalo.htm (accessed October 2004).

8. Lott, *American Bison: A Natural History*, 197.

9. Robert J. Hudson, "From Prairie to Paddock," in *International Symposium on Bison Ecology*, 233–37.

10. Craig Knowles, Carl Mitchell, and Mike Fox, "Trends in Bison Management," in *International Symposium on Bison Ecology*, 244–50.

11. Karen Conley, "The Future of the Bison Industry," *Bison World* 25, no. 1 (2000): 156–58.

12. National Bison Association, "Handling" (undated), http://www.bisoncentral. com/raising/handling.asp (accessed October 2004).

13. Jared Diamond, *Guns, Germs, and Steel: The Fates of Human Societies* (New York: W. W. Norton, 1997), 159.

14. Dan O'Brien, interview by Steve Curwood, *Living on Earth*, National Public Radio, 20 August 2002.

15. Bryan Hodgson, "Buffalo: Back Home on the Range," *National Geographic*, November 1994, 78.

16. Ernest Callenbach, *Bring Back the Buffalo! A Sustainable Future for America's Great Plains* (Washington, D.C.: Island Press, 1996), 10.

17. Ronald E. Walker, "Management Strategies for the Custer State Herd," in *International Symposium on Bison Ecology*, 262–67.

18. Keith Aune et al., "Preliminary Results on Home Range, Movements, Reproduction and Behavior of Female Bison in Northern Yellowstone National Park," in *International Symposium on Bison Ecology*, 61–70.

19. Walker, "Management Strategies for the Custer State Herd," 263.

20. Alaska Department of Fish and Game, "Delta Junction State Bison Range," 8 October 2003, http://www.wildlife.alaska.gov/refuge/bison.cfm.

21. Bill Rinehart, "Across the Fence at the Tallgrass Prairie," The Nature Conservancy, 9 February 2004, http://oklahomanature.org/OK/Rinehart/2004-02-09.html.

22. Glenn Plumb and Jerold Dodd, "Foraging Ecology of Bison and Cattle on a Mixed Prairie: Implications for Natural Area Management," *Ecological Applications* 3, no. 4 (1993): 631–43.

23. Hodgson, "Back Home on the Range," 80.

24. Natalie Halbert, "The Utilization of Genetic Markers to Resolve Modern Management Issues in Historic Bison Populations: Implications for Species Conservation" (Ph.D. dissertation, Texas A&M University, 2003), 44–45.

25. Knowles, Mitchell, and Fox, "Trends in Bison Management," 245, 249.

26. Buffalo Field Campaign, "Notes from the Field," 5 March 2003, http://www. wildrockies.org/buffalo/update02/030503.html.

27. Interagency Bison Management EIS, 2:183.

28. Cheville et al., *Brucellosis in the Greater Yellowstone Area*, 12.

29. Frank Gilbert Roe, *The North American Buffalo: A Critical Study of the Species in the Wild State* (Toronto: University of Toronto Press, 1951), 167–73.

30. Tom McHugh, "Social Behavior of the American buffalo," *Zoologica* 43, no. 1(1958): 1–40; Meagher, *Bison of Yellowstone National Park*, 46–47; Lott, *American Bison: A Natural History*, 32.

31. J. Dewey Soper, "History, Range and Home Life of the Northern Bison," *Ecological Monographs* 11, no. 4 (1941): 348–412; W. C. H. Green, J. G. Griswold, and A. Rothstein, "Post-Weaning Associations among Bison Mothers and Daughters," *Animal Behavior* 38 (1989): 847–58. The latter research was done at Wind Cave National Park.

32. Mary Meagher, pers. comm., 10 August 2003; Glenn Plumb, pers. comm., 24 September 2003.

33. Joe Templeton, pers. comm., 17 September 2003.

34. Karen Brandon, "As Buffalo Thrive, So Does Fight over Room to Roam," *Chicago Tribune*, 17 February 1999.

35. Liz Kearney, "Don't Bother to 'Manage' Park Bison for Horse Butte Residents," opinion, *Bozeman Daily Chronicle*, 7 July 2003.

36. Jack Rhyan, "Contraception: A Possible Means of Decreasing Transmission of Brucellosis in Bison," in *Brucellosis in Elk and Bison in the Greater Yellowstone Area*, 99–108.

37. Keith Aune and Jack Rhyan, "A Proposed Feasibility Study of Bison Quarantine Procedures," submitted to the Yellowstone National Park research committee, 24 September 2004.

Chapter 16. Thinking Outside the Box

1. Eisenberg, *Ecology of Eden*, 289.

2. William Cronon, "The Trouble with Wilderness; or, Getting Back to the Wrong Nature," in *Uncommon Ground: Toward Reinventing Nature*, ed. William Cronon (New York: W. W. Norton, 1995), 81–82.

3. Eisenberg, *Ecology of Eden*, 289.

4. Holmes Rolston III, "Natural and Unnatural; Wild and Cultural," *Western North American Naturalist* 61, no. 3 (2001): 267–76.

5. Peter S. White and Susan Bratton, "After Preservation: The Problems of Change," *Biological Conservation* 18, no. 4 (1980): 241–55.

6. Glenn Plumb, pers. comm., 23 September 2003.

7. Shaw and Meagher, "Bison," in *Ecology and Management of Large Mammals*, 447–66.

8. Cheville et al., *Brucellosis in the Greater Yellowstone Area*, 118.

9. Rebecca Huntington, "Bison in Yellowstone near Record Levels," *Jackson Hole Guide and News*, 2 July 2003.

10. Dan Flores, "Making the West Whole Again: A Historical Perspective on Restoration," in *Reclaiming the Native Home of Hope*, ed. Robert B. Keiter (Salt Lake City: University of Utah Press, 1998).

11. Frederic H. Wagner, "Principles for the Conservation of Wildlife Resources: Another Perspective," *Ecological Applications* 6, no. 2 (1996): 365–67.

12. Daniel B. Botkin, *Our Natural History: The Lessons of Lewis and Clark* (New York: Berkley Publishing, 1995), 119–21.

13. Rolston, "Natural and Unnatural," 275.

14. Robert Frost, pers. comm., 29 September 2004.

15. Glenn Plumb, pers. comm., 23 September 2003.

16. N. Scott Momaday, "Vision Statement for the Buffalo Trust," The Buffalo Trust, 14 July 2002, http://www.buffalotrust.org/mission.htm.

17. Loren Eiseley, "The Winter of Man," in *The Star Thrower* (New York: Random House, 1978), 202–206.

18. *Yellowstone Center for Resources Annual Report, 2001* (Mammoth Hot Springs, Wyo.: National Park Service, 2002), 52–53.

19. Paul Schullery and Lee Whittlesey, *Myth and History in the Creation of Yellowstone National Park* (Lincoln: University of Nebraska Press, 2003), 78.

20. Mary Midgley, *Beast and Man: The Roots of Human Nature* (Ithaca: Cornell University Press), 1978.

Selected References

Bison Ecology and Environmental History

Allen, Joel Asaph. 1876. "The American Bisons, Living and Extinct," *Memorial Museum of Comprehensive Zoology* 4, no. 10.

Barsness, Larry. 1985. *Heads, Hides, and Horns.* Fort Worth: Texas Christian University Press.

Cheville, Norman F., Dale R. McCullough, Lee R. Paulson, Norman Grossblatt, Kathrine Iverson, and Stephanie Parker. 1998. *Brucellosis in the Greater Yellowstone Area.* Washington D.C.: National Academy Press.

Flores, Daniel. 2001. *The Natural West: Environmental History in the Great Plains and Rocky Mountains.* Norman: University of Oklahoma Press.

Geist, Valerius. 1996. *Buffalo Nation: History and Legend of the North American Bison.* Stillwater, Minn.: Voyageur Press.

Guthrie, R. Dale. 1980. "Bison and Man in North America." *Canadian Journal of Anthropology* 1: 55–73.

Irby, Lynn R., and James E. Knight, eds. 1998. *International Symposium on Bison Ecology and Management in North America.* Bozeman: Montana State University, Extension Wildlife Program.

Isenberg, Andrew C. 2000. *The Destruction of the Bison: An Environmental History, 1750–1920.* Boston: Cambridge University Press.

Kreeger, Terry J., ed. 2002. *Brucellosis in Elk and Bison in the Greater Yellowstone Area.* Cheyenne: Wyoming Game and Fish Department.

Lott, Dale F. 2002. *American Bison: A Natural History.* Berkeley and Los Angeles: University of California Press.

McDonald, Jerry N. 1981. *North American Bison: Their Classification and Evolution.* Berkeley: University of California Press.

McHugh, Tom. 1972. *The Time of the Buffalo*. New York: Knopf.

Meagher, Mary. 1973. *The Bison of Yellowstone National Park*. National Park Service, Scientific Monographs 1. Washington, D.C: Government Printing Office.

Meagher, Mary, and Douglas B. Houston. 1998. *Yellowstone and the Biology of Time: Photographs across a Century*. Norman: University of Oklahoma Press.

National Park Service, U.S. Department of the Interior. 2000. *Bison Management for the State of Montana and Yellowstone National Park*. Final Environmental Impact Statement, 3 vols. (August), and Record of Decision (December 20).

Roe, Frank Gilbert. 1951. *The North American Buffalo: A Critical Study of the Species in the Wild State*. Toronto: University of Toronto Press.

Thorne, E. Tom, Mark S. Boyce, Paul Nicoletti, and Terry J. Kreeger, eds. 1997. *Bison, Elk and Cattle in the Greater Yellowstone Area: Defining the Problem, Exploring Solutions*. Cheyenne: Wyoming Game and Fish Department.

Yellowstone and Wildlife Management History

Bartlett, Richard A. 1985. *A Wilderness Besieged*. Tucson: University of Arizona Press.

Haines, Aubrey L. 1977. *The Yellowstone Story: A History of Our First National Park*. 2 vols. Boulder, Colo.: Yellowstone Library and Museum Association in cooperation with Colorado Associated University Press.

Hampton, H. Duane. 1971. *How the U.S. Cavalry Saved Our National Parks*. Bloomington: Indiana University Press.

Janetski, J. C. 2002. *Indians in Yellowstone National Park*. Revised edition. Salt Lake City: University of Utah Press.

Keiter, Robert, and Mark S. Boyce, eds. 1991. *The Greater Yellowstone Ecosystem: Redefining America's Wilderness Heritage*. New Haven: Yale University Press.

Magoc, Chris J. 1999. *Yellowstone, The Creation and Selling of an American Landscape, 1870–1903*. Albuquerque: University of New Mexico Press.

Nabokov, Peter, and Lawrence Loendorf. 2002. *American Indians and Yellowstone National Park: A Documentary Overview*. Yellowstone National Park: National Park Service, Yellowstone Center for Resources. An expanded version of this document has been published as *Restoring a Presence: A Documentary Overview of Native Americans and Yellowstone National Park*. Norman: University of Oklahoma Press, 2004.

National Research Council, Committee on Ungulate Management in Yellowstone National Park. 2002. *Ecological Dynamics on Yellowstone's Northern Range*. Washington, D.C.: National Academy Press.

Pritchard, James A. 1999. *Preserving Yellowstone's Natural Conditions: Science and the Perception of Nature*. Lincoln: University of Nebraska Press.

Schullery, Paul. 1997. *Searching for Yellowstone: Ecology and Wonder in the Last Wilderness*. Boston: Houghton Mifflin.

Sellars, Richard West. 1997. *Preserving Nature in the National Parks: A History*. New Haven: Yale University Press.

Skinner, Curtis K., and Wayne B. Alcorn. 1941; Supplement, 1942–1951. "History of the Bison in Yellowstone National Park." Unpublished report on file at Yellowstone National Park Research Library, Gardiner, Mont.

Spence, Mark David. 1999. *Dispossessing the Wilderness: Indian Removal and the Making of the National Parks*. New York: Oxford University Press.

Wagner, Frederic H., Ronald Foresta, R. Bruce Gill, Dale R. McCullough, Michael R. Pelton, William F. Porter, and Hal Salwasser. 1995. *Wildlife Policies in the U.S. National Parks*. Washington D.C.: Island Press.

Wright, R. Gerald. 1991. *Wildlife Research and Management in the National Parks*. Urbana: University of Illinois Press.

Index

Grassrope, Al, 243
Great Plains, 7, 19, 63; as bison habitat, 9, 13, 14, 43, 202, 254–55, 274
Greater Yellowstone Area, 7, 12, 130, 162–63
Greater Yellowstone Coalition, 148, 217
Greater Yellowstone Interagency Brucellosis Committee, 130, 155, 163–66, 169, 180–81, 266, 275
Grimm, Rudolph, 82, 89, 101
Grinnell, George Bird: on bison, 36, 47, 51, 61; on Indians, 30–32; on wilderness, 27, 49; on wildlife, 23, 24, 28, 29
Gros Ventres, 238, 241
Guthrie, Dale, 196
Guwande, Atul, 188

Haines, Aubrey, 44, 81
Halbert, Natalie, 261
Hansen, Clifford, 107
Hardy, Amanda, 213–14
Harris, Edward, 18
Harris, Moses, 30, 31, 32, 51
Hathaway, Stanley, 99
Hawks, Bill, 173
Hayden, Ferdinand, 21
Heckert, Mark, 239
Helicopters: used to capture bison, 91, 93, 95, 106, 187; used to haze bison, 109, 111, 179
Hemorrhagic septicemia, 67, 68
Henderson, A. Bart, 12
Hendry, Rob, 165–66, 168, 275
Henry Mountains, Utah, 70, 95–96, 223–24, 229–30
Highwood, Mont., 10
Hill, Frank Ernest, 79
Hillman, Bob, 135–36, 149, 160
Hitchcock, Ethan Allen, 53, 54, 61
Ho-Chunks, 244–45
Hockett, Glenn, 227
Holocene epoch, 7–8
Holt, Peter, 53, 56–58, 127, 129, 268–69, 272